THE PRINCIPLES OF ETHICS

HERBERT SPENCER

THE PRINCIPLES OF ETHICS

HERBERT SPENCER

Introduction by Tibor R. Machan

In Two Volumes
Vol. I

Liberty Fund
INDIANAPOLIS
1978

This book is published by Liberty Fund, Inc., a foundation established to encourage study of the ideal of a society of free and responsible individuals.

The cuneiform inscription that serves as the design motif for our endpapers is the earliest-known written appearance of the word "freedom" (*amagi*), or liberty. It is taken from a clay document written about 2300 B.C. in the Sumerian city-state of Lagash.

This edition of *The Principles of Ethics* follows the text of the edition published in New York in 1897 by D. Appleton and Company.

Frontispiece photograph: Bettmann Archive, Inc.

Library of Congress Cataloging in Publication Data

Spencer, Herbert, 1820–1903.
    The principles of ethics.

    Includes bibliographical references and index.
    1. Ethics. 2. Ethics, Evolutionary. I. Title.
BJ1311.S75 1977   170   77-1274

0-913966-33-9 Set (HC)
0-913966-76-2 Volume I (HC)
0-913966-74-6 Volume II (HC)
0-913966-34-7 Set (SC)
0-913966-77-0 Volume I (SC)
0-913966-75-4 Volume II (SC)

01 00 99 98 97 C 7 6 5 4 3
01 00 99 98 97 P 7 6 5 4 3a

CONTENTS OF VOLUME I

PART I
THE DATA OF ETHICS

Contents

PART II
THE INDUCTIONS OF ETHICS

PART III
THE ETHICS OF INDIVIDUAL LIFE

Herbert Spencer: A Century Later
By Tibor R. Machan

Classical liberalism, with its focus on individual political and economic liberty, brought millions a better life than they would have had under the influence of other systems of thought. Capitalism, where consistently implemented, has been better for people than all the alternatives known to mankind. History and common sense bear this out, despite relentless allegations to the contrary from left and right.

But the classical liberals never developed a theoretically sound ethical base for their political and economic system. Herbert Spencer is the most formidable among those who have made the effort.

What Spencer did for libertarianism is what Marx did for communism—provide it with what was to be a full-blown scientific justification, on the model of proper science prominent in his day.

Neither thinker succeeded. But while Marx is hailed everywhere as a messiah (in secular garb)—even as his theories are being patched up desperately to fit the facts—Herbert Spencer, a better scientist, and in his moral and political theory far more astute than Marx, is widely dismissed as a foolhardy fellow or crude Darwinian.

Much has occurred since Spencer's time, and the free society now enjoys a better theoretical base than ever. It is philosophically well grounded today, and eventually this may come to be recognized and have an impact on concrete political and economic affairs. We can, nevertheless, learn a great deal from Herbert Spencer, which is why the reissue of what he deemed his most important work is such a welcome event.

Triumph and Disappointment: Spencer's Life

Born in Derby, England, on April 27, 1820, Spencer was from the start an unusual individual among intellectuals. Of Quaker parents, Spencer grew up with an undistinguished educational background. He had no formal classical or humanist education, nor did he acquire literary sensitivities as so many of Great Britain's luminaries did. Instead Spencer started his studies in the sciences, mostly technology and mathematics. He even embarked on an engineering career at first, in 1837, in the railway industry. But this merely served to increase his intellectual curiosity within the various scientific fields. The enthusiasm he had for an understanding of nature along scientific paths led him at times to pursue odd roads of inquiry, ones that started off with great optimism only to end in disrepute—for example, phrenology.

Spencer's first intellectually creative work was a series of lectures published in *The Nonconformist,* entitled "The Proper Sphere of Government," in which the seeds of his subsequent thinking are clearly contained. Here Spencer demonstrated his confidence in the all-pervasive character of certain kinds of natural laws, scientific principles the ignorance of which can only spell destruction for us.

Although it is known that Spencer had occasional romantic attachments, including a relatively long-lasting one with the novelist George Eliot (Marian Evans), Spencer's personal life consisted almost exclusively of pursuing his philosophical and scientific studies. During most of his life he suffered from a nervous ailment for which doctors could find no explanation, and what we know of his life testifies to a case of total dedication, bordering on the obsessive, to the completion of work Spencer set out to accomplish in his thirties.

As for social life, the opportunity always existed. Spencer attained popularity early in his life, shortly after the publication of *Social Statics* in 1850. He soon became world-famous and was read by both professionals and lay people. His influence is still evident throughout the fields of biology and sociology, even when he is not explicitly acknowledged.

Though Spencer's evolutionism is different from and broader than Darwin's, the two theories are often identified in journalistic and polemical treatments of various related topics. In the area of social theory Spencer's thought developed much further than Darwin's, and while Darwin's evolutionism was theoretically superior to Spencer's in the field of biology, Spencer was ahead of his time in some of his extensions of the evolutionist ideas. For example, in the history of the development of scientific concepts, Spencer's principle of evolutionism could be made to apply in ways later alleged by Collingwood and today defended by Thomas S. Kuhn, in his *The Structure of Scientific Revolutions* (Chicago, 1962), and Stephen Toulmin, in his *Human Understanding*, vol. 1 (Princeton, 1972). (Toulmin regards Spencer's view as "providentialist." But the pattern of development, whatever its explanation, is Spencerian throughout Toulmin's discussion of the growth of scientific ideas.) Then also, the famous behavioral psychologist B. F. Skinner invokes the evolutionist scheme in his discussion of the survival of different cultures, thus employing an idea, rejected in its individualist application, to make a collectivist point.

Spencer's friends included John Stuart Mill, Thomas Huxley, Beatrice Webb, and others, all of whom discussed Spencer in their works. He was admired by thousands, including the American industrialist Andrew Carnegie; A. E. Taylor, Josiah Royce, and David Duncan wrote books about him. But in the later years of his life Spencer lost not only his stature but also a good deal of his optimism, vigor, and confidence, so that his second edition of *Social Statics* omitted the crucial chapter "The

Right to Ignore the State," and he changed some of his libertarian views. Most striking was his apparent abandonment of the universality of his social and political theory. He could declare late in his life that "the goodness of these or those institutions is purely relative to the nature of the men living under them."

There is not room here to explore why this indefatigable man relented on certain crucial elements of his doctrine late in his life, while at the same time he refused to yield to objections that had the fullest possible scientific backing. Anecdotes abound on Spencer's good-spirited stubbornness. He would at times construct elaborate explanations of minute phenomena and upon finding that his factual assumptions had been mistaken, he would laugh heartily but not readily abandon his stance. Yet on other occasions he would encourage the most detailed, minuscule research experimentation and recording so that scientists far into the twentieth century still relied on the facts his work brought to light.

Beatrice Webb said of Spencer, after the latter's declining last years had become an object of some discussion and speculation, that he had "a nature with so perfect an intellect and little else—save friendliness and the uprightness of a truth-loving mind." It is hardly surprising that such an individual would give up some of his most controversial ideas when the theoretical basis underlying most of what he believed began to receive severe and widespread scientific opposition. It is a pity. Because, if anything, it was Spencer's normative convictions that can still be shown, even better than in his own times, to deserve full confidence. Had Spencer realized this, he might have lived out his life with justifiable pride.

Spencer's Principles of Ethics

During his time Spencer achieved prominence and a degree of influence that prompted Justice Oliver Wendell Holmes to say in one of his opinions that "The 14th Amendment does not enact Mr. Herbert Spencer's *Social Statics*," referring to

Spencer's advocacy of laissez-faire economics. Spencer's ethical writing, however, did not become influential and is today mentioned mainly as part of a certain phase of philosophical explorations in moral theory. Yet Spencer produced some valuable insights in substantive moral theory. It is often pointed out, probably justly, that Spencer's attempt to achieve a fusion between the scientific—in his case, evolutionist—and ethical regard toward human affairs was unsuccessful. In essence the charge is simply that to take a scientific perspective in Spencer's sense implies determinism of the sort that excludes the very possibility of genuine human choices; and without the possibility of genuine human choices, the content of any ethical system must be meaningless. For example, if it be taken as true that each individual should strive to achieve happiness in life, then it must be true that each individual has a genuine choice in the matter of so striving or not so striving. But if individual behavior is governed by the complex lawful relations that govern less-evolved entities, then no choice as to what he will do is possible, so ethics is meaningless.

This criticism was placed before Spencer in some of the letters commenting on his ethical writings, and the Appendix of the present edition includes his replies. Hardly any serious student of ethics could fail to appreciate the significance of the issue being posed, and Spencer's efforts to meet the critics are of much more than academic interest. It is possible that had not the currents of thought in the last century been under the powerful sway of collectivist ideals even before Spencer produced his ethical and social philosophy, it would be the collectivist efforts at fusionism that would have succumbed under the pressures of the type Spencer faced. Marxism contains both claims as to its scientific character and claims of distinctly ethical or moral character. The same can be said of prominent contemporary thinkers like B. F. Skinner and Karl Menninger, to name but two.

What differentiates Spencer from these fusionists, then, is not the fusionism but the specifically ethical content of his thought. It is no secret that the bulk of ethical commentary, whether from the pulpit, editorials, the campaign trails, or the stages from which the oratory of commencement exercises rings forth, urges upon human beings acts of self-sacrifice. In this respect there is nothing revolutionary about Marxism, for example. Marx also places before us the ideals of self-sacrifice—his condemnation of the Lockean human-rights tradition consisted mainly of dismissing such rights as vehicles of selfishness. Spencer, however, advocated egoism. And his ethics could not be faulted for being of the hedonistic egoist variety, such as those of Jeremy Bentham and even John Stuart Mill. Instead, Spencer developed what he called a *rational* utilitarian moral theory. Omitting from consideration for now the difficulties of Spencer's fusionist efforts, we cannot deny that the substance of Spencer's ethical writings deserves extensive study. We have here a brilliant theory in which the mutually compatible selfish goals of individuals are demonstrated to be the proper end of human conduct. The principles that would further this goal are the principles of *rational* utilitarianism, gleaned through a consideration of the self-consistently enhancing course of conduct possible for human beings to undertake.

In developing his humanistic egoism, Spencer critically evaluates some of the greatest moral philosophers in Western history. His assessment of Aristotle is superb, especially since his own ethical views are probably closest to this great Greek thinker's own moral point of view. Spencer rightly perceives an idealistic tendency in Aristotle's conception of the happiness that is the goal of the moral life for every individual. He points out that Aristotle's ideas are "allied to the Platonic belief that there is an ideal or absolute good, which gives to particular and relative goods their property of goodness." Against this intrinsicist conception of good, Spencer makes the counter proposal that the virtues "are united by their common relation to [happiness]; while they are not united by their inner natures." What with the simplistic renditions of Herbert Spencer's philosophy that we can encounter in the caricatures of this man's intellectual contributions, hardly anyone is prepared for the complex philosophical explorations that Spencer's *Principles of Ethics* offers in such plentitude.

It should be noted that most moral philosophers either are concerned only with the consequences of conduct or focus exclusively on the purity of motives for action. Yet both the consequences and the grounds of action are of moral significance, and Spencer shows his awareness of this in his advocacy of rational utilitarianism. Actions should reap benefits, but they can do so only if rationally guided, if they are principled.

Spencer's egoism, unlike that of Hobbes, does not begin by conceiving of the ego—the individual—as a bundle of passions purposelessly striking out to sustain itself in motion. This is the type of egoism that is accepted by many economists and promptly ridiculed by most moral philosophers. So it is no wonder that egoism has become not only an absurd moral theory but almost a synonym for "immorality." Its Hobbesian version allows for callous, inconsiderate, or cruel conduct. By focusing on this variety of egoism—which, you will recall, means individualism—critics can throw out the baby with the bathwater. They can reject the importance of the individual for ethical purposes on grounds that the conception of the individual on the Hobbesian model is invalid and leads to absurd consequences. If we are all motivated by drives fixed within us by nature, pushing us toward self-aggrandizement qua purely passionate, unreasoning animals, then we will undoubtedly end in mortal combat with each other just a few steps down the social path. Such an ethics does imply dog-eat-dog, the caricature of the ethical base of laissez-faire capitalism.

Spencer will have none of this, and his discussion is highly illuminating. Unfortunately, it is mostly dismissed as a desperate attempt to rationalize capitalism with Victorian mores. And because of its problematic philosophical base, the charge rings true enough. (Never mind that charges of a similar type

could be made against virtually any other thinker, and that
Spencer's own life does not demonstrate the slightest undue
loyalty to either capitalism or the customs and etiquette of his
times.) What we find in Spencer's egoism is a system ensur-
ing the prospects of compatibility of interests among intelligent, good people, which should indicate why understanding
ethics along egoistic lines makes very good sense. This is one
reason why, of all of the many volumes Spencer produced, his
ethical writings are the most valuable and unorthodox. It is
furthermore an advantage in these works that Spencer is
concerned, not to defend his ethics via his evolutionary science, but to work out the dynamics of an ethical position.

A note is due here about certain developments in the classical liberal conception of society following Spencer's notable
efforts to give that conception a firm base. Why has liberalism
changed its colors in our day? How could a term used for a free
society in which government had as its proper role the protection and preservation of individual rights, take on a virtually
opposite meaning?

Unfortunately Spencer must take part of the blame for this
turn of events. Classical liberals accepted, willy-nilly (and
deliberately in Locke), that human beings are free and responsible for most of their conduct. This implied that under conditions of political freedom, the suffering people experience can
ordinarily be said to be their own fault. This idea made the
desirability of government along classical liberal lines quite
intelligible.

But in Hegel and Marx, for example, the idea that human
beings are free in the sense specified above lost out to a total
determinism. After Kant accounted for free will by reference
to something fundamentally mysterious—the unknowable
thing-in-itself—it was not surprising that those with a scientific bent rejected the idea altogether. But the notion *freedom*
was kept in use following the substantive change. And it is
easy to understand the sense in which it began to be used by
considering such expressions as "free from hunger," "free
from ignorance," "free from hardship," and "free from temp-

tation." Liberalism changed, then, because the underlying idea of human nature changed, leaving intact only a distorted idea of human freedom. Since most individualists *and* most collectivists believe that humanity is evolving, gradually or by leaps and bounds, toward a full maturation or the realization of human nature in some final social order, freedom was interpreted as the condition whereby progress toward this end is least impeded—that is, whereby all people can surge toward their final emancipation. The only freedom that makes sense by this account is freedom from our deprived conditions, freedom from our impediments, whether economic, psychological, spiritual, or whatnot. Since the earlier liberals convinced most people that government was established to protect and preserve the liberty or freedom to which we all have either a natural or a utilitarian right, it was consistent now to demand that the "rights" identified by this distorted conception of freedom receive government's equal protection.

Spencer helped this development by flatly rejecting the idea of human freedom of the will and endorsing a variety of progressivism (which he modified, but not sufficiently to escape the charge of being a prophet of eventual utopia). What he failed to realize is that without the fact of human choice clearly demonstrated, the ideal of political and economic liberty makes no sense at all. This ideal means that people *should* act so as not to violate one another's rights. But that implies that they have a choice. Spencer was challenged on this point and his attempts to cope with the issue—for example, in his Appendix C—fell short, because he always thought that any concession would commit him to some form of mysticism, the bane of a scientist.

There is, however, nothing unscientific about accepting the possibility, even the actuality, of freedom of the human will— indeed, it would be antiscientific to preclude it. Not science, but certain philosophical premises that many scientists accepted have led to the idea that science and free will contradict each other.

What is lamentable is that, while Spencer was constantly

challenged on this issue, Marx and his disciples were being honored for philosophical achievements despite their constant conflation of science with values and evaluations. Even today, such European intellectual luminaries as Sartre proclaim themselves to be Marxists, refusing to admit the fatal flaw in Marx, while they and their admirers will not give Spencer their respect.

Fortunately, some of this is changing. One of the best brief eye-openers on Herbert Spencer is Robert L. Carneiro's introduction to his edition of selections from Spencer's *Principles of Sociology: The Evolution of Society* (Chicago, 1974). J. D. Y. Peel's *Herbert Spencer: The Evolution of a Sociologist* (New York, 1971) is another valuable source on this often-forgotten genius. Both authors focus mainly on Spencer's sociology, however, and barely mention the insights he can contribute to the study of ethics.

Many of those who today embrace Spencer's political convictions fail in a different respect from those who ignore Spencer. They omit from consideration the serious inadequacies in Spencer's ethical and political theories. I have mentioned the most significant problem with Spencer's ethics. His politics suffers from yet another crucial difficulty. Spencer believes that although we all have natural rights, these rights do not take effect or come into existence before the emergence of the full development of human nature and society. Here, too, Spencer shares elements of Marxism. Marx rejected moral issues as irrelevant to societies in which human nature has not fully matured. He rejected the idea of natural rights as inapplicable in a precommunist society (and presumably unnecessary in communism). Spencer took a utilitarian perspective on rights, and although he insisted on regarding them as natural rights, he allowed their neglect until the time society would evolve into its most mature manifestation.

It seems to me that no one need humble himself before another to such an extent that the latter's theoretical problems are ignored in the process of paying him homage. Spencer would be the last one to accept such unqualified, blind compliments. What we need not do, on the other hand, is reject Spencer's numerous insights in the area of substantive ethics. Here his ideas were more independent of his evolutionist system than in other areas. Here he often relied on common sense to shed light on what simply could not be developed from what he regarded as scientific principles. And with his commitment both to the importance of human life and excellence and to political and economic liberty, what Spencer had to offer us in his ethical discussions can enhance our understanding of life in freedom, whatever our own arguments for the value of such a life.

These are some ideas, I believe, that are worth keeping in mind as we encounter Herbert Spencer's ethical writings. It should be added that Spencer was not only a keen systematic thinker but also an uncompromisingly thorough and honest man. He lived only for his ideas, so that even his *Autobiography* consists mainly of an interpretive history of one person's life in terms of the theoretical framework he had developed. For those who value the ideals Spencer defended, it is gratifying that Spencer himself made every effort to live by them, to integrate them into his own concrete existence. There is much in Spencer's thought that is philosophically and scientifically unacceptable; but read critically, as all serious works should be, Spencer provides us with an intellectual adventure rarely matched, especially in our own epoch. The study of Spencer's ethics can shed needed light on some of the intricacies of what is demonstrably the best perspective on the ethical and political aspects of human life, namely, the morality of rational self-interest and the politics of the free society.

Fredonia, New York
January 1978

THE PRINCIPLES OF ETHICS

GENERAL PREFACE

The divisions of which this work consists have been published in an irregular manner. Part I was issued in 1879; Part IV in 1891; Parts II and III, forming along with Part I, the first volume, were issued in 1892; and Parts V and VI, concluding the second volume, have now, along with Part IV, been just issued. The reasons for this seemingly eccentric order of publication, primarily caused by ill health, will be found stated in the respective prefaces; which, by those who care to understand why the succession named has been followed, should be read in the order: Preface to Part I; then that to Part IV; Preface to Vol. I; and then that to Vol. II.

The preservation of these respective prefaces, while intended to account for the anomalous course pursued, serves also to explain some repetitions which, I fancy, have been made requisite by the separate publication of the parts: the independence of each having been a desideratum.

Now that the work is complete, it becomes possible to prefix some general remarks, which could not rightly be prefixed to any one of the installments.

The ethical doctrine set forth is fundamentally a corrected and elaborated version of the doctrine set forth in *Social*

Statics, issued at the end of 1850. The correspondence between
the two is shown, in the first place, by the coincidence of their
constructive divisions. In *Social Statics* the subject matter of
morality is divided into parts which treat respectively of Private Conduct, Justice, Negative Beneficence, and Positive
Beneficence; and these severally answer to Part III, Part IV,
Part V, and Part VI, constituting the constructive portion of
this work: to which there are, however, here prefixed Part I,
The Data, and Part II, The Inductions; in conformity with the
course I have pursued throughout The Synthetic Philosophy.
In *Social Statics* one division only of the ethical system marked
out was developed—justice; and I did not, when it was written, suppose that I should ever develop the others.

Besides coinciding in their divisions, the two works agree in
their cardinal ideas. As in the one so in the other, man, in
common with lower creatures, is held to be capable of indefinite change by adaptation to conditions. In both he is regarded
as undergoing transformation from a nature appropriate to his
aboriginal wild life, to a nature appropriate to a settled
civilized life; and in both this transformation is described as a
molding into a form fitted for harmonious cooperation. In
both, too, this molding is said to be effected by the repression
of certain primitive traits no longer needed, and the development of needful traits. As in the first work, so in this last, the
great factor in the progressive modification is shown to be
sympathy. It was contended then, as it is contended now, that
harmonious social cooperation implies that limitation of individual freedom which results from sympathetic regard for the
freedoms of others; and that the law of equal freedom is the
law in conformity to which equitable individual conduct and
equitable social arrangements consist. Morality, truly so
called, was described in the original work as formulating the
law of the "straight man"; and this conception corresponds
with the conception of absolute ethics, set forth in this work.
The theory then was, as the theory still is, that those mental
products of sympathy constituting what is called the "moral
sense," arise as fast as men are disciplined into social life; and

that along with them arise intellectual perceptions of right human relations, which become clearer as the form of social life becomes better. Further, it was inferred at that time as at this, that there is being effected a conciliation of individual natures with social requirements; so that there will eventually be achieved the greatest individuation along with the greatest mutual dependence—an equilibrium of such kind that each, in fulfilling the wants of his own life, will spontaneously aid in fulfilling the wants of all other lives. Finally, in the first work there were drawn essentially the same corollaries respecting the rights of individuals and their relations to the state, that are drawn in this last work.

Of course it yields me no small satisfaction to find that these ideas which fell dead in 1850, have now become generally diffused; and, more especially since the publication of the *Data of Ethics* in 1879, have met with so wide an acceptance that the majority of recent works on ethics take cognizance of them, and, in many cases, tacitly assume them, or some of them. Sundry of these works convey either the impression that the evolutionary view of ethics has long been familiar, or else that it dates from 1859, when the doctrine of "natural selection" was promulgated. In this connection I may name Mr. S. Alexander's *Moral Order and Progress,* and still more the *Review of the Systems of Ethics Founded on Evolution* by Mr. C. M. Williams. Alike in the introductory remarks of this last volume, and in the paragraph closing the account given of the views of Darwin, Wallace, and Haeckel, it is alleged that these "great original authorities paved the way for a system of evolutionary ethics." Though in the exposition of my own views, which immediately succeeds, there is a recognition of the fact that they date back to 1851, yet the collocation, as well as the express statements, practically cancel this inconsistent admission; and leave the impression that they are sequences of those of Mr. Darwin. And this, indeed, is the established general belief; as is sufficiently shown by the phrase "Darwinism in ethics," frequently to be met with, and which I now have before me in a review of Mr. Williams' book.

Rectification of this misbelief is of course hopeless. The world resents any attempt to show that it has fallen into an error; so that I should perhaps best consult my personal interests by saying nothing. But it seems to me proper to point out, as a matter of historical truth, that in this case, as in other cases, the genesis of ideas does not always follow the order of logical sequence; and that the doctrine of organic evolution in its application to human character and intelligence, and, by implication, to society, is of earlier date than *The Origin of Species*.

Without entering at length upon the prolegomena of ethics, it may be well here to state briefly one of them. The tacit assumption made in this work, as more or less consistently in all modern works on ethics, is that the conduct dealt with is the conduct of and between like-natured individuals—individuals whose likenesses of nature are so great in comparison with their differences as to constitute them of the same kind.

The possibility of another assumption, and consequently of another ethics, may be best shown by an analogy. The several kinds of social insects, though they do not form societies proper (since a nest of them is one large family descended from the same parents) yet show us that there may exist a body of cooperators among which a marked inequality is an essential trait; and they illustrate the possibility of a social organization such that the normal conduct of class to class is guided by rules appropriate to each class, and not common to all classes. They suggest that dissimilar members of a community may work together harmoniously on principles adapted to inequalities of nature. And they draw attention to the fact that there have been, and are, human societies constituted in a way which is analogous, to the extent that its classes of units, clearly marked off from one another, and devoted to different kinds of activities, either have, or tend to acquire, contrasted characters proper to their relative positions, and reciprocal codes of conduct which are thought obligatory.

Societies formed of dominant and enslaved races obviously answer to this description. In the United States in slavery days, it was common for slaves to jeer at free Negroes as having no white man to take care of them. To such an extent may the sentiments become molded to relations of inequality that, as in South Africa, the servants of a mild master will speak contemptuously of him because he does not thrash them. With extreme cases such as these to give the clue, we may perceive that wherever there are ruling classes and servile classes, as throughout Europe in early days, there comes to be an adjustment of natures such that command on the one side and obedience on the other are the natural concomitants of the social type. By continuous breeding of each class within itself, there tends to arise a differentiation into two varieties, such that the one becomes organically adapted to supremacy and the other to subordination. And it needs but to recall the ancient feudal loyalty, running down through all grades, or the fealty shown by an ancient Highlander to his chief, to see that there grew up ethical conceptions adjusted to the conditions.

But systems of ethics appropriate to social systems characterized by these organized inequalities of *status* cannot be the highest systems of ethics. Manifestly they presuppose imperfect natures—natures which are not self-sufficing. On the one side there is the need for control from without for the proper regulation of conduct; and on the other side there is the need for exercise of control, which, in an opposite way, implies lack of self-sufficingness. Further, external regulation is less economical of energy than internal regulation. When classes of inferiors are governed by classes of superiors, there is a waste of action which does not occur when all are self-governed. But chiefly the imperfection of ethical systems appropriate to societies characterized by organized inequality, is that sympathy and all those emotions into which sympathy enters, and all that happiness of which sympathy is the root, remain incomplete. Alien natures cannot sympathize in full measure—can sympathize only in respect of those feelings which they have in common. Hence the unlikenesses pre-supposed between permanently ruling classes and permanently subject classes, negative that highest happiness which a rational ethics takes for its end.

Throughout this work, therefore, the tacit assumption will be that the beings spoken of have that substantial unity of nature which characterizes the same variety of man; and the work will not, save incidentally or by contrast, take account of mixed societies, such as that which we have established in India, and still less of slave societies.

H.S.

June 1893

PREFACE TO VOLUME I

Misapprehensions would probably arise in the absence of explanations respecting the order in which the several parts of *The Principles of Ethics* have been, and are to be, published; for the production of the work, and its appearance in print, have proceeded in an unusual manner.

As explained in the original preface fixed to Part I (which is reproduced on the pages which follow), that part was written, and issued by itself in 1879, under the impression that ill health might wholly prevent me from treating the subject of ethics, if I waited till it was reached in the prescribed course of my work. More than ten years followed, partly occupied in further elaboration of *The Principles of Sociology,* and partly passed in a state of prostration which prevented all serious work. Along with partial recovery there came the decision to write at once the most important of the further divisions of *The Principles of Ethics*—Part IV: Justice. This was issued separately in June 1891. As stated in the preface to it, I proposed thereafter to write, if possible, Parts II and III, completing the first volume. This purpose has fortunately now been compassed; and Parts II and III are herewith issued in conjunction with Part I, as proposed in the original program.

One object I have in describing this irregular course of

publication, is the excuse it affords for some small repetitions, and perhaps minor incongruities, which I suspect exist. The endeavor to make certain of the divisions comprehensible by themselves, has prompted inclusion in them of explanations belonging to other divisions, which publication of the work as a whole would have rendered superfluous.

There have still to be written and published the concluding parts of the second volume: Part V, "The Ethics of Social Life—Negative Beneficence"; and Part VI, "The Ethics of Social Life—Positive Beneficence." The writing of these parts I hope to complete before ability ends: being especially anxious to do this because, in the absence of them, the divisions at present published will leave, on nearly all minds, a very erroneous impression respecting the general tone of evolutionary ethics. In its full scope, the moral system to be set forth unites sternness with kindness; but thus far attention has been drawn almost wholly to the sternness. Extreme misapprehensions and gross misstatements have hence resulted.

London
June 1892

PREFACE TO PART I
When First Issued Separately

A reference to the program of the "System of Synthetic Philosophy" will show that the chapters herewith issued constitute the first division of the work on the *Principles of Morality*, with which the system ends. As the second and third volumes of the *Principles of Sociology* are as yet unpublished, this installment of the succeeding work appears out of its place.

I have been led thus to deviate from the order originally set down, by the fear that persistence in conforming to it might result in leaving the final work of the series unexecuted. Hints, repeated of late years with increasing frequency and distinctness, have shown me that health may permanently fail, even if life does not end, before I reach the last part of the task I have marked out for myself. This last part of the task it is, to which I regard all the preceding parts as subsidiary. Written as far back as 1842, my first essay, consisting of letters on *The Proper Sphere of Government*, vaguely indicated what I conceived to be certain general principles of right and wrong in political conduct; and from that time onwards my ultimate purpose, lying behind all proximate purposes, has been that of finding for the principles of right and wrong in conduct at large, a scientific basis. To leave this purpose unfulfilled after making so extensive a preparation for fulfilling it, would be a failure the probability of which I do not like to contemplate; and I am anxious to preclude it, if not wholly, still partially. Hence the step I now take. Though this first division of the work terminating the Synthetic Philosophy cannot, of course, contain the specific conclusions to be set forth in the entire work; yet it implies them in such wise that, definitely to formulate them requires nothing beyond logical deduction.

I am the more anxious to indicate in outline, if I cannot complete, this final work, because the establishment of rules of right conduct on a scientific basis is a pressing need. Now that moral injunctions are losing the authority given by their supposed sacred origin, the secularization of morals is becoming imperative. Few things can happen more disastrous than the decay and death of a regulative system no longer fit, before another and fitter regulative system has grown up to replace it. Most of those who reject the current creed, appear to assume that the controlling agency furnished by it may safely be thrown aside, and the vacancy left unfilled by any other controlling agency. Meanwhile, those who defend the current creed allege that in the absence of the guidance it yields, no guidance can exist: divine commandments they think the only possible guides. Thus between these extreme opponents there is a certain community. The one holds that the gap left by disappearance of the code of supernatural ethics, need not be filled by a code of natural ethics; and the other holds that it cannot be so filled. Both contemplate a vacuum, which the one wishes and the other fears. As the change which promises or threatens to bring about this state, desired or dreaded, is rapidly progressing, those who believe that the vacuum can be filled, and that it must be filled, are called on to do something in pursuance of their belief.

To this more special reason I may add a more general reason. Great mischief has been done by the repellent aspect habitually given to moral rule by its expositors; and immense benefits are to be anticipated from presenting moral rule under that attractive aspect which it has when undistorted by superstition and asceticism. If a father, sternly enforcing numerous commands, some needful and some needless, adds to his severe control a behavior wholly unsympathetic— if his children have to take their pleasures by stealth, or, when timidly looking up from their play, ever meet a cold glance or more frequently a frown; his government will inevitably be disliked, if not hated; and the aim will be to evade it as much as possible. Contrariwise, a father who, equally firm in maintaining restraints needful for the well-being of his children or the well-being of other persons, not only avoids needless restraints, but, giving his sanction to all legitimate gratifications and providing the means for them, looks on at their gambols with an approving smile, can scarcely fail to gain an influence which, no less efficient for the time being, will also be permanently efficient. The controls of such two fathers symbolize the controls of morality as it is and morality as it should be.

Nor does mischief result only from this undue severity of the ethical doctrine bequeathed us by the harsh past. Further mischief results from the impracticability of its ideal. In violent reaction against the utter selfishness of life as carried on in barbarous societies, it has insisted on a life utterly unselfish. But just as the rampant egoism of a brutal militancy, was not to be remedied by attempts at the absolute subjection of the ego in convents and monasteries; so neither is the misconduct of ordinary humanity as now existing, to be remedied by upholding a standard of abnegation beyond human achievement. Rather the effect is to produce a despairing abandonment of all attempts at a higher life. And not only does an effort to achieve the impossible, end in this way, but it simultaneously discredits the possible. By association with rules that cannot be obeyed, rules that can be obeyed lose their authority.

Much adverse comment will, I doubt not, be passed on the theory of right conduct which the following pages shadow forth. Critics of a certain class, far from rejoicing that ethical principles otherwise derived by them, coincide with ethical principles scientifically derived, are offended by the coincidence. Instead of recognizing essential likeness they enlarge on superficial difference. Since the days of persecution, a curious change has taken place in the behavior of so-called orthodoxy towards so-called heterodoxy. The time was when a heretic, forced by torture to recant, satisfied authority by external conformity: apparent agreement sufficed, however profound continued to be the real disagreement. But now that the heretic can no longer be coerced into professing the ordinary belief, his belief is made to appear as much opposed to the ordinary as possible. Does he diverge from established theological dogma? Then he shall be an atheist; however inadmissible he considers the term. Does he think spiritualistic interpretations of phenomena not valid? Then he shall be classed as a materialist; indignantly though he repudiates the name. And in like manner, what differences exist between natural morality and supernatural morality, it has become the policy to exaggerate into fundamental antagonisms. In pursuance of this policy, there will probably be singled out for reprobation from this volume, doctrines which, taken by themselves, may readily be made to seem utterly wrong. With a view to clearness, I have treated separately some correlative aspects of conduct, drawing conclusions either of which becomes untrue if divorced from the other; and have thus given abundant opportunity for misrepresentation.

The relations of this work to works preceding it in the series, are such as to involve frequent reference. Containing, as it does, the outcome of principles set forth in each of them, I have found it impracticable to dispense with restatements of those principles. Further, the presentation of them in their relations to different ethical theories, has made it needful, in every case, briefly to remind the reader what they are, and how they are derived. Hence an amount of repetition which to some will probably appear tedious. I do not, however, much regret this almost unavoidable result; for only by varied iteration can alien conceptions be forced on reluctant minds.

June 1879

PART I
THE DATA OF ETHICS

CHAPTER 1

Conduct in General

1. The doctrine that correlatives imply one another—that a
    father cannot be thought of without thinking of a child,
and that there can be no consciousness of superior without a
consciousness of inferior—has for one of its common examples the necessary connection between the conceptions of
whole and part. Beyond the primary truth that no idea of a
whole can be framed without a nascent idea of parts constituting it, and that no idea of a part can be framed without a
nascent idea of some whole to which it belongs, there is the
secondary truth that there can be no correct idea of a part
without a correct idea of the correlative whole. There are
several ways in which inadequate knowledge of the one involves inadequate knowledge of the other.

If the part is conceived without any reference to the whole,
it becomes itself a whole—an independent entity; and its
relations to existence in general are misapprehended. Further,
the size of the part as compared with the size of the whole,
must be misapprehended unless the whole is not only recognized as including it, but is figured in its total extent. And
again, the position which the part occupies in relation to other
parts, cannot be rightly conceived unless there is some conception of the whole in its distribution as well as in its amount.

Still more when part and whole, instead of being statically related only, are dynamically related, must there be a general understanding of the whole before the part can be understood. By a savage who has never seen a vehicle, no idea can be formed of the use and action of a wheel. To the unsymmetrically pierced disk of an eccentric, no place or purpose can be ascribed by a rustic unacquainted with machinery. Even a mechanician, if he has never looked into a piano, will, if shown a damper, be unable to conceive its function or relative value.

Most of all, however, where the whole is organic, does complete comprehension of a part imply extensive comprehension of the whole. Suppose a being ignorant of the human body to find a detached arm. If not misconceived by him as a supposed whole, instead of being conceived as a part, still its relations to other parts, and its structure, would be wholly inexplicable. Admitting that the cooperation of its bones and muscles might be divined, yet no thought could be framed of the share taken by the arm in the actions of the unknown whole it belonged to; nor could any interpretation be put upon the nerves and vessels ramifying through it, which severally refer to certain central organs. A theory of the structure of the arm implies a theory of the structure of the body at large.

And this truth holds not of material aggregates only, but of immaterial aggregates—aggregated motions, deeds, thoughts, words. The moon's movements cannot be fully interpreted without taking into account the movements of the solar system at large. The process of loading a gun is meaningless until the subsequent actions performed with the gun are known. A fragment of a sentence, if not unintelligible, is wrongly interpreted in the absence of the remainder. Cut off its beginning and end, and the rest of a demonstration proves nothing. Evidence given by a plaintiff often misleads until the evidence which the defendant produces is joined with it.

2. Conduct is a whole; and, in a sense, it is an organic whole—an aggregate of interdependent actions performed by

an organism. That division or aspect of conduct with which ethics deals, is a part of this organic whole—a part having its components inextricably bound up with the rest. As currently conceived, stirring the fire, or reading a newspaper, or eating a meal, are acts with which morality has no concern. Opening the window to air the room, putting on an overcoat when the weather is cold, are thought of as having no ethical significance. These, however, are all portions of conduct. The behavior we call good and the behavior we call bad, are included, along with the behavior we call indifferent, under the conception of behavior at large. The whole of which ethics forms a part, is the whole constituted by the theory of conduct in general; and this whole must be understood before the part can be understood. Let us consider this proposition more closely.

And first, how shall we define conduct? It is not co-extensive with the aggregate of actions, though it is nearly so. Such actions as those of an epileptic in a fit, are not included in our conception of conduct: the conception excludes purposeless actions. And in recognizing this exclusion, we simultaneously recognize all that is included. The definition of conduct which emerges is either—acts adjusted to ends, or else—the adjustment of acts to ends; according as we contemplate the formed body of acts, or think of the form alone. And conduct in its full acceptation must be taken as comprehending all adjustments of acts to ends, from the simplest to the most complex, whatever their special natures and whether considered separately or in their totality.

Conduct in general being thus distinguished from the somewhat larger whole constituted by actions in general, let us next ask what distinction is habitually made between the conduct on which ethical judgments are passed and the remainder of conduct. As already said, a large part of ordinary conduct is indifferent. Shall I walk to the waterfall today? Or shall I ramble along the seashore? Here the ends are ethically indifferent. If I go to the waterfall, shall I go over the moor or take the path through the wood? Here the means are ethically indifferent. And from hour to hour most of the things we do are not to be judged as either good or bad in respect of either ends or means. No less clear is it that the transition from indifferent acts to acts which are good or bad is gradual. If a friend who is with me has explored the seashore but has not seen the waterfall, the choice of one or other end is no longer ethically indifferent. And if, the waterfall being fixed on as our goal, the way over the moor is too long for his strength, while the shorter way through the wood is not, the choice of means is no longer ethically indifferent. Again, if a probable result of making the one excursion rather than the other, is that I shall not be back in time to keep an appointment, or if taking the longer route entails this risk while taking the shorter does not, the decision in favor of one or other end or means acquires in another way an ethical character; and if the appointment is one of some importance, or one of great importance, or one of life-and-death importance, to self or others, the ethical character becomes pronounced. These instances will sufficiently suggest the truth that conduct with which morality is not concerned, passes into conduct which is moral or immoral, by small degrees and in countless ways.

But the conduct that has to be conceived scientifically before we can scientifically conceive those modes of conduct which are the objects of ethical judgments, is a conduct immensely wider in range than that just indicated. Complete comprehension of conduct is not to be obtained by contemplating the conduct of human beings only: we have to regard this as a part of universal conduct—conduct as exhibited by all living creatures. For evidently this comes within our definition—acts adjusted to ends. The conduct of the higher animals as compared with that of man, and the conduct of the lower animals as compared with that of the higher, mainly differ in this, that the adjustments of acts to ends are relatively simple and relatively incomplete. And as in other cases, so in this case, we must interpret the more developed by the less developed. Just as, fully to understand the part of conduct which ethics deals with, we must study human conduct as a whole; so, fully to understand human conduct as a whole, we must study it as a part of that large whole constituted by the conduct of animate beings in general.

Nor is even this whole conceived with the needful fullness, so long as we think only of the conduct at present displayed around us. We have to include in our conception the less-developed conduct out of which this has arisen in course of time. We have to regard the conduct now shown us by creatures of all orders, as an outcome of the conduct which has brought life of every kind to its present height. And this is tantamount to saying that our preparatory step must be to study the evolution of conduct.

CHAPTER 2

The Evolution of Conduct

3.   We have become quite familiar with the idea of an evolution of structures throughout the ascending types of animals. To a considerable degree we have become familiar with the thought that an evolution of functions has gone on *pari passu* with the evolution of structures. Now advancing a step, we have to frame a conception of the evolution of conduct, as correlated with this evolution of structures and functions.

These three subjects are to be definitely distinguished. Obviously the facts comparative morphology sets forth, form a whole which, though it cannot be treated in general or in detail without taking into account facts belonging to comparative physiology, is essentially independent. No less clear is it that we may devote our attention exclusively to that progressive differentiation of functions, and combination of functions, which accompanies the development of structures—may say no more about the characters and connections of organs than is implied in describing their separate and joint actions. And the subject of conduct lies outside the subject of functions, if not as far as this lies outside the subject of structures, still, far enough to make it substantially separate. For those functions which are already variously compounded to achieve what we regard as single bodily acts, are endlessly recompounded to achieve that coordination of bodily acts which is known as conduct.

We are concerned with functions in the true sense, while we think of them as processes carried on within the body; and, without exceeding the limits of physiology, we may treat of their adjusted combinations, so long as these are regarded as parts of the vital *consensus*. If we observe how the lungs aerate the blood which the heart sends to them; how heart and lungs together supply aerated blood to the stomach, and so enable it to do its work; how these cooperate with sundry secreting and excreting glands to further digestion and to remove waste matter; and how all of them join to keep the brain in a fit condition for carrying on those actions which indirectly conduce to maintenance of the life at large; we are dealing with functions. Even when considering how parts that act directly on the environment—legs, arms, wings—perform their duties, we are still concerned with functions in that aspect of them constituting physiology, so long as we restrict our attention to internal processes, and to internal combinations of them. But we enter on the subject of conduct when we begin to study such combinations among the actions of sensory and motor organs as are externally manifested. Suppose that instead of observing those contractions of muscles by which the optic axes are converged and the foci of the eyes adjusted (which is a portion of physiology), and that instead of observing the cooperation of other nerves, muscles, and bones, by which a hand is moved to a particular place and the fingers closed (which is also a portion of physiology), we observe a weapon being seized by a hand under guidance of the eyes. We now pass from the thought of combined internal functions to the thought of combined external motions. Doubtless if we could trace the cerebral processes which accompany these, we should find an inner physiological coordination corresponding with the outer coordination of actions. But this admission is consistent with the assertion, that when we ignore the internal combination and attend only to the external combination, we pass from a portion of physiology to a portion of conduct. For though it may be objected that the external combination instanced, is too simple to be rightly included under the name conduct, yet a moment's thought shows that it is joined with what we call conduct by insensible gradations. Suppose the weapon seized is used to ward off a blow. Suppose a counterblow is given. Suppose the aggressor runs and is chased. Suppose there comes a struggle and a handing him over to the police. Suppose there follow the many and varied acts constituting a prosecution. Obviously the initial adjustment of an act to an end, inseparable from the rest, must be included with them under the same general head; and obviously from this initial simple adjustment, having intrinsically no moral character, we pass by degrees to the most complex adjustments and to those on which moral judgments are passed.

Hence, excluding all internal coordinations, our subject here is the aggregate of all external coordinations; and this aggregate includes not only the simplest as well as the most complex performed by human beings, but also those performed by all inferior beings considered as less or more evolved.

4. Already the question—What constitutes advance in the evolution of conduct, as we trace it up from the lowest types of living creatures to the highest? has been answered by implication. A few examples will now bring the answer into conspicuous relief.

We saw that conduct is distinguished from the totality of actions by excluding purposeless actions; but during evolution this distinction arises by degrees. In the very lowest creatures most of the movements from moment to moment made, have not more recognizable aims than have the struggles of an epileptic. An infusorium swims randomly about, determined in its course not by a perceived object to be pursued or escaped, but, apparently, by varying stimuli in its medium; and its acts, unadjusted in any appreciable way to ends, lead it now into contact with some nutritive substance which it absorbs, and now into the neighborhood of some creature by which it is swallowed and digested. Lacking those developed senses and motor powers which higher animals possess, ninety-nine in the hundred of these minute animals, severally living but for a few hours, disappear either by innutrition or by destruction. The conduct is constituted of actions so little adjusted to ends, that life continues only as long as the accidents of the environment are favorable. But when, among aquatic creatures, we observe one which, though still low in type, is much higher than the infusorium—say a rotifer—we see how, along with larger size, more developed structures, and greater power of combining functions, there goes an advance in conduct. We see how by its whirling cilia it sucks in as food these small animals moving around; how by its prehensile tail it fixes itself to some object; how by withdrawing its outer organs and contracting its body, it preserves itself from this or that injury from time to time threatened; and how thus, by better adjusting its own actions, it becomes less dependent on the actions going on around, and so preserves itself for a longer period.

A superior subkingdom, as the Mollusca, still better exemplifies this contrast. When we compare a low mollusc, such as a floating ascidian, with a high mollusc, such as a cephalopod, we are again shown that greater organic evolution is accompanied by more evolved conduct. At the mercy of every marine creature large enough to swallow it, and drifted about by currents which may chance to keep it at sea or may chance to leave it fatally stranded, the ascidian displays but little adjustment of acts to ends in comparison with the cephalopod; which, now crawling over the beach, now exploring the rocky crevices, now swimming through the open water, now darting after a fish, now hiding itself from some larger animal in a cloud of ink, and using its suckered arms at one time for anchoring itself and at another for holding fast its prey; selects, and combines, and proportions, its movements from minute to minute, so as to evade dangers which threaten, while utilizing chances of food which offer; so showing us varied activities which, in achieving special ends, achieve the general end of securing continuance of the activities.

Among vertebrate animals we similarly trace up, along with advance in structures and functions, this advance in conduct. A fish roaming about at hazard in search of something to eat, able to detect it by smell or sight only within short distances, and now and again rushing away in alarm on the approach of a bigger fish, makes adjustments of acts to ends that are relatively few and simple in their kinds; and shows us, as a consequence, how small is the average duration of life. So few survive to maturity that, to make up for destruction of unhatched young and small fry and half-grown individuals, a million ova have to be spawned by a codfish that two may reach the spawning age. Conversely, by a highly evolved mammal, such as an elephant, those general actions performed in common with the fish are far better adjusted to their ends. By sight as well, probably, as by odor, it detects food at relatively great distances; and when, at intervals, there arises a need for escape, relatively great speed is attained. But the chief difference arises from the addition of new sets of adjustments. We have combined actions which facilitate nutrition— the breaking off of succulent and fruit-bearing branches, the selecting of edible growths throughout a comparatively wide reach; and, in case of danger, safety can be achieved not by flight only, but, if necessary, by defense or attack: bringing into combined use tusks, trunk, and ponderous feet. Further, we see various subsidiary acts adjusted to subsidiary ends— now the going into a river for coolness, and using the trunk as a means of projecting water over the body; now the employment of a bough for sweeping away flies from the back; now the making of signal sounds to alarm the herd, and adapting the actions to such sounds when made by others. Evidently, the effect of this more highly evolved conduct is to secure the balance of the organic actions throughout far longer periods.

And now, on studying the doings of the highest of mammals, mankind, we not only find that the adjustments of acts to ends are both more numerous and better than among lower mammals; but we find the same thing on comparing the doings of higher races of men with those of lower races. If we take any one of the major ends achieved, we see greater completeness of achievement by civilized than by savage; and we also see an achievement of relatively numerous minor ends subserving major ends. Is it in nutrition? The food is obtained more regularly in response to appetite; it is far higher in quality; it is free from dirt; it is greater in variety; it is better prepared. Is it in warmth? The characters of the fabrics and forms of the articles used for clothing, and the adaptations of them to requirements from day to day and hour to hour, are much superior. Is it in dwelling? Between the shelter of boughs and grass which the lowest savage builds, and the mansion of the civilized man, the contrast in aspect is not more extreme than is the contrast in number and efficiency of the adjustments of acts to ends betrayed in their respective constructions. And when with the ordinary activities of the savage we compare the ordinary civilized activities—as the business of the trader, which involves multiplied and complex transactions extending over long periods, or as professional avocations, prepared for by elaborate studies and daily carried on in endlessly varied forms, or as political discussions and agitations, directed now to the carrying of this measure and now to the defeating of that—we see sets of adjustments of acts to ends, not only immensely exceeding those seen among lower races of men in variety and intricacy, but sets to which lower races of men present nothing analogous. And along with this greater elaboration of life produced by the pursuit of more numerous ends, there goes that increased duration of life which constitutes the supreme end.

And here is suggested the need for supplementing this conception of evolving conduct. For besides being an improving adjustment of acts to ends, such as furthers prolongation of life, it is such as furthers increased amount of life. Reconsideration of the examples above given, will show that length of life is not by itself a measure of evolution of conduct; but that quantity of life must be taken into account. An oyster, adapted by its structure to the diffused food contained in the water it draws in, and shielded by its shell from nearly all dangers, may live longer than a cuttlefish, which has such superior powers of dealing with numerous contingencies; but then, the sum of vital activities during any given interval is far less in the oyster than in the cuttlefish. So a worm, ordinarily sheltered from most enemies by the earth it burrows through, which also supplies a sufficiency of its poor food, may have greater longevity than many of its annulose relatives, the insects; but one of these during its existence as larva and imago, may experience a greater quantity of the changes which constitute life. Nor is it otherwise when we compare the more evolved with the less evolved among mankind. The difference between the average lengths of the lives of savage and civilized, is no true measure of the difference between the totalities of their two lives, considered as aggregates of thought, feeling, and action. Hence, estimating life by multiplying its length into its breadth, we must say that the augmentation of it which accompanies evolution of conduct, results from increase of both factors. The more multiplied and varied adjustments of acts to ends, by which the more developed creature from hour to hour fulfills more numerous requirements, severally add to the activities that are carried on abreast, and severally help to make greater the period through which such simultaneous activities endure. Each further evolution of conduct widens the aggregate of actions while conducing to elongation of it.

5. Turn we now to a further aspect of the phenomena, separate from, but necessarily associated with, the last. Thus far we have considered only those adjustments of acts to ends which have for their final purpose complete individual life. Now we have to consider those adjustments which have for their final purpose the life of the species.

Self-preservation in each generation has all along de-

pended on the preservation of offspring by preceding generations. And in proportion as evolution of the conduct
subserving individual life is high, implying high organization,
there must previously have been a highly evolved conduct
subserving nurture of the young. Throughout the ascending
grades of the animal kingdom, this second kind of conduct
presents stages of advance like those which we have observed
in the first. Low down, where structures and functions are
little developed, and the power of adjusting acts to ends but
slight, there is no conduct, properly so named, furthering
salvation of the species. Race-maintaining conduct, like
self-maintaining conduct, arises gradually out of that which
cannot be called conduct: adjusted actions are preceded by
unadjusted ones. Protozoa spontaneously divide and sub-
divide, in consequence of physical changes over which they
have no control; or, at other times, after a period of quiescence, break up into minute portions which severally grow
into new individuals. In neither case can conduct be alleged.
Higher up, the process is that of ripening, at intervals, germ
cells and sperm cells, which, on occasion, are sent forth into
the surrounding water and left to their fate: perhaps one in ten
thousand surviving to maturity. Here, again, we see only
development and dispersion going on apart from parental
care. Types above these, as fish which choose fit places in
which to deposit their ova, or as the higher crustaceans which
carry masses of ova about until they are hatched, exhibit
adjustments of acts to ends which we may properly call conduct; though it is of the simplest kind. Where, as among
certain fish, the male keeps guard over the eggs, driving away
intruders, there is an additional adjustment of acts to ends;
and the applicability of the name conduct is more decided.
Passing at once to creatures far superior, such as birds which,
building nests and sitting on their eggs, feed their broods for
considerable periods, and give them aid after they can fly; or
such as mammals which, suckling their young for a time,
continue afterwards to bring them food or protect them while
they feed, until they reach ages at which they can provide for

themselves; we are shown how this conduct which furthers race maintenance evolves hand-in-hand with the conduct which furthers self-maintenance. That better organization which makes possible the last, makes possible the first also. Mankind exhibit a great progress of like nature. Compared with brutes, the savage, higher in his self-maintaining conduct, is higher too in his race-maintaining conduct. A larger number of the wants of offspring are provided for; and parental care, enduring longer, extends to the disciplining of offspring in arts and habits which fit them for their conditions of existence. Conduct of this order, equally with conduct of the first order, we see becoming evolved in a still greater degree as we ascend from savage to civilized. The adjustments of acts to ends in the rearing of children become far more elaborate, alike in number of ends met, variety of means used, and efficiency of their adaptations; and the aid and oversight are continued throughout a much greater part of early life.

In tracing up the evolution of conduct, so that we may frame a true conception of conduct in general, we have thus to recognize these two kinds as mutually dependent. Speaking generally, neither can evolve without evolution of the other; and the highest evolutions of the two must be reached simultaneously.

6. To conclude, however, that on reaching a perfect adjustment of acts to ends subserving individual life and the rearing of offspring, the evolution of conduct becomes complete, is to conclude erroneously. Or rather, I should say, it is an error to suppose that either of these kinds of conduct can assume its highest form, without its highest form being assumed by a third kind of conduct yet to be named.

The multitudinous creatures of all kinds which fill the earth, cannot live wholly apart from one another, but are more or less in presence of one another—are interfered with by one another. In large measure the adjustments of acts to ends which we have been considering, are components of that "struggle for existence" carried on both between members of the same species and between members of different species; and, very generally, a successful adjustment made by one creature involves an unsuccessful adjustment made by another creature, either of the same kind or of a different kind. That the carnivore may live herbivores must die; and that its young may be reared the young of weaker creatures must be orphaned. Maintenance of the hawk and its brood involves the deaths of many small birds; and that small birds may multiply, their progeny must be fed with innumerable sacrificed worms and larvae. Competition among members of the same species has allied, though less conspicuous, results. The stronger often carries off by force the prey which the weaker has caught. Monopolizing certain hunting grounds, the more ferocious drive others of their kind into less favorable places. With plant-eating animals, too, the like holds: the better food is secured by the more vigorous individuals, while the less vigorous and worse fed, succumb either directly from innutrition or indirectly from resulting inability to escape enemies. That is to say, among creatures whose lives are carried on antagonistically, each of the two kinds of conduct delineated above, must remain imperfectly evolved. Even in such few kinds of them as have little to fear from enemies or competitors, as lions or tigers, there is still inevitable failure in the adjustments of acts to ends towards the close of life. Death by starvation from inability to catch prey, shows a falling short of conduct from its ideal.

This imperfectly evolved conduct introduces us to antithesis to conduct that is perfectly evolved. Contemplating these adjustments of acts to ends which miss completeness because they cannot be made by one creature without other creatures being prevented from making them, raises the thought of adjustments such that each creature may make them without preventing them from being made by other creatures. That the highest form of conduct must be so distinguished, is an inevitable implication; for while the form of conduct is such that adjustments of acts to ends by some necessitate non-adjustments by others, there remains room for modifications which bring conduct into a form avoiding this, and so making the totality of life greater.

From the abstract let us pass to the concrete. Recognizing men as the beings whose conduct is most evolved, let us ask under what conditions their conduct, in all three aspects of its evolution, reaches its limit. Clearly while the lives led are entirely predatory, as those of savages, the adjustments of acts to ends fall short of this highest form of conduct in every way. Individual life, ill carried on from hour to hour, is prematurely cut short; the fostering of offspring often fails, and is incomplete when it does not fail; and in so far as the ends of self-maintenance and race maintenance are met, they are met by destruction of other beings, of different kind or of like kind. In social groups formed by compounding and recompounding primitive hordes, conduct remains imperfectly evolved in proportion as there continue antagonisms between the groups and antagonisms between members of the same group—two traits necessarily associated; since the nature which prompts international aggression prompts aggression of individuals on one another. Hence the limit of evolution can be reached by conduct only in permanently peaceful societies. That perfect adjustment of acts to ends in maintaining individual life and rearing new individuals, which is effected by each without hindering others from effecting like perfect adjustments, is, in its very definition, shown to constitute a kind of conduct that can be approached only as war decreases and dies out.

A gap in this outline must now be filled up. There remains a further advance not yet even hinted. For beyond so behaving that each achieves his ends without preventing others from achieving their ends, the members of a society may give mutual help in the achievement of ends. And if, either indirectly by industrial cooperation, or directly by volunteered aid, fellow citizens can make easier for one another the adjustments of acts to ends, then their conduct assumes a still higher phase of evolution; since whatever facilitates the making of adjustments by each, increases the totality of the adjustments made, and serves to render the lives of all more complete.

7. The reader who recalls certain passages in *First Principles,* in the *Principles of Biology,* and in the *Principles of Psychology,* will perceive above a restatement, in another form, of generalizations set forth in those works. Especially will he be reminded of the proposition that life is "the definite combination of heterogeneous changes, both simultaneous and successive, in correspondence with external coexistences and sequences"; and still more of that abridged and less specific formula, in which life is said to be "the continuous adjustment of internal relations to external relations."

The presentation of the facts here made, differs from the presentations before made, mainly by ignoring the inner part of the correspondence and attending exclusively to that outer part constituted of visible actions. But the two are in harmony; and the reader who wishes further to prepare himself for dealing with our present topic from the evolution point of view, may advantageously join to the foregoing more special aspect of the phenomena, the more general aspects before delineated.

After this passing remark, I recur to the main proposition set forth in these two chapters, which has, I think, been fully justified. Guided by the truth that as the conduct with which ethics deals is part of conduct at large, conduct at large must be generally understood before this part can be specially understood; and guided by the further truth that to understand conduct at large we must understand the evolution of conduct; we have been led to see that ethics has for its subject matter, that form which universal conduct assumes during the last stages of its evolution. We have also concluded that these last stages in the evolution of conduct are those displayed by the highest type of being, when he is forced, by increase of numbers, to live more and more in presence of his fellows. And there has followed the corollary that conduct gains ethical sanction in proportion as the activities, becoming less and less militant and more and more industrial, are such as do not necessitate mutual injury or hindrance, but consist with, and are furthered by, cooperation and mutual aid.

These implications of the evolution hypothesis, we shall now see harmonize with the leading moral ideas men have otherwise reached.

CHAPTER 3

Good and Bad Conduct

8. **B**y comparing its meanings in different connections and observing what they have in common, we learn the essential meaning of a word; and the essential meaning of a word that is variously applied, may best be learnt by comparing with one another those applications of it which diverge most widely. Let us thus ascertain what good and bad mean.

In which cases do we distinguish as good, a knife, a gun, a house? And what trait leads us to speak of a bad umbrella or a bad pair of boots? The characters here predicated by the words good and bad, are not intrinsic characters; for apart from human wants, such things have neither merits nor demerits. We call these articles good or bad according as they are well or ill adapted to achieve prescribed ends. The good knife is one which will cut; the good gun is one which carries far and true; the good house is one which duly yields the shelter, comfort, and accommodation sought for. Conversely, the badness alleged of the umbrella or the pair of boots, refers to their failures in fulfilling the ends of keeping off the rain and comfortably protecting the feet, with due regard to appearances. So is it when we pass from inanimate objects to inanimate actions. We call a day bad in which storms prevent us from satisfying certain of our desires. A good season is the expression used when the weather has favored the production of valuable crops. If from lifeless things and actions we pass to living ones, we similarly find that these words in their current applications refer to efficient subservience. The goodness or badness of a pointer or a hunter, of a sheep or an ox, ignoring all other attributes of these creatures, refers in the one case to the fitness of their actions for effecting the ends men use them for, and in the other case to the qualities of their flesh as adapting it to support human life. And those doings of men which, morally considered, are indifferent, we class as good or bad according to their success or failure. A good jump is a jump which, remoter ends ignored, well achieves the immediate purpose of a jump; and a stroke at billiards is called good when the movements are skillfully adjusted to the requirements. Oppositely, the badness of a walk that is shuffling and an utterance that is indistinct, is alleged because of the relative nonadaptations of the acts to the ends.

Thus recognizing the meanings of good and bad as otherwise used, we shall understand better their meanings as used in characterizing conduct under its ethical aspects. Here, too, observation shows that we apply them according as the adjustments of acts to ends are, or are not, efficient. This truth is somewhat disguised. The entanglement of social relations is such, that men's actions often simultaneously affect the welfares of self, of offspring, and of fellow citizens. Hence results confusion in judging of actions as good or bad; since actions well fitted to achieve ends of one order, may prevent ends of the other orders from being achieved. Nevertheless, when we disentangle the three orders of ends, and consider each separately, it becomes clear that the conduct which achieves each kind of end is regarded as relatively good; and is regarded as relatively bad if it fails to achieve it.

Take first the primary set of adjustments—those subserving individual life. Apart from approval or disapproval of his ulterior aims, a man who fights is said to make a good defense, if his defense is well adapted for self-preservation; and, the judgments on other aspects of his conduct remaining the same, he brings down on himself an unfavorable verdict, in so far as his immediate acts are concerned, if these are futile. The goodness ascribed to a man of business, as such, is measured by the activity and ability with which he buys and sells to advantage; and may coexist with a hard treatment of dependents which is reprobated. Though in repeatedly lending money to a friend who sinks one loan after another, a man is doing that which, considered in itself is held praiseworthy; yet, if he does it to the extent of bringing on his own ruin, he is held blameworthy for a self-sacrifice carried too far. And thus is it with the opinions we express from hour to hour on those acts of people around which bear on their health and personal welfare. "You should not have done that," is the reproof given to one who crosses the street amid a dangerous rush of vehicles. "You ought to have changed your clothes," is said to another who has taken cold after getting wet. "You were right to take a receipt"; "you were wrong to invest without advice"; are common criticisms. All such approving and disapproving utterances make the tacit assertion that, other things equal, conduct is right or wrong according as its special acts, well or ill adjusted to special ends, do or do not further the general end of self-preservation.

These ethical judgments we pass on self-regarding acts are ordinarily little emphasized; partly because the promptings of the self-regarding desires, generally strong enough, do not need moral enforcement, and partly because the promptings of the other-regarding desires, less strong, and often overridden, do need moral enforcement. Hence results a contrast. On turning to that second class of adjustments of acts to ends which subserve the rearing of offspring, we no longer find any obscurity in the application of the words good and bad to them, according as they are efficient or inefficient. The expressions good nursing and bad nursing, whether they refer to the supply of food, the quality and amount of clothing, or the due ministration to infantine wants from hour to hour, tacitly recognize as special ends which ought to be fulfilled, the furthering of the vital functions, with a view to the general end of continued life and growth. A mother is called good who, ministering to all the physical needs of her children, also adjusts her behavior in ways conducive to their mental health; and a bad father is one who either does not provide the necessaries of life for his family, or otherwise acts in a manner injurious to their bodies or minds. Similarly of the education given to them, or provided for them. Goodness or badness is affirmed of it (often with little consistency, however) according as its methods are so adapted to physical and psychical requirements, as to further the children's lives for the time being, while preparing them for carrying on complete and prolonged adult life.

Most emphatic, however, are the applications of the words good and bad to conduct throughout that third division of it comprising the deeds by which men affect one another. In maintaining their own lives and fostering their offspring, men's adjustments of acts to ends are so apt to hinder the kindred adjustments of other men, that insistence on the needful limitations has to be perpetual; and the mischiefs caused by men's interferences with one another's life-subserving actions are so great, that the interdicts have to be peremptory. Hence the fact that the words good and bad have come to be specially associated with acts which further the complete living of others and acts which obstruct their complete living. Goodness, standing by itself, suggests, above all other things, the conduct of one who aids the sick in reacquiring normal vitality, assists the unfortunate to recover the means of maintaining themselves, defends those who are threatened with harm in person, property, or reputation, and aids whatever promises to improve the living of all his fellows. Contrariwise, badness brings to mind, as its leading correlative, the conduct of one who, in carrying on his own life, damages the lives of others by injuring their bodies, destroying their possessions, defrauding them, calumniating them.

Always, then, acts are called good or bad, according as they are well or ill adjusted to ends; and whatever inconsistency there is in our uses of the words, arises from inconsistency of the ends. Here, however, the study of conduct in general, and of the evolution of conduct, have prepared us to harmonize these interpretations. The foregoing exposition shows that the conduct to which we apply the name good, is the relatively more evolved conduct; and that bad is the name we apply to conduct which is relatively less evolved. We saw that evolution, tending ever towards self-preservation, reaches its limit when individual life is the greatest, both in length and breadth; and now we see that, leaving other ends aside, we regard as good the conduct furthering self-preservation, and as bad the conduct tending to self-destruction. It was shown that along with increasing power of maintaining individual life, which evolution brings, there goes increasing power of perpetuating the species by fostering progeny, and that in this direction evolution reaches its limit when the needful number of young, preserved to maturity, are then fit for a life that is complete in fullness and duration; and here it turns out that parental conduct is called good or bad as it approaches or falls short of this ideal result. Lastly, we inferred that establishment of an associated state, both makes possible and requires a form of conduct such that life may be completed in each and in his offspring, not only without preventing completion of it in others, but with furtherance of it in others; and we have found above, that this is the form of conduct most emphatically termed good. Moreover, just as we there saw that evolution becomes the highest possible when the conduct simultaneously achieves the greatest totality of life in self, in offspring, and in fellow men; so here we see that the conduct called good rises to the conduct conceived as best, when it fulfills all three classes of ends at the same time.

9. Is there any postulate involved in these judgments on conduct? Is there any assumption made in calling good the acts conducive to life, in self or others, and bad those which directly or indirectly tend towards death, special or general? Yes; an assumption of extreme significance has been made— an assumption underlying all moral estimates.

The question to be definitely raised and answered before entering on any ethical discussion, is the question of late much agitated—Is life worth living? Shall we take the pessimist view? or shall we take the optimist view? or shall we, after weighing pessimistic and optimistic arguments, conclude that the balance is in favor of a qualified optimism?

On the answer to this question depends entirely every decision concerning the goodness or badness of conduct. By those who think life is not a benefit but a misfortune, conduct which prolongs it is to be blamed rather than praised: the ending of an undesirable existence being the thing to be wished, that which causes the ending of it must be applauded; while actions furthering its continuance, either in self or others, must be reprobated. Those who, on the other hand, take an optimistic view, or who, if not pure optimists, yet hold that in life the good exceeds the evil, are committed to opposite estimates; and must regard as conduct to be approved that which fosters life in self and others, and as conduct to be disapproved that which injures or endangers life in self or others.

The ultimate question, therefore, is—Has evolution been a mistake; and especially that evolution which improves the adjustment of acts to ends in ascending stages of organization? If it is held that there had better not have been any animate existence at all, and that the sooner it comes to an end the better; then one set of conclusions with respect to conduct emerges. If, contrariwise, it is held that there is a balance in favor of animate existence, and if, still further, it is held that in the future this balance may be increased; then the opposite set of conclusions emerges. Even should it be alleged that the worth of life is not to be judged by its intrinsic character, but rather by its extrinsic sequences—by certain results to be anticipated when life has passed—the ultimate issue reappears in a new shape. For though the accompanying creed may negative a deliberate shortening of life that is miserable, it cannot justify a gratuitous lengthening of such life. Legislation conducive to increased longevity would, on the pessimistic view, remain blamable; while it would be praiseworthy on the optimistic view.

But now, have these irreconcilable opinions anything in common? Men being divisible into two schools differing on this ultimate question, the inquiry arises—Is there anything which their radically opposed views alike take for granted? In the optimistic proposition, tacitly made when using the words good and bad after the ordinary manner; and in the pessimistic proposition overtly made, which implies that the words good and bad should be used in the reverse senses; does examination disclose any joint proposition—any proposition which, contained in both of them, may be held more certain than either—any universally asserted proposition?

10. Yes, there is one postulate in which pessimists and optimists agree. Both their arguments assume it to be self-evident that life is good or bad, according as it does, or does not, bring a surplus of agreeable feeling. The pessimist says he condemns life because it results in more pain than pleasure. The optimist defends life in the belief that it brings more pleasure than pain. Each makes the kind of sentiency which accompanies life the test. They agree that the justification for life as a state of being, turns on this issue—whether the average consciousness rises above indifference-point into pleasurable feeling or falls below it into painful feeling. The implication common to their antagonist views is, that conduct should conduce to preservation of the individual, of the family, and of the society, only supposing that life brings more happiness than misery.

Changing the venue cannot alter the verdict. If either the pessimist, while saying that the pains of life predominate, or the optimist, while saying that the pleasures predominate, urges that the pains borne here are to be compensated by pleasures received hereafter; and that so life, whether or not justified in its immediate results, is justified in its ultimate results; the implication remains the same. The decision is still reached by balancing pleasures against pains. Animate existence would be judged by both a curse, if to a surplus of misery borne here, were added a surplus of misery to be borne hereafter. And for either to regard animate existence as a blessing, if here its pains were held to exceed its pleasures, he must hold that hereafter its pleasures will exceed its pains. Thus there is no escape from the admission that in calling good the conduct which subserves life, and bad the conduct which hinders or destroys it, and in so implying that life is a blessing and not a curse, we are inevitably asserting that conduct is good or bad according as its total effects are pleasurable or painful.

One theory only is imaginable in pursuance of which other interpretations of good and bad can be given. This theory is that men were created with the intention that they should be sources of misery to themselves; and that they are bound to continue living that their creator may have the satisfaction of contemplating their misery. Though this is not a theory avowedly entertained by many—though it is not formulated by any in this distinct way; yet not a few do accept it under a disguised form. Inferior creeds are pervaded by the belief that the sight of suffering is pleasing to the gods. Derived from bloodthirsty ancestors, such gods are naturally conceived as gratified by the infliction of pain: when living they delighted in torturing other beings; and witnessing torture is supposed still to give them delight. The implied conceptions long survive. It needs but to name Indian fakirs who hang on hooks and Eastern dervishes who gash themselves, to show that in societies considerably advanced, are still to be found many who think that submission to anguish brings divine favor. And without enlarging on fasts and penances, it will be clear that there has existed, and still exists, among Christian peoples, the belief that the Deity whom Jephthah thought to propitiate by sacrificing his daughter, may be propitiated by self-inflicted pains. Further, the conception accompanying this, that acts pleasing to self are offensive to God, has survived along with it, and still widely prevails; if not in formulated dogmas, yet in beliefs that are manifestly operative.

Doubtless, in modern days such beliefs have assumed qualified forms. The satisfaction which ferocious gods were supposed to feel in contemplating tortures, has been, in large measure, transformed into the satisfaction felt by a deity in contemplating that self-infliction of pain which is held to further eventual happiness. But clearly those who entertain this modified view, are excluded from the class whose position we are here considering. Restricting ourselves to this class—supposing that from the savage who immolates victims to a cannibal god, there are descendants among the civilized, who hold that mankind were made for suffering, and that it is their duty to continue living in misery for the delight of their maker, we can only recognize the fact that devil-worshippers are not yet extinct.

Omitting people of this class, if there are any, as beyond or beneath argument, we find that all others avowedly or tacitly hold that the final justification for maintaining life, can only be the reception from it of a surplus of pleasurable feeling over painful feeling; and that goodness or badness can be ascribed to acts which subserve life or hinder life, only on this supposition.

And here we are brought round to those primary meanings of the words good and bad, which we passed over when considering their secondary meanings. For on remembering that we call good and bad the things which immediately produce agreeable and disagreeable sensations, and also the sensations themselves—a good wine, a good appetite, a bad smell, a bad headache—we see that by referring directly to pleasures and pains, these meanings harmonize with those which indirectly refer to pleasures and pains. If we call good the enjoyable state itself, as a good laugh—if we call good the proximate cause of an enjoyable state, as good music—if we call good any agent which conduces immediately or remotely to an enjoyable state, as a good shop, a good teacher—if we call good considered intrinsically, each act so adjusted to its end as to further self-preservation and that surplus of enjoyment which makes self-preservation desirable—if we call good every kind of conduct which aids the lives of others, and do this under the belief that life brings more happiness than misery; then it becomes undeniable that, taking into account immediate and remote effects on all persons, the good is universally the pleasurable.

11. Sundry influences—moral, theological, and political—conspire to make people disguise from themselves this truth. As in narrower cases so in this widest case, they become so preoccupied with the means by which an end is achieved, as eventually to mistake it for the end. Just as money, which is a means of satisfying wants, comes to be regarded by a miser as the sole thing to be worked for, leaving the wants unsatisfied; so the conduct men have found preferable because most conducive to happiness, has come to be thought of as intrinsically preferable: not only to be made a proximate end (which it should be) but to be made an ultimate end, to the exclusion of the true ultimate end. And yet cross-examination quickly compels everyone to confess the true ultimate end. Just as the miser, asked to justify himself, is obliged to allege the power of money to purchase desirable things, as his reason for prizing it; so the moralist who thinks this conduct intrinsically good and that intrinsically bad, if pushed home, has no choice but to fall back on their pleasure-giving and pain-giving effects. To prove this it needs but to observe how impossible it would be to think of them as we do, if their effects were reversed.

Suppose that gashes and bruises caused agreeable sensations, and brought in their train increased power of doing work and receiving enjoyment; should we regard assault in the same manner as at present? Or suppose that self-mutilation, say by cutting off a hand, was both intrinsically pleasant and furthered performance of the processes by which personal welfare and the welfare of dependents is achieved; should we hold as now, that deliberate injury to one's own body is to be reprobated? Or again, suppose that picking a man's pocket excited in him joyful emotions, by brightening his prospects; would theft be counted among crimes, as in existing lawbooks and moral codes? In these extreme cases, no one can deny that what we call the badness of actions is ascribed to them solely for the reason that they entail pain, immediate or remote, and would not be so ascribed did they entail pleasure.

If we examine our conceptions on their obverse side, this general fact forces itself on our attention with equal distinctness. Imagine that ministering to a sick person always increased the pains of illness. Imagine that an orphan's relatives who took charge of it, thereby necessarily brought miseries upon it. Imagine that liquidating another man's pecuniary claims on you redounded to his disadvantage. Imagine that crediting a man with noble behavior hindered his social welfare and consequent gratification. What should we say to these acts which now fall into the class we call praiseworthy? Should we not contrariwise class them as blameworthy?

Using, then, as our tests, these most pronounced forms of good and bad conduct, we find it unquestionable that our ideas of their goodness and badness really originate from our consciousness of the certainty or probability that they will produce pleasures or pains somewhere. And this truth is brought out with equal clearness by examining the standards of different moral schools; for analysis shows that every one of them derives its authority from this ultimate standard. Ethical systems are roughly distinguishable according as they take for their cardinal ideas (1) the character of the agent; (2) the nature of his motive; (3) the quality of his deeds; and (4) the results. Each of these may be characterized as good or bad; and those who do not estimate a mode of life by its effects on happiness, estimate it by the implied goodness or badness in the agent, in his motive, or in his deeds. We have perfection in the agent set up as a test by which conduct is to be judged. Apart from the agent we have his feeling considered as moral. And apart from the feeling we have his action considered as virtuous.

Though the distinctions thus indicated have so little definiteness that the words marking them are used interchangeably, yet there correspond to them doctrines partially unlike one another; which we may here conveniently examine separately, with the view of showing that all their tests of goodness are derivative.

12. It is strange that a notion so abstract as that of perfection, or a certain ideal completeness of nature, should ever have been thought one from which a system of guidance can be evolved; as it was in a general way by Plato and more distinctly by Jonathan Edwards. Perfection is synonymous with goodness in the highest degree; and hence to define good conduct in terms of perfection, is indirectly to define good conduct in terms of itself. Naturally, therefore, it happens that the notion of perfection like the notion of goodness can be framed only in relation to ends.

We allege imperfection of any inanimate thing, as a tool, if it lacks some part needful for effectual action, or if some part is so shaped as not to fulfill its purpose in the best manner. Perfection is alleged of a watch if it keeps exact time, however plain its case; and imperfection is alleged of it because of inaccurate timekeeping, however beautifully it is ornamented. Though we call things imperfect if we detect in them any injuries or flaws, even when these do not detract from efficiency; yet we do this because they imply that inferior workmanship, or that wear and tear, with which inefficiency is commonly joined in experience: absence of minor imperfections being habitually associated with absence of major imperfections.

As applied to living things, the word perfection has the same meaning. The idea of perfect shape in a race horse is derived by generalization from those observed traits of race horses which have usually gone along with attainment of the highest speed; and the idea of perfect constitution in a race horse similarly refers to the endurance which enables him to continue that speed for the longest time. With men, physically considered, it is the same: we are able to furnish no other test of perfection, than that of complete power in all the organs to fulfill their respective functions. That our conception of perfect balance among the internal parts, and of perfect proportion among the external parts, originates thus, is made clear by observing that imperfection of any viscus, as lungs, heart, or liver, is ascribed for no other reason than inability to meet in full the demands which the activities of the organism make on it; and on observing that the conception of insufficient size, or of too great size, in a limb, is derived from accumulated experiences respecting that ratio among the limbs which furthers in the highest degree the performance of all needful actions.

And of perfection in mental nature we have no other measure. If imperfection of memory, of judgment, of temper, is alleged, it is alleged because of inadequacy to the requirements of life; and to imagine a perfect balance of the intellectual powers and of the emotions, is to imagine that proportion among them which ensures an entire discharge of each and every obligation as the occasion calls for it.

So that the perfection of man considered as an agent, means the being constituted for effecting complete adjustment of acts to ends of every kind. And since, as shown above, the complete adjustment of acts to ends is that which both secures and constitutes the life that is most evolved, alike in breadth and length; while, as also shown, the justification for whatever increases life is the reception from life of more happiness than misery; it follows that conduciveness to happiness is the ultimate test of perfection in a man's nature. To be fully convinced of this it needs but to observe how the proposition looks when inverted. It needs but to suppose that every approach towards perfection involved greater misery to self, or others, or both, to show by opposition that approach to perfection really means approach to that which secures greater happiness.

13. Pass we now from the view of those who make excellence of being the standard, to the view of those who make virtuousness of action the standard. I do not here refer to moralists who, having decided empirically or rationally, in-

ductively or deductively, that acts of certain kinds have the character we call virtuous, argue that such acts are to be performed without regard to proximate consequences: these have ample justification. But I refer to moralists who suppose themselves to have conceptions of virtue as an end, unde-rived from any other end—who think that the idea of virtue is not resolvable into simpler ideas.

This is the doctrine which appears to have been entertained by Aristotle. I say, appears to have been, because his state-ments are far from consistent with one another. Recognizing happiness as the supreme end of human endeavor, it would at first sight seem that he cannot be taken as typical of those who make virtue the supreme end. Yet he puts himself in this category by seeking to define happiness in terms of virtue, instead of defining virtue in terms of happiness. The imper-fect separation of words from things, which characterizes Greek speculation in general, seems to have been the cause of this. In primitive thought the name and the object named, are associated in such wise that the one is regarded as a part of the other—so much so, that knowing a savage's name is consid-ered by him as having some of his being, and a consequent power to work evil on him. This belief in a real connection between word and thing, continuing through lower stages of progress, and long surviving in the tacit assumption that the meanings of words are intrinsic, pervades the dialogues of Plato, and is traceable even in Aristotle. For otherwise it is not easy to see why he should have so incompletely dissociated the abstract idea of happiness from particular forms of happi-ness. Naturally where the divorcing of words as symbols, from things as symbolized, is imperfect, there must be diffi-culty in giving to abstract words a sufficiently abstract mean-ing. If in the first stages of language the concrete name cannot be separated in thought from the concrete object it belongs to, it is inferable that in the course of forming successively higher grades of abstract names, there will have to be resisted the tendency to interpret each more abstract name in terms of some one class of the less abstract names it covers. Hence, I think, the fact that Aristotle supposes happiness to be associated with some one order of human activities, rather than with all orders of human activities. Instead of including in it the pleasurable feelings accompanying actions that constitute mere living, which actions he says man has in common with vegetables; and instead of making it include the mental states which the life of external perception yields, which he says man has in common with animals at large; he excludes these from his idea of happiness, and includes in it only the modes of consciousness accompanying rational life. Asserting that the proper work of man "consists in the active exercise of the mental capacities conformably to reason," he concludes that "the supreme good of man will consist in performing this work with excellence or virtue: herein he will obtain happiness." And he finds confirmation for his view in its correspondence with views previously enunciated, saying—"our notion nearly agrees with theirs who place happiness in virtue; for we say that it consists in the action of virtue; that is, not merely in the possession, but in the use."

Now the implied belief that virtue can be defined otherwise than in terms of happiness (for else the proposition is that happiness is to be obtained by actions conducive to happiness) is allied to the Platonic belief that there is an ideal or absolute good, which gives to particular and relative goods their property of goodness; and an argument analogous to that which Aristotle uses against Plato's conception of good, may be used against his own conception of virtue. As with good so with virtue—it is not singular but plural: in Aristotle's own classification, virtue, when treated of at large, is transformed into virtues. Those which he calls virtues, must be so called in consequence of some common character that is either intrinsic or extrinsic. We may class things together either because they are made alike by all having in themselves some peculiarity, as we do vertebrate animals because they all have vertebral columns; or we may class them together because of some community in their outer relations, as when we group saws, knives, mallets, harrows, under the head of tools. Are

the virtues classed as such because of some intrinsic community of nature? Then there must be identifiable a common trait
in all the cardinal virtues which Aristotle specifies—
"Courage, Temperance, Liberality, Magnanimity, Magnifi-
cence, Meekness, Amiability or Friendliness, Truthfulness,
Justice." What now is the trait possessed in common by mag-
nificence and meekness? and if any such common trait can be
disentangled, is it that which also constitutes the essential
trait in truthfulness? The answer must be—no. The virtues,
then, not being classed as such because of an intrinsic community of character, must be classed as such because of something extrinsic; and this something can be nothing else than
the happiness which Aristotle says consists in the practice of
them. They are united by their common relation to this result;
while they are not united by their inner natures.

Perhaps still more clearly may the inference be drawn thus:
If virtue is primordial and independent, no reason can be
given why there should be any correspondence between virtuous conduct and conduct that is pleasure-giving in its total
effects on self, or others, or both; and if there is not a necessary
correspondence, it is conceivable that the conduct classed as
virtuous should be pain-giving in its total effects. That we may
see the consequence of so conceiving it, let us take the two
virtues considered as typically such in ancient times and in
modern times—courage and chastity. By the hypothesis,
then, courage, displayed alike in self-defense and in defense
of country, is to be conceived as not only entailing pains
incidentally, but as being necessarily a cause of misery to the
individual and to the state; while, by implication, the absence
of it redounds to personal and general well-being. Similarly,
by the hypothesis, we have to conceive that irregular sexual
relations are directly and indirectly beneficial—that adultery is
conducive to domestic harmony and the careful rearing of
children; while marital relations in proportion as they are
persistent, generate discord between husband and wife and
entail on their offspring, suffering, disease, and death. Unless
it is asserted that courage and chastity could still be thought of

as virtues though thus productive of misery, it must be admitted that the conceptions of virtue cannot be separated from the conception of happiness producing conduct; and that as this holds of all the virtues, however otherwise unlike, it is from their conduciveness to happiness that they come to be classed as virtues.

14. When from those ethical estimates which take perfection of nature, or virtuousness of action, as tests, we pass to those which take for test rectitude of motive, we approach the intuitional theory of morals; and we may conveniently deal with such estimates by a criticism on this theory.

By the intuitional theory I here mean, not that which recognizes as produced by the inherited effects of continued experiences, the feelings of liking and aversion we have to acts of certain kinds; but I mean the theory which regards such feelings as divinely given, and as independent of results experienced by self or ancestors. "There is therefore," says Hutcheson, "as each one by close attention and reflection may convince himself, a natural and immediate determination to approve certain affections, and actions consequent upon them"; and since, in common with others of his time, he believes in the special creation of man, and all other beings, this "natural sense of immediate excellence" he considers as a supernaturally derived guide. Though he says that the feelings and acts thus intuitively recognized as good, "all agree in one general character, of tending to the happiness of others"; yet he is obliged to conceive this as a preordained correspondence. Nevertheless, it may be shown that conduciveness to happiness, here represented as an incidental trait of the acts which receive these innate moral approvals, is really the test by which these approvals are recognized as moral. The intuitionists place confidence in these verdicts of conscience, simply because they vaguely, if not distinctly, perceive them to be consonant with the disclosures of that ultimate test. Observe the proof.

By the hypothesis, the wrongness of murder is known by a

moral intuition which the human mind was originally constituted to yield; and the hypothesis therefore negatives the
admission that this sense of its wrongness arises, immediately
or remotely, from the consciousness that murder involves
deduction from happiness, directly and indirectly. But if you
ask an adherent of this doctrine to contrast his intuition with
that of the Fijian, who, considering murder an honorable
action, is restless until he has distinguished himself by killing
someone; and if you inquire of him in what way the civilized
intuition is to be justified in opposition to the intuition of the
savage; no course is open save that of showing how conformity to the one conduces to well-being, while conformity
to the other entails suffering, individual and general. When
asked why the moral sense which tells him that it is wrong to
take another man's goods, should be obeyed rather than the
moral sense of a Turcoman, who proves how meritorious he
considers theft to be by making pilgrimages to the tombs of
noted robbers to make offerings; the intuitionist can do nothing but urge that, certainly under conditions like ours, if not
also under conditions like those of the Turkomans, disregard
of men's claims to their property not only inflicts immediate
misery, but involves a social state inconsistent with happiness. Or if, again, there is required from him a justification for
his feeling of repugnance to lying, in contrast with the feeling
of an Egyptian, who prides himself on skill in lying (even
thinking it praiseworthy to deceive without any further end
than that of practicing deception); he can do no more than
point to the social prosperity furthered by entire trust between
man and man, and the social disorganization that follows
universal untruthfulness—consequences that are necessarily
conducive to agreeable feelings and disagreeable feelings respectively.

The unavoidable conclusion is, then, that the intuitionist
does not, and cannot, ignore the ultimate derivations of right
and wrong from pleasure and pain. However much he may be
guided, and rightly guided, by the decisions of conscience
respecting the characters of acts; he has come to have confidence in these decisions because he perceives, vaguely but

positively, that conformity to them furthers the welfare of himself and others, and that disregard of them entails in the long-run suffering on all. Require him to name any moral-sense judgment by which he knows as right, some kind of act that will bring a surplus of pain, taking into account the totals in this life and in any assumed other life, and you find him unable to name one: a fact proving that underneath all these intuitions respecting the goodness or badness of acts, there lies the fundamental assumption that acts are good or bad according as their aggregate effects increase men's happiness or increase their misery.

15. It is curious to see how the devil worship of the savage, surviving in various disguises among the civilized, and leaving as one of its products that asceticism which in many forms and degrees still prevails widely, is to be found influencing in marked ways, men who have apparently emancipated themselves, not only from primitive superstitions but from more developed superstitions. Views of life and conduct which originated with those who propitiated deified ancestors by self-tortures, enter even still into the ethical theories of many persons who have years since cast away the theology of the past, and suppose themselves to be no longer influenced by it.

In the writings of one who rejects dogmatic Christianity together with the Hebrew cult which preceded it, a career of conquest costing tens of thousands of lives, is narrated with a sympathy comparable to that rejoicing which the Hebrew traditions show us over destruction of enemies in the name of God. You may find, too, a delight in contemplating the exercise of despotic power, joined with insistence on the salutariness of a state in which the wills of slaves and citizens, are humbly subject to the wills of masters and rules—a sentiment also reminding us of that ancient Oriental life which biblical narratives portray. Along with this worship of the strong man—along with this justification of whatever force may be needed for carrying out his ambition—along with this yearning for a form of society in which supremacy of the few is unrestrained and the virtue of the many consists in obedience to them; we not unnaturally find repudiation of the ethical theory which takes, in some shape or other, the greatest happiness as the end of conduct: we not unnaturally find this utilitarian philosophy designated by the contemptuous title of "pig-philosophy." And then, serving to show what comprehension there has been of the philosophy so nicknamed, we are told that not happiness but blessedness must be the end.

Obviously, the implication is that blessedness is not a kind of happiness; and this implication at once suggests the question—What mode of feeling is it? If it is a state of consciousness at all, it is necessarily one of three states—painful, indifferent, or pleasurable. Does it leave the possessor at the zero point of sentiency? Then it leaves him just as he would be if he had not got it. Does it not leave him at the zero point? Then it must leave him below zero or above zero.

Each of these possibilities may be conceived under two forms. That to which the term blessedness is applied, may be a particular state of consciousness—one among the many states that occur; and on this supposition we have to recognize it as a pleasurable state, an indifferent state, or a painful state. Otherwise, blessedness is a word not applicable to a particular state of consciousness, but characterizes the aggregate of its states; and in this case the average of the aggregate is to be conceived as one in which the pleasurable predominates, or one in which the painful predominates, or one in which pleasures and pains exactly cancel one another. Let us take in turn these two imaginable applications of the word.

"Blessed are the merciful"; "Blessed are the peacemakers"; "Blessed is he that considereth the poor"; are sayings which we may fairly take as conveying the accepted meaning of blessedness. What now shall we say of one who is, for the time being, blessed in performing an act of mercy? Is his mental state pleasurable? If so the hypothesis is abandoned: blessedness is a particular form of happiness. Is the state indifferent or painful? In that case the blessed man is so devoid of sympathy that relieving another from pain, or the fear of pain, leaves him either wholly unmoved, or gives him an unpleasant emotion. Again, if one who is blessed in making peace receives no gratification from the act, then seeing men injure each other does not affect him at all, or gives him a pleasure which is changed into a pain when he prevents the injury. Once more, to say that the blessedness of one who "considereth the poor" implies no agreeable feeling, is to say that his consideration for the poor leaves him without feeling or entails on him a disagreeable feeling. So that if blessedness is a particular mode of consciousness temporarily existing as a concomitant of each kind of beneficent action, those who deny that it is a pleasure, or constituent of happiness, confess themselves either not pleased by the welfare of others or displeased by it.

Otherwise understood, blessedness must, as we have seen, refer to the totality of feelings experienced during the life of one who occupies himself with the actions the word connotes. This also presents the three possibilities—surplus of pleasures, surplus of pains, equality of the two. If the pleasurable states are in excess, then the blessed life can be distinguished from any other pleasurable life only by the relative amount, or the quality, of its pleasures: it is a life which makes happiness of a certain kind and degree its end; and the assumption that blessedness is not a form of happiness, lapses. If the blessed life is one in which the pleasures and pains received balance one another, so producing an average that is indifferent; or if it is one in which the pleasures are outbalanced by the pains; then the blessed life has the character which the pessimist alleges of life at large, and therefore regards it as cursed. Annihilation is best, he will argue; since if an average that is indifferent is the outcome of the blessed life, annihilation at once achieves it; and if a surplus of suffering is the outcome of this highest kind of life called blessed, still more should life in general be ended.

A possible rejoinder must be named and disposed of. While it is admitted that the particular kind of consciousness accompanying conduct that is blessed, is pleasurable; it may be contended that pursuance of this conduct and receipt of the pleasure, brings by the implied self-denial, and persistent effort, and perhaps bodily injury, a suffering that exceeds it in amount. And it may then be urged that blessedness, characterized by this excess of aggregate pains over aggregate pleasures, should nevertheless be pursued as an end, rather than the happiness constituted by excess of pleasures over pains. But now, defensible though this conception of blessedness may be when limited to one individual, or some individuals, it becomes indefensible when extended to all individuals; as it must be if blessedness is taken for the end of conduct. To see this we need but ask for what purpose are these pains in excess of pleasures to be borne. Blessedness being the ideal state for all persons; and the self-sacrifices made by each person in pursuance of this ideal state, having for their end to help all other persons in achieving the like ideal state; it results that the blessed though painful state of each, is to be acquired by furthering the like blessed though painful states of others: the blessed consciousness is to be constituted by the contemplation of their consciousness in a condition of average suffering. Does any one accept this inference? If not, his rejection of it involves the admission that the motive for bearing pains in performing acts called blessed, is not the obtaining for others like pains of blessedness, but the obtaining of pleasures for others; and that thus pleasure somewhere is the tacitly implied ultimate end.

In brief, then, blessedness has for its necessary condition of existence, increased happiness, positive or negative, in some consciousness or other; and disappears utterly if we assume that the actions called blessed, are known to cause decrease of happiness in others as well as in the actor.

16. To make clear the meaning of the general argument set forth in this chapter, its successive parts must be briefly summarized.

That which in the last chapter we found to be highly evolved conduct, is that which, in this chapter, we find to be what is called good conduct; and the ideal goal to the natural evolution of conduct there recognized, we here recognize as the ideal standard of conduct ethically considered.

The acts adjusted to ends, which while constituting the outer visible life from moment to moment further the continuance of life, we saw become, as evolution progresses, better adjusted; until finally they make the life of each individual entire in length and breadth, at the same time that they efficiently subserve the rearing of young, and do both these not only without hindering other individuals from doing the like, but while giving aid to them in doing the like. And here we see that goodness is asserted of such conduct under each of these three aspects. Other things equal, well-adjusted self-conserving acts we call good; other things equal, we call good the acts that are well adjusted for bringing up progeny capable of complete living; and other things equal, we ascribe goodness to acts which further the complete living of others.

This judging as good, conduct which conduces to life in each and all, we found to involve the assumption that animate existence is desirable. By the pessimist, conduct which subserves life cannot consistently be called good: to call it good implies some form of optimism. We saw, however, that pessimists and optimists both start with the postulate that life is a blessing or a curse, according as the average consciousness accompanying it is pleasurable or painful. And since avowed or implied pessimists, and optimists of one or other shade, taken together constitute all men, it results that this postulate is universally accepted. Whence it follows that if we call good the conduct conducive to life, we can do so only with the implication that it is conducive to a surplus of pleasures over pains.

The truth that conduct is considered by us as good or bad, according as its aggregate results, to self or others or both, are pleasurable or painful, we found on examination to be involved in all the current judgments on conduct: the proof being that reversing the applications of the words creates absurdities. And we found that every other proposed standard of conduct derives its authority from this standard.

Whether perfection of nature is the assigned proper aim, or vituousness of action, or rectitude of motive, we saw that definition of the perfection, the virtue, the rectitude, inevitably brings us down to happiness experienced in some form, at some time, by some person, as the fundamental idea. Nor could we discover any intelligible conception of blessedness, save one which implies a raising of consciousness, individual or general, to a happier state; either by mitigating pains or increasing pleasures.

Even with those who judge of conduct from the religious point of view, rather than from the ethical point of view, it is the same. Men who seek to propitiate God by inflicting pains on themselves, or refrain from pleasures to avoid offending him, do so to escape greater ultimate pains or to get greater ultimate pleasures. If by positive or negative suffering here, they expected to achieve more suffering hereafter, they would not do as they do. That which they now think duty they would not think duty if it promised eternal misery instead of eternal happiness. Nay, if there be any who believe that human beings were created to be unhappy, and that they ought to continue living to display their unhappiness for the satisfaction of their creator, such believers are obliged to use this standard of judgment; for the pleasure of their diabolical god is the end to be achieved.

So that no school can avoid taking for the ultimate moral aim a desirable state of feeling called by whatever name— gratification, enjoyment, happiness. Pleasure somewhere, at some time, to some being or beings, is an inexpugnable element of the conception. It is as much a necessary form of moral intuition as space is a necessary form of intellectual intuition.*

---

* It has been remarked, quite truly, that this is a somewhat inconsistent comparison to be made by me; remembering my partial denial of the doctrine that space is a form of intellectual intuition (see *Principles of Psychology,* § 399). Contending, as I do, that space is a form of the intuitions yielded by touch and vision only, and is not a form of the intuitions which we know as sounds and odors, I ought to have said that happiness is *more* truly a form of moral intuition than space is a form of intellectual intuition: being, as we see, a universal form of it.

CHAPTER 4

Ways of Judging Conduct

17. Intellectual progress is by no one trait so adequately characterized, as by development of the idea of causation; since development of this idea involves development of so many other ideas. Before any way can be made, thought and language must have advanced far enough to render properties or attributes thinkable as such, apart from objects; which, in low stages of human intelligence, they are not. Again, even the simplest notion of cause, as we understand it, can be reached only after many like instances have been grouped into a simple generalization; and through all ascending steps, higher notions of causation imply wider notions of generality. Further, as there must be clustered in the mind, concrete causes of many kinds before there can emerge the conception of cause, apart from particular causes; it follows that progress in abstractness of thought is implied. Concomitantly, there is implied the recognition of constant relations among phenomena, generating ideas of uniformity of sequence and of coexistence—the idea of natural law. These advances can go on only as fast as perceptions and resulting thoughts, are made definite by the use of measures; serving to familiarize the mind with exact correspondence, truth, certainty. And only when growing science accumulates examples

of quantitative relations, foreseen and verified, throughout a widening range of phenomena, does causation come to be conceived as necessary and universal. So that though all these cardinal conceptions aid one another in developing, we may properly say that the conception of causation especially depends for its development on the developments of the rest; and therefore is the best measure of intellectual development at large.

How slowly, as a consequence of its dependence, the conception of causation evolves, a glance at the evidence shows. We hear with surprise of the savage who, falling down a precipice, ascribes the failure of his foothold to a malicious demon; and we smile at the kindred notion of the ancient Greek, that his death was prevented by a goddess who unfastened for him the thong of the helmet by which his enemy was dragging him. But daily, without surprise, we hear men who describe themselves as saved from shipwreck by "divine interposition," who speak of having "providentially" missed a train which met with a fatal disaster, and who call it a "mercy" to have escaped injury from a falling chimney pot—men who, in such cases, recognize physical causation no more than do the uncivilized or semicivilized. The Veddah who thinks that failure to hit an animal with his arrow, resulted from inadequate invocation of an ancestral spirit, and the Christian priest who says prayers over a sick man in the expectation that the course of his disease will so be stayed, differ only in respect of the agent from whom they expect supernatural aid and the phenomena to be altered by him: the necessary relations among causes and effects are tacitly ignored by the last as much as by the first. Deficient belief in causation is, indeed, exemplified even in those whose discipline has been specially fitted to generate this belief—even in men of science. For a generation after geologists had become uniformitarians in geology, they remained catastrophists in biology: while recognizing none but natural agencies in the genesis of the earth's crust, they ascribed to supernatural agency the genesis of the organisms on its surface. Nay more—among those who are convinced that living things in genera have been evolved by the continued interaction of forces everywhere operating, there are some who make an exception of man; or who, if they admit that his body has been evolved in the same manner as the bodies of other creatures, allege that his mind has been not evolved but specially created. If, then, universal and necessary causation is only now approaching full recognition, even by those whose investigations are daily reillustrating it, we may expect to find it very little recognized among men at large, whose culture has not been calculated to impress them with it; and we may expect to find it least recognized by them in respect of those classes of phenomena amid which, in consequence of their complexity, causation is most difficult to trace—the psychical, the social, the moral.

Why do I here make these reflections on what seems an irrelevant subject? I do it because on studying the various ethical theories, I am struck with the fact that they are all characterized either by entire absence of the idea of causation, or by inadequate presence of it. Whether theological, political, intuitional, or utilitarian, they all display, if not in the same degree, still, each in a large degree, the defects which result from this lack. We will consider them in the order named.

18. The school of morals properly to be considered as the still-extant representative of the most ancient school, is that which recognizes no other rule of conduct than the alleged will of God. It originates with the savage whose only restraint beyond fear of his fellow man, is fear of an ancestral spirit; and whose notion of moral duty as distinguished from his notion of social prudence, arises from this fear. Here the ethical doctrine and the religious doctrine are identical—have in no degree differentiated.

This primitive form of ethical doctrine, changed only by the gradual dying out multitudinous minor supernatural agents and accompanying development of one universal supernatural agent, survives in great strength down to our own day.

Religious creeds, established and dissenting, all embody the belief that right and wrong are right and wrong simply in virtue of divine enactment. And this tacit assumption has passed from systems of theology into systems of morality; or rather, let us say that moral systems in early stages of development, little differentiated from the accompanying theological systems, have participated in this assumption. We see this in the works of the Stoics, as well as in the works of certain Christian moralists. Among recent ones I may instance the *Essays on the Principles of Morality,* by Jonathan Dymond, a Quaker, which makes "the authority of the Deity the sole ground of duty, and His communicated will the only ultimate standard of right and wrong." Nor is it by writers belonging to so relatively unphilosophical a sect only, that this view is held; it is held with a difference by writers belonging to sects contrariwise distinguished. For these assert that in the absence of belief in a deity, there would be no moral guidance; and this amounts to asserting that moral truths have no other origin than the will of God, which, if not considered as revealed in sacred writings, must be considered as revealed in conscience.

This assumption when examined, proves to be suicidal. If there are no other origins for right and wrong than this enunciated or intuited divine will, then, as alleged, were there no knowledge of the divine will, the acts now known as wrong would not be known as wrong. But if men did not know such acts to be wrong because contrary to the divine will, and so, in committing them, did not offend by disobedience; and if they could not otherwise know them to be wrong; then they might commit them indifferently with the acts now classed as right: the results, practically considered, would be the same. In so far as secular matters are concerned, there would be no difference between the two; for to say that in the affairs of life, any evils would arise from continuing to do the acts called wrong and ceasing to do the acts called right, is to say that these produce in themselves certain mischievous consequences and certain beneficial consequences; which is to say there is another source for moral rules than the revealed or inferred divine will: they may be established by induction from these observed consequences.

From this implication I see no escape. It must be either admitted or denied that the acts called good and the acts called bad, naturally conduce, the one to human well-being and the other to human ill-being. Is it admitted? Then the admission amounts to an assertion that the conduciveness is shown by experience; and this involves abandonment of the doctrine that there is no origin for morals apart from divine injunctions. Is it denied, that acts classed as good and bad differ in their effects? Then it is tacitly affirmed that human affairs would go on just as well in ignorance of the distinction; and the alleged need for commandments from God disappears.

And here we see how entirely wanting is the conception of cause. This notion that such and such actions are made respectively good and bad simply by divine injunction, is tantamount to the notion that such and such actions have not in the nature of things such and such kinds of effects. If there is not an unconsciousness of causation there is an ignoring of it.

19. Following Plato and Aristotle, who make state enactments the sources of right and wrong; and following Hobbes, who holds that there can be neither justice nor injustice till a regularly constituted coercive power exists to issue and enforce commands; not a few modern thinkers hold that there is no other origin for good and bad in conduct than law. And this implies the belief that moral obligation originates with acts of Parliament, and can be changed this way or that way by majorities. They ridicule the idea that men have any natural rights, and allege that rights are wholly results of convention: the necessary implication being that duties are so too. Before considering whether this theory coheres with outside truths, let us observe how far it is coherent within itself.

In pursuance of his argument that rights and duties originate with established social arrangements, Hobbes says—

Where no covenant hath preceded, there hath no right been transferred, and every man has right to every thing; and consequently, no action can be unjust. But when a covenant is made, then to break it is *unjust;* and the definition of *injustice,* is no other than *the not performance of covenant.* And whatsoever is not unjust, is *just.* . . . Therefore before the names of just and unjust can have place, there must be some coercive power, to compel men equally to the performance of their covenants, by the terror of some punishment, greater than the benefit they expect by the breach of their covenant.*

In this paragraph the essential propositions are: justice is fulfillment of covenant; fulfillment of covenant implies a power enforcing it: "just and unjust *can* have no place" unless men are compelled to perform their covenants. But this is to say that men *cannot* perform their covenants without compulsion. Grant that justice is performance of covenant. Now suppose it to be performed voluntarily: there is justice. In such case, however, there is justice in the absence of coercion; which is contrary to the hypothesis. The only conceivable rejoinder is an absurd one: voluntary performance of covenant is impossible. Assert this, and the doctrine that right and wrong come into existence with the establishment of sovereignty is defensible. Decline to assert it, and the doctrine vanishes.

From inner incongruities pass now to outer ones. The justification for his doctrine of absolute civil authority as the source of rules of conduct, Hobbes seeks in the miseries entailed by the chronic war between man and man which must exist in the absence of society; holding that under any kind of government a better life is possible than in the state of nature. Now whether we accept the gratuitous and baseless theory that men surrendered their liberties to a sovereign power of some kind, with a view to the promised increase of satisfactions; or whether we accept the rational theory, inductively based, that a state of political subordination gradually became established through experience of the increased satisfactions derived under it; it equally remains obvious that the acts of the

---

* *Leviathan,* chap. 15.

sovereign power have no other warrant than their subservience to the purpose for which it came into existence. The
necessities which initiate government, themselves prescribe
the actions of government. If its actions do not respond to the
necessities, they are unwarranted. The authority of law is,
then, by the hypothesis, derived; and can never transcend the
authority of that from which it is derived. If general good, or
welfare, or utility, is the supreme end; and if state enactments
are justified as means to this supreme end; then, state enactments have such authority only as arises from conduciveness
to this supreme end. When they are right, it is only because
the original authority endorses them; and they are wrong if
they do not bear its endorsement. That is to say, conduct
cannot be made good or bad by law; but its goodness or
badness is to the last determined by its effects as naturally
furthering, or not furthering, the lives of citizens.

Still more when considered in the concrete, than when
considered in the abstract, do the views of Hobbes and his
disciples prove to be inconsistent. Joining in the general belief
that without such security for life as enables men to go fear-
lessly about their business, there can be neither happiness nor
prosperity, individual or general, they agree that measures for
preventing murder, manslaughter, assault, &c., are requisite;
and they advocate this or that penal system as furnishing the
best deterrents: so arguing, both in respect of the evils and the
remedies, that such and such causes will, by the nature of
things, produce such and such effects. They recognize as
inferable *a priori*, the truth that men will not lay by property
unless they can count with great probability on reaping advantages from it; that consequently where robbery is unchecked, or where a rapacious ruler appropriates whatever
earnings his subjects do not effectually hide, production will
scarcely exceed immediate consumption; and that necessarily
there will be none of that accumulation of capital required for
social development, with all its aids to welfare. In neither
case, however, do they perceive that they are tacitly asserting

the need of certain restraints on conduct as deducible from the necessary conditions to complete life in the social state; and are so making the authority of law derivative and not original.

If it be said by any belonging to this school, that certain moral obligations to be distinguished as cardinal, must be admitted to have a basis deeper than legislation, and that it is for legislation not to create but merely to enforce them—if, I say, admitting this, they go on to allege a legislative origin for minor claims and duties; then we have the implication that whereas some kinds of conduct do, in the nature of things, tend to work out certain kinds of results, other kinds of conduct do not, in the nature of things, tend to work out certain kinds of results. While of these acts the natural good or bad consequences must be allowed, it may be denied of those acts that they have naturally good or bad consequences. Only after asserting this can it be consistently asserted that acts of the last class are made right or wrong by law. For if such acts have any intrinsic tendencies to produce beneficial or mischievous effects, then these intrinsic tendencies furnish the warrant for legislative requirements or interdicts; and to say that the requirements or interdicts make them right or wrong, is to say that they have no intrinsic tendencies to produce beneficial or mischievous effects.

Here, then, we have another theory betraying deficient consciousness of causation. An adequate consciousness of causation yields the irresistible belief that from the most serious to the most trivial actions of men in society, there must flow consequences which, quite apart from legal agency, conduce to well-being or ill-being in greater or smaller degrees. If murders are socially injurious whether forbidden by law or not—if one man's appropriation of another's gains by force, brings special and general evils, whether it is or is not contrary to a ruler's edicts—if nonfulfillment of contract, if cheating, if adulteration, work mischiefs on a community in proportion as they are common, quite irrespective of prohibitions; then, is it not manifest that the like holds throughout all the details of men's behavior? Is it not clear that when legislation insists on certain acts which have naturally beneficial effects, and forbids others that have naturally injurious effects, the acts are not made good or bad by legislation; but the legislation derived its authority from the natural effects of the acts? Nonrecognition of this implies nonrecognition of natural causation.

20. Nor is it otherwise with the pure intuitionists, who hold that moral perceptions are innate in the original sense—thinkers whose view is that men have been divinely endowed with moral faculties; not that these have resulted from inherited modifications caused by accumulated experiences.

To affirm that we know some things to be right and other things to be wrong, by virtue of a supernaturally given conscience; and thus tacitly to affirm that we do not otherwise know right from wrong; is tacitly to deny any natural relations between acts and results. For if there exist any such relations, then we may ascertain by induction, or deduction, or both, what these are. And if it be admitted that because of such natural relations, happiness is produced by this kind of conduct, which is therefore to be approved, while misery is produced by that kind of conduct, which is therefore to be condemned; then it is admitted that the rightness or wrongness of actions is determinable, and must finally be determined, by the goodness or badness of the effects that flow from them; which is contrary to the hypothesis.

It may, indeed, be rejoined that effects are deliberately ignored by this school; which teaches that courses recognized by moral intuition as right, must be pursued without regard to consequences. But on inquiry it turns out that the consequences to be disregarded are particular consequences and not general consequences. When, for example, it is said that property lost by another ought to be restored irrespective of evil to the finder, who possibly may, by restoring it, lose that which would have preserved him from starvation; it is meant that in pursuance of the principle, the immediate and special consequences must be disregarded, not the diffused and remote consequences. By which we are shown that though the theory forbids overt recognition of causation, there is an un-avowed recognition of it.

And this implies the trait to which I am drawing attention. The conception of natural causation is so imperfectly de-veloped, that there is only an indistinct consciousness that throughout the whole of human conduct, necessary relations of causes and effects prevail; and that from them are ulti-mately derived all moral rules, however much these may be proximately derived from moral intuitions.

21. Strange to say, even the utilitarian school, which, at first sight, appears to be distinguished from the rest by recognizing natural causation, is, if not so far from complete recognition of it, yet very far.

Conduct, according to its theory, is to be estimated by ob-servation of results. When, in sufficiently numerous cases, it has been found that behavior of this kind works evil while behavior of that kind works good, these kinds of behavior are to be judged as wrong and right respectively. Now though it seems that the origin of moral rules in natural causes, is thus asserted by implication, it is but partially asserted. The impli-cation is simply that we are to ascertain by induction that such and such mischiefs or benefits *do* go along with such and such acts; and are then to infer that the like relations will hold in future. But acceptance of these generalizations and the infer-ences from them, does not amount to recognition of causation in the full sense of the word. So long as only *some* relation between cause and effect in conduct is recognized, and not *the* relation, a completely scientific form of knowledge has not been reached. At present, utilitarians pay no attention to this distinction. Even when it is pointed out, they disregard the fact that empirical utilitarianism is but a transitional form to be passed through on the way to rational utilitarianism.

In a letter to Mr. Mill, written some sixteen years ago, repudiating the title anti-utilitarian which he had applied to me (a letter subsequently published in Mr. Bain's work on

Mental and Moral Science), I endeavored to make clear the difference above indicated; and I must here quote certain passages from that letter.

> The view for which I contend is, that morality properly so-called—the science of right conduct—has for its object to determine *how* and *why* certain modes of conduct are detrimental, and certain other modes beneficial. These good and bad results cannot be accidental, but must be necessary consequences of the constitution of things; and I conceive it to be the business of moral science to deduce, from the laws of life and the conditions of existence, what kinds of action necessarily tend to produce happiness, and what kinds to produce unhappiness. Having done this, its deductions are to be recognized as laws of conduct; and are to be conformed to irrespective of a direct estimation of happiness or misery.
>
> Perhaps an analogy will most clearly show my meaning. During its early stages, planetary astronomy consisted of nothing more than accumulated observations respecting the positions and motions of the sun and planets; from which accumulated observations it came by and by to be empirically predicted, with an approach to truth, that certain of the heavenly bodies would have certain positions at certain times. But the modern science of planetary astronomy consists of deductions from the law of gravitation—deductions showing why the celestial bodies *necessarily* occupy certain places at certain times. Now, the kind of relation which thus exists between ancient and modern astronomy, is analogous to the kind of relation which, I conceive, exists between the expediency morality and moral science properly so-called. And the objection which I have to the current utilitarianism is, that it recognizes no more developed form of morality—does not see that it has reached but the initial stage of moral science.

Doubtless if utilitarians are asked whether it can be by mere chance that this kind of action works evil and that works good, they will answer no; they will admit that such sequences are parts of a necessary order among phenomena. But though this truth is beyond question; and though if there are causal relations between acts and their results, rules of conduct can become scientific only when they are deduced from these causal relations; there continues to be entire satisfaction with that form of utilitarianism in which these causal relations are practically ignored. It is supposed that in future, as now, utility is to be determined only by observation of results; and that there is no possibility of knowing by deduction from fundamental principles, what conduct *must* be detrimental and what conduct *must* be beneficial.

22. To make more specific that conception of ethical science here indicated, let me present it under a concrete aspect; beginning with a simple illustration and complicating this illustration by successive steps.

If, by tying its main artery, we stop most of the blood going to a limb, then, for as long as the limb performs its function, those parts which are called into play must be wasted faster than they are repaired: whence eventual disablement. The relation between due receipt of nutritive matters through its arteries, and due discharge of its duties by the limb, is a part of the physical order. If, instead of cutting off the supply to a particular limb, we bleed the patient largely, so drafting away the materials needed for repairing not one limb but all limbs, and not limbs only but viscera, there results both a muscular debility and an enfeeblement of the vital functions. Here, again, cause and effect are necessarily related. The mischief that results from great depletion, results apart from any divine command, or political enactment, or moral intuition. Now advance a step. Suppose the man to be prevented from taking in enough of the solid and liquid food containing those substances continually abstracted from his blood in repairing his tissues: suppose he has cancer of the esophagus and cannot swallow—what happens? By this indirect depletion, as by direct depletion, he is inevitably made incapable of performing the actions of one in health. In this case, as in the other cases, the connection between cause and effect is one that cannot be established, or altered, by any authority external to the phenomena themselves. Again, let us say that instead of being stopped after passing his mouth, that which he would swallow is stopped before reaching his mouth; so that day after day the man is required to waste his tissues in getting food, and day after day the food he has got to meet this waste, he is forcibly prevented from eating. As before, the progress towards death by starvation is inevitable—the connection between acts and effects is independent of any alleged theological or political authority. And similarly if, being forced by the whip to labor, no adequate return in food is supplied to him, there are equally certain evils, equally independent of sacred or secular enactment. Pass now to those actions more commonly thought of as the occasions for rules of conduct. Let us assume the man to be continually robbed of that which was given him in exchange for his labor, and by which he was to make up for nervo-muscular expenditure and renew his powers. No less than before is the connection between conduct and consequence rooted in the constitution of things; unchangeable by state-made law, and not needing establishment by empirical generalization. If the action by which the man is affected is a stage further away from the results, or produces results of a less decisive kind, still we see the same basis for morality in the physical order. Imagine that payment for his services is made partly in bad coin; or that it is delayed beyond the date agreed upon; or that what he buys to eat is adulterated with innutritive matter. Manifestly, by any of these deeds which we condemn as unjust, and which are punished by law, there is, as before, an interference with the normal adjustment of physiological repair to physiological waste. Nor is it otherwise when we pass to kinds of conduct still more remotely operative. If he is hindered from enforcing his claim—if class predominance prevents him from proceeding, or if a bribed judge gives a verdict contrary to evidence, or if a witness swears falsely; have not these deeds, though they affect him more indirectly, the same original cause for their wrongness? Even with actions which work diffused and indefinite mischiefs it is the same. Suppose that the man, instead of being dealt with fraudulently, is calumniated. There is, as before, a hindrance to the carrying on of life-sustaining activities; for the loss of character detrimentally affects his business. Nor is this all. The mental depression caused partially incapacitates him for energetic activity, and perhaps brings on ill-health. So that maliciously or carelessly propagating false statements, tends both to diminish his life and to diminish his ability to maintain life. Hence its flagitiousness. Moreover, if we trace to their ultimate ramifications the effects wrought by any of these acts which morality called intuitive reprobates—if we ask what results not to the individual himself only, but also to his belongings—if we observe how impoverishment hinders the rearing of his children, by entailing underfeeding or inadequate clothing, resulting perhaps in the death of some and the constitutional injury of others; we see that by the necessary connections of things these acts, besides tending primarily to lower the life of the individual aggressed upon, tend, secondarily, to lower the lives of all his family, and, thirdly, to lower the life of society at large; which is damaged by whatever damages its units.

A more distinct meaning will now be seen in the statement that the utilitarianism which recognizes only the principles of conduct reached by induction, is but preparatory to the utilitarianism which deduces these principles from the processes of life as carried on under established conditions of existence.

22a. Thus, then, is justified the allegation made at the outset, that, irrespective of their distinctive characters and their special tendencies, all the current methods of ethics have one general defect—they neglect ultimate causal connections. Of course I do not mean that they wholly ignore the natural consequences of actions; but I mean that they recognize them only incidentally. They do not erect into a method the ascertaining of necessary relations between causes and effects, and deducing rules of conduct from formulated statements of them.

Every science begins by accumulating observations, and presently generalizes these empirically; but only when it reaches the stage at which its empirical generalizations are included in a rational generalization, does it become developed science. Astronomy has already passed through its successive stages: first collections of facts; then inductions from them; and lastly deductive interpretations of these, as corollaries from a universal principle of action among masses in space. Accounts of structures and tabulations of strata, grouped and compared, have led gradually to the assigning of various classes of geological changes to igneous and aqueous actions; and it is now tacitly admitted that geology becomes a science proper, only as fast as such changes are explained in terms of those natural processes which have arisen in the cooling and solidifying earth, exposed to the sun's heat and the action of the moon upon its ocean. The science of life has been, and is still, exhibiting a like series of steps: the evolution of organic forms at large, is being affiliated on physical actions in operation from the beginning; and the vital phenomena each organism presents, are coming to be understood as connected sets of changes, in parts formed of matters that are affected by certain forces and disengage other forces. So is it with mind. Early ideas concerning thought and feeling ignored everything like cause, save in recognizing those effects of habit which were forced on men's attention and expressed in proverbs; but there are growing up interpretations of thought and feeling as correlates of the actions and reactions of a nervous structure, that is influenced by outer changes and works in the body adapted changes: the implication being that psychology becomes a science, as fast as these relations of phenomena are explained as consequences of ultimate principles. Sociology, too, represented down to recent times only by stray ideas about social organization, scattered through the masses of worthless gossip furnished us by historians, is coming to be recognized by some as also a science; and such adumbrations of it as have from time to time appeared in the shape of empirical generalizations, are now beginning to assume the character of generalizations made coherent by derivation from causes lying in human nature placed under given conditions. Clearly, then, ethics, which is a science dealing with the conduct of associated human beings, regarded under one of its aspects, has to undergo a like transformation; and, at present undeveloped, can be considered a developed science only when it has undergone this transformation.

A preparation in the simpler sciences is presupposed. Ethics has a physical aspect; since it treats of human activities which, in common with all expenditures of energy, conform to the law of the persistence of energy: moral principles must conform to physical necessities. It has a biological aspect; since it concerns certain effects, inner and outer, individual and social, of the vital changes going on in the highest type of animal. It has a psychological aspect; for its subject matter is an aggregate of actions that are prompted by feelings and guided by intelligence. And it has a sociological aspect; for these actions, some of them directly and all of them indirectly, affect associated beings.

What is the implication? Belonging under one aspect to each of these sciences—physical, biological, psychological, sociological—it can find its ultimate interpretations only in those fundamental truths which are common to all of them. Already we have concluded in a general way that conduct at large, including the conduct ethics deals with, is to be fully understood only as an aspect of evolving life; and now we are brought to this conclusion in a more special way.

23. Here, then, we have to enter on the consideration of moral phenomena as phenomena of evolution; being forced to do this by finding that they form a part of the aggregate of phenomena which evolution has wrought out. If the entire visible universe has been evolved—if the solar system as a whole, the earth as a part of it, the life in general which the earth bears, as well as that of each individual organism—if the mental phenomena displayed by all creatures, up to the highest, in common with the phenomena presented by aggregates of these highest—if one and all conform to the laws of evolution; then the necessary implication is that those phenomena

of conduct in these highest creatures with which morality is concerned, also conform.

The preceding volumes have prepared the way for dealing with morals as thus conceived. Utilizing the conclusions they contain, let us now observe what data are furnished by these. We will take in succession—the physical view, the biological view, the psychological view, and the sociological view.

CHAPTER 5

The Physical View

24.   Every moment we pass instantly from men's perceived
actions to the motives implied by them; and so are led
to formulate these actions in mental terms rather than in
bodily terms. Thoughts and feelings are referred to when we
speak of any one's deeds with praise or blame; not those outer
manifestations which reveal the thoughts and feelings. Hence
we become oblivious of the truth that conduct as actually
experienced, consists of changes recognized by touch, sight
and hearing.

This habit of contemplating only the psychical face of conduct, is so confirmed that an effort is required to contemplate
only the physical face. Undeniable as it is that another's
behavior to us is made up of movements of his body and
limbs, of his facial muscles, and of his vocal apparatus; it yet
seems paradoxical to say that these are the only elements of
conduct really known by us, while the elements of conduct
which we exclusively think of as constituting it, are not known
but inferred.

Here, however, ignoring for the time being the inferred
elements in conduct, we have to deal with the perceived
elements—we have to observe its traits considered as a set of
combined motions. Taking the evolution point of view, and

remembering that while an aggregate evolves, not only the matter composing it, but also the motion of that matter, passes from an indefinite incoherent homogeneity to a definite coherent heterogeneity, we have now to ask whether conduct as it rises to its higher forms, displays in increasing degrees these characters; and whether it does not display them in the greatest degree when it reaches that highest form which we call moral.

25. It will be convenient to deal first with the trait of increasing coherence. The conduct of lowly organized creatures is broadly contrasted with the conduct of highly organized creatures, in having its successive portions feebly connected. The random movements which an animalcule makes, have severally no reference to movements made a moment before; nor do they affect in specific ways the movements made immediately after. Today's wanderings of a fish in search of food, though perhaps showing by their adjustments to catching different kinds of prey at different hours, a slightly determined order, are unrelated to the wanderings of yesterday and tomorrow. But such more developed creatures as birds, show us in the building of nests, the sitting on eggs, the rearing of chicks, and the aiding of them after they fly, sets of motions which form a dependent series, extending over a considerable period. And on observing the complexity of the acts performed in fetching and fixing the fibres of the nest or in catching and bringing to the young each portion of food, we discover in the combined motions, lateral cohesion as well as longitudinal cohesion.

Man, even in his lowest state, displays in his conduct far more coherent combinations of motions. By the elaborate manipulations gone through in making weapons that are to serve for the chase next year, or in building canoes and wigwams for permanent uses—by acts of aggression and defense which are connected with injuries long since received or committed, the savage exhibits an aggregate of motions which, in some of its parts, holds together over great periods.

Moreover, if we consider the many movements implied by the transactions of each day, in the wood, on the water, in the camp, in the family; we see that this coherent aggregate of movements is composed of many minor aggregates, that are severally coherent within themselves and with one another. In civilized man this trait of developed conduct becomes more conspicuous still. Be his business what it may, its processes involve relatively numerous dependent motions; and day by day it is so carried on as to show connections between present motions and motions long gone by, as well as motions anticipated in the distant future. Besides the many doings, related to one another, which the farmer goes through in looking after his cattle, directing his laborers, keeping an eye on his dairy, buying his implements, selling his produce, &c.; the business of getting his lease involves numerous combined movements on which the movements of subsequent years depend; and in manuring his fields with a view to larger returns, or putting down drains with the like motive, he is performing acts which are parts of a coherent combination relatively extensive. That the like holds of the shopkeeper, manufacturer, banker, is manifest; and this increased coherence of conduct among the civilized, will strike us even more when we remember how its parts are often continued in a connected arrangement through life, for the purpose of making a fortune, founding a family, gaining a seat in Parliament.

Now mark that a greater coherence among its component motions, broadly distinguishes the conduct we call moral from the conduct we call immoral. The application of the word dissolute to the last, and of the word self-restrained to the first, implies this—implies that conduct of the lower kind, constituted of disorderly acts, has its parts relatively loose in their relations with one another; while conduct of the higher kind, habitually following a fixed order, so gains a characteristic unity and coherence. In proportion as the conduct is what we call moral, it exhibits comparatively settled connections between antecedents and consequents; for the doing right implies that under given conditions the combined motions constituting conduct will follow in a way that can be specified. Contrariwise, in the conduct of one whose principles are not high, the sequences of motions are doubtful. He may pay the money or he may not; he may keep his appointment or he may fail; he may tell the truth or he may lie. The words trustworthiness and untrustworthiness, as used to characterize the two respectively, sufficiently imply that the actions of the one can be foreknown while those of the other can not; and this implies that the successive movements composing the one bear more constant relations to one another than do those composing the other—are more coherent.

26. Indefiniteness accompanies incoherence in conduct that is little evolved; and throughout the ascending stages of evolving conduct, there is an increasingly definite coordination of the motions constituting it.

Such changes of form as the rudest protozoa show us, are utterly vague—admit of no precise description; and though in higher kinds the movements of the parts are more definable, yet the movement of the whole in respect of direction is indeterminate: there is no adjustment of it to this or the other point in space. In such coelenterate animals as polypes, we see the parts moving in ways which lack precision; and in one of the locomotive forms, as a medusa, the course taken, otherwise at random, can be described only as one which carries it towards the light, where degrees of light and darkness are present. Among annulose creatures the contrast between the track of a worm, turning this way or that at hazard, and the definite course taken by a bee in its flight from flower to flower or back to the hive, shows us the same thing: the bee's acts in building cells and feeding larvae further exhibiting precision in the simultaneous movements as well as in the successive movements. Though the motions made by a fish in pursuing its prey have considerable definiteness, yet they are of a simple kind, and are in this respect contrasted with the many definite motions of body, head, and limbs gone through by a carnivorous mammal in the course of waylaying, running down, and seizing a herbivore; and further, the fish shows us none of those definitely adjusted sets of motions which in the mammal subserve the rearing of young.

Much greater definiteness, if not in the combined movements forming single acts, still in the adjustments of many combined acts to various purposes, characterizes human conduct, even in its lowest stages. In making and using weapons and in the maneuverings of savage warfare, numerous movements all precise in their adaptations to proximate ends, are arranged for the achievement of remote ends, with a precision not paralleled among lower creatures. The lives of civilized men exhibit this trait far more conspicuously. Each industrial art exemplifies the effects of movements which are severally definite; and which are definitely arranged in simultaneous and successive order. Business transactions of every kind are characterized by exact relations between the sets of motions constituting acts, and the purposes fulfilled, in time, place, and quantity. Further, the daily routine of each person shows us in its periods and amounts of activity, of rest, of relaxation, a measured arrangement which is not shown us by the doings of the wandering savage; who has no fixed times for hunting, sleeping, feeding, or any one kind of action.

Moral conduct differs from immoral conduct in the same manner and in a like degree. The conscientious man is exact in all his transactions. He supplies a precise weight for a specified sum; he gives a definite quality in fulfillment of understanding; he pays the full amount he bargained to do. In times as well as in quantities, his acts answer completely to anticipations. If he has made a business contract he is to the day; if an appointment he is to the minute. Similarly in respect to truth: his statements correspond accurately with the facts. It is thus too in his family life. He maintains marital relations that are definite in contrast with the relations that result from breach of the marriage contract; and as a father, fitting his behavior with care to the nature of each child and to the occasion, he avoids the too much and the too little of praise or

blame, reward or penalty. Nor is it otherwise in his miscellaneous acts. To say that he deals equitably with those he
employs, whether they behave well or ill, is to say that he
adjusts his acts to their deserts; and to say that he is judicious
in his charities, is to say that he portions out his aid with
discrimination instead of distributing it indiscriminately to
good and bad, as do those who have no adequate sense of
their social responsibilities.

That progress towards rectitude of conduct is progress
towards duly proportioned conduct, and that duly proportioned conduct is relatively definite, we may see from another
point of view. One of the traits of conduct we call immoral, is
excess; while moderation habitually characterizes moral conduct. Now excesses imply extreme divergences of actions
from some medium, while maintenance of the medium is
implied by moderation; whence it follows that actions of the
last kind can be defined more nearly than those of the first.
Clearly conduct which, being unrestrained, runs into great
and incalculable oscillations, therein differs from restrained
conduct of which, by implication, the oscillations fall within
narrower limits. And falling within narrower limits necessitates relative definiteness of movements.

27. That throughout the ascending forms of life, along with
increasing heterogeneity of structure and function, there goes
increasing heterogeneity of conduct—increasing diversity in
the sets of external motions and combined sets of such
motions—needs not be shown in detail. Nor need it be shown
that becoming relatively great in the motions constituting the
conduct of the uncivilized man, this heterogeneity has become still greater in those which the civilized man goes
through. We may pass at once to that further degree of the like
contrast which we see on ascending from the conduct of the
immoral to that of the moral.

Instead of recognizing this contrast, most readers will be
inclined to identify a moral life with a life little varied in its
activities. But here we come upon a defect in the current

conception of morality. This comparative uniformity in the aggregate of motions, which goes along with morality as commonly conceived, is not only not moral but is the reverse of moral. The better a man fulfills every requirement of life, alike as regards his own body and mind, as regards the bodies and minds of those dependent on him, and as regards the bodies and minds of his fellow citizens, the more varied do his activities become. The more fully he does all these things, the more heterogeneous must be his movements.

One who satisfies personal needs only, goes through, other things equal, less multiform processes than one who also administers to the needs of wife and children. Supposing there are no other differences, the addition of family relations necessarily renders the actions of the man who fulfills the duties of husband and parent, more heterogeneous than those of the man who has no such duties to fulfill, or, having them, does not fulfill them; and to say that his actions are more heterogeneous is to say that there is a greater heterogeneity in the combined motions he goes through. The like holds of social obligations. These, in proportion as a citizen duly performs them, complicate his movements considerably. If he is helpful to inferiors dependent on him, if he takes a part in political agitation, if he aids in diffusing knowledge, he, in each of these ways, adds to his kinds of activity—makes his sets of movements more multiform; so different from the man who is the slave of one desire or group of desires.

Though it is unusual to consider as having a moral aspect, those activities which culture involves, yet to the few who hold that due exercise of all the higher faculties, intellectual and aesthetic, must be included in the conception of complete life, here identified with the ideally moral life, it will be manifest that a further heterogeneity is implied by them. For each of such activities, constituted by that play of these faculties which is eventually added to their life-subserving uses, adds to the multiformity of the aggregated motions.

Briefly, then, if the conduct is the best possible on every

occasion, it follows that as the occasions are endlessly varied the acts will be endlessly varied to suit—the heterogeneity in the combinations of motions will be extreme.

28. Evolution in conduct considered under its moral aspect, is, like all other evolution, toward equilibrium. I do not mean that it is toward the equilibrium reached at death, though this is, of course, the final state which the evolution of the highest man has in common with all lower evolution; but I mean that it is towards a moving equilibrium.

We have seen that maintaining life, expressed in physical terms, is maintaining a balanced combination of internal actions in face of external forces tending to overthrow it; and we have seen that advance towards a higher life, has been an acquirement of ability to maintain the balance for a longer period, by the successive additions of organic appliances which by their actions counteract, more and more fully, the disturbing forces. Here, then, we are led to the conclusion that the life called moral is one in which this maintenance of the moving equilibrium reaches completeness, or approaches most nearly to completeness.

This truth is clearly disclosed on observing how those physiological rhythms which vaguely show themselves when organization begins, become more regular as well as more various in their kinds, as organization advances. Periodicity is but feebly marked in the actions, inner and outer, of the rudest types. Where life is low there is passive dependence on the accidents of the environment; and this entails great irregularities in the vital processes. The taking in of food by a polype is at intervals now short, now very long, as circumstances determine; and the utilization of it is by a slow dispersion of the absorbed part through the tissues, aided only by the irregular movements of the creature's body; while such aeration as is effected is similarly without a trace of rhythm. Much higher up we still find very imperfect periodicities; as in the inferior molluscs which, though possessed of vascular systems, have no proper circulation, but merely a slow movement of the crude blood, now in one direction through the vessels and then, after a pause, in the opposite direction. Only with well-developed structures do there come a rhythmical pulse and a rhythm of the respiratory actions. And then in birds and mammals, along with great rapidity and regularity in these essential rhythms, and along with a consequently great vital activity and therefore great expenditure, comparative regularity in the rhythm of the alimentary actions is established, as well as in the rhythm of activity and rest; since the rapid waste to which rapid pulsation and respiration are instrumental, necessitates tolerably regular supplies of nutriment, as well as recurring intervals of sleep during which repair may overtake waste. And from these stages the moving equilibrium characterized by such interdependent rhythms, is continually made better by the counteracting of more and more of those actions which tend to perturb it. So it is as we ascend from savage to civilized and from the lowest among the civilized to the highest. The rhythm of external actions required to maintain the rhythm of internal actions, becomes at once more complicated and more complete; making them into a better moving equilibrium. The irregularities which their conditions of existence entail on primitive men, continually cause wide deviations from the mean state of the moving equilibrium—wide oscillations; which imply imperfection of it for the time being, and bring about its premature overthrow. In such civilized men as we call ill-conducted, frequent perturbations of the moving equilibrium are caused by those excesses characterizing a career in which the periodicities are much broken; and a common result is that the rhythm of the internal actions being often deranged, the moving equilibrium, rendered by so much imperfect, is generally shortened in duration. While one in whom the internal rhythms are best maintained is one by whom the external actions required to fulfill all needs and duties, severally performed on the recurring occasions, conduce to a moving equilibrium that is at once involved and prolonged.

Of course the implication is that the man who thus reaches

the limit of evolution, exists in a society congruous with his nature—is a man among men similarly constituted, who are severally in harmony with that social environment which they have formed. This is, indeed, the only possibility. For the production of the highest type of man, can go on only *pari passu* with the production of the highest type of society. The implied conditions are those before described as accompanying the most evolved conduct—conditions under which each can fulfill at his needs and rear the due number of progeny, not only without hindering others from doing the like, but while aiding them in doing the like. And evidently, considered under its physical aspect, the conduct of the individual so constituted, and associated with like individuals, is one in which all the actions, that is the combined motions of all kinds, have become such as duly to meet every daily process, every ordinary occurrence, and every contingency in his environment. Complete life in a complete society is but another name for complete equilibrium between the coordinated activities of each social unit and those of the aggregate of units.

29. Even to readers of preceding volumes, and still more to other readers, there will seem a strangeness, or even an absurdity, in this presentation of moral conduct in physical terms. It has been needful to make it however. If that redistribution of matter and motion constituting evolution goes on in all aggregates, its laws must be fulfilled in the most developed being as in every other thing; and his actions, when decomposed in motions, must exemplify its laws. This we find that they do. There is an entire correspondence between moral evolution and evolution as physically defined.

Conduct as actually known to us in perception and not as interpreted into the accompanying feelings and ideas, consists of combined motions. On ascending through the various grades of animate creatures, we find these combined motions characterized by increasing coherence, increasing definiteness considered singly and in their coordinated groups, and increasing heterogeneity; and in advancing from lower to higher types of man, as well as in advancing from the less moral to the more moral type of man, these traits of evolving conduct become more marked still. Further, we see that the increasing coherence, definiteness, and heterogeneity, of the combined motions, are instrumental to the better maintenance of a moving equilibrium. Where the evolution is small this is very imperfect and soon cut short; with advancing evolution, bringing greater power and intelligence, it becomes more steady and longer continued in face of adverse actions; in the human race at large it is comparatively regular and enduring; and its regularity and enduringness are greater in the highest.

CHAPTER 6

The Biological View

30. The truth that the ideally moral man is one in whom the moving equilibrium is perfect, or approaches nearest to perfection, becomes, when translated into physiological language, the truth that he is one in whom the functions of all kinds are duly fulfilled. Each function has some relation, direct or indirect, to the needs of life: the fact of its existence as a result of evolution, being itself a proof that it has been entailed, immediately or remotely, by the adjustment of inner actions to outer actions. Consequently, nonfulfillment of it in normal proportion is nonfulfillment of a requisite to complete life. If there is defective discharge of the function, the organism experiences some detrimental result caused by the inadequacy. If the discharge is in excess, there is entailed a reaction upon the other functions, which in some way diminishes their efficiencies.

It is true that during full vigor, while the momentum of the organic actions is great, the disorder caused by moderate excess or defect of any one function, soon disappears—the balance is reestablished. But it is nonetheless true that always some disorder results from excess or defect, that it influences every function bodily and mental, and that it constitutes a lowering of the life for the time being.

Beyond the temporary falling short of complete life implied by undue or inadequate discharge of a function, there is entailed, as an ultimate result, decreased length of life. If some function is habitually performed in excess of the requirement, or in defect of the requirement; and if, as a consequence, there is an often-repeated perturbation of the functions at large; there results some chronic derangement in the balance of the functions. Necessarily reacting on the structures, and registering in them its accumulated effects, this derangement works a general deterioration; and when the vital energies begin to decline, the moving equilibrium, further from the perfection than it would else have been, is sooner overthrown: death is more or less premature.

Hence the moral man is one whose functions—many and varied in their kinds as we have seen—are all discharged in degrees duly adjusted to the conditions of existence.

31. Strange as the conclusion looks, it is nevertheless a conclusion to be here drawn, that the performance of every function is, in a sense, a moral obligation.

It is usually thought that morality requires us only to restrain such vital activities as, in our present state, are often pushed to excess, or such as conflict with average welfare, special or general; but it also requires us to carry on these vital activities up to their normal limits. All the animal functions, in common with all the higher functions, have, as thus understood, their imperativeness. While recognizing the fact that in our state of transition, characterized by very imperfect adaptation of constitution to conditions, moral obligations of supreme kinds often necessitate conduct which is physically injurious; we must also recognize the fact that, considered apart from other effects, it is immoral so to treat the body as in any way to diminish the fullness or vigor of its vitality.

Hence results one test of actions. There may in every case be put the questions—Does the action tend to maintenance of complete life for the time being? And does it tend to prolongation of life to its full extent? To answer yes or no to either of these questions, is implicitly to class the action as right or wrong in respect of its immediate bearings, whatever it may be in respect of its remote bearings.

The seeming paradoxicalness of this statement results from the tendency, so difficult of avoidance, to judge a conclusion which presupposes an ideal humanity, by its applicability to humanity as now existing. The foregoing conclusion refers to that highest conduct in which, as we have seen, the evolution of conduct terminates—that conduct in which the making of all adjustments of acts to ends subserving complete individual life, together with all those subserving maintenance of offspring and preparation of them for maturity, not only consist with the making of like adjustments by others, but furthers it. And this conception of conduct in its ultimate form, implies the conception of a nature having such conduct for its spontaneous outcome—the product of its normal activities. So understanding the matter, it becomes manifest that under such conditions, any falling short of function, as well as any excess of function, implies deviation from the best conduct or from perfectly moral conduct.

32. Thus far in treating of conduct from the biological point of view, we have considered its constituent actions under their physiological aspects only; leaving out of sight their psychological aspects. We have recognized the bodily changes and have ignored the accompanying mental changes. And at first sight it seems needful for us here to do this; since taking account of states of consciousness, apparently implies an inclusion of the psychological view in the biological view.

This is not so, however. As we pointed out in the *Principles of Psychology* (secs. 52, 53), we enter upon psychology proper, only when we begin to treat of mental states and their relations, considered as referring to external agents and their relations. While we concern ourselves exclusively with modes of mind as correlatives of nervous changes, we are treating of what was there distinguished as aesthophysiology. We pass to psychology only when we consider the correspondence between the connections among subjective states and the connections among objective actions. Here, then, without transgressing the limits of our immediate topic, we may deal with feelings and functions in their mutual dependencies.

We cannot omit doing this; because the psychical changes which accompany many of the physical changes in the organism, are biological factors in two ways. Those feelings, classed as sensations, which, directly initiated in the bodily framework, go along with certain states of the vital organs and more conspicuously with certain states of the external organs, now serve mainly as guides to the performance of functions but partly as stimuli, and now serve mainly as stimuli but in a smaller degree as guides. Visual sensations which, as coordinated, enable us to direct our movements, also, if vivid, raise the rate of respiration; while sensations of cold and heat, greatly depressing or raising the vital actions, serve also for purposes of discrimination. So, too, the feelings classed as emotions, which are not localizable in the bodily framework, act in more general ways, alike as guides and stimuli—having influences over the performance of functions more potent even than have most sensations. Fear, at the same time that it urges flight and evolves the forces spent in it, also affects the heart and the alimentary canal; while joy, prompting persistence in the actions bringing it, simultaneously exalts the visceral processes.

Hence in treating of conduct under its biological aspect, we are compelled to consider that interaction of feelings and functions, which is essential to animal life in all its more developed forms.

33. In the *Principles of Psychology*, section 124, it was shown that necessarily, throughout the animate world at large, "pains are the correlatives of actions injurious to the organism, while pleasures are the correlatives of actions conducive to its welfare"; since "it is an inevitable deduction from the hypothesis of evolution, that races of sentient creatures could have come into existence under no other conditions." The argument was as follows:

> If we substitute for the word *pleasure* the equivalent phrase—a feeling which we seek to bring into consciousness and retain there,

and if we substitute for the word *pain* the equivalent phrase—a feeling which we seek to get out of consciousness and to keep out; we see at once that, if the states of consciousness which a creature endeavors to maintain are the correlatives of injurious actions, and if the states of consciousness which it endeavors to expel are the correlatives of beneficial actions, it must quickly disappear through persistence in the injurious and avoidance of the beneficial. In other words, those races of beings only can have survived in which, on the average, agreeable or desired feelings went along with activities conducive to the maintenance of life, while disagreeable and habitually avoided feelings went along with activities directly or indirectly destructive of life; and there must ever have been, other things equal, the most numerous and long-continued survivals among races in which these adjustments of feelings to actions were the best, tending ever to bring about perfect adjustment.

Fit connections between acts and results must establish themselves in living things, even before consciousness arises; and after the rise of consciousness these connections can change in no other way than to become better established. At the very outset, life is maintained by persistence in acts which conduce to it, and desistance from acts which impede it; and whenever sentiency makes its appearance as an accompaniment, its forms must be such that in the one case the produced feeling is of a kind that will be sought—pleasure, and in the other case is of a kind that will be shunned—pain. Observe the necessity of these relations as exhibited in the concrete.

A plant which envelops a buried bone with a plexus of rootlets, or a potato which directs its blanched shoots towards a grating through which light comes into the cellar, shows us that the changes which outer agents themselves set up in its tissues are changes which aid the utilization of these agents. If we ask what would happen if a plant's roots grew not towards the place where there was moisture but away from it, or if its leaves, enabled by light to assimilate, nevertheless bent themselves toward the darkness; we see that death would result in the absence of the existing adjustments. This general relation is still better shown in an insectivorous plant, such as the *Dionoea muscipula,* which keeps its trap closed round animal matter but not round other matter. Here it is manifest that the stimulus arising from the first part of the absorbed substance, itself sets up those actions by which the mass of the substance is utilized for the plant's benefit. When we pass from vegetal organisms to unconscious animal organisms, we see a like connection between proclivity and advantage. On observing how the tentacles of a polyp attach themselves to, and begin to close round, a living creature, or some animal substance, while they are indifferent to the touch of other substance; we are similarly shown that diffusion of some of the nutritive juices into the tentacles, which is an incipient assimilation, causes the motions effecting prehension. And it is obvious that life would cease were these relations reversed. Nor is it otherwise with this fundamental connection between contact with food and taking in of food, among conscious creatures, up to the very highest. Tasting a substance implies the passage of its molecules through the mucous membrane of the tongue and palate; and this absorption, when it occurs with a substance serving for food, is but a commencement of the absorption carried on throughout the alimentary canal. Moreover, the sensation accompanying this absorption, when it is of the kind produced by food, initiates at the place where it is strongest, in front of the pharynx, an automatic act of swallowing, in a manner rudely analogous to that in which the stimulus of absorption in a polyp's tentacles initiates prehension.

If from these processes and relations that imply contact between a creature's surface and the substance it takes in, we turn to those set up by diffused particles of the substance, constituting to conscious creatures its odor, we meet a kindred general truth. Just as, after contact, some molecules of a mass of food are absorbed by the part touched, and excite the act of prehension; so are absorbed such of its molecules as, spreading through the water, reach the organism; and, being absorbed by it, excite those actions by which contact with the mass is effected. If the physical stimulation caused by the dispersed particles is not accompanied by consciousness, still the motor changes set up must conduce to survival of the

organism if they are such as end in contact; and there must be
relative innutrition and mortality of organisms in which the
produced contractions do not bring about this result. Nor can
it be questioned that whenever and wherever the physical
stimulation has a concomitant sentiency, this must be such as
consists with, and conduces to, movement towards the nutritive matter: it must be not a repulsive but an attractive sentiency. And this which holds with the lowest consciousness,
must hold throughout; as we see it do in all such superior
creatures as are drawn to their food by odor.

Besides those movements which cause locomotion, those
which effect seizure must no less certainly become thus adjusted. The molecular changes caused by absorption of nutritive matter from organic substance in contact, or from adjacent
organic substance, initiate motions which are indefinite where
the organization is low, and which become more definite
with the advance of organization. At the outset, while the
undifferentiated protoplasm is everywhere absorbent and
everywhere contractile, the changes of form initiated by the
physical stimulation of adjacent nutritive matter are vague,
and ineffectually adapted to utilization of it; but gradually,
along with the specialization into parts that are contractile and
parts that are absorbent, these motions become better
adapted; for necessarily individuals in which they are least
adapted disappear faster than those in which they are
most adapted. Recognizing this necessity we have here especially to recognize a further necessity. The relation between
these stimulations and adjusted contractions must be such
that increase of the one causes increase of the other; since the
directions of the discharges being once established, greater
stimulation causes greater contraction, and the greater contraction causing closer contact with the stimulating agent,
causes increase of stimulus and is thereby itself further
increased. And now we reach the corollary which more par-
ticularly concerns us. Clearly as fast as an accompanying
sentiency arises, this cannot be one that is disagreeable,
prompting desistance, but must be one that is agreeable,

prompting persistence. The pleasurable sensation must be itself the stimulus to the contraction by which the pleasurable sensation is maintained and increased; or must be so bound up with the stimulus that the two increase together. And this relation which we see is directly established in the case of a fundamental function, must be indirectly established with all other functions; since nonestablishment of it in any particular case implies, in so far, unfitness to the conditions of existence.

In two ways then, it is demonstrable that there exists a primordial connection between pleasure-giving acts and continuance or increase of life, and, by implication, between pain-giving acts and decrease or loss of life. On the one hand, setting out with the lowest living things, we see that the beneficial act and the act which there is a tendency to perform, are originally two sides of the same; and cannot be disconnected without fatal results. On the other hand, if we contemplate developed creatures as now existing, we see that each individual and species is from day to day kept alive by pursuit of the agreeable and avoidance of the disagreeable.

Thus approaching the facts from a different side, analysis brings us down to another face of that ultimate truth disclosed by analysis in a preceding chapter. We found it was no more possible to frame ethical conceptions from which the consciousness of pleasure, of some kind, at some time, to some being, is absent, than it is possible to frame the conception of an object from which the consciousness of space is absent. And now we see that this necessity of thought originates in the very nature of sentient existence. Sentient existence can evolve only on condition that pleasure-giving acts are life-sustaining acts.

34. Notwithstanding explanations already made, the naked enunciation of this as an ultimate truth, underlying all estimations of right and wrong, will in many, if not in most, cause astonishment. Having in view certain beneficial results that are preceded by disagreeable states of consciousness, such as those commonly accompanying labor; and having in

view the injurious results that follow the receipt of certain
gratifications, such as those which excess in drinking produces; the majority tacitly or avowedly believe that the bearing of pains is on the whole beneficial, and that the receipt of
pleasures is on the whole detrimental. The exceptions so fill
their minds as to exclude the rule.

When asked, they are obliged to admit that the pains accompanying wounds, bruises, sprains, are the concomitants
of evils, alike to the sufferer and to those around him; and that
the anticipations of such pains serve as deterrents from careless or dangerous acts. They cannot deny that the tortures of
burning or scalding, and the miseries which intense cold,
starvation, and thirst produce, are indissolubly connected
with permanent or temporary mischiefs, tending to inca-
pacitate one who bears them for doing things that should be
done, either for his own welfare or the welfare of others. The
agony of incipient suffocation they are compelled to recognize
as a safeguard to life, and must allow that avoidance of it is
conducive to all that life can bring or achieve. Nor will they
refuse to own that one who is chained in a cold, damp,
dungeon, in darkness and silence, is injured in health and
efficiency; alike by the positive pains thus inflicted on him and
by the accompanying negative pains due to absence of light,
of freedom, of companionship. Conversely, they do not doubt
that notwithstanding occasional excesses the pleasure which
accompanies the taking of food, goes along with physical
benefit; and that the benefit is the greater the keener the
satisfaction of appetite. They have no choice but to acknowl-
edge that the instincts and sentiments which so over-
poweringly prompt marriage, and those which find their
gratification in the fostering of offspring, work out an immense surplus of benefit after deducting all evils. Nor dare
they question that the pleasure taken in accumulating property, leaves a large balance of advantage, private and public,
after making all drawbacks. Yet many and conspicuous as are
the cases in which pleasures and pains, sensational and emotional, serve as incentives to proper acts and deterrents from

improper acts, these pass unnoticed; and notice is taken only of those cases in which men are directly or indirectly misled by them. The well-working in essential matters is ignored; and the ill-working in unessential matters is alone recognized.

Is it replied that the more intense pains and pleasures, which have immediate reference to bodily needs, guide us rightly; while the weaker pains and pleasures, not immediately connected with the maintenance of life, guide us wrongly? Then the implication is that the system of guidance by pleasures and pains, which has answered with all types of creatures below the human, fails with the human. Or rather, the admission being that with mankind it succeeds in so far as fulfillment of certain imperative wants goes, it fails in respect of wants that are not imperative. Those who think this are required, in the first place, to show us how the line is to be drawn between the two; and then to show us why the system which succeeds in the lower will not succeed in the higher.

35. Doubtless, however, after all that has been said, there will be raised afresh the same difficulty—there will be instanced the mischievous pleasures and the beneficent pains. The drunkard, the gambler, the thief, who severally pursue gratifications, will be named in proof that the pursuit of gratifications misleads; while the self-sacrificing relative, the worker who perseveres through weariness, the honest man who stints himself to pay his way, will be named in proof that disagreeable modes of consciousness accompany acts that are really beneficial. But after recalling the fact pointed out in section 20, that this objection does not tell against guidance by pleasures and pains at large, since it merely implies that special and proximate pleasures and pains must be disregarded out of consideration for remote and diffused pleasures and pains; and after admitting that in mankind as at present constituted, guidance by proximate pleasures and pains fails throughout a wide range of cases; I go on to set forth the interpretation biology gives of these anomalies, as being not necessary and permanent but incidental and temporary.

Already while showing that among inferior creatures, pleasures and pains have all along guided the conduct by which life has been evolved and maintained, I have pointed out that since the conditions of existence for each species have been occasionally changing, there have been occasionally arising partial misadjustments of the feelings to the requirements, necessitating readjustments. This general cause of derangement operating on all sentient beings, has been operating on human beings in a manner unusually decided, persistent, and involved. It needs but to contrast the mode of life followed by primitive men, wandering in the forests and living on wild food, with the mode of life followed by rustics, artisans, traders, and professional men in a civilized community; to see that the constitution, bodily and mental, well adjusted to the one is ill adjusted to the other. It needs but to observe the emotions kept awake in each savage tribe, chronically hostile to neighboring tribes, and then to observe the emotions which peaceful production and exchange bring into play, to see that the two are not only unlike but opposed. And it needs but to note how, during social evolution, the ideas and sentiments appropriate to the militant activities carried on by coercive cooperation, have been at variance with the ideas and sentiments appropriate to the industrial activities, carried on by voluntary cooperation; to see that there has ever been within each society, and still continues, a conflict between the two moral natures adjusted to these two unlike modes of life. Manifestly, then, this readjustment of constitution to conditions, involving readjustment of pleasures and pains for guidance, which all creatures from time to time undergo, has been in the human race during civilization, especially difficult; not only because of the greatness of the change from small nomadic groups to vast settled societies, and from predatory habits to peaceful habits; but also because the old life of enmity between societies has been maintained along with the new life of amity within each society. While there coexist two ways of life so radically opposed as the militant and the industrial, human nature cannot become properly adapted to either.

That hence results such failure of guidance by pleasures and pains as is daily exhibited, we discover on observing in what parts of conduct the failure is most conspicuous. As above shown, the pleasurable and painful sensations are fairly well adjusted to the peremptory physical requirements: the benefits of conforming to the sensations which prompt us in respect of nutrition, respiration, maintenance of temperature, &c., immensely exceed the incidental evils; and such mis-adjustments as occur may be ascribed to the change from the outdoor life of the primitive man to the indoor life which the civilized man is often compelled to lead. It is the emotional pleasures and pains which are in so considerable a degree out of adjustment to the needs of life as carried on in society; and it is of these that the readjustment is made, in the way above shown, so tardy because so difficult.

From the biological point of view then, we see that the connections between pleasure and beneficial action and between pain and detrimental action, which arose when sentient existence began, and have continued among animate creatures up to man, are generally displayed in him also throughout the lower and more completely organized part of his nature; and must be more and more fully displayed throughout the higher part of his nature, as fast as his adaptation to the conditions of social life increases.

36. Biology has a further judgment to pass on the relations of pleasures and pains to welfare. Beyond the connections between acts beneficial to the organism and the pleasures accompanying performance of them, and between acts detrimental to the organism and the pains causing desistance from them, there are connections between pleasure in general and physiological exaltation, and between pain in general and physiological depression. Every pleasure increases vitality; every pain decreases vitality. Every pleasure raises the tide of life; every pain lowers the tide of life. Let us consider, first, the pains.

By the general mischiefs that result from submission to pains, I do not mean those arising from the diffused effects of local organic lesions, such as follow an aneurism caused by intense effort spite of protesting sensations, or such as follow the varicose veins brought on by continued disregard of fatigue in the legs, or such as follow the atrophy set up in muscles that are persistently exerted when extremely weary; but I mean the general mischiefs caused by that constitutional disturbance which pain forthwith sets up. These are conspicuous when the pains are acute, whether they be sensational or emotional. Bodily agony long borne, produces death by exhaustion. More frequently, arresting the action of the heart for a time, it causes that temporary death we call fainting. On other occasions vomiting is a consequence. And where such manifest derangements do not result, we still, in the pallor and trembling, trace the general prostration. Beyond the actual loss of life caused by subjection to intense cold, there are depressions of vitality less marked caused by cold less extreme—temporary enfeeblement following too long an immersion in icy water; enervation and pining away consequent on inadequate clothing. Similarly is it with submission to great heat: we have lassitude reaching occasionally to exhaustion; we have, in weak persons, fainting, succeeded by temporary debilitation; and in steaming tropical jungles. Europeans contract fevers which when not fatal often entail lifelong incapacities. Consider, again, the evils that follow violent exertion continued in spite of painful feelings—now a fatigue which destroys appetite or arrests digestion if food is taken, implying failure of the reparative processes when they are most needed; and now a prostration of the heart, here lasting for a time and there, where the transgression has been repeated day after day, made permanent: reducing the rest of life to a lower level. No less conspicuous are the depressing effects of emotional pains. There are occasional cases of death from grief; and in other cases the mental suffering which a calamity causes, like bodily suffering, shows its effects by syncope. Often a piece of bad news is succeeded by sickness; and continued anxiety will produce loss of appetite, perpetual indigestion, and diminished strength. Excessive fear, whether aroused by physical or moral danger, will, in like manner, arrest for a time the processes of nutrition; and, not unfrequently, in pregnant women brings on miscarriage; while, in less extreme cases, the cold perspiration and unsteady hands indicate a general lowering of the vital activities, entailing partial incapacity of body or mind or both. How greatly emotional pain deranges the visceral actions is shown us by the fact that incessant worry is not unfrequently followed by jaundice. And here, indeed, the relation between cause and effect happens to have been proved by direct experiment. Making such arrangements that the bile duct of a dog delivered its product outside the body, Claude Bernard observed that so long as he petted the dog and kept him in good spirits, secretion went on at its normal rate; but on speaking angrily, and for a time so treating him as to produce depression, the flow of bile was arrested. Should it be said that evil results of such kinds are proved to occur only when the pains, bodily or mental, are great; the reply is that in healthy persons the injurious perturbations caused by small pains, though not easily traced, are still produced; and that in those whose vital powers are much reduced by illness, slight physical irritations and trifling moral annoyances, often cause relapses.

Quite opposite are the constitutional effects of pleasure. It sometimes, though rarely, happens that in feeble persons intense pleasure—pleasure that is almost pain—gives a nervous shock that is mischievous; but it does not do this in those who are undebilitated by voluntary or enforced submission to actions injurious to the organism. In the normal order, pleasures, great and small, are stimulants to the processes by which life is maintained. Among the sensations may be instanced those produced by bright light. Sunshine is enlivening in comparison with gloom—even a gleam excites a wave of pleasure; and experiments have shown that sunshine raises the rate of respiration: raised respiration being an index of raised vital activities in general. A warmth that is agreeable in degree favors the heart's action, and furthers the various functions to which this is instrumental. Though those who are in full vigor and fitly clothed, can maintain their temperature in winter, and can digest additional food to make up for the loss of heat, it is otherwise with the feeble; and, as vigor declines, the beneficence of warmth becomes conspicuous. That benefits accompany the agreeable sensations produced by fresh air, and the agreeable sensations that accompany muscular action after due rest, and the agreeable sensations caused by rest after exertion, cannot be questioned. Receipt of these pleasures conduces to the maintenance of the body in fit condition for all the purposes of life. More manifest still are the physiological benefits of emotional pleasures. Every power, bodily and mental, is increased by "good spirits"; which is our name for a general emotional satisfaction. The truth that the fundamental vital actions—those of nutrition—are furthered by laughter-moving conversation, or rather by the pleasurable feeling causing laughter, is one of old standing; and every dyspeptic knows that in exhilarating company, a large and varied dinner including not very digestible things, may be eaten with impunity, and indeed with benefit, while a small, carefully chosen dinner of simple things, eaten in solitude, will be followed by indigestion. This striking effect on the alimentary system is accompanied by effects, equally certain though less manifest, on the circulation and the respiration. Again, one who, released from daily labors and anxieties, receives delights from fine scenery or is enlivened by the novelties he sees abroad, comes back showing by toned-up face and vivacious manner, the greater energy with which he is prepared to pursue his avocation. Invalids especially, on whose narrowed margin of vitality the influence of conditions is most visible, habitually show the benefits derived from agreeable states of feeling. A lively social circle, the call of an old friend, or even removal to a brighter room, will, by the induced cheerfulness, much improve the physical state. In brief, as every medical man knows, there is no such tonic as happiness.

These diffused physiological effects of pleasures and pains, which are joined with the local or special physiological effects, are, indeed, obviously inevitable. We have seen (*Principles of Psychology,* secs. 123–25) that while craving, or negative pain, accompanies the underactivity of an organ, and while positive pain accompanies its overactivity, pleasure accompanies its normal activity. We have seen that by evolution no other relations could be established; since, through all inferior types of creatures, if defect or excess of function produced no disagreeable sentiency, and medium function no agreeable sentiency, there would be nothing to ensure a proportioned performance of function. And as it is one of the laws of nervous action that each stimulus, beyond a direct discharge to the particular organ acted on, indirectly caused a general discharge throughout the nervous system (*Prin. of Psy.*, §§ 21, 39), it results that the rest of the organs, all influenced as they are by the nervous system, participate in the stimulation. So that beyond the aid, more slowly shown, which the organs yield to one another through the physiological division of labor, there is the aid, more quickly shown, which mutual excitation gives. While there is a benefit to be presently felt by the whole organism from the due performance of each function, there is an immediate benefit from the exaltation of its functions at large caused by the accompanying pleasure; and from pains, whether of excess or defect, there also come these double effects, immediate and remote.

37. Nonrecognition of these general truths vitiates moral speculation at large. From the estimate of right and wrong habitually framed, these physiological effects wrought on the actor by his feelings are entirely omitted. It is tacitly assumed that pleasures and pains have no reactions on the body of the recipient, affecting his fitness for the duties of life. The only reactions recognized are those on character; respecting which the current supposition is, that acceptance of pleasures is detrimental and submission to pains beneficial. The notion, remotely descended from the ghost theory of the savage, that mind and body are independent, has, among its various implications, this belief that states of consciousness are in no

wise related to bodily states. "You have had your gratifi-cation—it is past; and you are as you were before," says the moralist to one. And to another he says, "You have borne the suffering—it is over; and there the matter ends." Both state-ments are false. Leaving out of view indirect results, the direct results are that the one has moved a step away from death and the other has moved a step toward death.

Leaving out of view, I say, the indirect results. It is these indirect results, here for the moment left out of view, which the moralist has conclusively in view: being so occupied by them that he ignores the direct results. The gratification, perhaps purchased at undue cost, perhaps enjoyed when work should have been done, perhaps snatched from the rightful claimant, is considered only in relation to remote injurious effects, and no setoff is made for immediate benefi-cial effects. Conversely, from positive and negative pains, borne now in the pursuit of some future advantage, now in discharge of responsibilities, now in performing a generous act, the distant good is alone dwelt on and the proximate evil ignored. Consequences, pleasurable and painful, experi-enced by the actor forthwith, are of no importance; and they become of importance only when anticipated as occurring hereafter to the actor or to other persons. And further, future evils borne by the actor are considered of no account if they result from self-denial, and are emphasized only when they result from self-gratification. Obviously, estimates so framed are erroneous; and obviously, the pervading judgments of conduct based on such estimates must be distorted. Mark the anomalies of opinion produced.

If, as the sequence of a malady contracted in pursuit of illegitimate gratification, an attack of iritis injures vision, the mischief is to be counted among those entailed by immoral conduct; but if, regardless of protesting sensations, the eyes are used in study too soon after ophthalmia, and there follows blindness for years or for life, entailing not only personal unhappiness but a burden on others, moralists are silent. The broken leg which a drunkard's accident causes, counts among those miseries brought on self and family by intemperance, which form the ground for reprobating it; but if anxiety to fulfill duties prompts the continued use of a sprained knee spite of the pain, and brings on a chronic lameness involving lack of exercise, consequent ill-health, inefficiency, anxiety, and unhappiness, it is supposed that ethics has no verdict to give in the matter. A student who is plucked because he has spent in amusement the time and money that should have gone in study, is blamed for thus making parents unhappy and preparing for himself a miserable future; but another who, thinking exclusively of claims on him, reads night after night with hot or aching head, and, breaking down, cannot take his degree, but returns home shattered in health and unable to support himself, is named with pity only, as not subject to any moral judgment; or rather, the moral judgment passed is wholly favorable.

Thus recognizing the evils caused by some kinds of conduct only, men at large, and moralists as exponents of their beliefs, ignore the suffering and death daily caused around them by disregard of that guidance which has established itself in the course of evolution. Led by the tacit assumption, common to pagan Stoics and Christian ascetics, that we are so diabolically organized that pleasures are injurious and pains beneficial, people on all sides yield examples of lives blasted by persisting in actions against which their sensations rebel. Here is one who, drenched to the skin and sitting in a cold wind, poohpoohs his shiverings and gets rheumatic fever and subsequent heart-disease, which makes worthless the short life remaining to him. Here is another who, disregarding painful feelings, works too soon after a debilitating illness, and establishes disordered health that lasts for the rest of his days, and makes him useless to himself and others. Now the account is of a youth who, persisting in gymnastic feats spite of scarcely bearable straining, bursts a blood vessel, and, long laid on the shelf, is permanently damaged; while now it is of a man in middle life who, pushing muscular effort to painful excess, suddenly brings on hernia. In this family is a case of aphasia, spreading paralysis, and death, caused by eating too little and doing too much; in that, softening of the brain has been brought on by ceaseless mental efforts against which the feelings hourly protested; and in others, less-serious brain affections have been contracted by overstudy continued regardless of discomfort and the cravings for fresh air and exercise.* Even without accumulating special examples, the truth is forced on us by the visible traits of classes. The careworn man of business too long at his office, the cadaverous barrister poring half the night over his briefs, the feeble factory hands and unhealthy seamstresses passing long hours in bad air, the anemic, flat-chested schoolgirls, bending over many lessons and forbidden boisterous play, no less than Sheffield grinders who die of suffocating dust, and peasants crippled with rheumatism due to exposure, show us the widespread miseries caused by persevering in actions repugnant to the sensations and neglecting actions which the sensations prompt. Nay the evidence is still more extensive and conspicuous. What are the puny malformed children, seen in poverty-stricken districts, but children whose appetites for food and desires for warmth have not been adequately satisfied? What are populations stinted in growth and prematurely aged, such as parts of France show us, but populations injured by work in excess and food in defect: the one implying positive pain, the other negative pain? What is the implication of that greater mortality which occurs among people who are weakened by privations, unless it is that bodily miseries conduce to fatal illnesses? Or once more, what must we infer from the frightful amount of disease and death suffered by armies in the field, fed on scanty and bad provisions, lying on damp ground, exposed to extremes of heat and cold, inadequately sheltered from rain, and subject to exhausting efforts; unless it be the terrible mischiefs caused by continuously subjecting the body to treatment which the feelings protest against?

---

* I can count up more than a dozen such cases among those personally well known to me.

It matters not to the argument whether the actions entailing such effects are voluntary or involuntary. It matters not from the biological point of view, whether the motives prompting them are high or low. The vital functions accept no apologies on the ground that neglect of them was unavoidable, or that the reason for neglect was noble. The direct and indirect sufferings caused by nonconformity to the laws of life, are the same whatever induces the nonconformity; and cannot be omitted in any rational estimate of conduct. If the purpose of ethical inquiry is to establish rules of right living; and if the rules of right living are those of which the total results, individual and general, direct and indirect, are most conducive to human happiness; then it is absurd to ignore the immediate results and recognize only the remote results.

38. Here might be urged the necessity for preluding the study of moral science, by the study of biological science. Here might be dwelt on the error men make in thinking they can understand those special phenomena of human life with which ethics deals, while paying little or no attention to the general phenomena of human life, and while utterly ignoring the phenomena of life at large. And doubtless there would be truth in the inference that such acquaintance with the world of living things as discloses the part which pleasures and pains have played in organic evolution, would help to rectify these one-sided conceptions of moralists. It cannot be held, however, that lack of this knowledge is the sole cause, or the main cause, of their one-sidedness. For facts of the kind above instanced, which, duly attended to, would prevent such distortions of moral theory, are facts which it needs no biological inquiries to learn, but which are daily thrust before the eyes of all. The truth is, rather, that the general consciousness is so possessed by sentiments and ideas at variance with the conclusions necessitated by familiar evidence, that the evidence gets no attention. These adverse sentiments and ideas have several roots.

There is the theological root. As before shown, from the

worship of cannibal ancestors who delighted in witnessing tortures, there resulted the primitive conception of deities who were propitiated by the bearing of pains, and, consequently, angered by the receipt of pleasures. Through the religions of the semicivilized, in which this conception of the divine nature remains conspicuous, it has persisted, in progressively modified forms, down to our own times; and still colors the beliefs, both of those who adhere to the current creed and of those who nominally reject it. There is another root in the primitive and still-surviving militancy. While social antagonisms continue to generate war, which consists in endeavors to inflict pain and death while submitting to the risks of pain and death, and which necessarily involves great privations; it is needful that physical suffering, whether considered in itself or in the evils it bequeaths, should be thought little of, and that among pleasures recognized as most worthy should be those which victory brings. Nor does partially developed industrialism fail to furnish a root. With social evolution, which implies transition from the life of wandering hunters to the life of settled peoples engaged in labor, and which therefore entails activities widely unlike those to which the aboriginal constitution is adapted, there comes an underexercise of faculties for which the social state affords no scope, and an overtaxing of faculties required for the social state: the one implying denial of certain pleasures, and the other submission to certain pains. Hence, along with that growth of population which makes the struggle for existence intense, bearing of pains and sacrifice of pleasures is daily necessitated.

Now always and everywhere, there arises among men a theory conforming to their practice. The savage nature, originating the conception of a savage deity, evolves a theory of supernatural control sufficiently stringent and cruel to influence his conduct. With submission to despotic government severe enough in its restraints to keep in order barbarous natures, there grows up a theory of divine right to rule, and the duty of absolute submission. Where war is made the business of life by the existence of warlike neighbors, virtues which are required for war come to be regarded as supreme virtues; while, contrariwise, when industrialism has grown predominant, the violence and the deception which warriors glory in come to be held criminal. In like manner, then, there arises a tolerable adjustment of the actually accepted (not the nominally accepted) theory of right living, to living as it is daily carried on. If the life is one that necessitates habitual denial of pleasures and bearing of pains, there grows up an answering ethical system under which the receipt of pleasures is tacitly disapproved and the bearing of pains avowedly approved. The mischiefs entailed by pleasures in excess are dwelt on, while the benefits which normal pleasures bring are ignored; and the good results achieved by submission to pains are fully set forth while the evils are overlooked.

But while recognizing the desirableness of, and indeed the necessity for, systems of ethics adapted, like religious systems and political systems, to their respective times and places; we have here to regard the first as, like the others, transitional. We must infer that like a purer creed and a better government, a truer ethics belongs to a more advanced social state. Led, *a priori,* to conclude that distortions must exist, we are enabled to recognize as such, the distortions we find: answering in nature, as these do, to expectation. And there is forced on us the truth that a scientific morality arises only as fast as the one-sided conceptions adapted to transitory conditions, are developed into both-sided conceptions. The science of right living has to take account of all consequences in so far as they affect happiness, personally or socially, directly or indirectly; and by as much as it ignores any class of consequences, by so much does it fail to be science.

39. Like the physical view, then, the biological view corresponds with the view gained by looking at conduct in general from the standpoint of evolution.

That which was physically defined as a moving equilibrium, we define biologically as a balance of functions. The implication of such a balance is that the several functions in their kinds, amounts, and combinations, are adjusted to the several activities which maintain and constitute complete life; and to be so adjusted is to have reached the goal towards which the evolution of conduct continually tends.

Passing to the feelings which accompany the performance of functions, we see that of necessity during the evolution of organic life, pleasures have become the concomitants of normal amounts of functions, while pains, positive and negative, have become the concomitants of excesses and defects of functions. And though in every species derangements of these relations are often caused by changes of conditions, they ever reestablish themselves: disappearance of the species being the alternative.

Mankind, inheriting from creatures of lower kinds, such adjustments between feelings and functions as concern fundamental bodily requirements; and daily forced by peremptory feelings to do the things which maintain life and avoid those which bring immediate death; has been subject to a change of conditions unusually great and involved. This has considerably deranged the guidance by sensations, and has deranged in a much greater degree the guidance by emotions. The result is that in many cases pleasures are not connected with actions which must be performed, nor pains with actions which must be avoided, but contrariwise.

Several influences have conspired to make men ignore the well-working of these relations between feelings and functions, and to observe whatever of ill-working is seen in them. Hence, while the evils which some pleasures entail are dilated upon, the benefits habitually accompanying receipt of pleasures are unnoticed; at the same time that the benefits achieved through certain pains are magnified while the immense mischiefs which pains bring are made little of.

The ethical theories characterized by these perversions, are products of, and are appropriate to, the forms of social life which the imperfectly adapted constitutions of men produce. But with the progress of adaptation, bringing faculties and requirements into harmony, such incongruities of experience,

and consequent distortions of theory, must diminish; until,
along with complete adjustment of humanity to the social
state, will go recognition of the truths that actions are completely right only when, besides being conducive to future
happiness, special and general, they are immediately pleasurable, and that painfulness, not only ultimate but proximate, is the concomitant of actions which are wrong.

So that from the biological point of view, ethical science
becomes a specification of the conduct of associated men who
are severally so constituted that the various self-preserving
activities, the activities required for rearing offspring, and
those which social welfare demands, are fulfilled in the spontaneous exercise of duly proportioned faculties, each yielding
when in action its quantum of pleasure; and who are, by
consequence, so constituted that excess or defect in any one of
these actions brings its quantum of pain, immediate and remote.

NOTE TO SECTION 33. In his *Physical Ethics*, Mr. Alfred Barratt has expressed
a view which here calls for notice. Postulating evolution and its general
laws, he refers to certain passages in the *Principles of Psychology* (1st ed., pt.
III., ch. viii., pp. 395, sqq. cf. pt. IV., ch. iv.) in which I have treated of the
relation between irritation and contraction which "marks the dawn of
sensitive life:" have pointed out that "the primordial tissue must be differently affected by contact with nutritive and with innutritive matters"—
the two being for aquatic creatures respectively the soluble and the insoluble; and have argued that the contraction by which a protruded part of a
rhizopod draws in a fragment of assimilable matter "is caused by a com-
mencing absorption of the assimilable matter." Mr. Barratt, holding that
consciousness "must be considered as an invariable property of animal life,
and ultimately, in its elements, of the material universe" (p. 43), regards
these responses of animal tissue to stimuli, as implying feeling of one or
other kind. "Some kinds of impressed force," he says, "are followed by
movements of retraction and withdrawal, others by such as secure a continuance of the impression. These two kinds of contraction are the
phenomena and external marks of pain and pleasure respectively. Hence
the tissue acts so as to secure pleasure and avoid pain by a law as truly
physical and natural as that whereby a needle turns to the pole, or a tree to
the light" (p. 52). Now without questioning that the raw material of consciousness is present even in undifferentiated protoplasm, and everywhere

exists potentially in that Unknowable Power which, otherwise conditioned, is manifested in physical action (*Prin. of Psy.*, §§ 272–73), I demur to the conclusion that it at first exists under the forms of pleasure and pain. These, I conceive, arise, as the more special feelings do, by a compounding of the ultimate elements of consciousness (*Prin. of Psy.*, §§ 60, 61): being, indeed, general aspects of these more special feelings when they reach certain intensities. Considering that even in creatures which have developed nervous systems, a great part of the vital processes are carried on by unconscious reflex actions, I see no propriety in assuming the existence of what we understand by consciousness in creatures not only devoid of nervous systems but devoid of structures in general.

NOTE TO SECTION 36. More than once in the *Emotions and the Will*, Dr. Bain insists on the connection between pleasure and exaltation of vitality, and the connection between pain and depression of vitality. As above shown, I concur in the view taken by him; which is, indeed, put beyond dispute by general experience as well as by the more special experience of medical men.

When, however, from the invigorating and relaxing effects of pleasure and pain respectively, Dr. Bain derives the original tendencies to persist in acts which give pleasure and to desist from those which give pain, I find myself unable to go with him. He says—"We suppose movements spontaneously begun, and accidentally causing pleasure; we then assume that with the pleasure there will be an increase of vital energy, in which increase the fortunate movements will share, and thereby increase the pleasure. Or, on the other hand, we suppose the spontaneous movements to give pain, and assume that, with the pain, there will be a decrease of energy, extending to the movements that cause the evil, and thereby providing a remedy" (3rd ed., p. 315). This interpretation, implying that "the fortunate movements" merely *share* in the effects of augmented vital energy caused by the pleasure, does not seem to me congruous with observation. The truth appears rather to be that though there is a concomitant general increase of muscular tone, the muscles specially excited are those which, by their increased contraction, conduce to increased pleasure. Conversely, the implication that desistance from spontaneous movements which cause pain, is due to a general muscular relaxation shared in by the muscles causing these particular movements, seems to me at variance with the fact that the retraction commonly takes the form not of a passive lapse but of an active withdrawal. Further, it may be remarked that depressing as pain eventually is to the system at large, we cannot say that it at once depresses the muscular energies. Not simply, as Dr. Bain admits, does an acute smart produce spasmodic movements, but pains of all kinds, both sensational and emotional stimulate the muscles (*Essays*, 1st series, p. 360, 1, or 2nd ed., vol. I., pp. 211, 12). Pain however (and also pleasure when very intense) simultaneously has an inhibitory effect on all the reflex actions; and as the vital functions in general are carried on by reflex actions, this inhibition, increasing with the intensity of the pain, proportionately depresses the vital functions. Arrest of the heart's action and fainting is an extreme result of this inhibition; and the viscera at large feel its effects in degrees proportioned to the degrees of pain. Pain, therefore, while directly causing a discharge of muscular energy as pleasure does, eventually lowers muscular power by lowering those vital processes on which the supply of energy depends. Hence we cannot, I think, ascribe the prompt desistance from muscular movements causing pain, to decrease in the flow of energy; for this decrease is felt only after an interval. Conversely, we cannot ascribe the persistence in a muscular act which yields pleasure to the resulting exaltation of energy; but must, as indicated in section 33, ascribe it to the establishment of lines of discharge between the place of pleasurable stimulation and those contractile structures which maintain and increase the act causing the stimulation—connections allied with the reflex, into which they pass by insensible gradations.

CHAPTER 7

The Psychological View

40.   The last chapter, in so far as it dealt with feelings in their relation to conduct, recognized only their physiological aspects: their psychological aspects were passed over. In this chapter, conversely, we are not concerned with the constitutional connections between feelings, as incentives or deterrents, and physical benefits to be gained or mischiefs to be avoided; nor with the reactive effects of feelings on the state of the organism, as fitting or unfitting it for future action. Here we have to consider represented pleasures and pains, sensational and emotional, as constituting deliberate motives—as forming factors in the conscious adjustments of acts to ends.

41. The rudimentary psychical act, not yet differentiated from a physical act, implies an excitation and a motion. In a creature of low type the touch of food excites prehension. In a somewhat higher creature the odor from nutritive matter sets up motion of the body towards the matter. And where rudimentary vision exists, sudden obscuration of light, implying the passage of something large, causes convulsive muscular movements which mostly carry the body away from the source of danger. In each of these cases we may distinguish four factors. There is (a) that property of the external object

which primarily affects the organism—the taste, smell, or capacity; and, connected with such property, there is in the external object that character (b) which renders seizure of it, or escape from it, beneficial. Within the organism there is (c) the impression or sensation which the property (a) produces, serving as stimulus; and there is, connected with it, the motor change (d) by which seizure or escape is effected. Now psychology is chiefly concerned with the connection between the relation *a b*, and the relation *c d*, under all those forms which they assume in the course of evolution. Each of the factors, and each of the relations, grows more involved as organization advances. Instead of being single the identifying attribute *a* often becomes, in the environment of a superior animal, a cluster of attributes; such as the size, form, colors, motions, displayed by a distant creature that is dangerous. The factor *b*, with which this combination of attributes is associated, becomes the congeries of characters, powers, habits, which constitute it an enemy. Of the subjective factors, *c* becomes a complicated set of visual sensations coordinated with one another and with the ideas and feelings established by experience of such enemies, and constituting the motive to escape; while *d* becomes the intricate, and often prolonged, series of runs, leaps, doubles, dives, &c., made in eluding the enemy. In human life we find the same four outer and inner factors still more multiform and entangled in their compositions and connections. The entire assemblage of physical attributes *a*, presented by an estate that is advertised for sale, passes enumeration; and the assemblage of various utilities, *b*, going along with these attributes, is also beyond brief specification. The perceptions and ideas, likes and dislikes, *c*, set up by the aspect of the estate, and which, compounded and recompounded, eventually form the motive for buying it, make a whole too large and complex for description; and the transactions, legal, pecuniary, and other, gone through in making the purchase and taking possession, are scarcely less numerous and elaborate. Nor must we overlook the fact that as evolution progresses, not only do the factors increase in complexity but also the relations among them. Originally, *a* is directly and simply connected with *b*, while *c* is directly and simply connected with *d*. But eventually, the connections between *a* and *b*, and between *c* and *d*, become very indirect and involved. On the one hand, as the first illustration shows us, sapidity and nutritiveness are closely bound together; as are also the stimulation caused by the one and the contraction which utilizes the other. But, as we see in the last illustration, the connection between the visible traits of an estate and those characters which constitute its value, is at once remote and complicated; while the transition from the purchaser's highly composite motive to the numerous actions of sensory and motor organs, severally intricate, which effect the purchase, is through an entangled plexus of thoughts and feelings constituting his decision.

After this explanation will be apprehended a truth otherwise set forth in the *Principles of Psychology*. Mind consists of feelings and the relations among feelings. By composition of the relations, and ideas of relations, intelligence arises. By composition of the feelings, and ideas of feelings, emotion arises. And, other things equal, the evolution of either is great in proportion as the composition is great. One of the necessary implications is that cognition becomes higher in proportion as it is remoter from reflex action; while emotion becomes higher in proportion as it is remoter from sensation.

And now of the various corollaries from this broad view of psychological evolution, let us observe those which concern the motives and actions that are classed as moral and immoral.

42. The mental process by which, in any case, the adjustment of acts to ends is effected, and which, under its higher forms, becomes the subject matter of ethical judgments, is, as above implied, divisible into the rise of a feeling or feelings constituting the motive, and the thought or thoughts through which the motive is shaped and finally issues in action. The first of these elements, originally an excitement, becomes a simple sensation; then a compound sensation; then a cluster

of partially presentative and partially representative sensations, forming an incipient emotion; then a cluster of exclusively ideal or representative sensations, forming an emotion proper; then a cluster of such clusters, forming a compound emotion; and eventually becomes a still more involved emotion composed of the ideal forms of such compound emotions. The other element, beginning with that immediate passage of a single stimulus into a single motion, called reflex action, presently comes to be a set of associated discharges of stimuli producing associated motions, constituting instinct. Step by step arise more entangled combinations of stimuli, somewhat variable in their modes of union, leading to complex motions similarly variable in their adjustments; whence occasional hesitations in the sensori-motor processes. Presently is reached a stage at which the combined clusters of impressions, not all present together, issue in actions not all simultaneous; implying representation of results, or thought. Afterwards follow stages in which various thoughts have time to pass before the composite motives produce the appropriate actions. Until at last arise those long deliberations during which the probabilities of various consequences are estimated, and the promptings of the correlative feelings balanced; constituting calm judgment. That under either of its aspects the later forms of this mental process are the higher, ethically considered as well as otherwise considered, will be readily seen.

For from the first, complication of sentiency has accompanied better and more numerous adjustments of acts to ends; as also has complication of movement, and complication of the coordinating or intellectual process uniting the two. Whence it follows that the acts characterized by the more complex motives and the more involved thoughts, have all along been of higher authority for guidance. Some examples will make this clear.

Here is an aquatic creature guided by the odor of organic matter towards things serving for food; but a creature which, lacking any other guidance, is at the mercy of larger creatures coming near. Here is another which, also guided to food by odor, possesses rudimentary vision; and so is made to start spasmodically away from a moving body which diffuses this odor, in those cases where it is large enough to produce sudden obscuration of light—usually an enemy. Evidently life will frequently be saved by conforming to the later and higher stimulus, instead of to the earlier and lower. Observe at a more advanced stage a parallel conflict. This is a beast which pursues others for prey, and, either lacking experience or prompted by raging hunger, attacks one more powerful than itself and gets destroyed. Conversely, that is a beast which, prompted by a hunger equally keen, but either by individual experience or effects of inherited experience, made conscious of evil by the aspect of one more powerful than itself, is deterred from attacking, and saves its life by subordinating the primary motive, consisting of craving sensations, to the secondary motive, consisting of ideal feelings, distinct or vague. Ascending at once from these examples of conduct in animals to examples of human conduct, we shall see that the contrasts between inferior and superior have habitually the same traits. The savage of lowest type devours all the food captured by today's chase; and, hungry, on the morrow, has perhaps for days to bear the pangs of starvation. The superior savage, conceiving more vividly the entailed sufferings if no game is to be found, is deterred by his complex feeling from giving way entirely to his simple feeling. Similarly are the two contrasted in the inertness which goes along with lack of forethought, and the activity which due forethought produces. The primitive man, idly inclined, and ruled by the sensation of the moment, will not exert himself until actual pains have to be escaped; but the man somewhat advanced, able more distinctly to imagine future gratifications and sufferings, is prompted by the thought of these to overcome his love of ease: decrease of misery and mortality resulting from this predominance of the representative feelings over the presentative feelings. Without dwelling on the fact that among the civilized, those who lead the life of the senses are contrasted in the same way with those whose lives are largely occupied with pleasures not of a sensual kind, let me point out that there are analogous contrasts between guidance by the less complex representative feelings, or lower emotions, and guidance by the more complex representative feelings, or higher emotions. When led by his acquisitiveness—a re-representative feeling which, acting under due control, conduces to welfare—the thief takes another man's property; his act is determined by certain imagined proximate pleasures of relatively simple kinds, rather than by less clearly imagined possible pains that are more remote and of relatively involved kinds. But in the conscientious man, there is an adequate restraining motive, still more re-representative in its nature, including not only ideas of punishment, and not only ideas of lost reputation and ruin, but including ideas of the claims of the person owning the property, and of the pains which loss of it will entail on him; all joined with a general aversion to acts injurious to others, which arises from the inherited effects of experience. And here at the end we see, as we saw at the beginning, that guidance by the more complex feeling, on the average conduces to welfare more than does guidance by the simpler feeling.

The like holds with the intellectual coordinations through which stimuli issue in motions. The lowest actions, called reflex, in which an impression made on an afferent nerve causes by discharge through an efferent nerve a contraction, shows us a very limited adjustment of acts to ends: the impression being simple, and the resulting motion simple, the internal coordination is also simple. Evidently when there are several senses which can be together affected by an outer object; and when, according as such object is discriminated as of one or other kind, the movements made in response are combined in one or other way; the intermediate coordinations are necessarily more involved. And evidently each further step in the evolution of intelligence, always instrumental to better self-preservation, exhibits this same general trait. The adjustments by which the more involved actions are made appropriate to the more involved circumstances, imply more intricate, and consequently more deliberate and conscious, coordinations; until, when we come to civilized men, who in their daily business taking into account many data and conditions adjust their proceedings to various consequences, we see that the intellectual actions, becoming of the kind we call judicial, are at once very elaborate and very deliberate.

Observe, then, what follows respecting the relative authorities of motives. Throughout the ascent from low creatures up to man, and from the lowest types of man up to the highest, self-preservation has been increased by the subordination of simple excitations to compound excitations—the subjection of immediate sensations to the ideas of sensations to come—the overruling of presentative feelings by representative feelings, and of representative feelings by re-representative feelings. As life has advanced, the accompanying sentiency has become increasingly ideal; and among feelings produced by the compounding of ideas, the highest, and those which have evolved latest, are the recompounded or doubly ideal. Hence it follows that as guides, the feelings have authorities proportionate to the degrees in which they are removed by their complexity and their ideality from simple sensations and appetites. A further implication is made clear by studying the intellectual sides of these mental processes by which acts are adjusted to ends. Where they are low and simple, these comprehend the guiding only of immediate acts by immediate stimuli—the entire transaction in each case, lasting but a moment, refers only to a proximate result. But with the development of intelligence and the growing ideality of the motives, the ends to which the acts are adjusted cease to be exclusively immediate. The more ideal motives concern ends that are more distant; and with approach to the highest types, present ends become increasingly subordinate to those future ends which the ideal motives have for their objects. Hence there arises a certain presumption in favor of a motive which refers to a remote good, in comparison with one which refers to a proximate good.

43. In the last chapter I hinted that besides the several influences there named as fostering the ascetic belief that doing things which are agreeable is detrimental while bearing disagreeable things is beneficial, there remained to be named an influence of deeper origin. This is shadowed forth in the foregoing paragraphs.

For the general truth that guidance by such simple pleasures and pains as result from fulfilling or denying bodily desires, is, under one aspect, inferior to guidance by those pleasures and pains which the complex ideal feelings yield, has led to the belief that the promptings of bodily desires should be disregarded. Further, the general truth that pursuit of proximate satisfactions is, under one aspect, inferior to pursuit of ultimate satisfactions, has led to the belief that proximate satisfactions must not be valued.

In the early stages of every science, the generalizations reached are not qualified enough. The discriminating statements of the truths formulated, arise afterwards, by limitation of the undiscriminating statements. As with bodily vision, which at first appreciates only the broadest traits of objects, and so leads to rude classings which developed vision, impressible by minor differences, has to correct; so with mental vision in relation to general truths, it happens that at first the inductions, wrongly made all-embracing, have to wait for skepticism and critical observation to restrict them, by taking account of unnoticed differences. Hence, we may expect to find the current ethical conclusions too sweeping. Let us note how, in three ways, these dominant beliefs, alike of professed moralists and of people at large, are made erroneous by lack of qualifications.

In the first place, the authority of the lower feelings as guides is by no means always inferior to the authority of the higher feelings, but is often superior. Daily occur occasions on which sensations must be obeyed rather than sentiments. Let any one think of sitting all night naked in a snowstorm, or going a week without food, or letting his head be held under water for ten minutes, and he will see that the pleasures and pains directly related to maintenance of life, may not be wholly subordinated to the pleasures and pains indirectly related to maintenance of life. Though in many cases guidance by the simple feelings rather than by the complex feelings is injurious, in other cases guidance by the complex feelings rather than by the simple feelings is fatal; and throughout a wide range of cases their relative authorities as guides are indeterminate. Grant that in a man pursued, the protesting feelings accompanying intense and prolonged effort, must, to preserve life, be overruled by the fear of his pursuers; it may yet happen that, persisting till he drops, the resulting exhaustion causes death, though, the pursuit having been abandoned, death would not otherwise have resulted. Grant that a widow left in poverty, must deny her appetite that she may give enough food to her children to keep them alive; yet the denial of her appetite pushed too far, may leave them not only entirely without food but without guardianship. Grant that, working his brain unceasingly from dawn till dark, the man in pecuniary difficulties must disregard rebellious bodily sensations in obedience to the conscientious desire to liquidate the claims on him; yet he may carry this subjection of simple feelings to complex feelings to the extent of shattering his health, and failing in that end which, with less of this subjection, he might have achieved. Clearly, then, the subordination of lower feelings must be a conditional subordination. The supremacy of higher feelings must be a qualified supremacy.

In another way does the generalization ordinarily made err by excess. With the truth that life is high in proportion as the simple presentative feelings are under the control of the compound representative feelings, it joins, as though they were corollaries, certain propositions which are not corollaries. The current conception is, not that the lower must yield to the higher when the two conflict, but that the lower must be disregarded even when there is no conflict. This tendency which the growth of moral ideas has generated, to condemn obedience to inferior feelings when superior feelings protest, has begotten a tendency to condemn inferior feelings considered intrinsically. "I really think she does things because she likes to do them," once said to me one lady concerning another: the form of expression and the manner both implying the belief not only that such behavior is wrong, but also that every one must recognize it as wrong. And there prevails widely a notion of this kind. In practice, indeed, the notion is very generally inoperative. Though it prompts various incidental asceticisms, as of those who think it alike manly and salutary to go without a great coat in cold weather, or to persevere through the winter in taking an out-of-door plunge, yet, generally, the pleasurable feelings accompanying due fulfillment of bodily needs, are accepted: acceptance being, indeed, sufficiently peremptory. But oblivious of these contradictions in their practice, men commonly betray a vague idea that there is something degrading, or injurious, or both, in doing that which is agreeable and avoiding that which is disagreeable. "Pleasant but wrong," is a phrase frequently used in a way implying that the two are naturally connected. As above hinted, however, such beliefs result from a confused apprehension of the general truth that the more compound and representative feelings are, on the average, of higher authority than the simple and presentative feelings. Apprehended with discrimination, this truth implies that the authority of the simple, ordinarily less than that of the compound but occasionally greater, is habitually to be accepted when the compound do not oppose.

In yet a third way is this principle of subordination misconceived. One of the contrasts between the earlier-evolved feelings and the later-evolved feelings, is that they refer respectively to the more immediate effects of actions and to the more remote effects; and speaking generally, guidance by that which is near is inferior to guidance by that which is distant. Hence has resulted the belief that, irrespective of their kinds, the pleasures of the present must be sacrificed to the pleasures of the future. We see this in the maxim often impressed on children when eating their meals, that they should reserve the nicest morsel till the last: the check on improvident yielding to immediate impulse, being here joined with the tacit teaching that the same gratification becomes more valuable as it becomes more distant. Such thinking is traceable throughout daily conduct; by no means indeed in all, but in those who are distinguished as prudent and well regulated in their conduct. Hurrying over his breakfast that he may catch the train, snatching a sandwich in the middle of the day, and eating a late dinner when he is so worn out that he is incapacitated for evening recreation, the man of business pursues a life in which not only the satisfactions of bodily desires, but also those of higher tastes and feelings, are, as far as may be, disregarded, that distant ends may be achieved; and yet if you ask what are these distant ends, you find (in cases where there are no parental responsibilities) that they are included under the conception of more comfortable living in time to come. So ingrained is this belief that it is wrong to seek immediate enjoyments and right to seek remote ones only, that you may hear from a busy man who has been on a pleasure excursion, a kind of apology for his conduct. He deprecates the unfavorable judgments of his friends by explaining that the state of his health had compelled him to take a holiday. Nevertheless, if you sound him with respect to his future, you find that his ambition is by and by to retire and devote himself wholly to the relaxations which he is now somewhat ashamed of taking.

The general truth disclosed by the study of evolving conduct, subhuman and human, that for the better preservation of life the primitive, simple, presentative feelings must be controlled by the later-evolved, compound, and representative feelings, has thus come, in the course of civilization, to be recognized by men; but necessarily at first in too indiscriminate a way. The current conception, while it errs by implying that the authority of the higher over the lower is unlimited, errs also by implying that the rule of the lower must be resisted even when it does not conflict with the rule of the higher, and further errs by implying that a gratification which forms a proper aim if it is remote, forms an improper aim if it is proximate.

44. Without explicitly saying so, we have been here tracing the genesis of the moral consciousness. For unquestionably the essential trait in the moral consciousness, is the control of some feeling or feelings by some other feeling or feelings.

Among the higher animals we may see, distinctly enough, the conflict of feelings and the subjection of simpler to more compound; as when a dog is restrained from snatching food by fear of the penalties which may come if he yields to his appetite; or as when he desists from scratching at a hole lest he should lose his master, who has walked on. Here, however, though there is subordination, there is not conscious subordination—there is no introspection revealing the fact that one feeling has yielded to another. So is it even with human beings when little developed mentally. The presocial man, wandering about in families and ruled by such sensations and emotions as are caused by the circumstances of the moment, though occasionally subject to conflicts of motives, meets with comparatively few cases in which the advantage of postponing the immediate to the remote is forced on his attention; nor has he the intelligence requisite for analyzing and generalizing such of these cases as occur. Only as social evolution renders the life more complex, the restraints many and strong, the evils of impulsive conduct marked, and the comforts to be gained by providing for the future tolerably certain, can there come experiences numerous enough to make familiar the benefit of subordinating the simpler feelings to the more complex ones. Only then, too, does there arise a sufficient intellectual power to make an induction from these experiences, followed by a sufficient massing of individual inductions into a public and traditional induction impressed on each generation as it grows up.

And here we are introduced to certain facts of profound significance. This conscious relinquishment of immediate and special good to gain distant and general good, while it is a cardinal trait of the self-restraint called moral, is also a cardinal trait of self-restraints other than those called moral—the restraints that originate from fear of the visible ruler, of the invisible ruler, and of society at large. Whenever the individual refrains from doing that which the passing desire prompts, lest he should afterward suffer legal punishment, or divine vengeance, or public reprobation, or all of them, he surrenders the near and definite pleasure rather than risk the remote and greater, though less definite, pains, which taking it may bring on him; and, conversely, when he undergoes some present pain, that he may reap some probable future pleasure, political, religious, or social. But though all these four kinds of internal control have the common character that the simpler and less ideal feelings are consciously overruled by the more complex and ideal feelings; and though, at first, they are practically coextensive and undistinguished; yet, in the course of social evidence they differentiate; and, eventually, the moral control with its accompanying conceptions and sentiments, emerges as independent. Let us glance at the leading aspects of the process.

While, as in the rudest groups, neither political nor religious rule exists, the leading check to the immediate satisfaction of each desire as it arises, is consciousness of the evils which the anger of fellow savages may entail, if satisfaction of the desire is obtained at their cost. In this early stage the imagined pains which constitute the governing motive, are those apt to be inflicted by beings of like nature, undistinguished in power: the political, religious, and social restraints, are as yet represented only by this mutual dread of vengeance. When special strength, skill, or courage makes one of them a leader in battle, he necessarily inspires greater fear than any other; and there comes to be a more decided check on such satisfactions of the desires as will injure or offend him. Gradually as, by habitual war, chieftainship is established, the evils thought of as likely to arise from angering the chief, not only by aggression upon him but by disobedience to him, because distinguishable both from the smaller evils which other personal antagonisms cause, and from the more diffused evils thought of as arising from social reprobation. That is, political control begins to differentiate from the more indefinite control of

mutual dread. Meanwhile there has been developing the
ghost-theory. In all but the rudest groups, the double of a
deceased man, propitiated at death and afterward is conceived as able to injure the survivors. Consequently, as fast as
the ghost-theory becomes established and definite, there
grows up another kind of check on immediate satisfaction of
the desires—a check constituted by ideas of the evils which
ghosts may inflict if offended; and when political headships
get settled, and the ghosts of dead chiefs, thought of as more
powerful and more relentless than other ghosts, are especially
dreaded, there begins to take shape the form of restraint
distinguished as religious. For a long time these three sets of
restraints, with their correlative sanctions, though becoming
separate in consciousness, remain coextensive; and do so
because they mostly refer to one end—success in war. The
duty of blood-revenge is insisted on even while yet nothing to
be called social organization exists. As the chief gains predominance, the killing of enemies becomes a political duty;
and as the anger of the dead chief comes to be dreaded, the
killing of enemies becomes a religious duty. Loyalty to the
ruler while he lives and after he dies, is increasingly shown by
holding life at his disposal for purposes of war. The earliest
enacted punishments are those for insubordination and for
breaches of observances which express subordination—all of
them militant in origin. While the divine injunctions, originally traditions of the dead king's will, mainly refer to the
destruction of peoples with whom he was at enmity; and
divine anger or approval are conceived as determined by the
degrees in which subjection to him is shown, directly by
worship and indirectly by fulfilling these injunctions. The
Fijian, who is said on entering the other world to commend
himself by narrating his successes in battle, and who, when
alive, is described as sometimes greatly distressed if he thinks
he has not killed enemies enough to please his gods, shows us
the resulting ideas and feelings; and reminds us of kindred
ideas and feelings betrayed by ancient races. To all which add
that the control of social opinion, besides being directly exer-

cised, as in the earliest stage, by praise of the brave and blame of the cowardly, comes to be indirectly exercised, with a kindred general effect by applause of loyalty to the ruler and piety to the god. So that the three differentiated forms of control which grow up along with militant organization and action, while enforcing kindred restraints and incentives, also enforce one another; and their separate and joint disciplines have the common character that they involve the sacrifice of immediate special benefits to obtain more distant and general benefits.

At the same time there have been developing under the same three sanctions, restraints and incentives of another order, similarly characterized by subordination of the proximate to the remote. Joint aggressions upon men outside the society, cannot prosper if there are many aggressions of man on man within the society. War implies cooperation; and cooperation is prevented by antagonisms among those who are to cooperate. We saw that in the primitive ungoverned group, the main check on immediate satisfaction of his desires by each man, is the fear of other men's vengeance if they are injured by taking the satisfaction; and through early stages of social development, this dread of retaliation continues to be the chief motive to such forbearance as exists. But though long after political authority has become established the taking of personal satisfaction for injuries persists, the growth of political authority gradually checks it. The fact that success in war is endangered if his followers fight among themselves, forces itself on the attention of the ruler. He has a strong motive for restraining quarrels, and therefore for preventing the aggressions which cause quarrels; and as his power becomes greater he forbids the aggressions and inflicts punishments for disobedience. Presently, political restraints of this class, like those of the preceding class, are enforced by religious restraints. The sagacious chief, succeeding in war partly because he thus enforces order among his followers, leaves behind him a tradition of the commands he habitually gave. Dread of his ghost tends to produce regard for these commands; and they eventually acquire sacredness. With further social evolution come, in like manner, further interdicts, checking aggressions of less serious kinds; until eventually there grows up a body of civil laws. And then in the way shown, arise beliefs concerning the divine disapproval of these minor, as well as of the major, civil offenses: ending, occasionally, in a set of religious injunctions harmonizing with, and enforcing, the political injunctions. While simultaneously there develops, as before, a social sanction for these rules of internal conduct, strengthening the political and religious sanctions.

But now observe that while these three controls, political, religious, and social, severally lead men to subordinate proximate satisfactions to remote satisfactions; and while they are in this respect like the moral control, which habitually requires the subjection of simple presentative feelings to complex representative feelings and postponement of present to future; yet they do not constitute the moral control, but are only preparatory to it—are controls within which the moral control evolves. The command of the political ruler is at first obeyed, not because of its perceived rectitude; but simply because it is his command, which there will be a penalty for disobeying. The check is not a mental representation of the evil consequences which the forbidden act will, in the nature of things, cause; but it is a mental representation of the factitious evil consequences. Down to our own time we trace in legal phrases, the original doctrine that the aggression of one citizen on another is wrong, and will be punished, not so much because of the injury done him, as because of the implied disregard of the king's will. Similarly, the sinfulness of breaking a divine injunction was universally at one time, and is still by many, held to consist in the disobedience to God, rather than in the deliberate entailing of injury; and even now it is a common belief that acts are right only if performed in conscious fulfillment of the divine will: nay, are even wrong if otherwise performed. The like holds, too, with that further control exercised by public opinion. On listening to the re-

marks made respecting conformity to social rules, it is noticeable that breach of them is condemned not so much because of
any essential impropriety as because the world's authority is
ignored. How imperfectly the truly moral control is even now
differentiated from these controls within which it has been
evolving, we see in the fact that the systems of morality
criticized at the outset, severally identify moral control with
one or other of them. For moralists of one class derive moral
rules from the commands of a supreme political power. Those
of another class recognize no other origin for them than the
revealed divine will. And though men who take social
prescription for their guide do not formulate their doctrine,
yet the belief, frequently betrayed, that conduct which society
permits is not blameworthy, implies that there are those who
think right and wrong can be made such by public opinion.

Before taking a further step we must put together the results
of this analysis. The essential truths to be carried with us
respecting these three forms of external control to which the
social unit is subject, are these: First, that they have evolved
with the evolution of society, as means to social self-
preservation, necessary under the conditions; and that, by
implication, they are in the main congruous with one another.
Second, that the correlative internal restraints generated in
the social unit, are representations of remote results which are
incidental rather than necessary—a legal penalty, a supernatural punishment, a social reprobation. Third, that these
results, simpler and more directly wrought by personal agencies, can be more vividly conceived than can the results
which, in the course of things, actions naturally entail; and the
conceptions of them are therefore more potent over undeveloped minds. Fourth, that as with the restraints thus generated is always joined the thought of external coercion, there
arises the notion of obligation; which so becomes habitually
associated with the surrender of immediate special benefits
for the sake of distant and general benefits. Fifth, that the
moral control corresponds in large measure with the three
controls thus originating, in respect of its injunctions; and

corresponds, too, in the general nature of the mental processes producing conformity to those injunctions; but differs in their special nature.

45. For now we are prepared to see that the restraints properly distinguished as moral, are unlike these restraints out of which they evolve, and with which they are long confounded, in this—they refer not to the extrinsic effects of actions but to their intrinsic effects. The truly moral deterrent from murder, is not constituted by a representation of hanging as a consequence, or by a representation of tortures in hell as a consequence, or by a representation of the horror and hatred excited in fellow men; but by a representation of the necessary natural results—the infliction of death-agony on the victim, the destruction of all his possibilities of happiness, the entailed sufferings to his belongings. Neither the thought of imprisonment, nor of divine anger, nor of social disgrace, is that which constitutes the moral check on theft; but the thought of injury to the person robbed, joined with a vague consciousness of the general evils caused by disregard of proprietary rights. Those who reprobate the adulterer on moral grounds, have their minds filled, not with ideas of an action for damages, or of future punishment following the breach of a commandment, or of loss of reputation; but they are occupied with ideas of unhappiness entailed on the aggrieved wife or husband, the damaged lives of children, and the diffused mischiefs which go along with disregard of the marriage tie. Conversely, the man who is moved by a moral feeling to help another in difficulty, does not picture to himself any reward here or hereafter; but pictures only the better condition he is trying to bring about. One who is morally prompted to fight against a social evil, has neither material benefit nor popular applause before his mind; but only the mischiefs he seeks to remove and the increased well-being which will follow their removal. Throughout, then, the moral motive differs from the motives it is associated with in this,

that instead of being constituted by representations of incidental, collateral, nonnecessary consequences of acts, it is constituted by representations of consequences which the acts naturally produce. These representations are not all distinct, though some of such are usually present; but they form an assemblage of indistinct representations accumulated by experience of the results of like acts in the life of the individual, superposed on a still more indistinct but voluminous consciousness due to the inherited effects of such experiences in progenitors: forming a feeling that is at once massive and vague.

And now we see why the moral feelings and correlative restraints have arisen later than the feelings and restraints that originate from political, religious, and social authorities; and have so slowly, and even yet so incompletely, disentangled themselves. For only by these lower feelings and restraints could be maintained the conditions under which the higher feelings and restraints evolve. It is thus alike with the self-regarding feelings and with the other-regarding feelings. The pains which improvidence will bring, and the pleasures to be gained by storing up things for future use and by laboring to get such things, can be habitually contrasted in thought, only as fast as settled social arrangements make accumulation possible; and that there may arise such settled arrangements, fear of the seen ruler, of the unseen ruler, and of public opinion, must come into play. Only after political, religious, and social restraints have produced a stable community, can there be sufficient experience of the pains, positive and negative, sensational and emotional, which crimes of aggression cause, as to generate that moral aversion to them constituted by consciousness of their intrinsically evil results. And more manifest still is it that such a moral sentiment as that of abstract equity, which is offended not only by material injuries done to men but also by political arrangements that place them at a disadvantage, can evolve only after the social stage reached gives familiar experience both of the pains flowing directly from injustices and also of those flowing indirectly from the class privileges which make injustices easy.

That the feelings called moral have the nature and origin alleged, is further shown by the fact that we associate the name with them in proportion to the degree in which they have these characters—first of being re-representative; second of being concerned with indirect rather than with direct effects, and generally with remote rather than immediate; and thirdly of referring to effects that are mostly general rather than special. Thus, though we condemn one man for extravagance and approve the economy shown by another man, we do not class their acts as respectively vicious and virtuous: these words are too strong: the present and future results here differ too little in concreteness and ideality to make the words fully applicable. Suppose, however, that the extravagance necessarily brings distress on wife and children—brings pains diffused over the lives of others as well as of self, and the viciousness of the extravagance becomes clear. Suppose, further, that prompted by the wish to relieve his family from the misery he has brought on them, the spendthrift forges a bill or commits some other fraud. Though, estimated apart, we characterize his overruling emotion as moral, and make allowance for him in consideration of it, yet his action taken as a whole we condemn as immoral: we regard as of superior authority, the feelings which respond to men's proprietary claims—feelings which are re-representative in a higher degree and refer to more remote diffused consequences. The difference, habitually recognized, between the relative elevations of justice and generosity, well illustrates this truth. The motive causing a generous act has reference to effects of a more concrete, special, and proximate kind, than has the motive to do justice; which, beyond the proximate effects, usually themselves less concrete than those that generosity contemplates, includes a consciousness of the distant, involved, diffused effects of maintaining equitable relations. And justice we hold to be higher generosity.

Comprehension of this long argument will be aided by here quoting a further passage from the before-named letter to Mr. Mill, following the passage already quoted from it.

> To make any position fully understood, it seems needful to add that, corresponding to the fundamental propositions of a developed Moral Science, there have been, and still are, developing in the race, certain fundamental moral intuitions; and that, though these moral intuitions are the results of accumulated experiences of Utility, gradually organized and inherited, they have come to be quite independent of conscious experience. Just in the same way that I believe the intuition of space, possessed by any living individual, to have arisen from organized and consolidated experiences of all antecedent individuals who bequeathed to him their slowly developed nervous organizations—just as I believe that this intuition, requiring only to be made definite and complete by personal experiences, has practically become a form of thought, apparently quite independent of experience; so do I believe that the experiences of utility organized and consolidated through all past generations of the human race, have been producing corresponding nervous modifications, which, by continued transmission and accumulation, have become in us certain faculties of moral intuition—certain emotions responding to right and wrong conduct, which have no apparent basis in the individual experiences of utility. I also hold that just as the space-intuition responds to the exact demonstrations of Geometry, and has its rough conclusions interpreted and verified by them; so will moral intuitions respond to the demonstrations of Moral Science, and will have their rough conclusions interpreted and verified by them.

To this, in passing, I will add only that the evolution hypothesis thus enables us to reconcile opposed moral theories, as it enables us to reconcile opposed theories of knowledge. For as the doctrine of innate forms of intellectual intuition falls into harmony with the experiential doctrine, when we recognize the production of intellectual faculties by inheritance of effects wrought by experience; so the doctrine of innate powers of moral perception becomes congruous with the utilitarian doctrine, when it is seen that preferences and aversions are rendered organic by inheritance of the effects of pleasurable and painful experiences in progenitors.

46. One further question has to be answered—How does there arise the feeling of moral obligation in general? Whence comes the sentiment of duty, considered as distinct from the several sentiments which prompt temperance, providence, kindness, justice, truthfulness, &c.? The answer is that it is an abstract sentiment generated in a manner analogous to that in which abstract ideas are generated.

The idea of each color had originally entire concreteness given to it by an object possessing the color; as some of the unmodified names, such as orange and violet, show us. The dissociation of each color from the object specially associated with it in thought at the outset, went on as fast as the color came to be associated in thought with objects unlike the first, and unlike one another. The idea of orange was conceived in the abstract more fully in proportion as the various orange-colored objects remembered, canceled one another's diverse attributes, and left outstanding their common attribute. So is it if we ascend a stage and note how there arises the abstract idea of color apart from particular colors. Were all things red the conception of color in the abstract could not exist. Imagine that every object was either red or green, and it is manifest that the mental habit would be to think of one or other of these two colors in connection with anything named. But multiply the colors so that thought rambles undecidedly among the ideas of them that occur along with any object named, and there results the notion of indeterminate color—the common property which objects possess of affecting us by light from their surfaces, as well as by their forms. For evidently the notion of this common property is that which remains constant while imagination is picturing every possible variety of color. It is the uniform trait in all colored things; that is—color in the abstract. Words referring to quantity furnish cases of more marked dissociation of abstract from concrete. Grouping various things as small in comparison either with those of their kind or with those of other kinds; and similarly grouping some objects as comparatively great; we get the opposite abstract notions of smallness and greatness. Applied as these are to innumerable very diverse things—not objects only, but forces, times, numbers, values—they have become so little connected with concretes, that their abstract meanings are very vague. Further, we must note that an abstract idea thus formed often acquires an illusive independence; as we may perceive in the case of motion, which, dissociated in thought from all particular bodies and velocities and directions, is sometimes referred to as though it could be conceived apart from something moving. Now all this holds of the subjective as well as of the objective; and among other states of consciousness, holds of the emotions as known by introspection. By the grouping of those re-representative feelings above described, which, differing among themselves in other respects have a component in common; and by the consequent mutual canceling of their diverse components; this common component is made relatively appreciable, and becomes an abstract feeling. Thus is produced the sentiment of moral obligation or duty. Let us observe its genesis.

We have seen that during the progress of animate existence, the later-evolved, more compound and more representative feelings, serving to adjust the conduct to more distant and general needs, have all along had an authority as guides superior to that of the earlier and simpler feelings—excluding cases in which these last are intense. This superior authority, unrecognizable by lower types of creatures which cannot generalize, and little recognizable by primitive men, who have but feeble powers of generalization, has become distinctly recognized as civilization and accompanying mental development have gone on. Accumulated experiences have produced the consciousness that guidance by feelings which refer to remote and general results, is usually more conducive to welfare than guidance by feelings to be immediately gratified. For what is the common character of the feelings that prompt honesty, truthfulness, diligence, providence, &c., which men habitually find to be better prompters than the appetites and simple impulses? They are all complex, re-representative feelings, occupied with the future rather than the present. The idea of authoritativeness has therefore come to be connected with feelings having these traits: the implication being that the lower and simpler feelings are without authority. And this idea of authoritativeness is one element in the abstract consciousness of duty.

But there is another element—the element of coerciveness. This originates from experience of those several forms of restraint that have, as above described, established themselves in the course of civilization—the political, religious, and social. To the effects of punishments inflicted by law and public opinion on conduct of certain kinds, Dr. Bain ascribes the feeling of moral obligation. And I agree with him to the extent of thinking that by them is generated the sense of compulsion which the consciousness of duty includes, and which the word obligation indicates. The existence of an earlier and deeper element, generated as above described, is, however, I think, implied by the fact that certain of the higher self-regarding feelings, instigating prudence and economy, have a moral authority in opposition to the simpler self-regarding feelings: showing that apart from any thought of factitious penalties on improvidence, the feeling constituted by representation of the natural penalties has acquired an acknowledged superiority. But accepting in the main the view that fears of the political and social penalties (to which, I think, the religious must be added) have generated that sense of coerciveness which goes along with the thought of postponing present to future and personal desires to the claims of others, it here chiefly concerns us to note that this sense of coerciveness becomes indirectly connected with the feelings distinguished as moral. For since the political, religious, and social restraining motives, are mainly formed of represented future results; and since the moral restraining motive is mainly formed of represented future results; it happens that the representations, having much in common, and being often aroused at the same time, the fear joined with three sets of them becomes, by association, joined with the fourth. Thinking of the extrinsic effects of a forbidden act, excites a dread which continues present while the intrinsic effects of the act are thought of; and being thus linked with these intrinsic effects causes a vague sense of moral compulsion. Emerging as the moral motive does but slowly from amidst the political, religious, and social motives, it long participates in that consciousness of subordination to some external agency which is joined with them; and only as it becomes distinct and predominant does it lose this associated consciousness—only then does the feeling of obligation fade.

This remark implies the tacit conclusion, which will be to most very startling, that the sense of duty or moral obligation is transitory, and will diminish as fast as moralization increases. Startling though it is, this conclusion may be satisfactorily defended. Even now progress towards the implied ultimate state is traceable. The observation is not infrequent that persistence in performing a duty ends in making it a pleasure; and this amounts to the admission that while at first the motive contains an element of coercion, at last this element of coercion dies out, and the act is performed without any consciousness of being obliged to perform it. The contrast between the youth on whom diligence is enjoined, and the man in business so absorbed in affairs that he cannot be induced to relax, shows us how the doing of work, originally under the consciousness that it *ought* to be done, may eventually cease to have any such accompanying consciousness. Sometimes, indeed, the relation comes to be reversed; and the man of business persists in work from pure love of it when told that he ought not. Nor is it thus with self-regarding feelings only. That the maintaining and protecting of wife by husband often result solely from feelings directly gratified by these actions, without any thought of *must*; and that the fostering of children by parents is in many cases made an absorbing occupation without any coercive feeling of *ought*; are obvious truths which show us that even now, with some of the fundamental other-regarding duties, the sense of obligation has retreated into the background of the mind. And it is in some degree so with other-regarding duties of a higher kind.

Conscientiousness has in many outgrown that stage in which the sense of a compelling power is joined with rectitude of action. The truly honest man here and there to be found, is not only without thought of legal, religious, or social compulsion, when he discharges an equitable claim on him; but he is without thought of self-compulsion. He does the right thing with a simple feeling of satisfaction in doing it; and is, indeed, impatient if anything prevents him from having the satisfaction of doing it.

Evidently, then, with complete adaptation to the social state, that element in the moral consciousness which is expressed by the word obligation, will disappear. The higher actions required for the harmonious carrying on of life, will be as much matters of course as are these lower actions which the simple desires prompt. In their proper times and places and proportions, the moral sentiments will guide men just as spontaneously and adequately as now do the sensations. And though, joined with their regulating influence when this is called for, will exist latent ideas of the evils which nonconformity would bring; these will occupy the mind no more than do ideas of the evils of starvation at the time when a healthy appetite is being satisfied by a meal.

47. This elaborate exposition, which the extreme complexity of the subject has necessitated, may have its leading ideas restated thus:

Symbolizing by a and b, related phenomena in the environment, which in some way concern the welfare of the organism; and symbolizing by c and d, the impressions, simple or compound, which the organism receives from the one, and the motions, single or combined, by which its acts are adapted to meet the other; we saw that psychology in general is concerned with the connection between the relation $a\,b$ and the relation $c\,d$. Further, we saw that by implication the psychological aspect of ethics, is that aspect under which the adjustment of $c\,d$ to $a\,b$, appears, not as an intellectual coordination simply, but as a coordination in which pleasures and pains are alike factors and results.

It was shown that throughout evolution, motive and act become more complex, as the adaptation of inner related actions to outer related actions extends in range and variety. Whence followed the corollary that the later-evolved feelings, more representative and re-representative in their constitution, and referring to remoter and wider needs, have, on the average, an authority as guides greater than have the earlier and simpler feelings.

After thus observing that even an inferior creature is ruled by a hierarchy of feelings so constituted that general welfare depends on a certain subordination of lower to higher, we saw that in man, as he passes into the social state, there arises the need for sundry additional subordinations of lower to higher: cooperation being made possible only by them. To the restraints constituted by mental representations of the intrinsic effects of actions, which, in their simpler forms, have been evolving from the beginning, are added the restraints caused by mental representations of extrinsic effects, in the shape of political, religious, and social penalties.

With the evolution of society, made possible by institutions maintaining order, and associating in men's minds the sense of obligation with prescribed acts and with desistances from forbidden acts, there arose opportunities for seeing the bad consequences naturally flowing from the conduct interdicted and the good consequences from the conduct required. Hence eventually grew up moral aversions and approvals: experience of the intrinsic effects necessarily here coming later than experience of the extrinsic effects, and therefore producing its results later.

The thoughts and feelings constituting these moral aversions and approvals, being all along closely connected with the thoughts and feelings constituting fears of political, religious, and social penalties, necessarily came to participate in the accompanying sense of obligation. The coercive element in the consciousness of duties at large, evolved by converse with external agencies which enforce duties, diffused itself by association through that consciousness of duty, properly called moral, which is occupied with intrinsic results instead of extrinsic results.

But this self-compulsion, which at a relatively high stage becomes more and more a substitute for compulsion from without, must itself, at a still higher stage, practically disappear. If some action to which the special motive is insufficient, is performed in obedience to the feeling of moral obligation, the fact proves that the special faculty concerned is not yet equal to its function—has not acquired such strength that the required activity has become its normal activity, yielding its due amount of pleasure. With complete evolution then, the sense of obligation, not ordinarily present in consciousness, will be awakened only on those extraordinary occasions that prompt breach of the laws otherwise spontaneously conformed to.

And this brings us to the psychological aspect of that conclusion which, in the last chapter, was reached under its biological aspect. The pleasures and pains which the moral sentiments originate, will, like bodily pleasures and pains, become incentives and deterrents so adjusted in their strengths to the needs, that the moral conduct will be the natural conduct.

CHAPTER 8

The Sociological View

48. Not for the human race only, but for every race, there are laws of right living. Given its environment and its structure, and there is for each kind of creature a set of actions adapted in their kinds, amounts, and combinations, to secure the highest conservation its nature permits. The animal, like the man, has needs for food, warmth, activity, rest, and so forth; which must be fulfilled in certain relative degrees to make its life whole. Maintenance of its race implies satisfaction of special desires, sexual and philoprogenitive, in due proportions. Hence there is a supposable formula for the activities of each species, which, could it be drawn out, would constitute a system of morality for that species. But such a system of morality would have little or no reference to the welfare of others than self and offspring. Indifferent to individuals of its own kind, as an inferior creature is, and habitually hostile to individuals of other kinds, the formula for its life could take no cognizance of the lives of those with which it came in contact; or rather, such formula would imply that maintenance of its life was at variance with maintenance of their lives.

But on ascending from beings of lower kinds to the highest kind of being, man; or, more strictly, on ascending from man in his presocial stage to man in his social stage; the formula has to include an additional factor. Though not peculiar to human life under its developed form, the presence of this factor is still, in the highest degree, characteristic of it. Though there are inferior species displaying considerable degrees of sociality; and though the formulas for their complete lives would have to take account of the relations arising from union; yet our own species is, on the whole, to be distinguished as having a formula for complete life which specially recognizes the relations of each individual to others, in presence of whom, and in cooperation with whom, he has to live.

This additional factor in the problem of complete living, is, indeed, so important that the necessitated modifications of conduct have come to form a chief part of the code of conduct. Because the inherited desires which directly refer to the maintenance of individual life, are fairly adjusted to the requirements, there has been no need to insist on that conformity to them which furthers self-conservation. Conversely, because these desires prompt activities that often conflict with the activities of others; and because the sentiments responding to others' claims are relatively weak; moral codes emphasize those restraints on conduct which the presence of fellow men entails.

From the sociological point of view, then, ethics becomes nothing else than a definite account of the forms of conduct that are fitted to the associated state, in such wise that the lives of each and all may be the greatest possible, alike in length and breadth.

49. But here we are met by a fact which forbids us thus to put in the foreground the welfares of citizens, individually considered, and requires us to put in the foreground the welfare of the society as a whole. The life of the social organism must, as an end, rank above the lives of its units. These two ends are not harmonious at the outset; and though the tendency is towards harmonization of them, they are still partially conflicting.

As fast as the social state establishes itself, the preservation of the society becomes a means of preserving its units. Living together arose because, on the average, it proved more advantageous to each than living apart; and this implies that maintenance of combination is maintenance of the conditions to more satisfactory living than the combined persons would otherwise have. Hence, social self-preservation becomes a proximate aim taking precedence of the ultimate aim, individual self-preservation.

This subordination of personal to social welfare is, however, contingent: it depends on the presence of antagonistic societies. So long as the existence of a community is endangered by the actions of communities around, it must remain true that the interests of individuals must be sacrificed to the interests of the community, as far as is needful for the community's salvation. But if this is manifest, it is, by implication, manifest, that when social antagonisms cease, this need for sacrifice of private claims to public claims ceases also; or rather, there cease to be any public claims at variance with private claims. All along, furtherance of individual lives has been the ultimate end; and if this ultimate end has been postponed to the proximate end of preserving the community's life, it has been so only because this proximate end was instrumental to the ultimate end. When the aggregate is no longer in danger, the final object of pursuit, the welfare of the units, no longer needing to be postponed, becomes the immediate object of pursuit.

Consequently, unlike sets of conclusions respecting human conduct emerge, according as we are concerned with a state of habitual or occasional war, or are concerned with a state of permanent and general peace. Let us glance at these alternative states and the alternative implications.

50. At present the individual man has to carry on his life with due regard to the lives of others belonging to the same society; while he is sometimes called on to be regardless of the lives of those belonging to other societies. The same mental

constitution having to fulfill both these requirements, is necessarily incongruous; and the correlative conduct, adjusted first to the one need and then to the other, cannot be brought within any consistent ethical system.

Hate and destroy your fellow man, is now the command; and then the command is, love and aid your fellow man. Use every means to deceive, says the one code of conduct; while the other code says, be truthful in word and deed. Seize what property you can and burn all you cannot take away, are injunctions which the religion of enmity countenances; while by the religion of amity, theft and arson are condemned as crimes. And as conduct has to be made up of parts thus at variance with one another, the theory of conduct remains confused. There coexists a kindred irreconcilability between the sentiments answering to the forms of cooperation required for militancy and industrialism respectively. While social antagonisms are habitual, and while, for efficient action against other societies, there needs great subordination to men who command, the virtue of loyalty and the duty of implicit obedience have to be insisted on: disregard of the ruler's will is punished with death. But when war ceases to be chronic, and growing industrialism habituates men to maintaining their own claims while respecting the claims of others, loyalty becomes less profound, the authority of the ruler is questioned or denied in respect of various private actions and beliefs. State dictation is in many directions successfully defied, and the political independence of the citizen comes to be regarded as a claim which it is virtuous to maintain and vicious to yield up. Necessarily during the transition, these opposite sentiments are incongruously mingled. So is it, too, with domestic institutions under the two regimes. While the first is dominant, ownership of a slave is honorable, and in the slave submission is praiseworthy; but as the last grows dominant, slave-owning becomes a crime and servile obedience excites contempt. Nor is it otherwise in the family. The subjection of women to men, complete while war is habitual but qualified as fast as peaceful occupations replace it, comes eventually to be thought wrong; and equality before the law is asserted. At the same time the opinion concerning paternal power changes. The once unquestioned right of the father to take his children's lives is denied; and the duty of absolute submission to him, long insisted on, is changed into the duty of obedience within reasonable limits.

Were the ratio between the life of antagonism with alien societies, and the life of peaceful cooperation within each society, a constant ratio, some permanent compromise between the conflicting rules of conduct appropriate to the two lives might be reached. But since this ratio is a variable one, the compromise can never be more than temporary. Ever the tendency is towards congruity between beliefs and requirements. Either the social arrangements are gradually changed until they come into harmony with prevailing ideas and sentiments; or, if surrounding conditions prevent change in the social arrangements, the necessitated habits of life modify the prevailing ideas and sentiments to the requisite extent. Hence, for each kind and degree of social evolution determined by external conflict and internal friendship, there is an appropriate compromise between the moral code of enmity and the moral code of amity: not, indeed, a definable, consistent compromise, but a compromise fairly well understood.

This compromise, vague, ambiguous, illogical, though it may be, is nevertheless for the time being authoritative. For if, as above shown, the welfare of the society must take precedence of the welfares of its component individuals, during those stages in which the individuals have to preserve themselves by preserving their society; then such temporary compromise between the two codes of conduct as duly regards external defense, while favoring internal cooperation to the greatest extent practicable, subserves the maintenance of life in the highest degree; and thus gains the ultimate sanction. So that the perplexed and inconsistent moralities of which each society and each age shows us a more or less different one, are severally justified as being approximately the best under the circumstances.

But such moralities are, by their definitions, shown to belong to incomplete conduct; not to conduct that is fully evolved. We saw that the adjustments of acts to ends which, while constituting the external manifestations of life conduce to the continuance of life, have been rising to a certain ideal form now approached by the civilized man. But this form is not reached so long as there continue aggressions of one society upon another. Whether the hindrances to complete living result from the trespasses of fellow citizens, or from the trespasses of aliens, matters not: if they occur there does not yet exist the state defined. The limit to the evolution of conduct is arrived at by the members of each society only when, being arrived at by members of other societies also, the causes of international antagonism end simultaneously with the causes of antagonism between individuals.

And now having from the sociological point of view recognized the need for, and authority of, these changing systems of ethics, proper to changing ratios between warlike activities and peaceful activities, we have, from the same point of view, to consider the system of ethics proper to the state in which peaceful activities are undisturbed.

51. If, excluding all thought of dangers or hindrances from causes external to a society, we set ourselves to specify those conditions under which the life of each person, and therefore of the aggregate, may be the greatest possible; we come upon certain simple ones which, as here stated, assume the form of truisms.

For, as we have seen, the definition of that highest life accompanying completely-evolved conduct, itself excludes all acts of aggression—not only murder, assault, robbery, and the major offenses generally, but minor offenses, such as libel, injury to property, and so forth. While directly deducting from individual life, these indirectly cause perturbations of social life. Trespasses against others rouse antagonisms in them; and if these are numerous the group loses coherence. Hence, whether the integrity of the group itself is considered as the end; or whether the end considered is the benefit ultimately secured to its units by maintaining its integrity; or whether the immediate benefit of its units taken separately, is considered the end; the implication is the same: such acts are at variance with achievement of the end. That these inferences are self-evident and trite (as indeed the first inferences drawn from the data of every science that reaches the deductive stage naturally are) must not make us pass lightly over the all-important fact that, from the sociological point of view, the leading moral laws are seen to follow as corollaries from the definition of complete life carried on under social conditions.

Respect for these primary moral laws is not enough, however. Associated men pursuing their several lives without injuring one another but without helping one another, reap no advantages from association beyond those of companionship. If, while there is no cooperation for defensive purposes (which is here excluded by the hypothesis) there is also no cooperation for satisfying wants, the social state loses its *raison d'être*—almost, if not entirely. There are, indeed, people who live in a condition little removed from this; as the Esquimaux. But though these, exhibiting none of the cooperation necessitated by war, which is unknown to them, lead lives such that each family is substantially independent of others, occasional cooperation occurs. And, indeed, that families should live in company without ever yielding mutual aid, is scarcely conceivable.

Nevertheless, whether actually existing or only approached, we must here recognize as hypothetically possible, a state in which these primary moral laws alone are conformed to; for the purpose of observing, in their uncomplicated forms, what are the negative conditions to harmonious social life. Whether the members of a social group do or do not cooperate, certain limitations to their individual activities are necessitated by their association; and after recognizing these as arising in the absence of cooperation, we shall be the better prepared to understand how conformity to them is effected when cooperation begins.

52. For whether men live together in quite independent ways, careful only to avoid aggressing; or whether, advancing from passive association to active association, they cooperate; their conduct must be such that the achievement of ends by each shall at least not be hindered. And it becomes obvious that when they cooperate, there must not only be no resulting hindrance but there must be facilitation; since in the absence of facilitation there can be no motive to cooperate. What shape, then, must the mutual restraints take when cooperation begins? Or rather—What, in addition to the primary mutual restraints already specified, are those secondary mutual restraints required to make cooperation possible?

One who, living in an isolated way, expends effort in pursuit of an end, gets compensation for the effort by securing the end; and so achieves satisfaction. If he expends the effort without achieving the end, there results dissatisfaction. The satisfaction and the dissatisfaction, are measures of success and failure in life-sustaining acts; since that which is achieved by effort is something which directly or indirectly furthers life, and so pays for the cost of the effort; while if the effort fails there is nothing to pay for the cost of it, and so much life is wasted. What must result from this when men's efforts are joined? The reply will be made clearer if we take the successive forms of cooperation in the order of ascending complexity. We may distinguish as homogeneous cooperation, (1) that in which like efforts are joined for like ends that are simultaneously enjoyed. As cooperation that is not completely homogeneous, we may distinguish, (2) that in which like efforts are joined for like ends that are not simultaneously enjoyed. A cooperation of which the heterogeneity is more distinct is, (3) that in which unlike efforts are joined for like ends. And lastly comes the decidedly heterogeneous cooperation, (4) that in which unlike efforts are joined for unlike ends.

The simplest and earliest of these, in which men's powers, similar in kind and degree, are united in pursuit of a benefit which, when obtained, they all participate in, is most familiarly exemplified in the catching of game by primitive men:

this simplest and earliest form of industrial cooperation being also that which is least differentiated from militant cooperation; for the cooperators are the same, and the processes, both destructive of life, are carried on in analogous ways. The condition under which such cooperation may be successfully carried on, is that the cooperators shall share alike in the produce. Each thus being enabled to repay himself in food for the expended effort, and being further enabled to achieve other such desired ends as maintenance of family, obtains satisfaction: there is no aggression of one on another, and the cooperation is harmonious. Of course the divided produce can be but roughly proportioned to the several efforts joined in obtaining it; but there is actually among savages, as we see that for harmonious cooperation there must be, a recognition of the principle that efforts when combined shall severally bring equivalent benefits, as they would do if they were separate. Moreover, beyond the taking equal shares in return for labors that are approximately equal, there is generally an attempt at proportioning benefit to achievement, by assigning something extra, in the shape of the best part of the trophy, to the actual slayer of the game. And obviously, if there is a wide departure from this system of sharing benefits when there has been a sharing of efforts, the cooperation will cease. Individual hunters will prefer to do the best they can for themselves separately.

Passing from this simplest case of cooperation to a case not quite so simple—a case in which the homogeneity is incomplete—let us ask how a member of the group may be led without dissatisfaction to expend effort in achieving a benefit which, when achieved, is enjoyed exclusively by another? Clearly he may do this on condition that the other shall afterward expend a like effort, the beneficial result of which shall be similarly rendered up by him in return. This exchange of equivalents of effort is the form which social cooperation takes while yet there is little or no division of labor save that between the sexes. For example, the Bodo and Dhimals "mutually assist each other for the nonce, as well in constructing their houses as in clearing their plots for cultivation." And this principle—I will help you if you will help me—common in simple communities where the occupations are alike in kind, and occasionally acted upon in more advanced communities, is one under which the relation between effort and benefit, no longer directly maintained, is maintained indirectly. For whereas when men's activities are carried on separately, or are joined in the way exemplified above, effort is immediately paid for by benefit, in this form of cooperation the benefit achieved by effort is exchanged for a like benefit to be afterward received when asked for. And in this case as in the preceding case, cooperation can be maintained only by fulfillment of the tacit agreements. For if they are habitually not fulfilled, there will commonly be refusal to give aid when asked; and each man will be left to do the best he can by himself. All those advantages to be gained by union of efforts in doing things that are beyond the powers of the single individual, will be unachievable. At the outset, then, fulfillment of contracts that are implied if not expressed, becomes a condition to social cooperation; and therefore to social development.

From these simple forms of cooperation in which the labors men carry on are of like kinds, let us turn to the more complex forms in which they carry on labors of unlike kinds. Where men mutually aid in building huts or felling trees, the number of days' work now given by one to another, is readily balanced by an equal number of days' work afterward given by the other to him. And no estimation of the relative values of the labors being required, a definite understanding is little needed. But when division of labor arises—when there come transactions between one who makes weapons and another who dresses skins for clothing, or between a grower of roots and a catcher of fish—neither the relative amounts nor the relative qualities of their labors admit of easy measure; and with the multiplication of businesses, implying numerous kinds of skill and power, there ceases to be anything like manifest equivalence between either the bodily and mental efforts set against one another, or between their products. Hence the arrangement cannot now be taken for granted, as while the things exchanged are like in kind: it has to be stated. If A allows B to appropriate a product of his special skill, on condition that he is allowed to appropriate a different product of B's special skill, it results that as equivalence of the two products cannot be determined by direct comparison of their quantities and qualities, there must be a distinct understanding as to how much of the one may be taken in consideration of so much of the other.

Only under voluntary agreement, then, no longer tacit and vague but overt and definite, can cooperation be harmoniously carried on when division of labor becomes established. And as in the simplest cooperation, where like efforts are joined to secure a common good, the dissatisfaction caused in those who, having expended their labors do not get their shares of the good, prompts them to cease cooperating; as in the more advanced cooperation, achieved by exchanging equal labors of like kind expended at different times, aversion to cooperate is generated if the expected equivalent of labor is not rendered; so in this developed cooperation, the failure of either to surrender to the other that which was avowedly recognized as of like value with the labor or product given, tends to prevent cooperation by exciting discontent with its results. And evidently, while antagonisms thus caused impede the lives of the units, the life of the aggregate is endangered by diminished cohesion.

53. Beyond these comparatively direct mischiefs, special and general, there have to be noted indirect mischiefs. As already implied by the reasoning in the last paragraph, not only social integration but also social differentiation, is hindered by breach of contract.

In Part II of the *Principles of Sociology,* it was shown that the fundamental principles of organization are the same for an individual organism and for a social organism; because both consist of mutually dependent parts. In the one case as in the other, the assumption of unlike activities by the component members, is possible only on condition that they severally benefit in due degrees by one another's activities. That we may the better see what are the implications in respect of social structures, let us first note the implications in respect of individual structures.

The welfare of a living body implies an approximate equilibrium between waste and repair. If the activities involve an expenditure not made good by nutrition, dwindling follows. If the tissues are enabled to take up from the blood enriched by food, fit substances enough to replace those used up in efforts made, the weight may be maintained. And if the gain exceeds the loss, growth results. That which is true of the whole in its relations to the external world, is no less true of the parts in their relations to one another. Each organ, like the entire organism, is wasted by performing its function, and has to restore itself from the materials brought to it. If the quantity of materials furnished by the joint agency of the other organs is deficient, the particular organ dwindles. If they are sufficient, it can maintain its integrity. If they are in excess, it is enabled to increase. To say that this arrangement constitutes the physiological contract, is to use a metaphor which, though not true in aspect is true in essence. For the relations of structures are actually such that, by the help of a central regulative system, each organ is supplied with blood in proportion to the work it does. As was pointed out (*Principles of Sociology*, sec. 254) well-developed animals are so constituted that each muscle or viscus, when called into action, sends to the vasomotor centers through certain nerve fibers, an impulse caused by its action; whereupon through other nerve fibers, there comes an impulse causing dilatation of its blood vessels. That is to say, all other parts of the organism when they jointly require it to labor, forthwith begin to pay it in blood. During the ordinary state of physiological equilibrium, the loss and the gain balance, and the organ does not sensibly change. If the amount of its function is increased within such moderate limits that the local blood vessels can bring adequately increased supplies, the organ grows: beyond replacing its losses by its gains, it makes a profit on its extra transactions; so being enabled by extra structures to meet extra demands. But if the demands made on it become so great that the supply of materials cannot keep pace with the expenditure, either because the local blood vessels are not large enough or for any other reason; then the organ begins to decrease from excess of waste over repair: there sets in what is known as atrophy. Now since each of the organs has thus to be paid in nutriment for its services by the rest; it follows that the due balancing of their respective claims and payments is requisite, directly for the welfare of each organ, and indirectly for the welfare of the organism. For in a whole formed of mutually dependent parts, anything which prevents due performance of its duty by one part reacts injuriously on all the parts.

With change of terms these statements and inferences hold of a society. That social division of labor which parallels in so many other respects the physiological division of labor, parallels it in this respect also. As was shown at large in the *Principles of Sociology,* Part II, each order of functionaries and each group of producers, severally performing some action or making some article not for direct satisfaction of their own needs but for satisfaction of the needs of fellow citizens in general, otherwise occupied, can continue to do this only so long as the expenditures of effort and returns of profit are approximately equivalent. Social organs like individual organs remain stationary if there come to them normal proportions of the commodities produced by the society as a whole. If because the demands made on an industry or profession are unusually great, those engaged in it make excessive profits, more citizens flock to it and the social structure constituted by its members grows; while decrease of the demands and therefore of the profits, either leads its members to choose other careers or stops the accessions needful to replace those who die, and the structure dwindles. Thus is maintained that proportion among the powers of the component parts which is most conducive to the welfare of the whole.

And now mark that the primary condition to achievement of this result is fulfillment of contract. If from the members of any part payment is frequently withheld, or falls short of the promised amount, then, through ruin of some and abandonment of the occupation by others, the part diminishes; and if it was before not more than competent to its duty, it now becomes incompetent, and the society suffers. Or if social needs throw on some part great increase of function, and the members of it are enabled to get for their services unusually high prices; fulfillment of the agreements to give them these high prices, is the only way of drawing to the part such additional number of members as will make it equal to the augmented demands. For citizens will not come to it if they find the high prices agreed upon are not paid.

Briefly, then, the universal basis of cooperation is the proportioning of benefits received to services rendered. Without this there can be no physiological division of labor; without this there can be no sociological division of labor. And since division of labor, physiological or sociological, profits the whole and each part; it results that on maintenance of the arrangements necessary to do it, depend both special and general welfare. In a society such arrangements are maintained only if bargains, overt or tacit, are carried out. So that beyond the primary requirement to harmonious coexistence in a society, that its units shall not directly aggress on one another; there comes this secondary requirement, that they shall not indirectly aggress by breaking agreements.

54. But now we have to recognize the fact that complete fulfillment of these conditions, original and derived, is not enough. Social cooperation may be such that no one is impeded in the obtainment of the normal return for effort, but contrariwise is aided by equitable exchange of services; and yet much may remain to be achieved. There is a theoretically

possible form of society, purely industrial in its activities, which, though approaching nearer to the moral idea in its code of conduct than any society not purely industrial, does not fully reach it.

For while industrialism requires the life of each citizen to be such that it may be carried on without direct or indirect aggressions on other citizens, it does not require his life to be such that it shall directly further the lives of other citizens. It is not a necessary implication of industrialism, as thus far defined, that each, beyond the benefits given and received by exchange of services, shall give and receive other benefits. A society is conceivable formed of men leading perfectly inoffensive lives, scrupulously fulfilling their contracts, and efficiently rearing their offspring, who yet, yielding to one another no advantages beyond those agreed upon, fall short of that highest degree of life which the gratuitous rendering of services makes possible. Daily experiences prove that every one would suffer many evils and lose many goods, did none give him unpaid assistance. The life of each would be more or less damaged had he to meet all contingencies single-handed. Further, if no one did for his fellows anything more than was required by strict performance of contract, private interests would suffer from the absence of attention to public interests. The limit of evolution of conduct is consequently not reached, until, beyond avoidance of direct and indirect injuries to others, there are spontaneous efforts to further the welfare of others.

It may be shown that the form of nature which thus to justice adds beneficence, is one which adaptation to the social state produces. The social man has not reached that harmonization of constitution with conditions forming the limit of evolution, so long as there remains space for the growth of faculties which, by their exercise, bring positive benefit to others and satisfaction to self. If the presence of fellow men, while putting certain limits to each man's sphere of activity, opens certain other spheres of activity in which feelings while achieving their gratifications, do not diminish but add to the gratifications of others, then such spheres will inevitably be occupied. Recognition of this truth does not, however, call on us to qualify greatly that conception of the industrial state above set forth; since sympathy is the root of both justice and beneficence.

55. Thus the sociological view of ethics supplements the physical, the biological, and the psychological views, by disclosing those conditions under which only associated activities can be so carried on, that the complete living of each consists with, and conduces to, the complete living of all.

At first the welfare of social groups, habitually in antagonism with other groups, takes precedence of individual welfare; and the rules of conduct which are authoritative for the time being, involve incompleteness of individual life that the general life may be maintained. At the same time the rules have to enforce the claims of individual life as far as may be; since on the welfare of the units the welfare of the aggregate largely depends.

In proportion as societies endanger one another less, the need for subordinating individual lives to the general life, decreases; and with approach to a peaceful state, the general life, having from the beginning had furtherance of individual lives as its ultimate purpose, comes to have this as its proximate purpose.

During the transitional stages there are necessitated successive compromises between the moral code which asserts the claims of the society versus those of the individual, and the moral code which asserts the claims of the individual versus those of the society. And evidently each such compromise, though for the time being authoritative, admits of no consistent or definite expression.

But gradually as war declines—gradually as the compulsory cooperation needful in dealing with external enemies becomes unnecessary, and leaves behind the voluntary cooperation which effectually achieves internal sustentation; there grows increasingly clear the code of conduct which voluntary cooperation implies. And this final permanent code alone admits of being definitely formulated, and so constituting ethics as a science in contrast with empirical ethics.

The leading traits of a code under which complete living through voluntary cooperation is secured, may be simply stated. The fundamental requirement is that the life-sustaining actions of each shall severally bring him the amounts and kinds of advantage naturally achieved by them; and this implies firstly that he shall suffer no direct aggressions on his person or property, and secondly that he shall suffer no indirect aggressions by breach of contract. Observance of these negative conditions to voluntary cooperation having facilitated life to the greatest extent by exchange of services under agreement, life is to be further facilitated by exchange of services beyond agreement: the highest life being reached only when, besides helping to complete one another's lives by specified reciprocities of aid, men otherwise help to complete one another's lives.

CHAPTER 9

Criticisms and Explanations

56. Comparisons of the foregoing chapters with one another, suggest sundry questions which must be answered partially, if not completely, before anything can be done towards reducing ethical principles from abstract forms to concrete forms.

We have seen that to admit the desirableness of conscious existence, is to admit that conduct should be such as will produce a consciousness which is desirable—a consciousness which is as much pleasurable and as little painful as may be. We have also seen that this necessary implication corresponds with the *a priori* inference, that the evolution of life has been made possible only by the establishment of connections between pleasures and beneficial actions and between pains and detrimental actions. But the general conclusion reached in both of these ways, though it covers the area within which our special conclusions must fall, does not help us to reach those special conclusions.

Were pleasures all of one kind, differing only in degree; were pains all of one kind, differing only in degree; and could pleasures be measured against pains with definite results; the problems of conduct would be greatly simplified. Were the pleasures and pains serving as incentives and deterrents, simultaneously present to consciousness with like vividness, or were they all immediately impending, or were they all equidistant in time; the problems would be further simplified. And they would be still further simplified if the pleasures and pains were exclusively those of the actor. But both the desirable and the undesirable feelings are of various kinds, making quantitative comparisons difficult; some are present and some are future, increasing the difficulty of quantitative comparison; some are entailed on self and some are entailed on others; again increasing the difficulty. So that the guidance yielded by the primary principle reached, is of little service unless supplemented by the guidance of secondary principles.

Already, in recognizing the needful subordination of presentative feelings to representative feelings, and the implied postponement of present to future throughout a wide range of cases, some approach towards a secondary principle of guidance has been made. Already, too, in recognizing the limitations which men's associated state puts to their actions, with the implied need for restraining feelings of some kinds by feelings of other kinds, we have come in sight of another secondary principle of guidance. Still, there remains much to be decided respecting the relative claims of these guiding principles, general and special.

Some elucidation of the questions involved, will be obtained by here discussing certain views and arguments set forth by past and present moralists.

57. Using the name hedonism for that ethical theory which makes happiness the end of action; and distinguishing hedonism into the two kinds, egoistic and universalistic, according as the happiness sought is that of the actor himself or is that of all, Mr. Sidgwick alleges its implied belief to be that pleasures and pains are commensurable. In his criticism on (empirical) egoistic hedonism he says:

> The fundamental assumption of Hedonism, clearly stated, is that
> all feelings considered merely as feelings can be arranged in a certain

scale of desirability, so that the desirability or pleasantness of each bears a definite ratio to that of all the others. [*Methods of Ethics*, 2d ed., p. 115.]

And asserting this to be its assumption, he proceeds to point out difficulties in the way of the hedonistic calculation; apparently for the purpose of implying that these difficulties tell against the hedonistic theory.

Now though it may be shown that by naming the intensity, the duration, the certainty, and the proximity, of a pleasure or a pain, as traits entering into the estimation of its relative value, Bentham has committed himself to the specified assumption; and though it is perhaps reasonably taken for granted that hedonism as represented by him, is identical with hedonism at large; yet it seems to me that the hedonist, empirical or other, is not necessarily committed to this assumption. That the greatest surplus of pleasures over pains ought to be the end of action, is a belief which he may still consistently hold after admitting that the valuations of pleasures and pains are commonly vague and often erroneous. He may say that though indefinite things do not admit of definite measurements, yet approximately true estimates of their relative values may be made when they differ considerably; and he may further say that even when their relative values are not determinable, it remains true that the most valuable should be chosen. Let us listen to him.

A debtor who cannot pay me, offers to compound for his debt by making over one of sundry things he possesses—a diamond ornament, a silver vase, a picture, a carriage. Other questions being set aside, I assert it to be my pecuniary interest to choose the most valuable of these; but I cannot say which is the most valuable. Does the proposition that it is my pecuniary interest to choose the most valuable therefore become doubtful? Must I not choose as well as I can; and if I choose wrongly must I give up my ground of choice? Must I infer that in matters of business I may not act on the principle that, other things equal, the more profitable transaction is to be preferred; because in many cases I cannot say which is the more profitable, and have often chosen the less profitable? Because I believe that of many dangerous courses I ought to take the least dangerous, do I make "the fundamental assumption" that courses can be arranged according to a scale of dangerousness; and must I abandon my belief if I cannot so arrange them? If I am not by consistency bound to do this, then I am no more by consistency bound to give up the principle that the greatest surplus of pleasures over pains should be the end of action, because the "commensurability of pleasures and pains" cannot be asserted.

At the close of his chapters on empirical hedonism, Mr. Sidgwick himself says he does "not think that the common experience of mankind, impartially examined, really sustains the view that egoistic Hedonism is necessarily suicidal"; adding, however, that the "uncertainty of hedonistic calculation cannot be denied to have great weight." But here the fundamental assumption of hedonism, that happiness is the end of action, is still supposed to involve the assumption that "feelings can be arranged in a certain scale of desirability." This we have seen it does not: its fundamental assumption is in no degree invalidated by proof that such arrangement of them is impracticable.

To Mr. Sidgwick's argument there is the further objection, no less serious, that to whatever degree it tells against egoistic hedonism, it tells in a greater degree against universalistic hedonism, or utilitarianism. He admits that it tells as much; saying "whatever weight is to be attached to the objections brought against this assumption [the commensurability of pleasures and pains] must of course tell against the present method." Not only does it tell, but it tells in a double way. I do not mean merely that, as he points out, the assumption becomes greatly complicated if we take all sentient beings into account, and if we include posterity along with existing individuals. I mean that, taking as the end to be achieved the greatest happiness of the existing individuals forming a single community, the set of difficulties standing in the way of egoistic hedonism, is compounded with another set of difficulties no less great, when we pass from it to universalistic hedonism. For if the dictates of universalistic hedonism are to be fulfilled, it must be under the guidance of individual judgments, or of corporate judgments, or of both. Now any one of such judgments issuing from a single mind, or from any aggregate of minds, necessarily embodies conclusions respecting the happinesses of other persons; few of them known, and the great mass never seen. All these persons have natures differing in countless ways and degrees from the natures of those who form the judgments; and the happinesses of which they are severally capable differ from one another, and differ from the happinesses of those who form the judgments. Consequently, if against the method of egoistic hedonism there is the objection that a man's own pleasures and pains, unlike in their kinds, intensities, and times of occurrence, are incommensurable; then against the method of universalistic hedonism it may be urged that to the incommensurability of each judge's own pleasures and pains (which he must use as standards) has now to be added the much more decided incommensurability of the pleasures and pains which he conceives to be experienced by innumerable other persons; all differently constituted from himself and from one another.

Nay more—there is a triple set of difficulties in the way of universalistic hedonism. To the double indeterminateness of the end has to be added the indeterminateness of the means. If hedonism, egoistic or universalistic, is to pass from dead theory into living practice, acts of one or other kind must be decided on to achieve proposed objects; and in estimating the two methods we have to consider how far the fitness of the acts respectively required can be judged. If, in pursuing his own ends, the individual is liable to be led by erroneous opinions to adjust his acts wrongly, much more liable is he to be led by erroneous opinions to adjust wrongly more complex acts to the more complex ends constituted by other men's welfares. It is so if he operates singly to benefit a few others; and it is still more so if he cooperates with many to benefit all. Making general happiness the immediate object of pursuit, implies numerous and complicated instrumentalities officered by thousands of unseen and unlike persons, and working on millions of other persons unseen and unlike. Even the few factors in this immense aggregate of appliances and processes which are known, are very imperfectly known; and the great mass of them are unknown. So that even supposing valuation of pleasures and pains for the community at large is more practicable than, or even as practicable as, valuation of his own pleasures and pains by the individual; yet the ruling of conduct with a view to the one end is far more difficult than the ruling of it with a view to the other. Hence if the method of egoistic hedonism is unsatisfactory, far more unsatisfactory for the same and kindred reasons, is the method of universalistic hedonism, or utilitarianism.

And here we come in sight of the conclusion which it has been the purpose of the foregoing criticism to bring into view. The objection made to the hedonistic method contains a truth, but includes with it an untruth. For while the proposition that happiness, whether individual or general, is the end of action, is not invalidated by proof that it cannot under either form be estimated by measurement of its components; yet it may be admitted that guidance in the pursuit of happiness by a mere balancing of pleasures and pains, is, if partially practicable throughout a certain range of conduct, futile throughout a much wider range. It is quite consistent to assert that happiness is the ultimate aim of action, and at the same time to deny that it can be reached by making it the immediate aim. I go with Mr. Sidgwick as far as the conclusion that "we must at least admit the desirability of confirming or correcting the results of such comparisons [of pleasures and pains] by any other method upon which we may find reason to rely"; and I then go further, and say that throughout a large part of conduct guidance by such comparisons is to be entirely set aside and replaced by other guidance.

58. The antithesis here insisted upon between the hedonistic and considered in the abstract, and the method which current hedonism, whether egoistic or universalistic, associates with that end; and the joining acceptance of the one with rejection of the other; commits us to an overt discussion of these two cardinal elements of ethical theory. I may conve-

niently initiate this discussion by criticizing another of Mr. Sidgwick's criticisms on the methods of hedonism.

Though we can give no account of those simple pleasures which the senses yield, because they are undecomposable, yet we distinctly know their characters as states of consciousness. Conversely, the complex pleasures formed by compounding and re-compounding the ideas of simple pleasures, though theoretically resolvable into their components, are not easy to resolve; and in proportion as they are heterogeneous in composition, the difficulty of framing intelligible conceptions of them increases. This is especially the case with the pleasures which accompany our sports. Treating of these, along with the pleasures of pursuit in general, for the purpose of showing that "in order to get them one must forget them," Mr. Sidgwick remarks:

> A man who maintains throughout an epicurean mood, fixing his aim on his own pleasure, does not catch the full spirit of the chase; his eagerness never gets just the sharpness of edge which imparts to the pleasure its highest zest and flavor. Here comes into view what we may call the fundamental paradox of Hedonism, that the impulse towards pleasure, if too predominant, defeats its own aim. This effect is not visible, or at any rate is scarcely visible, in the case of passive sensual pleasures. But our active employments generally, whether the activities on which they attend are classed as "bodily" or as "intellectual" (as well as of many emotional pleasures), it may certainly be said that we cannot attain them, at least in their best form, so long as we concentrate our aim on them. [*Methods of Ethics*, 2d ed., p. 41.]

Now I think we shall not regard this truth as paradoxical after we have duly analyzed the pleasure of pursuit. The chief components of this pleasure are—first, a renewed consciousness of personal efficiency (made vivid by actual success and partially excited by impending success) which consciousness of personal efficiency, connected in experience with achieved ends of every kind, arouses a vague but massive consciousness of resulting gratifications; and, second, a representation of the applause which recognition of this efficiency by others has before brought, and will again bring. Games of skill show us this clearly. Considered as an end in itself, the good cannon which a billiard player makes yields no pleasure. Whence then does the pleasure of making it arise? Partly from the fresh proof of capability which the player gives to himself, and partly from the imagined admiration of those who witness the proof of his capability: the last being the chief, since he soon tires of making cannons in the absence of witnesses. When from games which, yielding the pleasures of success, yield no pleasure derived from the end considered intrinsically, we pass to sports in which the end has intrinsic value as a source of pleasure, we see substantially the same thing. Though the bird which the sportsman brings down is useful as food, yet his satisfaction arises mainly from having made a good shot, and from having added to the bag which will presently bring praise of his skill. The gratification of self-esteem he immediately experiences; and the gratification of receiving applause he experiences, if not immediately and in full degree, yet by representation; for the ideal pleasure is nothing else than a faint revival of the real pleasure. These two kinds of agreeable excitement present in the sportsman during the chase, constitute the mass of the desires stimulating him to continue it; for all desires are nascent forms of the feelings to be obtained by the efforts they prompt. And though while seeking more birds these representative feelings are not so vividly excited as by success just achieved, yet they are excited by imaginations of further successes; and so make enjoyable the activities constituting the pursuit. Recognizing, then, the truth that the pleasures of pursuit are much more those derived from the efficient use of means than those derived from the end itself, we see that "the fundamental paradox of hedonism" disappears.

These remarks concerning end and means, and the pleasure accompanying use of the means as added to the pleasure derived from the end, I have made for the purpose of drawing attention to a fact of profound significance. During evolution there has been a superposing of new and more complex sets of means upon older and simpler sets of means; and a superposing of the pleasures accompanying the uses of these successive sets of means; with the result that each of these pleasures has itself eventually become an end. We begin with a simple animal which, without ancillary appliances, swallows such food as accident brings in its way; and so, as we may assume, stills some kind of craving. Here we have the primary end of nutrition with its accompanying satisfaction, in their simple forms. We pass to higher types having jaws for seizing and biting—jaws which thus, by their actions, facilitate achievement of the primary end. On observing animals furnished with these organs, we get evidence that the use of them becomes in itself pleasurable irrespective of the end: instance a squirrel, which, apart from food to be so obtained, delights in nibbling everything it gets hold of. Turning from jaws to limbs we see that these, serving some creatures for pursuit and others for escape, similarly yield gratification by their exercise; as in lambs which skip and horses which prance. How the combined use of limbs and jaws, originally subserving the satisfaction of appetite, grows to be in itself pleasurable, is daily illustrated in the playing of dogs. For that throwing down and worrying which, when prey is caught, precedes eating, is, in their mimic fights, carried by each as far as he dares. Coming to means still more remote from the end, namely, those by which creatures chased are caught, we are again shown by dogs that when no creature is caught there is still a gratification in the act of catching. The eagerness with which a dog runs after stones, or dances and barks in anticipation of jumping into the water after a stick, proves that apart from the satisfaction of appetite, and apart even from the satisfaction of killing prey, there is a satisfaction in the successful pursuit of a moving object. Throughout, then, we see that the pleasure attendant on the use of means to achieve an end, itself becomes an end.

Now if we contemplate these as phenomena of conduct in general, some facts worthy of note may be discerned—facts which, if we appreciate their significance, will aid us in developing our ethical conceptions. One of them is that among the successive sets of means, the later are the more remote from the primary end; are, as coordinating earlier and simpler means, the more complex; and are accompanied by feelings which are more representative. Another fact is that each set of means, with its accompanying satisfactions, eventually becomes in its turn dependent on one originating later than itself. Before the gullet swallows, the jaws must lay hold; before the jaws tear out and bring within the grasp of the gullet a piece fit for swallowing, there must be that cooperation of limbs and senses required for killing the prey; before this cooperation can take place, there needs the much longer cooperation constituting the chase; and even before this there must be persistent activities of limbs, eyes, and nose, in seeking prey. The pleasure attending each set of acts, while making possible the pleasure attending the set of acts which follows, is joined with a representation of this subsequent set of acts and its pleasure, and of the other which succeed in order; so that along with the feelings accompanying the search for prey, are partially aroused the feelings accompanying the actual chase, the actual destruction, the actual devouring, and the eventual satisfaction of appetite. A third fact is that the use of each set of means in due order, constitutes an obligation. Maintenance of its life being regarded as the end of its conduct, the creature is obliged to use in succession the means of finding prey, the means of catching prey, the means of killing prey, the means of devouring prey. Lastly, it follows that though the assuaging of hunger, directly associated with sustentation, remains to the last the ultimate end; yet the successful use of each set of means in its turn is the proximate end—the end which takes temporary precedence in authoritativeness.

59. The relations between means and ends thus traced throughout the earlier stages of evolving conduct, are traceable throughout later stages; and hold true of human conduct, up even to its highest forms. As fast as, for the better mainte-

nance of life, the simpler sets of means and the pleasures accompanying the uses of them, come to be supplemented by the more complex sets of means and their pleasures, these begin to take precedence in time and in imperativeness. To use effectually each more complex set of means becomes the proximate end, and the accompanying feeling becomes the immediate gratification sought; though there may be, and habitually is, an associated consciousness of the remoter ends and remoter gratifications to be obtained. An example will make clear the parallelism.

Absorbed in his business the trader, if asked what is his main end, will say—making money. He readily grants that achievement of this end is desired by him in furtherance of ends beyond it. He knows that in directly seeking money he is indirectly seeking food, clothes, house room, and the comforts of life for self and family. But while admitting that money is but a means to these ends, he urges that the money-getting actions precede in order of time and obligation, the various actions and concomitant pleasures subserved by them; and he testifies to the fact that making money has become itself an end, and success in it a source of satisfaction, apart from these more distant ends. Again, on observing more closely the trader's proceedings, we find that though to the end of living comfortably he gets money, and though to the end of getting money he buys and sells at a profit, which so becomes a means more immediately pursued, yet he is chiefly occupied with means still more remote from ultimate ends, and in relation to which even the selling at a profit becomes an end. For leaving to subordinates the actual measuring out of goods and receiving of proceeds, he busies himself mainly with his general affairs—inquiries concerning markets, judgments of future prices, calculations, negotiations, correspondence: the anxiety from hour to hour being to do well each one of these things indirectly conducive to the making of profits. And these ends precede in time and obligation the effecting of profitable sales, just as the effecting of profitable sales precedes the end of moneymaking, and just as the end of moneymaking precedes the end of satisfactory living. His bookkeeping best exemplifies the principle at large. Entries to the debtor or creditor sides are being made all through the day; the items are classified and arranged in such way that at a moment's notice the state of each account may be ascertained; and then, from time to time, the books are balanced, and it is required that the result shall come right to a penny: satisfaction following proved correctness, and annoyance being caused by error. If you ask why all this elaborate process, so remote from the actual getting of money, and still more remote from the enjoyments of life, the answer is that keeping accounts correctly is fulfilling a condition to the end of moneymaking, and becomes in itself a proximate end—a duty to be discharged, that there may be discharged the duty of getting an income, that there may be discharged the duty of maintaining self, wife, and children.

Approaching as we here do to moral obligation, are we not shown its relations to conduct at large? Is it not clear that observance of moral principles is fulfillment of certain general conditions to the successful carrying on of special activities? That the trader may prosper, he must not only keep his books correctly, but must pay those he employs according to agreement, and must meet his engagements with creditors. May we not say, then, that conformity to the second and third of these requirements is, like conformity to the first, an indirect means to effectual use of the more direct means of achieving welfare? May we not say, too, that as the use of each more indirect means in due order becomes itself an end, and a source of gratification; so, eventually, becomes the use of this most indirect means? And may we not infer that though conformity to moral requirements precedes in imperativeness conformity to other requirements; yet that this imperativeness arises from the fact that fulfillment of the other requirements, by self or others or both, is thus furthered?

60. This question brings us round to another side of the issue before raised. When alleging that empirical utili-

tarianism is but introductory to rational utilitarianism, I pointed out that the last does not take welfare for its immediate object of pursuit, but takes for its immediate object of pursuit conformity to certain principles which, in the nature of things, causally determine welfare. And now we see that this amounts to recognition of that law, traceable throughout the evolution of conduct in general, that each later and higher order of means takes precedence in time and authoritativeness of each earlier and lower order of means. The contrast between the ethical methods thus distinguished, made tolerably clear by the above illustrations, will be made still clearer by contemplating the two as put in opposition by the leading exponent of empirical utilitarianism. Treating of legislative aims, Bentham writes:

> But justice, what is it that we are to understand by justice: and why not happiness but justice? What happiness is, every man knows, because, what pleasure is, every man knows, and what pain is, every man knows. But what justice is—this is what on every occasion is the subject-matter of dispute. Be the meaning of the word justice what it will, what regard is it entitled to otherwise than as a means of happiness.*

Let us first consider the assertion here made respecting the relative intelligibilities of these two ends; and let us afterwards consider what is implied by the choice of happiness instead of justice.

Bentham's positive assertion that "what happiness is every man knows, because, what pleasure is, every man knows," is met by counterassertions equally positive. "Who can tell," asks Plato, "what pleasure really is, or know it in its essence, except the philosopher, who alone is conversant with realities."† Aristotle, too, after commenting on the different opinions held by the vulgar, by the political, by the contemplative, says of happiness that "to some it seems to be virtue, to others

---

* *Constitutional Code,* chap. xvi, Supreme Legislative—Section vi, *Omnicompetence.*
† *Republic,* Bk. ix.

prudence, and to others a kind of wisdom: to some again, these, or some one of these, with pleasure, or at least, not without pleasure; others again include external prosperity."* And Aristotle, like Plato, comes to the remarkable conclusion that the pleasures of the intellect, reached by the contemplative life, constitute the highest happiness!† How disagreements concerning the nature of happiness and the relative values of pleasures, thus exhibited in ancient times, continue down to modern times, is shown in Mr. Sidgwick's discussion of egoistic hedonism, above commented upon. Further, as was pointed out before, the indefiniteness attending the estimations of pleasures and pains, which stands in the way of egoistic hedonism as ordinarily conceived, is immensely increased on passing to universalistic hedonism as ordinarily conceived; since its theory implies that the imagined pleasures and pains of others are to be estimated by the help of these pleasures and pains of self, already so difficult to estimate. And that anyone after observing the various pursuits into which some eagerly enter but which others shun, and after listening to the different opinions concerning the likableness of this or that occupation or amusement, expressed at every table, should assert that the nature of happiness can be fully agreed upon, so as to render it a fit end for direct legislative action, is surprising.

The accompanying proposition that justice is unintelligible as an end, is no less surprising. Though primitive men have no words for either happiness or justice; yet even among them an approach to the conception of justice is traceable. The law of retaliation, requiring that a death inflicted by one tribe on another, shall be balanced by the death either of the murderer or of some member of his tribe, shows us in a vague shape that notion of equalness of treatment which forms an essential element in it. When we come to early races who have given

---

* *Nicomachean Ethics*, Bk. i. chap. 8.
† Bk. x., chap. 7.

their thoughts and feelings literary form, we find this conception of justice, as involving equalness of action, becoming distinct. Among the Jews, David expressed in words this association of ideas when, praying to God to "hear the right," he said—"Let my sentence come forth from thy presence; let thine eyes behold the things that are equal"; as also, among early Christians, did Paul when to the Colossians he wrote— "Masters, give unto your servants that which is just and equal." Commenting on the different meanings of justice, Aristotle concludes that "the just will therefore be the lawful and the equal; and the unjust the unlawful and the unequal. But since the unjust man is also one who takes more than his share," &c. And that justice was similarly conceived by the Romans they proved by including under it such meanings as exact, proportionate, impartial, severally implying fairness of division; and still better by identification of it with equity, which is a derivative of *æquus:* the word *æquus* itself having for one of its meanings just or impartial. This coincidence of view among ancient peoples respecting the nature of justice, has extended to modern peoples; who by a general agreement in certain cardinal principles which their systems of law embody, forbidding direct aggressions, which are forms of unequal actions, and forbidding indirect aggressions by breaches of contract, which are other forms of unequal actions, one and all show us the identification of justice with equalness. Bentham, then, is wrong when he says—"But what justice is—this is what on every occasion is the subject-matter of dispute." He is more wrong, indeed, than has thus far appeared. For, in the first place, he misrepresents utterly by ignoring the fact that in ninety-nine out of every hundred daily transactions between men, no dispute about justice arises; but the business done is recognized on both sides as justly done. And in the second place if, with respect to the hundredth transaction there is a dispute, the subject matter of it is not "what justice is," for it is admitted to be equity or equalness; but the subject matter of dispute always is—what, under these particular circumstances, constitutes equalness?—a widely different question.

It is not then self-evident, as Bentham alleges, that happiness is an intelligible end while justice is not; but, contrariwise, examination makes evident the greater intelligibility of justice as an end. And analysis shows why it is the more intelligible. For justice, or equity, or equalness, is concerned exclusively with *quantity* under *stated conditions;* whereas happiness is concerned with both *quantity* and *quality* under *conditions not stated.* When, as in case of theft, a benefit is taken while no equivalent benefit is yielded—when, as in case of adulterated goods bought or base coin paid, that which is agreed to be given in exchange as of equal value is not given, but something of less value—when, as in case of broken contract, the obligation on one side has been discharged while there has been no discharge, or incomplete discharge, of the obligation on the other; we see that, *the circumstances being specified,* the injustice complained of refers to the relative amounts of actions, or products, or benefits, the natures of which are recognized only so far as is needful for saying whether *as much* has been given, or done, or allowed, by each concerned, as was implied by tacit or overt understanding to be *an equivalent.* But when the end proposed is happiness, *the circumstances remaining unspecified,* the problem is that of estimating both quantities and qualities, unhelped by any such definite measures as acts of exchange imply, or as contracts imply, or as are implied by the differences between the doings of one aggressing and one aggressed upon. The mere fact that Bentham himself includes as elements in the estimation of each pleasure or pain, its intensity, duration, certainty, and proximity, suffices to show how difficult is this problem. And when it is remembered that all pleasures and pains, not felt in particular cases only but in the aggregate of cases, and severally regarded under these four aspects, have to be compared with one another and their relative values determined, simply by introspection; it will be manifest both that the problem is complicated by the addition of indefinite judgments of qualities to indefinite measures of quantities, and that it is further complicated by the multitudinousness of these vague estimations to be gone through and summed up.

But now passing over this assertion of Bentham that happiness is a more intelligible end than justice, which we find to be the reverse of truth, let us note the several implications of the doctrine that the supreme legislative body ought to make the greatest happiness of the greatest number its immediate aim.

It implies, in the first place, that happiness may be compassed by methods framed directly for the purpose, without any previous inquiry respecting the conditions that must be fulfilled; and this presupposes a belief that there are no such conditions. For if there are any conditions without fulfillment of which happiness cannot be compassed, then the first step must be to ascertain these conditions with a view to fulfilling them; and to admit this is to admit that not happiness itself must be the immediate end, but fulfillment of the conditions to its attainment must be the immediate end. The alternatives are simple: Either the achievement of happiness is not conditional, in which case one mode of action is as good as another, or it is conditional, in which case the required mode of action must be the direct aim and not the happiness to be achieved by it.

Assuming it conceded, as it will be, that there exist conditions which must be fulfilled before happiness can be attained, let us next ask what is implied by proposing modes of so controlling conduct as to further happiness, without previously inquiring whether any such modes are already known? The implication is that human intelligence throughout the past, operating on experiences, has failed to discover any such modes; whereas present human intelligence may be expected forthwith to discover them. Unless this be asserted, it must be admitted that certain conditions to the achievement of happiness have already been partially, if not wholly, ascertained; and if so, our first business should be to look for them. Having found them, our rational course is to bring existing intelligence to bear on these products of past intelligence, with the expectation that it will verify the substance of them while possibly correcting the form. But to suppose that no regulative principles for the conduct of associated human beings have thus far been established, and that they are now to be established *de novo*, is to suppose that man as he is differs from man as he was in an incredible degree.

Beyond ignoring the probability, or rather the certainty, that past experience generalized by past intelligence, must by this time have disclosed partially, if not wholly, some of the essential conditions to the achievement of happiness, Bentham's proposition ignores the formulated knowledge of them actually existing. For whence come the conception of justice and the answering sentiment. He will scarcely say that they are meaningless, although his proposition implies as much; and if he admits that they have meanings, he must choose between two alternatives either of which is fatal to his hypothesis. Are they supernaturally caused modes of thinking and feeling, tending to make men fulfill the conditions to happiness? If so their authority is peremptory. Are they modes of thinking and feeling naturally caused in men by experience of these conditions? If so, their authority is no less peremptory. Not only, then, does Bentham fail to infer that certain principles of guidance must by this time have been ascertained, but he refuses to recognize these principles as actually reached and present to him.

And then after all, he tacitly admits that which he overtly denies, by saying that—"Be the meaning of the word justice what it will, what regard is it entitled to otherwise than as a means to happiness?" For if justice is a means having happiness as its end, then justice must take precedence of happiness, as every other means takes precedence of every other end. Bentham's own elaborate polity is a means having happiness as its end, as justice is, by his own admission, a means having happiness as an end. If, then, we may properly skip justice, and go directly to the end happiness, we may properly skip Bentham's polity, and go directly to the end happiness. In short, we are led to the remarkable conclusion that in all cases we must contemplate exclusively the end and must disregard the means.

61. This relation of ends to means, underlying all ethical speculation, will be further elucidated if we join with some of

the above conclusions, certain conclusions drawn in the last chapter. We shall see that while greatest happiness may vary widely in societies which, though ideally constituted, are subject to unlike physical circumstances, certain fundamental conditions to the achievement of this greatest happiness, are common to all such societies.

Given a people inhabiting a tract which makes nomadic habits necessary, and the happiness of each individual will be greatest when his nature is so molded to the requirements of his life, that all his faculties find their due activities in daily driving and tending cattle, milking, migrating, and so forth. The members of a community otherwise similar, which is permanently settled, will severally achieve their greatest happiness when their natures have become such that a fixed habitat, and the occupations necessitated by it, supply the spheres in which each instinct and emotion is exercised and brings the concomitant pleasure. The citizens of a large nation industrially organized, have reached their possible ideal of happiness, when the producing, distributing, and other activities, are such in their kinds and amounts, that each citizen finds in them a place for all his energies and aptitudes, while he obtains the means of satisfying all his desires. Once more we may recognize as not only possible but probable, the eventual existence of a community, also industrial, the members of which, having natures similarly responding to these requirements, are also characterized by dominant aesthetic faculties, and achieve complete happiness only when a large part of life is filled with æsthetic activities. Evidently these different types of men, with their different standards of happiness, each finding the possibility of that happiness in his own society, would not find it if transferred to any of the other societies. Evidently though they might have in common such kinds of happiness as accompany the satisfaction of vital needs, they would not have in common sundry other kinds of happiness.

But now mark that while, to achieve greatest happiness in each of such societies, the special conditions to be fulfilled must differ from those to be fulfilled in the other societies, certain general conditions must be fulfilled in all the societies. Harmonious cooperation, by which alone in any of them the greatest happiness can be attained, is, as we saw, made possible only by respect for one another's claims: there must be neither those direct aggressions which we class as crimes against person and property, nor must there be those indirect aggressions constituted by breaches of contracts. So that maintenance of equitable relations between men, is the condition to attainment of greatest happiness in all societies; however much the greatest happiness attainable in each may differ in nature, or amount, or both.

And here a physical analogy may fitly be used to give the greatest definiteness to this cardinal truth. A mass of matter of whatever kind, maintains its state of internal equilibrium, so long as its component particles severally stand toward their neighbors in equidistant positions. Accepting the conclusions of modern physicists, which imply that each molecule moves rhythmically, then a balanced state implies that each performs its movements within a space bounded by the like spaces required for the movements of those around. If the molecules have been so aggregated that the oscillations of some are more restrained than the oscillations of others, there is a proportionate instability. If the number of them thus unduly restrained is considerable, the instability is such that the cohesion in some part is liable to fail, and a crack results. If the excesses of restraint are great and multitudinous, a trifling disturbance causes the mass to break up into small fragments. To which add that the recognized remedy for this unstable state, is an exposure to such physical condition (ordinarily high temperature) as enables the molecules so to change their relative positions that their mutual restraints become equal on all sides. And now observe that this holds whatever be the natures of the molecules. They may be simple; they may be compound; they may be composed of this or that matter in this or that way. In other words, the special activities of each molecule, constituted by the relative movements of its units, may be various in their kinds and degrees; and yet, be they what they may, it remains true that to preserve internal equilibrium throughout the mass of molecules, the mutual limitations of their activities must be everywhere alike.

And this is the above-described prerequisite to social equilibrium, whatever the special natures of the associated persons. Assuming that within each society such persons are of the same type, needing for the fulfillment of their several lives kindred activities, and though these activities may be of one kind in one society and of another kind in another, so admitting of indefinite variation, this condition to social equilibrium does not admit of variation. It must be fulfilled before complete life, that is greatest happiness, can be attained in any society; be the particular quality of that life, or that happiness, what it may.*

62. After thus observing how means and ends in conduct stand to one another, and how there emerge certain conclusions respecting their relative claims, we may see a way to reconcile sundry conflicting ethical theories. These severally embody portions of the truth; and simply require combining in proper order to embody the whole truth.

The theological theory contains a part. If for the divine will, supposed to be supernaturally revealed, we substitute the naturally revealed end towards which the Power manifested throughout evolution works; then, since evolution has been, and is still, working towards the highest life, it follows that conforming to those principles by which the highest life is achieved, is furthering that end. The doctrine that perfection or excellence of nature should be the object of pursuit, is in one sense true; for it tacitly recognizes that ideal form of being which the highest life implies, and to which evolution tends. There is a truth, also, in the doctrine that virtue must be the aim; for this is another form of the doctrine that the aim must be to fulfill the conditions to achievement of the highest life.

---

* This universal requirement it was which I had in view when choosing for my first work, published in 1850, the title *Social Statics*.

That the intuitions of a moral faculty should guide our conduct, is a proposition in which a truth is contained; for these
intuitions are the slowly organized results of experiences received by the race while living in presence of these conditions.
And that happiness is the supreme end is beyond question
true; for this is the concomitant of that highest life which every
theory of moral guidance has distinctly or vaguely in view.

So understanding their relative positions, those ethical systems which make virtue, right, obligation, the cardinal aims,
are seen to be complementary to those ethical systems which
make welfare, pleasure, happiness, the cardinal aims.
Though the moral sentiments generated in civilized men by
daily conduct with social conditions and gradual adaptation
to them, are indispensable as incentives and deterrents; and
though the intuitions corresponding to these sentiments,
have, in virtue of their origin, a general authority to be rever-
ently recognized; yet the sympathies and antipathies hence
originating, together with the intellectual expressions of
them, are, in their primitive forms, necessarily vague. To
make guidance by them adequate to all requirements, their
dictates have to be interpreted and made definite by science;
to which end there must be analysis of those conditions to
complete living which they respond to, and from converse
with which they have arisen. And such analysis necessitates
the recognition of happiness for each and all, as the end to be
achieved by fulfillment of these conditions.

Hence, recognizing in due degrees all the various ethical
theories, conduct in its highest form will take as guides,
innate perceptions of right duly enlightened and made precise
by an analytic intelligence; while conscious that these guides
are proximately supreme solely because they lead to the ultimately supreme end, happiness special and general.

CHAPTER 10

The Relativity of Pains and Pleasures

63.   A truth of cardinal importance as a datum of ethics, which was incidentally referred to in the last chapter, must here be set forth at full length. I mean the truth that not only men of different races, but also different men of the same race, and even the same men at different periods of life, have different standards of happiness. Though there is some recognition of this by moralists, the recognition is inadequate; and the far-reaching conclusions to be drawn when the relativity of happiness is fully recognized, are scarcely suspected.

It is a belief universal in early life—a belief which in most people is but partially corrected in later life, and in very few wholly dissipated—that there is something intrinsic in the pleasantness of certain things, while other things are intrinsically unpleasant. The error is analogous to, and closely allied with, the error crude realism makes. Just as to the uncultured mind it appears self-evident that the sweetness of sugar is inherent in sugar, that sound as we perceive it is sound as it exists in the external world, and that the warmth from a fire is in itself what it seems; so does it appear self-evident that the sweetness of sugar is necessarily grateful, that there is in a beautiful sound something that must be beautiful to all crea-

tures, and that the agreeable feeling produced by warmth is a
feeling which every other consciousness must find agreeable.

But as criticism proves the one set of conclusions to be
wrong, so does it prove to be wrong the other set. Not only are
the qualities of external things as intellectually apprehended
by us, relative to our own organisms; but the pleasurableness
or painfulness of the feelings which we associate with such
qualities, are also relative to our own organisms. They are so
in a double sense—they are relative to its structures, and they
are relative to the states of its structures.

That we may not rest in a mere nominal acceptance of these
general truths, but may so appreciate them as to see their full
bearings on ethical theory, we must here glance at them as
exemplified by animate creatures at large. For after contemplating the wide divergences of sentiency accompanying
the wide divergences of organization which evolution in general has brought about, we shall be enabled the better to see
the divergences of sentiency to be expected from the further
evolution of humanity.

64. Because they can be most quickly disposed of, let us
first deal with pains: a further reason for first dealing with
pains being that we may thus forthwith recognize, and then
leave out of consideration, those sentient states the qualities
of which may be regarded as absolute rather than relative.

The painfulness of the feelings produced by forces which
tend to destroy organic structures, wholly or in part, is of
course common to all creatures capable of feeling. We saw it to
be inevitable that during evolution there must everywhere be
established such connections between external actions and
the modes of consciousness they cause, that the injurious
ones are accompanied by disagreeable feelings and the beneficial ones by agreeable feelings. Consequently, pressures or
strains which tear or bruise, and heats which burn or scald,
being in all cases partially or wholly destructive, are in all
cases painful. But even here the relativity of the feelings may
in one sense be asserted. For the effect of a force of given

quantity or intensity, varies partly with the size and partly with the structure of the creature exposed to it. The weight which is scarcely felt by a large animal crushes a small one; the blow which breaks the limb of a mouse produces little effect on a horse; the weapon which lacerates a horse leaves a rhinoceros uninjured. And with these differences of injuriousness doubtless go differences of feeling. Merely glancing at the illustrations of this truth furnished by sentient beings in general, let us consider the illustrations mankind furnish.

Comparisons of robust laboring men with women or children, show us that degrees of mechanical stress which the first bear with impunity, produce on the others injuries and accompanying pains. The blistering of a tender skin by an amount of friction which does not even redden a coarse one, or the bursting of superficial blood vessels, and consequent discoloration, caused in a person of lax tissues by a blow which leaves in well-toned tissues no trace, will sufficiently exemplify this contrast. Not only, however, are the pains due to violent incident forces, relative to the characters or constitutional qualities of the parts directly affected, but they are relative in equally marked ways, or even in more marked ways, to the characters of the nervous structures. The common assumption is that equal bodily injuries excite equal pains. But this is a mistake. Pulling out a tooth or cutting off a limb, gives to different persons widely different amounts of suffering: not the endurance only, but the feeling to be endured, varies greatly: and the variation largely depends on the degree of nervous development. This is well shown by the great insensibility of idiots—blows, cuts, and extremes of heat and cold, being borne by them with indifference.* The relation thus shown in the most marked manner where the development of the central nervous system is abnormally low, is shown in a less marked manner where the development of the central nervous system is normally low; namely, among inferior races of men. Many travellers have commented on the

---

* William W. Ireland, M.D., *On Idiocy and Imbecility*, pp. 255–56.

strange callousness shown by savages who have been mangled in battle or by accident; and surgeons in India say that wounds and operations are better borne by natives than by Europeans. Further, there comes the converse fact that among the higher types of men, larger-brained and more sensitive to pain than the lower, the most sensitive are those whose nervous developments, as shown by their mental powers, are the highest: part of the evidence being the relative intolerance of disagreeable sensations common among men of genius,* and the general irritability characteristic of them.

That pain is relative not to structures only, but to their states as well, is also manifest—more manifest indeed. The sensibility of an external part depends on its temperature. Cool it below a certain point and it becomes, as we say, numb; and if by ether-spray it is made very cold, it may be cut without any feeling being produced. Conversely, heat the part so that its blood-vessels dilate, and the pain which any injury or irritation causes is greater than usual. How largely the production of pain depends on the condition of the part affected, we see in the extreme tenderness of an inflamed surface—a tenderness such that a slight touch causes shrinking, and such that rays from the fire which ordinarily would be indifferent become intolerable. Similarly with the special senses. A light which eyes that are in good order bear without disagreeable feeling, cannot be borne by inflamed eyes. And beyond the local state, the state of the system as a whole, and the state of the nervous centers, are both factors. Those enfeebled by illness are distressed by noises which those in health bear with equanimity; and men with overwrought brains are irritated in unusual degrees by annoyances, both physical and moral. Further, the temporary condition known as exhaustion enters into the relation. Limbs overworn by prolonged exertion, cannot without aching perform acts which would at other times cause no appreciable feeling. After reading continuously for very many hours, even strong eyes begin to

---

* For instances, see *Fortnightly Review,* vol. 24 *(New Series),* p. 712.

smart. And noises that can be listened to for a short time with indifference, become, if there is no cessation, causes of suffering.

So that though there is absoluteness in the relation between positive pains and actions that are positively injurious, in so far that wherever there is sentiency it exists; yet even here partial relativity may be asserted. For there is no fixed relation between the acting force and the produced feeling. The amount of feeling varies with the size of the organism, with the character of its outer structures, with the character of its nervous system; and also with the temporary states of the part affected, of the body at large, and of the nervous centers.

65. The relativity of pleasures is far more conspicuous; and the illustrations of it furnished by the sentient world at large are innumerable.

It needs but to glance round at the various things which different creatures are prompted by their desires to eat and are gratified in eating—flesh for predaceous animals, grass for the herbivora, worms for the mole, flies for the swallow, seeds for the finch, honey for the bee, a decaying carcase for the maggot—to be reminded that the tastes for foods are relative to the structures of the creatures. And this truth, made conspicuous by a survey of animals in general, is forced on our attention even by a survey of different races of men. Here human flesh is abhorred, and there regarded as the greatest delicacy; in this country roots are allowed to putrefy before they are eaten, and in that the taint of decay produces disgust; the whale's blubber which one race devours with avidity, will in another by its very odor produce nausea. Nay, without looking abroad we may, in the common saying that "one man's meat is another man's poison," see the general admission that members of the same society so far differ, that a taste which is to these pleasurable is to those displeasurable. So is it with the other senses. Assafoetida, which by us is singled out as typical of the disgusting in odor, ranks among the Estonians as a favorite perfume; and even those around us vary so far in their likings that the scents of flowers grateful to some are repugnant to others. Analogous differences in the preferences for colors, we daily hear expressed. And in a greater or less degree the like holds with all sensations, down even to those of touch: the feeling yielded by velvet, which is to most agreeable, setting the teeth on edge in some.

It needs but to name appetite and satiety to suggest multitudinous facts showing that pleasures are relative not only to the organic structures but also to their states. The food which yields keen gratification when there is great hunger ceases to be grateful when hunger is satisfied; and if then forced on the eater is rejected with aversion. So, too, a particular kind of food, seeming when first tasted so delicious that daily repetition would be a source of endless enjoyment, becomes, in a few days, not only unenjoyable but repugnant. Brilliant colors which, falling on unaccustomed eyes give delight, pall on the sense if long looked at; and there is relief in getting away from the impressions they yield. Sounds sweet in themselves and sweet in their combinations, which yield to unfatigued ears intense pleasure, become, at the end of a long concert, not only wearisome but, if there is no escape from them, causes of irritation. The like holds down even to such simple sensations as those of heat and cold. The fire so delightful on a winter's day is, in hot weather, oppressive; and pleasure is then taken in the cold water from which, in winter, there would be shrinking. Indeed, experiences lasting over but a few moments suffice to show how relative to the states of the structures are pleasurable sensations of these kinds; for it is observable that on dipping the cold hand into hot water, the agreeable feeling gradually diminishes as the hand warms.

These few instances will carry home the truth, manifest enough to all who observe, that the receipt of each agreeable sensation depends primarily on the existence of a structure which is called into play; and, secondarily, on the condition of that structure, as fitting it or unfitting it for activity.

66. The truth that emotional pleasures are made possible, partly by the existence of correlative structures and partly by the states of those structures, is equally undeniable.

Observe the animal which, leading a life demanding solitary habits, has an adapted organization, and it gives no sign of need for the presence of its kind. Observe, conversely, a gregarious animal separated from the herd, and you see marks of unhappiness while the separation continues, and equally distinct marks of joy on joining its companions. In the one case there is no nervous structure which finds its sphere of action in the gregarious state; and in the other case such a structure exists. As was implied by instances cited in the last chapter for another purpose, animals leading lives involving particular kinds of activities, have become so constituted that pursuance of those activities, exercising the correlative structures, yields the associated pleasures. Beasts of prey confined in dens, show us by their pacings from side to side the endeavor to obtain, as well as they can, the satisfactions that accompany roaming about in their natural habitats; and that gratification in the expenditure of their locomotive energies shown us by porpoises playing round a vessel, is shown us by the similarly unceasing excursions from end to end of its cell which a captured porpoise makes. The perpetual hoppings of the canary from bar to bar of its cage, and the ceaseless use of claws and bill in climbing about its perch by the parrot, are other activities which, severally related to the needs of the species, have severally themselves become sources of agreeable feelings. Still more clearly are we shown by the efforts which a caged beaver makes to build with such sticks and pieces of wood as are at hand, how dominant in its nature has become the building instinct; and how, apart from any advantage gained, it gets gratification by repeating, as well as it can, the processes of construction it is organized to carry on. The cat which, lacking something to tear with her claws, pulls at the mat with them, the confined giraffe which, in default of branches to lay hold of wears out the upper angles of the doors to its house by continually grasping them with its prehensile tongue, the rhinoceros which, having no enemy to fight, ploughs up the ground with his horn, all yield us analogous evidence. Clearly, these various actions performed by these various creatures are not intrinsically pleasurable; for they differ more or less in each species and are often utterly unlike. The pleasurableness is simply in the exercise of nervomuscular structures adapted to the performance of the actions.

Though races of men are contrasted with one another so much less than genera and orders of animals are, yet, as we saw in the last chapter, along with visible differences there go invisible differences, with accompanying likings for different modes of life. Among some, as the Mantras, the love of unrestrained action and the disregard of companionship, are such that they separate if they quarrel, and hence live scattered; while among others, as the Damaras, there is little tendency to resist, but instead, an admiration for any one who assumes power over them. Already when exemplifying the indefiniteness of happiness as an end of action, I have referred to the unlike ideals of life pursued by the nomadic and the settled, the warlike and the peaceful—unlike ideals which imply unlikenesses of nervous structures caused by the inherited effects of unlike habits accumulating through generations. These contrasts, various in their kinds and degrees among the various types of mankind, everyone can supplement by analogous contrasts observable among those around. The occupations some delight in are to those otherwise constituted intolerable; and men's hobbies, severally appearing to themselves quite natural, often appear to their friends ludicrous and almost insane: facts which alone might make us see that the pleasurableness of actions of this or that kind, is due not to anything in the natures of the actions but to the existence of faculties which find exercise in them.

It must be added that each pleasurable emotion, like each pleasurable sensation, is relative not only to a certain structure but also to the state of that structure. The parts called into action must have had proper rest—must be in a condition fit for action; not in the condition which prolonged action produces. Be the order of emotion what it may, an unbroken continuity in the receipt of it eventually brings satiety. The pleasurable consciousness becomes less and less vivid, and there arises the need for a temporary cessation during which the parts that have been active may recover their fitness for activity; and during which also, the activities of other parts and receipt of the accompanying emotions may find due place.

67. I have insisted on these general truths with perhaps needless iteration, to prepare the reader for more fully recognizing a corollary that is practically ignored. Abundant and clear as is the evidence, and forced though it is daily on everyone's attention, the conclusions respecting life and conduct which should be drawn, are not drawn; and so much at variance are these conclusions with current beliefs, that enunciation of them causes a stare of incredulity. Pervaded as all past thinking has been, and as most present thinking is, by the assumption that the nature of every creature has been specially created for it, and that human nature, also specially created, is, like other natures, fixed—pervaded too as this thinking has been, and is, by the allied assumption that the agreeableness of certain actions depends on their essential qualities, while other actions are by their essential qualities made disagreeable; it is difficult to obtain a hearing for the doctrine that the kinds of action which are now pleasurable will, under conditions requiring the change, cease to be pleasurable, while other kinds of action will become pleasurable. Even those who accept the doctrine of evolution mostly hear with skepticism, or at best with nominal faith, the inferences to be drawn from it respecting the humanity of the future.

And yet as shown in myriads of instances indicated by the few above given, those natural processes which have produced multitudinous forms of structure adapted to multitudinous forms of activity, have simultaneously made these forms of activity pleasurable. And the inevitable implication is that within the limits imposed by physical laws, there will be evolved, in adaptation to any new sets of conditions that may be established, appropriate structures of which the functions will yield their respective gratifications.

When we have got rid of the tendency to think that certain modes of activity are necessarily pleasurable because they give us pleasure, and that other modes which do not please us are necessarily unpleasing; we shall see that the remolding of human nature into fitness for the requirements of social life, must eventually make all needful activities pleasurable, while it makes displeasurable all activities at variance with these requirements. When we have come fully to recognize the truth that there is nothing intrinsically more gratifying in the efforts by which wild animals are caught, than in the efforts expended in rearing plants, and that the combined actions of muscles and senses in rowing a boat are not by their essential natures more productive of agreeable feeling than those gone through in reaping corn, but that everything depends on the cooperating emotions, which at present are more in accordance with the one than with the other; we shall infer that along with decrease of those emotions for which the social state affords little or no scope, and increase of those which it persistently exercises, the things now done with dislike from a sense of obligation will be done with immediate liking, and the things desisted from as a matter of duty will be desisted from because they are repugnant.

This conclusion, alien to popular beliefs and in ethical speculation habitually ignored, or at most recognized but partially and occasionally, will be thought by the majority so improbable that I must give further justification of it: enforcing the *a priori* argument by an *a posteriori* one. Small as is the attention given to the fact, yet is the fact conspicuous that the corollary above drawn from the doctrine of evolution at large, coincides with the corollary which past and present changes in human nature force on us. The leading contrasts of character between savage and civilized, are just those contrasts to be expected from the process of adaptation.

The life of the primitive man is passed mainly in the pursuit of beasts, birds, and fish, which yields him a gratifying excitement; but though to the civilized man the chase gives gratification, this is neither so persistent nor so general. There are among us keen sportsmen; but there are many to whom shooting and fishing soon become wearisome; and there are not a few to whom they are altogether indifferent or even distasteful. Conversely, the power of continued application which in the primitive man is very small, has among ourselves become considerable. It is true that most are coerced into industry by necessity; but there are sprinkled throughout society men to whom active occupation is a need—men who are restless when away from business and miserable when they eventually give it up; men to whom this or that line of investigation is so attractive, that they devote themselves to it day after day, year after year; men who are so deeply interested in public affairs that they pass lives of labor in achieving political ends they think advantageous, hardly giving themselves the rest necessary for health. Yet again, and still more strikingly, does the change become manifest when we compare undeveloped with developed humanity in respect of the conduct prompted by fellow feeling. Cruelty rather than kindness is characteristic of the savage, and is in many cases a source of marked gratification to him; but though among the civilized are some in whom this trait of the savage survives, yet a love of inflicting pain is not general, and besides numbers who show benevolence, there are those who devote their whole time and much of their money to philanthropic ends, without thought of reward either here or hereafter. Clearly these major, along with many minor, changes of nature, conform to the law set forth. Activities appropriate to their needs which give pleasures to savages have ceased to be pleasurable to many of the civilized; while the civilized have acquired capacities for other appropriate activities and accompanying pleasures which savages had no capacities for.

Now, not only is it rational to infer that changes like those which have been going on during civilization, will continue to go on, but it is irrational to do otherwise. Not he who believes that adaptation will increase is absurd, but he who doubts that it will increase is absurd. Lack of faith in such further evolution of humanity as shall harmonize its nature with its conditions, adds but another to the countless illustrations of inadequate consciousness of causation. One who, leaving behind both primitive dogmas and primitive ways of looking at things, has, while accepting scientific conclusions acquired those habits of thought which science generates, will regard the conclusion above drawn as inevitable. He will find it impossible to believe that the processes which have heretofore so molded all beings to the requirements of their lives that they get satisfactions in fulfilling them, will not hereafter continue so molding them. He will infer that the type of nature to which the highest social life affords a sphere such that every faculty has its due amount, and no more than the due amount, of function and accompanying gratification, is the type of nature toward which progress cannot cease till it is reached. Pleasure being producible by the exercise of any structure which is adjusted to its special end, he will see the necessary implication to be that, supposing it consistent with the maintenance of life, there is no kind of activity which will not become a source of pleasure if continued; and that therefore pleasure will eventually accompany every mode of action demanded by social conditions.

This corollary I here emphasize because it will presently play an important part in the argument.

CHAPTER 11

Egoism Versus Altruism

68.   If insistence on them tends to unsettle established systems of unbelief, self-evident truths are by most people silently passed over; or else there is a tacit refusal to draw from them the most obvious inferences.

Of self-evident truths so dealt with, the one which here concerns us is that a creature must live before it can act. From this it is a corollary that the acts by which each maintains his own life must, speaking generally, precede in imperativeness all other acts of which he is capable. For if it be asserted that these other acts must precede in imperativeness the acts which maintain life; and if this, accepted as a general law of conduct, is conformed to by all; then by postponing the acts which maintain life to the other acts which life makes possible, all must lose their lives. That is to say, ethics has to recognize the truth, recognized in unethical thought, that egoism comes before altruism. The acts required for continued self-preservation, including the enjoyment of benefits achieved by such acts, are the first requisites to universal welfare. Unless each duly cares for himself, his care for all others is ended by death; and if each thus dies, there remain no others to be cared for.

This permanent supremacy of egoism over altruism, made

manifest by contemplating existing life, is further made manifest by contemplating life in course of evolution.

69. Those who have followed with assent the recent course of thought, do not need telling that throughout past eras, the life, vast in amount and varied in kind, which has overspread the earth, has progressed in subordination to the law that every individual shall gain by whatever aptitude it has for fulfilling the conditions to its existence. The uniform principle has been that better adaptation shall bring greater benefit; which greater benefit, while increasing the prosperity of the better adapted, shall increase also its ability to leave offspring inheriting more or less its better adaptation. And, by implication, the uniform principle has been that the ill adapted, disadvantaged in the struggle for existence, shall bear the consequent evils: either disappearing when its imperfections are extreme, or else rearing fewer offspring, which, inheriting its imperfections, tend to dwindle away in posterity.

It has been thus with innate superiorities; it has been thus also with acquired ones. All along the law has been that increased function brings increased power; and that therefore such extra activities as aid welfare in any member of a race, produce in its structures greater ability to carry on such extra activities: the derived advantages being enjoyed by it to the heightening and lengthening of its life. Conversely, as lessened function ends in lessened structure, the dwindling of unused faculties has ever entailed loss of power to achieve the correlative ends: the result of inadequate fulfillment of the ends being diminished ability to maintain life. And by inheritance, such functionally produced modifications have respectively furthered or hindered survival in posterity.

As already said, the law that each creature shall take the benefits and the evils of its own nature, be they those derived from ancestry or those due to self-produced modifications, has been the law under which life has evolved thus far; and it must continue to be the law however much further life may evolve. Whatever qualifications this natural course of action may now or hereafter undergo, are qualifications that cannot, without fatal results, essentially change it. Any arrangements which in a considerable degree prevent superiority from profiting by the rewards of superiority, or shield inferiority from the evils it entails—any arrangements which tend to make it as well to be inferior as to be superior; are arrangements diametrically opposed to the progress of organization and the reaching of a higher life.

But to say that each individual shall reap the benefits brought to him by his own powers, inherited and acquired, is to enunciate egoism as an ultimate principle of conduct. It is to say that egoistic claims must take precedence of altruistic claims.

70. Under its biological aspect this proposition cannot be contested by those who agree in the doctrine of evolution; but probably they will not at once allow that admission of it under its ethical aspect is equally unavoidable. While, as respects development of life, the well-working of the universal principle described is sufficiently manifest; the well-working of it as respects increase of happiness may not be seen at once. But the two cannot be disjoined.

Incapacity of every kind and of whatever degree, causes unhappiness directly and indirectly—directly by the pain consequent on the overtaxing of inadequate faculty, and indirectly by the nonfulfillment, or imperfect fulfillment, of certain conditions to welfare. Conversely, capacity of every kind sufficient for the requirement, conduces to happiness immediately and remotely—immediately by the pleasure accompanying the normal exercise of each power that is up to its work, and remotely by the pleasures which are furthered by the ends achieved. A creature that is weak or slow of foot, and so gets food only by exhausting efforts or escapes enemies with difficulty, suffers the pains of overstrained powers, of unsatisfied appetites, of distressed emotions; while the strong and swift creature of the same species delights in its efficient activities, gains more fully the satisfactions yielded by food as

well as the renewed vivacity this gives, and has to bear fewer
and smaller pains in defending itself against foes or escaping
from them. Similarly with duller and keener senses, or higher
and lower degrees of sagacity. The mentally inferior individual of any race suffers negative and positive miseries;
while the mentally superior individual receives negative and
positive gratifications. Inevitably, then, this law in conformity
with which each member of a species takes the consequences
of its own nature; and in virtue of which the progeny of each
member, participating in its nature, also takes such consequences; is one that tends ever to raise the aggregate happiness of the species, by furthering the multiplication of the
happier and hindering that of the less happy.

All this is true of human beings as of other beings. The
conclusion forced on us is that the pursuit of individual happiness within those limits prescribed by social conditions, is
the first requisite to the attainment of the greatest general
happiness. To see this it needs but to contrast one whose
self-regard has maintained bodily well-being, with one whose
regardlessness of self has brought its natural results; and then
to ask what must be the contrast between two societies
formed of two such kinds of individuals.

Bounding out of bed after an unbroken sleep, singing or
whistling as he dresses, coming down with beaming face
ready to laugh on the smallest provocation, the healthy man
of high powers, conscious of past successes and by his energy,
quickness, resource, made confident of the future, enters on
the day's business not with repugnance but with gladness;
and from hour to hour experiencing satisfactions from work
effectually done, comes home with an abundant surplus of
energy remaining for hours of relaxation. Far otherwise is it
with one who is enfeebled by great neglect of self. Already
deficient, his energies are made more deficient by constant
endeavors to execute tasks that prove beyond his strength,
and by the resulting discouragement. Besides the depressing
consciousness of the immediate future, there is the depressing
consciousness of the remoter future, with its probability of

accumulated difficulties and diminished ability to meet them. Hours of leisure which, rightly passed, bring pleasures that raise the tide of life and renew the powers of work, cannot be utilized: there is not vigor enough for enjoyments involving action, and lack of spirits prevents passive enjoyments from being entered upon with zest. In brief, life becomes a burden. Now if, as must be admitted, in a community composed of individuals like the first the happiness will be relatively great, while in one composed of individuals like the last there will be relatively little happiness, or rather much misery; it must be admitted that conduct causing the one result is good and conduct causing the other is bad.

But diminutions of general happiness are produced by inadequate egoism in several other ways. These we will successively glance at.

71. If there were no proofs of heredity—if it were the rule that the strong are usually begotten by the weak while the weak usually descend from the strong, that vivacious children form the families of melancholy parents while fathers and mothers with overflowing spirits mostly have dull progeny, that from stolid peasants there ordinarily come sons of high intelligence while the sons of the cultured are commonly fit for nothing but following the plough—if there were no transmission of gout, scrofula, insanity, and did the diseased habitually give birth to the healthy and the healthy to the diseased, writers on ethics might be justified in ignoring those effects of conduct which are felt by posterity through the natures they inherit.

As it is, however, the current ideas concerning the relative claims of egoism and altruism are vitiated by the omission of this all-important factor. For if health, strength and capacity, are usually transmitted; and if disease, feebleness, stupidity, generally reappear in descendants; then a rational altruism requires insistence on that egoism which is shown by receipt of the satisfactions accompanying preservation of body and mind in the best state. The necessary implication is that blessings are provided for offspring by due self-regard, while disregard of self carried too far provides curses. When, indeed, we remember how commonly it is remarked that high health and overflowing spirits render any lot in life tolerable, while chronic ailments make gloomy a life most favorably circumstanced, it becomes amazing that both the world at large and writers who make conduct their study, should ignore the terrible evils which disregard of personal well-being inflicts on the unborn, and the incalculable good laid up for the unborn by attention to personal well-being. Of all bequests of parents to children the most valuable is a sound constitution. Though a man's body is not a property that can be inherited, yet his constitution may fitly be compared to an entailed estate; and if he rightly understands his duty to posterity, he will see that he is bound to pass on that estate uninjured if not improved. To say this is to say that he must be egoistic to the extent of satisfying all those desires associated with the due performance of functions. Nay, it is to say more. It is to say that he must seek in due amounts the various pleasures which life offers. For beyond the effect these have in raising the tide of life and maintaining constitutional vigor, there is the effect they have in preserving and increasing a capacity of receiving enjoyment. Endowed with abundant energies and various tastes, some can get gratifications of many kinds on opportunities hourly occurring; while others are so inert, and so uninterested in things around, that they cannot even take the trouble to amuse themselves. And unless heredity be denied, the inference must be that due acceptance of the miscellaneous pleasures life offers, conduces to the capacity for enjoyment in posterity; and that persistence in dull monotonous lives by parents, diminishes the ability of their descendants to make the best of what gratifications fall to them.

72. Beyond the decrease of general happiness which results in this indirect way if egoism is unduly subordinated, there is a decrease of general happiness which results in a

direct way. He who carries self-regard far enough to keep himself in good health and high spirits, in the first place thereby becomes an immediate source of happiness to those around, and in the second place maintains the ability to increase their happiness by altruistic actions. But one whose bodily vigor and mental health are undermined by self-sacrifice carried too far, in the first place becomes to those around a cause of depression, and in the second place renders himself incapable, or less capable, of actively furthering their welfare.

In estimating conduct we must remember that there are those who by their joyousness beget joy in others, and that there are those who by their melancholy cast a gloom on every circle they enter. And we must remember that by display of overflowing happiness a man of the one kind may add to the happiness of others more than by positive efforts to benefit them; and that a man of the other kind may decrease their happiness more by his presence than he increases it by his actions. Full of vivacity, the one is ever welcome. For his wife he has smiles and jocose speeches; for his children stores of fun and play; for his friends pleasant talk interspersed with the sallies of wit that come from buoyancy. Contrariwise, the other is shunned. The irritability resulting now from ailments, now from failures caused by feebleness, his family has daily to bear. Lacking adequate energy for joining in them, he has at best but a tepid interest in the amusements of his children; and he is called a wet blanket by his friends. Little account as our ethical reasonings take note of it, yet is the fact obvious that since happiness and misery are infectious, such regard for self as conduces to health and high spirits is a benefaction to others, and such disregard of self as brings on suffering, bodily or mental, is a malefaction to others. The duty of making one's self agreeable by seeming to be pleased, is, indeed, often urged; and thus to gratify friends is applauded so long as self-sacrificing effort is implied. But though display of real happiness gratifies friends far more than display of sham happiness, and has no drawback in the shape either of hypocrisy or of strain, yet it is not thought a duty to fulfill the conditions which favor the display of real happiness. Nevertheless, if quantity of happiness produced is to be the measure, the last is more imperative than the first.

And then, as above indicated, beyond this primary series of effects produced on others there is a secondary series of effects. The adequately egoistic individual retains those powers which make altruistic activities possible. The individual who is inadequately egoistic, loses more or less of his ability to be altruistic. The truth of the one proposition is self-evident; and the truth of the other is daily forced on us by examples. Note a few of them. Here is a mother who, brought up in the insane fashion usual among the cultivated, has a physique not strong enough for suckling her infant, but who, knowing that its natural food is the best, and anxious for its welfare, continues to give it milk for a longer time than her system will bear. Eventually the accumulating reaction tells. There comes exhaustion running, it may be, into illness caused by depletion; occasionally ending in death, and often entailing chronic weakness. She becomes, perhaps for a time, perhaps permanently, incapable of carrying on household affairs; her other children suffer from the loss of maternal attention; and where the income is small, payments for nurse and doctor tell injuriously on the whole family. Instance, again, what not unfrequently happens with the father. Similarly prompted by a high sense of obligation, and misled by current moral theories into the notion that self-denial may rightly be carried to any extent, he daily continues his office work for long hours regardless of hot head and cold feet; and debars himself of social pleasures, for which he thinks he can afford neither time nor money. What comes of this entirely unegoistic course? Eventually a sudden collapse, sleeplessness, inability to work. That rest which he would not give himself when his sensations prompted, he has now to take in long measure. The extra earnings laid by for the benefit of his family, are quickly swept away by costly journeys in aid of recovery, and by the many expenses which illness entails. Instead of increased ability to do his duty by his offspring, there comes now inability. Lifelong evils on them replace hoped-for goods. And so is it, too, with the social effects of inadequate egoism. All grades furnish examples of the mischiefs, positive and negative, inflicted on society by excessive neglect of self. Now the case is that of a laborer who, conscientiously continuing his work under a broiling sun, spite of violent protest from his feelings, dies of sunstroke; and leaves his family a burden to the parish. Now the case is that of a clerk whose eyes permanently fail from overstraining, or who, daily writing for hours after his fingers are painfully cramped, is attacked with "scrivener's palsy," and, unable to write at all, sinks with aged parents into poverty which friends are called on to mitigate. And now the case is that of a man devoted to public ends who, shattering his health by ceaseless application, fails to achieve all he might have achieved by a more reasonable apportionment of his time between labor on behalf of others and ministration to his own needs.

73. In one further way is the undue subordination of egoism to altruism injurious. Both directly and indirectly unselfishness pushed to excess generates selfishness.

Consider first the immediate effects. That one man may yield up to another a gratification, it is needful that the other shall accept it; and where the gratification is of a kind to which their respective claims are equal, or which is no more required by the one than by the other, acceptance implies a readiness to get gratification at another's cost. The circumstances and needs of the two being alike, the transaction involves as much culture of egoism in the last as it involves culture of altruism in the first. It is true that not unfrequently, difference between their means or difference between their appetites for a pleasure which the one has had often and the other rarely, divests the acceptance of this character; and it is true that in other cases the benefactor manifestly takes so much pleasure in giving pleasure, that the sacrifice is partial, and the reception of it not wholly selfish. But to see the effect above indicated we must exclude such inequalities, and consider what happens where wants are approximately alike and where the sacrifices, not reciprocated at intervals, are perpetually on one side. So restricting the inquiry all can name instances verifying the alleged result. Everyone can remember circles in which the daily surrender of benefits by the generous to the greedy, has caused increase of greediness; until there has been produced an unscrupulous egoism intolerable to all around. There are obvious social effects of kindred nature. Most thinking people now recognize the demoralization caused by indiscriminate charity. They see how in the mendicant there is, besides destruction of the normal relation between labor expended and benefit obtained, a genesis of the expectation that others shall minister to his needs; showing itself sometimes in the venting of curses on those who refuse.

Next consider the remote results. When the egoistic claims are so much subordinated to the altruistic as to produce physical mischief, the tendency is towards a relative decrease in the number of the altruistic, and therefore an increased predominance of the egoistic. Pushed to extremes, sacrifice of self for the benefit of others, leads occasionally to death before the ordinary period of marriage; leads sometimes to abstention from marriage, as in sisters of charity; leads sometimes to an ill-health or a loss of attractiveness which prevents marriage; leads sometimes to nonacquirement of the pecuniary means needed for marriage; and in all these cases, therefore, the unusually altruistic leave no descendants. Where the postponement of personal welfare to the welfare of others has not been carried so far as to prevent marriage, it yet not unfrequently occurs that the physical degradation resulting from years of self-neglect causes infertility; so that again the most altruistically natured leave no like-natured posterity. And then in less marked and more numerous cases, the resulting enfeeblement shows itself by the production of relatively weak offspring; of whom some die early, while the rest are less likely than usual to transmit the parental type to future generations. Inevitably, then, by this dying out of the especially unegoistic, there is prevented that desirable mitigation of egoism in the average nature which would else have taken place. Such disregard of self as brings down bodily vigor below the normal level, eventually produces in the society a counterbalancing excess of regard for self.

74. That egoism precedes altruism in order of imperativeness, is thus clearly shown. The acts which make continued life possible, must, on the average, be more peremptory than all those other acts which life makes possible; including the acts which benefit others. Turning from life as existing to life as evolving, we are equally shown this. Sentient beings have progressed from low to high types, under the law that the superior shall profit by their superiority and the inferior shall suffer from their inferiority. Conformity to this law has been, and is still, needful, not only for the continuance of life but for the increase of happiness; since the superior are those having faculties better adjusted to the requirements—faculties, therefore, which bring in their exercise greater pleasure and less pain.

More special considerations join these more general ones in showing us this truth. Such egoism as preserves a vivacious mind in a vigorous body furthers the happiness of descendants, whose inherited constitutions make the labors of life easy and its pleasures keen; while, conversely, unhappiness is entailed on posterity by those who bequeath them constitutions injured by self-neglect. Again, the individual whose well-conserved life shows itself in overflowing spirits, becomes, by his mere existence, a source of pleasure to all around; while the depression which commonly accompanies ill-health diffuses itself through family and among friends. A further contrast is that whereas one who has been duly regardful of self retains the power of being helpful to others, there results from self-abnegation in excess, not only an inability to help others but the infliction of positive burdens on them. Lastly, we come upon the truth that undue altruism increases egoism; both directly in contemporaries and indirectly in posterity.

And now observe that though the general conclusion enforced by these special conclusions, is at variance with nominally accepted beliefs, it is not at variance with actually accepted beliefs. While opposed to the doctrine which men are taught should be acted upon, it is in harmony with the doctrine which they do act upon and dimly see must be acted upon. For omitting such abnormalities of conduct as are instanced above, everyone, alike by deed and word, implies that in the business of life personal welfare is the primary consideration. The laborer looking for wages in return for work done, no less than the merchant who sells goods at a profit, the doctor who expects fees for advice, the priest who calls the scene of his ministrations "a living," assumes as beyond question the truth that selfishness, carried to the extent of enforcing his claims and enjoying the returns his efforts bring, is not only legitimate but essential. Even persons who avow a contrary conviction prove by their acts that it is inoperative. Those who repeat with emphasis the maxim "Love your neighbor as yourself" do not render up what they possess so as to satisfy the desires of all as much as they satisfy their own desires. Nor do those whose extreme maxim is "Live for others" differ appreciably from people around in their regards for personal welfare, or fail to appropriate their shares of life's pleasures. In short, that which is above set forth as the belief to which scientific ethics leads us, is that which men do really believe, as distinguished from that which they believe they believe.

Finally it may be remarked that a rational egoism, so far from implying a more egoistic human nature, is consistent with a human nature that is less egoistic. For excesses in one direction do not prevent excesses in the opposite direction; but rather, extreme deviations from the mean on one side lead to extreme deviations on the other side. A society in which the most exalted principles of self-sacrifice for the benefit of neighbors are enunciated, may be a society in which unscrupulous sacrifice of alien fellow creatures is not only tolerated but applauded. Along with professed anxiety to spread these exalted principles among heathens, there may go the deliberate fastening of a quarrel upon them with a view to annexing their territory. Men who every Sunday have listened approvingly to injunctions carrying the regard for other men to an impracticable extent, may yet hire themselves out to slay, at the word of command, any people in any part of the world, utterly indifferent to the right or wrong of the matter fought about. And as in these cases transcendent altruism in theory coexists with brutal egoism in practice, so, conversely, a more qualified altruism may have for its concomitant a greatly moderated egoism. For asserting the due claims of self, is, by implication, drawing a limit beyond which the claims are undue; and is, by consequence, bringing into greater clearness the claims of others.

CHAPTER 12

Altruism Versus Egoism

75. If we define altruism as being all action which, in the normal course of things, benefits others instead of benefiting self, then, from the dawn of life, altruism has been no less essential than egoism. Though primarily it is dependent on egoism, yet secondarily egoism is dependent on it.

Under altruism in this comprehensive sense, I take in the acts by which offspring are preserved and the species maintained. Moreover, among these acts must be included not such only as are accompanied by consciousness, but also such as conduce to the welfare of offspring without mental representation of the welfare—acts of automatic altruism as we may call them. Nor must there be left out those lowest altruistic acts which subserve race maintenance without implying even automatic nervous processes—acts not in the remotest sense psychical, but in a literal sense physical. Whatever action, unconscious or conscious, involves expenditure of individual life to the end of increasing life in other individuals, is unquestionably altruistic in a sense, if not in the usual sense; and it is here needful to understand it in this sense that we may see how conscious altruism grows out of unconscious altruism.

The simplest beings habitually multiply by spontaneous fission. Physical altruism of the lowest kind, differentiating

231

from physical egoism, may in this case be considered as not yet independent of it. For since the two halves which before fission constituted the individual, do not on dividing disappear, we must say that though the individuality of the parent infusorium or other protozoon is lost in ceasing to be single, yet the old individual continues to exist in each of the new individuals. When, however, as happens generally with these smallest animals, an interval of quiescence ends in the breaking up of the whole body into minute parts, each of which is the germ of a young one, we see the parent entirely sacrificed in forming progeny.

Here might be described how among creatures of higher grades, by fission or gemmation, parents bequeath parts of their bodies, more or less organized, to form offspring at the cost of their own individualities. Numerous examples might also be given of the ways in which the development of ova is carried to the extent of making the parental body little more than a receptacle for them: the implication being that the accumulations of nutriment which parental activities have laid up, are disposed of for the benefit of posterity. And then might be dwelt on the multitudinous cases where, as generally throughout the insect world, maturity having been reached and a new generation provided for, life ends: death follows the sacrifices made for progeny.

But leaving these lower types in which the altruism is physical only, or in which it is physical and automatically-psychical only, let us ascend to those in which it is also, to a considerable degree, conscious. Though in birds and mammals such parental activities as are guided by instinct, are accompanied by either no representations or but vague representations of the benefits which the young receive; yet there are also in them actions which we may class as altruistic in the higher sense. The agitation which creatures of these classes show when their young are in danger, joined often with efforts on their behalf, as well as the grief displayed after loss of their young, make it manifest that in them parental altruism has a concomitant of emotion.

Those who understand by altruism only the conscious sacrifice of self to others among human beings, will think it strange, or even absurd, to extend its meaning so widely. But the justification for doing this is greater than has thus far appeared. I do not mean merely that in the course of evolution, there has been a progress through infinitesimal gradations from purely physical and unconscious sacrifices of the individual for the welfare of the species, up to sacrifices consciously made. I mean that from first to last the sacrifices are, when reduced to their lowest terms, of the same essential nature: to the last, as at first, there is involved a loss of bodily substance. When a part of the parental body is detached in the shape of gemmule, or egg, or foetus, the material sacrifice is conspicuous; and when the mother yields milk by absorbing which the young one grows, it cannot be questioned that there is also a material sacrifice. But though a material sacrifice is not manifest when the young are benefited by activities on their behalf; yet, as no effort can be made without an equivalent waste of tissue, and as the bodily loss is proportionate to the expenditure that takes place without reimbursement in food consumed, it follows that efforts made in fostering offspring do really represent a part of the parental substance; which is now given indirectly instead of directly.

Self-sacrifice, then, is no less primordial than self-preservation. Being in its simple physical form absolutely necessary for the continuance of life from the beginning; and being extended under its automatic form, as indispensable to maintenance of race in types considerably advanced; and being developed to its semiconscious and conscious forms, along with the continued and complicated attendance by which the offspring of superior creatures are brought to maturity; altruism has been evolving simultaneously with egoism. As was pointed out in an early chapter, the same superiorities which have enabled the individual to preserve itself better, have enabled it better to preserve the individuals derived from it; and each higher species, using its improved faculties primarily for egoistic benefit, has spread in proportion as it has used them secondarily for altruistic benefit.

The imperativeness of altruism as thus understood, is, indeed, no less than the imperativeness of egoism was shown to be in the last chapter. For while, on the one hand, a falling short of normal egoistic acts entails enfeeblement or loss of life, and therefore loss of ability to perform altruistic acts; on the other hand, such defect of altruistic acts as causes death of offspring or inadequate development of them, involves disappearance from future generations of the nature that is not altruistic enough—so decreasing the average egoism. In short, every species is continually purifying itself from the unduly egoistic individuals, while there are being lost to it the unduly altruistic individuals.

76. As there has been an advance by degrees from unconscious parental altruism to conscious parental altruism of the highest kind, so has there been an advance by degrees from the altruism of the family to social altruism.

A fact to be first noted is that only where altruistic relations in the domestic group have reached highly developed forms, do there arise conditions making possible full development of altruistic relations in the political group. Tribes in which promiscuity prevails or in which the marital relations are transitory, and tribes in which polyandry entails in another way indefinite relationships, are incapable of much organization. Nor do peoples who are habitually polygamous, show themselves able to take on those high forms of social cooperation which demand due subordination of self to others. Only where monogamic marriage has become general and eventually universal—only where there have consequently been established the closest ties of blood—only where family altruism has been most fostered, has social altruism become conspicuous. It needs but to recall the compound forms of the Aryan family as described by Sir Henry Maine and others, to see that family feeling, first extending itself to the gens and the tribe, and afterwards to the society formed of related tribes, prepared the way for fellow feeling among citizens not of the same stock.

Recognizing this natural transition, we are here chiefly concerned to observe that throughout the latter stages of the progress, as throughout the former, increase of egoistic satisfactions has depended on growth of regard for the satisfactions of others. On contemplating a line of successive parents and offspring, we see that each, enabled while young to live by the sacrifices predecessors make for it, itself makes, when adult, equivalent sacrifices for successors; and that in default of this general balancing of benefits received by benefits given, the line dies out. Similarly, it is manifest that in a society each generation of members, indebted for such benefits as social organization yields them to preceding generations, who have by their sacrifices elaborated this organization, are called on to make for succeeding generations such kindred sacrifices as shall at least maintain this organization, if they do not improve it: the alternative being decay and eventual dissolution of the society, implying gradual decrease in the egoistic satisfactions of its members.

And now we are prepared to consider the several ways in which, under social conditions, personal welfare depends on due regard for the welfare of others. Already the conclusions to be drawn have been foreshadowed. As in the chapter on the biological view were implied the inferences definitely set forth in the last chapter; so in the chapter on the sociological view were implied the inferences to be definitely set forth here. Sundry of these are trite enough; but they must nevertheless be specified, since the statement would be incomplete without them.

77. First to be dealt with comes that negative altruism implied by such curbing of the egoistic impulses as prevents direct aggression.

As before shown, if men instead of living separately are to unite for defense or for other purposes, they must severally reap more good than evil from the union. On the average, each must lose less from the antagonisms of those with whom he is associated, than he gains by the association. At the outset, therefore, that increase of egoistic satisfactions which the social state brings, can be purchased only by altruism sufficient to cause some recognition of others' claims: if not a voluntary recognition, still, a compulsory recognition.

While the recognition is but of that lowest kind due to dread of retaliation, or of prescribed punishment, the egoistic gain from association is small; and it becomes considerable only as the recognition becomes voluntary—that is, more altruistic. Where, as among some of the wild Australians, there exists no limit to the right of the strongest, and the men fight to get possession of women while the wives of one man fight among themselves about him, the pursuit of egoistic satisfactions is greatly impeded. Besides the bodily pain occasionally given to each by conflict, and the more or less of subsequent inability to achieve personal ends, there is the waste of energy entailed in maintaining readiness for self-defense, and there is the accompanying occupation of consciousness by emotions that are on the average of cases disagreeable. Moreover, the primary end of safety in presence of external foes is ill-attained in proportion as there are internal animosities; such furtherance of satisfactions as industrial cooperation brings cannot be had; and there is little motive to labor for extra benefits when the products of labor are insecure. And from this early stage to comparatively late stages, we may trace in the wearing of arms, in the carrying on of family feuds, and in the taking of daily precautions for safety, the ways in which the egoistic satisfactions of each are diminished by deficiency of that altruism which checks overt injury of others.

The private interests of the individual are on the average better subserved, not only in proportion as he himself refrains from direct aggression, but also, on the average, in proportion as he succeeds in diminishing the aggression of his fellows on one another. The prevalence of antagonisms among those around, impedes the activities carried on by each in pursuit of satisfactions; and by causing disorder makes the beneficial results of activities more doubtful. Hence, each profits egoistically from the growth of an altruism which leads each to aid in preventing or diminishing others' violence.

The like holds when we pass to that altruism which restrains the undue egoism displayed in breaches of contract. General acceptance of the maxim that honesty is the best policy, implies general experience that gratification of the self-regarding feelings is eventually furthered by such checking of them as maintains equitable dealings. And here, as before, each is personally interested in securing good treatment of his fellows by one another. For in countless ways evils are entailed on each by the prevalence of fraudulent transactions. As everyone knows, the larger the number of a shopkeeper's bills left unpaid by some customers, the higher must be the prices which other customers pay. The more manufacturers lose by defective raw materials or by carelessness of workmen, the more must they charge for their fabrics to buyers. The less trustworthy people are, the higher rises the rate of interest, the larger becomes the amount of capital hoarded, the greater are the impediments to industry. The further traders and people in general go beyond their means, and hypothecate the property of others in speculation, the more serious are those commercial panics which bring disasters on multitudes and injuriously affect all.

This introduces us to yet a third way in which such personal welfare as results from the proportioning of benefits gained to labors given, depends on the making of certain sacrifices for social welfare. The man who, expending his energies wholly on private affairs refuses to take trouble about public affairs, pluming himself on his wisdom in minding his own business, is blind to the fact that his own business is made possible only by maintenance of a healthy social state, and that he loses all round by defective governmental arrangements. Where there are many like-minded with himself—where, as a consequence, offices come to be filled by political adventurers and opinion is swayed by demagogues—where bribery vitiates the administration of the law and makes fraudulent state-transactions habitual; heavy penalties fall on the community at large, and, among others, on those who have thus done everything for self and nothing for society. Their investments are insecure; recovery of their debts is difficult; and even their lives are less safe than they would otherwise have been.

So that on such altruistic actions as are implied, first in being just, second in seeing justice done between others, and third in upholding and improving the agencies by which justice is administered, depend, in large measure, the egoistic satisfactions of each.

78. But the identification of personal advantage with the advantage of fellow citizens is much wider than this. In various other ways the well-being of each rises and falls with the well-being of all.

A weak man left to provide for his own wants, suffers by getting smaller amounts of food and other necessaries than he might get were he stronger. In a community formed by weak men, who divide their labors and exchange the products, all suffer evils from the weakness of their fellows. The quantity of each kind of product is made deficient by the deficiency of laboring power; and the share each gets for such share of his own product as he can afford to give, is relatively small. Just as the maintenance of paupers, hospital patients, inmates of asylums, and others who consume but do not produce, leaves to be divided among producers a smaller stock of commodities than would exist were there no incapables; so must there be left a smaller stock of commodities to be divided, the greater the number of inefficient producers, or the greater the average deficiency of producing power. Hence, whatever decreases the strength of men in general restricts the gratifications of each by making the means to them dearer.

More directly, and more obviously, does the bodily well-being of his fellows concern him; for their bodily ill-being, when it takes certain shapes, is apt to bring similar bodily ill-being on him. If he is not himself attacked by cholera, or smallpox or typhus, when it invades his neighborhood, he often suffers a penalty through his belongings. Under conditions spreading it, his wife catches diphtheria, or his servant is laid up with scarlet fever, or his children take now this and

now that infectious disorder. Add together the immediate
and remote evils brought on him year after year by epidemics,
and it becomes manifest that his egoistic satisfactions are
greatly furthered by such altruistic activities as render disease
less prevalent.

With the mental, as well as with the bodily, states of fellow
citizens, his enjoyments are in multitudinous ways bound up.
Stupidity like weakness raises the cost of commodities. Where
farming is unimproved, the prices of food are higher than they
would else be; where antiquated routine maintains itself in
trade, the needless expense of distribution weighs on all;
where there is no inventiveness, everyone loses the benefits
which improved appliances diffuse. Other than economic
evils come from the average unintelligence—periodically
through the manias and panics that arise because traders rush
in herds all to buy or all to sell; and habitually through the
maladministration of justice, which people and rulers alike
disregard while pursuing this or that legislative will-o'-the-
wisp. Closer and clearer is the dependence of his personal
satisfactions on others' mental states, which each experiences
in his household. Unpunctuality and want of system are perpetual sources of annoyance. The unskillfulness of the cook
causes frequent vexation and occasional indigestion. Lack of
forethought in the housemaid leads to a fall over a bucket in a
dark passage. And inattention to a message or forgetfulness in
delivering it, entails failure in an important engagement.
Each, therefore, benefits egoistically by such altruism as aids
in raising the average intelligence. I do not mean such altruism as taxes ratepayers that children's minds may be filled
with dates, and names, and gossip about kings, and narratives of battles, and other useless information, no amount of
which will make them capable workers or good citizens; but I
mean such altruism as helps to spread a knowledge of the
nature of things and to cultivate the power of applying that
knowledge.

Yet again, each has a private interest in public morals and
profits by improving them. Not in large ways only, by aggres-

sions and breaches of contract, by adulterations and short measures, does each suffer from the general unconscientiousness; but in more numerous small ways. Now it is through the untruthfulness of one who gives a good character to a bad servant; now it is by the recklessness of a laundress who, using bleaching agents to save trouble in washing, destroys his linen; now it is by the acted falsehood of railway passengers who, by dispersed coats, make him believe that all the seats in a compartment are taken when they are not. Yesterday the illness of his child due to foul gases, led to the discovery of a drain that had become choked because it was ill-made by a dishonest builder under supervision of a careless or bribed surveyor. Today workmen employed to rectify it bring on him cost and inconvenience by dawdling; and their low standard of work, determined by the unionist principle that the better workers must not discredit the worse by exceeding them in efficiency, he may trace to the immoral belief that the unworthy should fare as well as the worthy. Tomorrow it turns out that business for the plumber has been provided by damage which the bricklayers have done.

Thus the improvement of others, physically, intellectually, and morally, personally concerns each; since their imperfections tell in raising the cost of all the commodities he buys, in increasing the taxes and rates he pays, and in the losses of time, trouble, and money daily brought on him by others' carelessness, stupidity, or unconscientiousness.

79. Very obvious are certain more immediate connections between personal welfare and ministration to the welfare of those around. The evils suffered by those whose behavior is unsympathetic, and the benefits to self which unselfish conduct brings, show these.

That anyone should have formulated his experience by saying that the conditions to success are a hard heart and a sound digestion, is marvellous considering the many proofs that success, even of a material kind, greatly depending as it does on the good offices of others, is furthered by whatever creates goodwill in others. The contrast between the prosperity of those who to but moderate abilities join natures which beget friendships by their kindliness, and the adversity of those who, though possessed of superior faculties and greater acquirements, arouse dislikes by their hardness or indifference, should force upon all the truth that egoistic enjoyments are aided by altruistic actions.

This increase of personal benefit achieved by benefiting others, is but partially achieved where a selfish motive prompts the seemingly unselfish act: it is fully achieved only where the act is really unselfish. Though services rendered with the view of some time profiting by reciprocated services, answer to a certain extent; yet, ordinarily, they answer only to the extent of bringing equivalents of reciprocated services. Those which bring more than equivalents are those not prompted by any thoughts of equivalents. For obviously it is the spontaneous outflow of good nature, not in the larger acts of life only but in all its details, which generates in those around the attachments prompting unstinted benevolence.

Besides furthering prosperity, other-regarding actions conduce to self-regarding gratifications by generating a genial environment. With the sympathetic being everyone feels more sympathy than with others. All conduct themselves with more than usual amiability to a person who hourly discloses a lovable nature. Such a one is practically surrounded by a world of better people than one who is less attractive. If we contrast the state of a man possessing all the material means to happiness, but isolated by his absolute egoism, with the state of an altruistic man relatively poor in means but rich in friends, we may see that various gratifications not to be purchased by money, come in abundance to the last and are inaccessible to the first.

While, then, there is one kind of other-regarding action, furthering the prosperity of fellow citizens at large, which admits of being deliberately pursued from motives that are remotely self-regarding—the conviction being that personal well-being depends in large measure on the well-being of society—there is an additional kind of other-regarding action having in it no element of conscious self-regard, which nevertheless conduces greatly to egoistic satisfactions.

80. Yet other modes exist in which egoism unqualified by altruism habitually fails. It diminishes the totality of egoistic pleasure by diminishing in several directions the capacity for pleasure.

Self-gratifications, considered separately or in the aggregate, lose their intensities by that too great persistence in them which results if they are made the exclusive objects of pursuit. The law that function entails waste, and that faculties yielding pleasure by their action cannot act incessantly without exhaustion and accompanying satiety, has the implication that intervals during which altruistic activities absorb the energies, are intervals during which the capacity for egoistic pleasure is recovering its full degree. The sensitiveness to purely personal enjoyments is maintained at a higher pitch by those who minister to the enjoyment of others, than it is by those who devote themselves wholly to personal enjoyments.

This which is manifest even while the tide of life is high, becomes still more manifest as life ebbs. It is in maturity and old age that we especially see how, as egoistic pleasures grow faint, altruistic actions come in to revive them in new forms. The contrast between the child's delight in the novelties daily revealed, and the indifference which comes as the world around grows familiar, until in adult life there remain comparatively few things that are greatly enjoyed, draws from all the reflection that as years go by pleasures pall. And to those who think, it becomes clear that only through sympathy can pleasures be indirectly gained from things that have ceased to yield pleasures directly. In the gratifications derived by parents from the gratifications of their offspring, this is conspicuously shown. Trite as is the remark that men live afresh in their children, it is needful here to set it down as reminding us of the way in which, as the egoistic satisfactions in life fade, altruism renews them while it transfigures them.

We are thus introduced to a more general consideration—the egoistic aspect of altruistic pleasure. Not, indeed, that this is the place for discussing the question whether the egoistic element can be excluded from altruism; nor is it the place for distinguishing between the altruism which is pursued with a foresight of the pleasurable feeling to be achieved through it, and the altruism which, though it achieves this pleasurable feeling, does not make pursuit of it a motive. Here we are concerned with the fact that, whether knowingly or unknowingly gained, the state of mind accompanying altruistic action, being a pleasurable state, is to be counted in the sum of pleasures which the individual can receive; and in this sense cannot be other than egoistic. That we must so regard it is proved on observing that this pleasure, like pleasures in general, conduces to the physical prosperity of the ego. As every other agreeable emotion raises the tide of life, so does the agreeable emotion which accompanies a benevolent deed. As it cannot be denied that the pain caused by the sight of suffering, depresses the vital functions—sometimes even to the extent of arresting the heart's action, as in one who faints on seeing a surgical operation; so neither can it be denied that the joy felt in witnessing others' joy exalts the vital functions. Hence, however much we may hesitate to class altruistic pleasure as a higher kind of egoistic pleasure, we are obliged to recognize the fact that its immediate effects in augmenting life and so furthering personal well-being, are like those of pleasures that are directly egoistic. And the corollary drawn must be that pure egoism is, even in its immediate results, less successfully egoistic than is the egoism duly qualified by altruism which, besides achieving additional pleasures, achieves also, through raised vitality, a greater capacity for pleasures in general.

That the range of æsthetic gratifications is wider for the altruistic nature than for the egoistic nature, is also a truth not to be overlooked. The joys and sorrows of human beings form a chief element in the subject matter of art; and evidently the pleasures which art gives increase as the fellow feeling with these joys and sorrows strengthens. If we contrast early poetry occupied mainly with war and gratifying the savage instincts by descriptions of bloody victories, with the poetry of modern times, in which the sanguinary forms but a small part while a large part, dealing with the gentler affections, enlists the feelings of readers on behalf of the weak; we are shown that with the development of a more altruistic nature, there has been opened a sphere of enjoyment inaccessible to the callous egoism of barbarous times. So, too, between the fiction of the past and the fiction of the present, there is the difference that while the one was almost exclusively occupied with the doings of the ruling classes, and found its plots in their antagonisms and deeds of violence, the other, chiefly taking stories of peaceful life for its subjects, and to a considerable extent the life of the humbler classes, discloses a new world of interest in the everyday pleasures and pains of ordinary people. A like contrast exists between early and late forms of plastic art. When not representing acts of worship, the wall sculptures and wall paintings of the Assyrians and Egyptians, or the decorations of temples among the Greeks, represented deeds of conquest; whereas in modern times, while the works which glorify destructive activities are less numerous, there are an increasing number of works gratifying to the kindlier sentiments of spectators. To see that those who care nothing about the feelings of other beings are, by implication, shut out from a wide range of æsthetic pleasures, it needs but to ask whether men who delight in dogfights may be expected to appreciate Beethoven's *Adelaida*, or whether Tennyson's *In Memoriam* would greatly move a gang of convicts.

81. From the dawn of life, then, egoism has been dependent upon altruism as altruism has been dependent upon egoism; and in the course of evolution the reciprocal services of the two have been increasing.

The physical and unconscious self-sacrifice of parents to form offspring, which the lowest living things display from hour to hour, shows us in its primitive form the altruism which makes possible the egoism of individual life and growth. As we ascend to higher grades of creatures, this parental altruism becomes a direct yielding up of only part of the body, joined with an increasing contribution from the remainder in the shape of tissue wasted in efforts made on behalf of progeny. This indirect sacrifice of substance, replacing more and more the direct sacrifice as parental altruism becomes higher, continues to the last to represent also altruism which is other than parental; since this, too, implies loss of substance in making efforts that do not bring their return in personal aggrandizement.

After noting how among mankind parental altruism and family altruism pass into social altruism, we observed that a society, like a species, survives only on condition that each generation of its members shall yield to the next, benefits equivalent to those it has received from the last. And this implies that care for the family must be supplemented by care for the society.

Fullness of egoistic satisfactions in the associated state, depending primarily on maintenance of the normal relation between efforts expended and benefits obtained, which underlies all life, implies an altruism which both prompts equitable conduct and prompts the enforcing of equity. The well-being of each is involved with the well-being of all in sundry other ways. Whatever conduces to their vigor concerns him; for it diminishes the cost of everything he buys. Whatever conduces to their freedom from disease concerns him; for it diminishes his own liability to disease. Whatever raises their intelligence concerns him; for inconveniences are daily entailed on him by others' ignorance or folly. Whatever raises their moral characters concerns him; for at every turn he suffers from the average unconscientiousness.

Much more directly do his egoistic satisfactions depend on those altruistic activities which enlist the sympathies of others. By alienating those around, selfishness loses the unbought aid they can render; shuts out a wide range of social enjoyments; and fails to receive those exaltations of pleasure and mitigations of pain, which come from men's fellow feeling with those they like.

Lastly, undue egoism defeats itself by bringing on an incapacity for happiness. Purely egoistic gratifications are rendered less keen by satiety, even in the earlier part of life, and almost disappear in the later; the less satiating gratifications of altruism are missed throughout life, and especially in that latter part when they largely replace egoistic gratifications; and there is a lack of susceptibility to æsthetic pleasures of the higher orders.

An indication must be added of the truth, scarcely at all recognized, that this dependence of egoism upon altruism ranges beyond the limits of each society, and tends ever towards universality. That within each society it becomes greater as social evolution, implying increase of mutual dependence, progresses, needs not be shown; and it is a corollary that as fast as the dependence of societies on one another is increased by commercial intercourse, the internal welfare of each becomes a matter of concern to the others. That the impoverishment of any country, diminishing both its producing and consuming powers, tells detrimentally on the people of countries trading with it, is a commonplace of political economy. Moreover, we have had of late years, abundant experience of the industrial derangements through which distress is brought on nations not immediately concerned, by wars between other nations. And if each community has the egoistic satisfactions of its members diminished by aggressions of neighboring communities on one another, still more does it have them diminished by its own aggressions. One who marks how, in various parts of the world, the unscrupulous greed of conquest cloaked by pretenses of spreading the blessings of British rule and British religion, is now reacting to the immense detriment of the industrial classes at home, alike by increasing expenditure and paralyzing trade, may see that these industrial classes, absorbed in questions about capital and labor, and thinking themselves unconcerned in our doings abroad, are suffering from lack of that wide-reaching altruism which should insist on just dealings with other peoples, civilized or savage. And he may also see that beyond these immediate evils, they will for a generation to come suffer the evils that must flow from resuscitating the type of social organization which aggressive activities produce, and from the lowered moral tone which is its accompaniment.

CHAPTER 13

Trial and Compromise

82. In the foregoing two chapters the case on behalf of egoism and the case on behalf of altruism have been stated. The two conflict; and we have now to consider what verdict ought to be given.

If the opposed statements are severally valid, or even if each of them is valid in part, the influence must be that pure egoism and pure altruism are both illegitimate. If the maxim "Live for self" is wrong, so also is the maxim "Live for others." Hence a compromise is the only possibility.

This conclusion, though already seeming unavoidable, I do not here set down as proved. The purpose of this chapter is to justify it in full; and I enunciate it at the outset because the arguments used will be better understood, if the conclusion to which they converge is in the reader's view.

How shall we so conduct the discussion as most clearly to bring out this necessity for a compromise? Perhaps the best way will be that of stating one of the two claims in its extreme form, and observing the implied absurdities. To deal thus with the principle of pure selfishness, would be to waste space. Every one sees that an unchecked satisfaction of personal desires from moment to moment, in absolute disregard of all other beings, would cause universal conflict and social dissolution. The principle of pure unselfishness, less obviously mischievous, may therefore better be chosen.

There are two aspects under which the doctrine that others' happiness is the true ethical aim presents itself. The "others" may be conceived personally, as individuals with whom we stand in direct relations; or they may be conceived impersonally, as constituting the community. Insofar as the self-abnegation implied by pure altruism is concerned, it matters not in which sense "others" is used. But criticism will be facilitated by distinguishing between these two forms of it. We will take the last form first.

83. This commits us to an examination of "the greatest happiness principle," as enunciated by Bentham and his followers. The doctrine that "the general happiness" ought to be the object of pursuit, is not, indeed, overtly identified with pure altruism. But as if general happiness is the proper end of action, the individual actor must regard his own share of it simply as a unit in the aggregate, no more to be valued by him than any other unit, it results that since this unit is almost infinitesimal in comparison with the aggregate, his action, if directed exclusively to achievement of general happiness, is, if not absolutely altruistic, as nearly so as may be. Hence the theory which makes general happiness the immediate object of pursuit, may rightly be taken as one form of the pure altruism to be here criticized.

Both as justifying this interpretation and as furnishing a definite proposition with which to deal, let me set out by quoting a passage from Mr. Mill's *Utilitarianism:*

> The Greatest-Happiness Principle is a mere form of words without rational signification, unless one person's happiness, supposed equal in degree (with the proper allowance made for kind), is counted for exactly as much as another's. Those conditions being supplied, Bentham's dictum, "everybody to count for one, nobody for more than one," might be written under the principle of utility as an explanatory commentary. [P. 91.]

Now though the meaning of "greatest happiness" as an end, is here to a certain degree defined, the need for further definition is felt the moment we attempt to decide on ways of regulating conduct so as to attain the end. The first question which arises is—Must we regard this "greatest happiness principle" as a principle of guidance for the community in its corporate capacity, or as a principle of guidance for its members separately considered, or both? If the reply is that the principle must be taken as a guide for governmental action rather than for individual action, we are at once met by the inquiry—What is to be the guide for individual action? If individual action is not to be regulated solely for the purpose of achieving "the greatest happiness of the greatest number," some other principle of regulation for individual action is required; and "the greatest happiness principle" fails to furnish the needful ethical standard. Should it be rejoined that the individual in his capacity of political unit, is to take furtherance of general happiness as his end, giving his vote or otherwise acting on the legislature with a view to this end, and that in so far guidance is supplied to him, there comes the further inquiry—Whence is to come guidance for the remainder of individual conduct, constituting by far the greater part of it? If this private part of individual conduct is not to have general happiness as its direct aim, then an ethical standard other than that offered has still to be found.

Hence, unless pure altruism as thus formulated confesses its inadequacy, it must justify itself as a sufficient rule for all conduct, individual and social. We will first deal with it as the alleged right principle of public policy; and then as the alleged right principle of private action.

84. On trying to understand precisely the statement that when taking general happiness as an end, the rule must be, "everybody to count for one, nobody for more than one," there arises the idea of distribution. We can form no idea of distribution without thinking of something distributed and recipients of this something. That we may clearly conceive the proposition we must clearly conceive both these elements of it. Let us take first the recipients.

"Everybody to count for one, nobody for more than one."

Does this mean that, in respect of whatever is portioned out, each is to have the same share whatever his character, whatever his conduct? Shall he if passive have as much as if active? Shall he if useless have as much as if useful? Shall he if criminal have as much as if virtuous? If the distribution is to be made without reference to the natures and deeds of the recipients, then it must be shown that a system which equalizes, as far as it can, the treatment of good and bad, will be beneficial. If the distribution is not to be indiscriminate, then the formula disappears. The something distributed must be apportioned otherwise than by equal division. There must be adjustment of amounts to deserts; and we are left in the dark as to the mode of adjustment—we have to find other guidance.

Let us next ask what is the something to be distributed? The first idea which occurs is that happiness itself must be divided out among all. Taken literally, the notions that the greatest happiness should be the end sought, and that in apportioning it everybody should count for one and nobody for more than one, imply that happiness is something that can be cut up into parts and handed round. This, however, is an impossible interpretation. But after recognizing the impossibility of it, there returns the question—What is it in respect of which everybody is to count for one and nobody for more than one?

Shall the interpretation be that the concrete means to happiness are to be equally divided? Is it intended that there shall be distributed to all in equal portions the necessaries of life, the appliances to comfort, the facilities for amusement? As a conception simply, this is more defensible. But passing over the question of policy—passing over the question whether greatest happiness would *ultimately* be secured by such a process (which it obviously would not) it turns out on examination that greatest happiness could not even *proximately* be so secured. Differences of age, of growth, of constitutional need, differences of activity and consequent expenditure, differences of desires and tastes, would entail the inevitable result that the material aids to happiness which each received would be more or less unadapted to his requirements. Even if purchasing power were equally divided, the greatest happiness would not be achieved if everybody counted for one and nobody for more than one; since, as the capacities for utilizing the purchased means to happiness would vary both with the constitution and the stage of life, the means which would approximately suffice to satisfy the wants of one would be extremely insufficient to satisfy the wants of another, and so the greatest total of happiness would not be obtained: means might be unequally apportioned in a way that would produce a greater total.

But now if happiness itself cannot be cut up and distributed equally, and if equal division of the material aids to happiness would not produce greatest happiness, what is the thing to be thus apportioned?—what is it in respect of which everybody is to count for one and nobody for more than one? There seems but a single possibility. There remains to be equally distributed nothing but the conditions under which each may pursue happiness. The limitations to action—the degrees of freedom and restraint, shall be alike for all. Each shall have as much liberty to pursue his ends as consists with maintaining like liberties to pursue their ends by others; and one as much as another shall have the enjoyment of that which his efforts, carried on within these limits, obtain. But to say that in respect of these conditions everybody shall count for one and nobody for more than one, is simply to say that equity shall be enforced.

Thus considered as a principle of public policy, Bentham's principle, when analyzed, transforms itself into the principle he slights. Not general happiness becomes the ethical standard by which legislative action is to be guided, but universal justice. And so the altruistic theory under this form collapses.

85. From examining the doctrine that general happiness should be the end of public action, we pass now to examine the doctrine that it should be the end of private action.

It is contended that from the standpoint of pure reason, the happiness of others has no less a claim as an object of pursuit for each than personal happiness. Considered as parts of a total, happiness felt by self and like happiness felt by another, are of equal values; and hence it is inferred that, rationally estimated, the obligation to expend effort for others' benefit, is as great as the obligation to expend effort for one's own benefit. Holding that the utilitarian system of morals, rightly understood, harmonizes with the Christian maxim "Love your neighbor as yourself," Mr. Mill says that "as between his own happiness and that of others, utilitarianism requires him to be as strictly impartial as a disinterested and benevolent spectator" (p. 24). Let us consider the alternative interpretations which may be given to this statement.

Suppose, first, that a certain quantum of happiness has in some way become available, without the special instrumentality of A, B, C, or D, constituting the group concerned. Then the proposition is that each shall be ready to have this quantum of happiness as much enjoyed by one or more of the others as by himself. The disinterested and benevolent spectator would clearly, in such a case, rule that no one ought to have more of the happiness than another. But here, assuming as we do that the quantum of happiness has become available without the agency of any among the group, simple equity dictates as much. No one having in any way established a claim different from the claims of others, their claims are equal; and due regard for justice by each will not permit him to monopolize the happiness.

Now suppose a different case. Suppose that the quantum of happiness has been made available by the efforts of one member of the group. Suppose that A has acquired by labor some material aid to happiness. He decides to act as the disinterested and benevolent spectator would direct. What will he decide?—what would the spectator direct? Let us consider the possible suppositions; taking first the least reasonable.

The spectator may be conceived as deciding that the labor expended by A in acquiring this material aid to happiness, originates no claim to special use of it; but that it ought to be given to B, C, or D, or that it ought to be divided equally among B, C, and D, or that it ought to be divided equally among all members of the group, including A who has labored for it. And if the spectator is conceived as deciding thus today, he must be conceived as deciding thus day after day; with the result that one of the group expends all the effort, getting either none of the benefit or only his numerical share, while the others get their shares of the benefit without expending any efforts. That A might conceive the disinterested and benevolent spectator to decide in this way, and might feel bound to act in conformity with the imagined decision, is a strong supposition; and probably it will be admitted that such kind of impartiality, so far from being conducive to the general happiness, would quickly be fatal to everyone. But this is not all. Action in pursuance of such a decision would in reality be negatived by the very principle enunciated. For not only A, but also B, C, and D have to act on this principle. Each of them must behave as he conceives an impartial spectator would decide. Does B conceive the impartial spectator as awarding to him, B, the product of A's labor? Then the assumption is that B conceives the impartial spectator as favoring himself, B, more than A conceives him as favoring himself, A; which is inconsistent with the hypothesis. Does B, in conceiving the impartial spectator, exclude his own interests as completely as A does? Then how can he decide so much to his own advantage, so partially, as to allow him to take from A an equal share of the benefit gained by A's labor, towards which he and the rest have done nothing?

Passing from this conceivable, though not credible, decision of the spectator, here noted for the purpose of observing that habitual conformity to it would be impossible, there remains to be considered the decision which a spectator really impartial would give. He would say that the happiness, or material aid to happiness, which had been purchased by A's labor, was to be taken by A. He would say that B, C, and D had no claims to it, but only to such happiness, or aids to happiness, as their respective labors had purchased. Consequently, A, acting as the imaginary impartial spectator would direct, is, by this test, justified in appropriating such happiness or aid to happiness as his own efforts have achieved.

And so under its special form as under its general form, the principle is true only in so far as it embodies a disguised justice. Analysis again brings out the result that making "general happiness" the end of action, really means maintaining what we call equitable relations among individuals. Decline to accept in its vague form "the greatest-happiness principle," and insist on knowing what is the implied conduct, public or private, and it turns out that the principle is meaningless save as indirectly asserting that the claims of each should be duly regarded by all. The utilitarian altruism becomes a duly qualified egoism.

86. Another point of view from which to judge the altruistic theory may now be taken. If, assuming the proper object of pursuit to be general happiness, we proceed rationally, we must ask in what different ways the aggregate, general happiness, may be composed; and must then ask what composition of it will yield the largest sum.

Suppose that each citizen pursues his own happiness independently, not to the detriment of others but without active concern for others; then their united happinesses constitute a certain sum—a certain general happiness. Now suppose that each, instead of making his own happiness the object of pursuit, makes the happiness of others the object of pursuit; then, again, there results a certain sum of happiness. This sum must be less than, or equal to, or greater than, the first. If it is admitted that this sum is either less than the first or only equal to it, the altruistic course of action is confessedly either worse than, or no better than, the egoistic. The assumption must be that the sum of happiness obtained is greater. Let us observe what is involved in this assumption.

If each pursues exclusively the happiness of others; and if each is also a recipient of happiness (which he must be, for otherwise no aggregate happiness can be formed out of their individual happinesses); then the implication is that each gains the happiness due to altruistic action exclusively; and that in each this is greater in amount than the egoistic happiness obtainable by him, if he devoted himself to pursuit of it. Leaving out of consideration for a moment these relative amounts of the two, let us note the conditions to the receipt of altruistic happiness by each. The sympathetic nature gets pleasure by giving pleasure; and the proposition is that if the general happiness is the object of pursuit, each will be made happy by witnessing others' happiness. But what in such case constitutes the happiness of others? These others are also, by the hypothesis, pursuers and receivers of altruistic pleasure. The genesis of altruistic pleasure in each is to depend on the display of pleasures by others; which is again to depend on the display of pleasures by others; and so on perpetually. Where, then, is the pleasure to begin? Obviously there must be egoistic pleasure somewhere, before there can be the altruistic pleasure caused by sympathy with it. Obviously, therefore, each must be egoistic in due amount, even if only with the view of giving others the possibility of being altruistic. So far from the sum of happiness being made greater if all make greatest happiness the exclusive end, the sum disappears entirely.

How absurd is the supposition that the happiness of all can be achieved without each pursuing his own happiness, will be best shown by a physical simile. Suppose a cluster of bodies, each of which generates heat; and each of which is, therefore, while a radiator of heat to those around, also a receiver of heat from them. Manifestly each will have a certain proper heat irrespective of that which it gains from the rest; and, each will have a certain heat gained from the rest irrespective of its proper heat. What will happen? So long as each of the bodies continues to be a generator of heat, each continues to maintain a temperature partly derived from itself and partly derived from others. But if each ceases to generate heat for itself and depends on the heat radiated to it by the rest, the entire

cluster becomes cold. Well, the self-generated heat stands for
egoistic pleasure; the heat radiated and received stands for
sympathetic pleasure; and the disappearance of all heat if each
ceases to be an originator of it, corresponds to the disappearance of all pleasure if each ceases to originate it egoistically.

A further conclusion may be drawn. Besides the implication
that before altruistic pleasure can exist, egoistic pleasure must
exist, and that if the rule of conduct is to be the same for all,
each must be egoistic in due degree; there is the implication
that, to achieve the greatest sum of happiness, each must be
more egoistic than altruistic. For, speaking generally, sympathetic pleasures must ever continue less intense than the
pleasures with which there is sympathy. Other things equal,
ideal feelings cannot be as vivid as real feelings. It is true that
those having strong imaginations may, especially in cases
where the affections are engaged, feel the moral pain if not the
physical pain of another, as keenly as the actual sufferer of it,
and may participate with like intensity in another's pleasure:
sometimes even mentally representing the received pleasure
as greater than it really is, and so getting reflex pleasure
greater than the recipients' direct pleasure. Such cases, however, and cases in which even apart from exaltation of
sympathy caused by attachment, there is a body of feeling
sympathetically aroused equal in amount to the original feeling, if not greater, are necessarily exceptional. For in such
cases the total consciousness includes many other elements
besides the mentally represented pleasure or pain—notably
the luxury of pity and the luxury of goodness; and genesis of
these can occur but occasionally: they could not be habitual
concomitants of sympathetic pleasures if all pursued these
from moment to moment. In estimating the possible totality of
sympathetic pleasures, we must include nothing beyond the
representations of the pleasures others experience. And unless it be asserted that we can have others' states of consciousness perpetually reproduced in us more vividly than the
kindred states of consciousness are aroused in ourselves by
their proper personal causes, it must be admitted that the

totality of altruistic pleasures cannot become equal to the totality of egoistic pleasures. Hence, beyond the truth that before there can be altruistic pleasures there must be the egoistic pleasures from sympathy with which they arise, there is the truth that, to obtain the greatest sum of altruistic pleasures, there must be a greater sum of egoistic pleasures.

87. That pure altruism is suicidal may be yet otherwise demonstrated. A perfectly moral law must be one which becomes perfectly practicable as human nature becomes perfect. If its practicableness decreases as human nature improves; and if an ideal human nature necessitates its impracticability; it cannot be the moral law sought.

Now opportunities for practicing altruism are numerous and great in proportion as there is weakness, or incapacity, or imperfection. If we pass beyond the limits of the family, in which a sphere for self-sacrificing activities must be preserved as long as offspring have to be reared; and if we ask how there can continue a social sphere for self-sacrificing activities; it becomes obvious that the continued existence of serious evils, caused by prevalent defects of nature, is implied. As fast as men adapt themselves to the requirements of social life, so fast will the demands for efforts on their behalf diminish. And with arrival at finished adaptation, when all persons are at once completely self-conserved and completely able to fulfill the obligations which society imposes on them, those occasions for postponement of self to others which pure altruism contemplates, disappear.

Such self-sacrifices become, indeed, doubly impracticable. Carrying on successfully their several lives, men not only cannot yield to those around the opportunities for giving aid, but aid cannot ordinarily be given them without interfering with their normal activities, and so diminishing their pleasures. Like every inferior creature, led by its innate desires spontaneously to do all that its life requires, man, when completely molded to the social state, must have desires so adjusted to his needs that he fulfills the needs in gratifying the desires. And if his desires are severally gratified by the performance of required acts, none of these can be performed for him without balking his desires. Acceptance from others of the results of their activities can take place only on condition of relinquishing the pleasures derived from his own activities. Diminution rather than increase of happiness would result, could altruistic action in such case be enforced.

And here, indeed, we are introduced to another baseless assumption which the theory makes.

88. The postulate of utilitarianism as formulated in the statements above quoted, and of pure altruism as otherwise expressed, involves the belief that it is possible for happiness, or the means to happiness, or the conditions to happiness, to be transferred. Without any specified limitation the proposition taken for granted is, that happiness in general admits of detachment from one and attachment to another—that surrender to any extent is possible by one and appropriation to any extent is possible by another. But a moment's thought shows this to be far from the truth. On the one hand, surrender carried to a certain point is extremely mischievous and to a further point fatal; and on the other hand, much of the happiness each enjoys is self-generated and can neither be given nor received.

To assume that egoistic pleasures may be relinquished to any extent, is to fall into one of those many errors of ethical speculation which result from ignoring the truths of biology. When taking the biological view of ethics we saw that pleasures accompany normal amounts of functions, while pains accompany defects or excesses of functions; further, that complete life depends on complete discharge of functions, and therefore on receipt of the correlative pleasures. Hence, to yield up normal pleasures is to yield up so much life; and there arises the question—to what extent may this be done? If he is to continue living, the individual *must* take certain amounts of those pleasures which go along with fulfillment of the bodily functions, and *must* avoid the pains which entire nonfulfillment of them entails. Complete abnegation means death; excessive abnegation means illness; abnegation less excessive means physical degradation and consequent loss of power to fulfill obligations, personal and other. When, therefore, we attempt to specialize the proposal to live not for self-satisfaction but for the satisfaction of others, we meet with the difficulty that beyond a certain limit this cannot be done. And when we have decided what decrease of bodily welfare, caused by sacrifice of pleasures and acceptance of pains, it is proper for the individual to make, there is forced on us the fact that the portion of happiness, or means to happiness, which it is possible for him to yield up for redistribution, is a limited portion.

Even more rigorous on another side is the restriction put upon the transfer of happiness, or the means to happiness. The pleasures gained by efficient action—by successful pursuit of ends, cannot by any process be parted with, and cannot in any way be appropriated by another. The habit of arguing about general happiness sometimes as though it were a concrete product to be portioned out, and sometimes as though it were coextensive with the use of those material aids to pleasure which may be given and received, has caused inattention to the truth that the pleasures of achievement are not transferable. Alike in the boy who has won a game of marbles, the athlete who has performed a feat, the statesman who has gained a party triumph, the inventor who has devised a new machine, the man of science who has discovered a truth, the novelist who has well delineated a character, the poet who has finely rendered an emotion, we see pleasures which must, in the nature of things, be enjoyed exclusively by those to whom they come. And if we look at all such occupations as men are not impelled to by their necessities—if we contemplate the various ambitions which play so large a part in life; we are reminded that so long as the consciousness of efficiency remains a dominant pleasure, there will remain a dominant pleasure which cannot be pursued altruistically but must be pursued egoistically.

Cutting off, then, at the one end, those pleasures which are inseparable from maintenance of the physique in an uninjured state; and cutting off at the other end the pleasures of successful action; the amount that remains is so greatly diminished, as to make untenable the assumption that happiness at large admits of distribution after the manner which utilitarianism assumes.

89. In yet one more way may be shown the inconsistency of this transfigured utilitarianism which regards its doctrine as embodying the Christian maxim "Love your neighbor as yourself," and of that altruism which, going still further, enunciates the maxim "Live for others."

A right rule of conduct must be one which may with advantage be adopted by all. "Act according to that maxim only, which you can wish, at the same time, to become a universal law," says Kant. And clearly a passing over needful qualifications of this maxim, we may accept it to the extent of admitting that a mode of action which becomes impracticable as it approaches universality, must be wrong. Hence, if the theory of pure altruism, implying that effort should be expended for the benefit of others and not for personal benefit, is defensible, it must be shown that it will produce good results when acted upon by all. Mark the consequences if all are purely altruistic.

First, an impossible combination of moral attributes is implied. Each is supposed by the hypothesis to regard self so little and others so much, that he willingly sacrifices his own pleasures to give pleasures to them. But if this is a universal trait, and if action is universally congruous with it, we have to conceive each as being not only a sacrificer but also one who accepts sacrifices. While he is so unselfish as willingly to yield up the benefit for which he has labored, he is so selfish as willingly to let others yield up to him the benefits they have labored for. To make pure altruism possible for all, each must be at once extremely unegoistic and extremely egoistic. As a giver, he must have no thought for self; as a receiver, no thought for others. Evidently, this implies an inconceivable mental constitution. The sympathy which is so solicitous for others as willingly to injure self in benefiting them, cannot at the same time be so regardless of others as to accept benefits which they injure themselves in giving.

The incongruities that emerge if we assume pure altruism to be universally practiced, may be otherwise exhibited thus. Suppose that each, instead of enjoying such pleasures as come to him, or such consumable appliances to pleasure as he has worked for, or such occasions for pleasure as reward his efforts, relinquishes these to a single other, or adds them to a common stock from which others benefit; what will result? Different answers may be given according as we assume that there are, or are not, additional influences brought into play. Suppose there are no additional influences. Then, if each transfers to another his happiness, or means to happiness, or occasions for happiness, while some one else does the like to him, the distribution of happiness is, on the average, unchanged; or if each adds to a common stock his happiness, or means to happiness, or occasions for happiness, from which common stock each appropriates his portion, the average state is still, as before, unchanged. The only obvious effect is that transactions must be gone through in the redistribution; and loss of time and labor must result. Now suppose some additional influence which makes the process beneficial; what must it be? The totality can be increased only if the acts of transfer increase the quantity of that which is transferred. The happiness, or that which brings it, must be greater to one who derives it from another's efforts, than it would have been had his own efforts procured it; or otherwise, supposing a fund of happiness, or of that which brings it, has been formed by contributions from each, then each, in appropriating his share, must find it larger than it would have been had no such aggregation and dispersion taken place. To justify belief in such increase two conceivable assumptions may be made. One is that though the sum of pleasures, or of pleasure-yielding things, remains the same yet the kind of pleasure, or of pleasure-yielding things, which each receives in exchange from another, or from the aggregate of others, is one which he appreciates more than that for which he labored. But to assume this is to assume that each labors directly for the thing which he enjoys less, rather than for the thing which he enjoys more, which is absurd. The other assumption is that while the exchanged or redistributed pleasure of the egoistic kind, remains the same in amount for each, there is added to it the altruistic pleasure accompanying the exchange. But this assumption is clearly inadmissible if, as is implied, the transaction is universal—is one through which each becomes giver and receiver to equal extents. For if the transfer of pleasures, or of pleasure-yielding things, from one to another or others, is always accompanied by the consciousness that there will be received from him or them an equivalent; there results merely a tacit exchange, either direct or roundabout. Each becomes altruistic in no greater degree than is implied by being equitable; and each, having nothing to exalt his happiness, sympathetically or otherwise, cannot be a source of sympathetic happiness to others.

90. Thus, when the meanings of its words are inquired into, or when the necessary implications of its theory are examined, pure altruism, in whatever form expressed, commits its adherents to various absurdities.

If "the greatest happiness of the greatest number," or in other words, "the general happiness," is the proper end of action, then not only for all public action but for all private action, it must be the end; because, otherwise, the greater part of action remains unguided. Consider its fitness for each. If corporate action is to be guided by the principle, with its interpreting comment—"everybody to count for one, nobody for more than one"—there must be an ignoring of all differences of character and conduct, merits and demerits, among citizens, since no discrimination is provided for; and moreover, since that in respect of which all are to count alike cannot be happiness itself, which is indistributable, and since equal sharing of the concrete means to happiness, besides failing utimately would fail proximately to produce the greatest happiness; it results that equal distribution of the conditions under which happiness may be pursued is the only tenable meaning: we discover in the principle nothing but a roundabout insistence on equity. If, taking happiness at large as the aim of private action, the individual is required to judge between his own happiness and that of others as an impartial spectator would do, we see that no supposition concerning the spectator save one which suicidally ascribes partiality to him, can bring out any other result than that each shall enjoy such happiness, or appropriate such means to happiness, as his own efforts gain: equity is again the sole content. When, adopting another method, we consider how the greatest sum of happiness may be composed, and, recognizing the fact that equitable egoism will produce a certain sum, ask how pure altruism is to produce a greater sum; we are shown that if all, exclusively pursuing altruistic pleasures, are so to produce a greater sum of pleasures, the implication is that altruistic pleasures, which arise from sympathy, can exist in the absence of egoistic pleasures with which there may be sympathy—an impossibility; and another implication is that if, the necessity for egoistic pleasures being admitted, it is said that the greatest sum of happiness will be attained if all individuals are more altruistic than egoistic, it is indirectly said that as a general truth, representative feelings are stronger than presentative feelings—another impossibility. Again the doctrine of pure altruism assumes that happiness may be to any extent transferred or redistributed; whereas the fact is that pleasures of one order cannot be transferred in large measure without results which are fatal or extremely injurious, and that pleasures of another order cannot be transferred in any degree. Further, pure altruism presents this fatal anomaly; that while a right principle of action must be more and more practiced as men improve, the altruistic principle becomes less and less practicable as men approach an ideal form, because the sphere for practicing it continually decreases. Finally, its self-destructiveness is made manifest on observing that for all to adopt it as a principle of action, which they must do if it is a sound principle, implies that all are at once extremely unegoistic and extremely egoistic—ready to injure self for others' benefit, and ready to accept benefit at the cost of injury to others: traits which cannot coexist.

The need for a compromise between egoism and altruism is thus made conspicuous. We are forced to recognize the claims which his own well-being has on the attention of each by noting how, in some directions we come to a deadlock, in others to contradictions, and in others to disastrous results, if they are ignored. Conversely, it is undeniable that disregard of others by each, carried to a great extent is fatal to society, and carried to a still greater extent is fatal to the family, and eventually to the race. Egoism and altruism are therefore coessential.

91. What form is the compromise between egoism and altruism to assume? how are their respective claims to be satisfied in due degree?

It is a truth insisted on by moralists and recognized in common life, that the achievement of individual happiness is not proportionate to the degree in which individual happiness is made the object of direct pursuit; but there has not yet become current the belief that, in like manner, the achievement of general happiness is not proportionate to the degree in which general happiness is made the object of direct pursuit. Yet failure of direct pursuit in the last case is more reasonably to be expected than in the first.

When discussing the relations of means and ends, we saw that as individual conduct evolves, its principle becomes more and more that of making fulfillment of means the proximate end, and leaving the ultimate end, welfare or happiness, to come as a result. And we saw that when general welfare or happiness is the ultimate end, the same principle holds even more rigorously; since the ultimate end under its impersonal form, is less determinate than under its personal form, and the difficulties in the way of achieving it by direct pursuit still greater. Recognizing, then, the fact that corporate happiness still more than individual happiness, must be pursued not directly but indirectly, the first question for us is—What must be the general nature of the means through which it is to be achieved.

It is admitted that self-happiness is, in a measure, to be obtained by furthering the happiness of others. May it not be true that, conversely, general happiness is to be obtained by furthering self-happiness? If the well-being of each unit is to be reached partly through his care for the well-being of the aggregate, is not the well-being of the aggregate to be reached partly through the care of each unit for himself? Clearly, our conclusion must be that general happiness is to be achieved mainly through the adequate pursuit of their own happinesses by individuals; while, reciprocally, the happinesses of individuals are to be achieved in part by their pursuit of the general happiness.

And this is the conclusion embodied in the progressing ideas and usages of mankind. This compromise between egoism and altruism has been slow establishing itself; and towards recognition of its propriety, men's actual beliefs, as distinguished from their nominal beliefs, have been gradually approaching. Social evolution has been bringing about a state in which the claims of the individual to the proceeds of his activities, and to such satisfactions as they bring, are more and more positively asserted; at the same time that insistence on others' claims, and habitual respect for them, have been increasing. Among the rudest savages personal interests are very vaguely distinguished from the interests of others. In early stages of civilization, the proportioning of benefits to efforts is extremely rude: slaves and serfs get for work, arbitrary amounts of food and shelter: exchange being infrequent, there is little to develop the idea of equivalence. But as civilization advances and status passes into contract, there comes daily experience of the relation between advantages enjoyed and labor given: the industrial system maintaining, through supply and demand, a due adjustment of the one to the other.

And this growth of voluntary cooperation—this exchange of services under agreement, has been necessarily accompanied by decrease of aggressions one upon another, and increase of sympathy: leading to exchange of services beyond agreement. That is to say, the more distinct assertions of individual claims and more rigorous apportioning of personal enjoyments to efforts expended, has gone hand in hand with growth of that negative altruism shown in equitable conduct and that positive altruism shown in gratuitous aid.

A higher phase of this double change has in our own times become conspicuous. If, on the one hand, we note the struggles for political freedom, the contests between labor and capital, the judicial reforms made to facilitate enforcement of rights, we see that the tendency still is towards complete appropriation by each of whatever benefits are due to him, and consequent exclusion of his fellows from such benefits. On the other hand, if we consider what is meant by the surrender of power to the masses, the abolition of class privileges, the efforts to diffuse knowledge, the agitations to spread temperance, the multitudinous philanthropic societies; it becomes clear that regard for the well-being of others is increasing *pari passu* with the taking of means to secure personal well-being.

What holds of the relations within each society holds to some extent, if to a less extent, of the relations between societies. Though to maintain national claims, real or imaginary, often of a trivial kind, the civilized still make war on one another; yet their several nationalities are more respected than in past ages. Though by victors portions of territory are taken and money compensations exacted; yet conquest is not now, as of old, habitually followed by entire appropriation of territories and enslavement of peoples. The individualities of societies are in a larger measure preserved. Meanwhile the altruistic intercourse is greater: aid is rendered on occasions of disaster by flood, by fire, by famine, or otherwise. And in international arbitration as lately exemplified, implying the recognition of claims by one nation upon another, we see a further progress in this wider altruism. Doubtless there is much to be said by way of setoff; for in the dealings of the civilized with the uncivilized, little of this progress can be traced. It may be urged that the primitive rule "Life for life" has been developed by us into the rule "For one life many lives," as in the cases of Bishop Patteson and Mr. Birch; but then there is the qualifying fact that we do not torture our prisoners or mutilate them. If it be said that as the Hebrews thought themselves warranted in seizing the lands God promised to them, and in some cases exterminating the inhabitants, so we, to fulfill the "manifest intention of Providence," dispossess inferior races whenever we want their territories; it may be replied that we do not kill many more than seems needful, and tolerate the existence of those who submit. And should any one point out that as Attila, while conquering or destroying peoples and nations, regarded himself as "the scourge of God," punishing men for their sins, so we, as represented by a High Commissioner and a priest he quotes, think ourselves called on to chastise with rifles and cannon, heathens who practice polygamy; there is the rejoinder that not even the most ferocious disciple of the teacher of mercy would carry his vengeance so far as to depopulate whole territories and erase scores of cities. And when, on the other hand, we remember that there is an Aborigines Protection Society, that there are commissioners in certain colonies appointed to protect native interests, and that in some cases the lands of natives have been purchased in ways which, however unfair, have implied some recognition of their claims; we may say that little as the compromise between egoism and altruism has progressed in international affairs, it has still progressed somewhat in the direction indicated.

CHAPTER 14

Conciliation

92. As exhibited in the last chapter, the compromise between the claims of self and the claims of others seems to imply permanent antagonism between the two. The pursuit by each of his own happiness while paying due regard to the happiness of his fellows, apparently necessitates the ever-recurring question—how far must the one end be sought and how far the other? suggesting, if not discord in the life of each, still, an absence of complete harmony. This is not the inevitable inference however.

When, in the *Principles of Sociology*, Part III, the phenomena of race-maintenance among living things at large were discussed, that the development of the domestic relations might be the better understood, it was shown that during evolution there has been going on a conciliation between the interests of the species, the interests of the parents, and the interests of the offspring. Proof was given that as we ascend from the lowest forms of life to the highest, race-maintenance is achieved with a decreasing sacrifice of life, alike of young individuals and of adult individuals, and also with a decreasing sacrifice of parental lives to the lives of offspring. We saw that, with the progress of civilization, like changes go on among human beings; and that the highest domestic relations are those in which the conciliation of welfare within the family becomes greatest, while the welfare of the society is best subserved. Here it remains to be shown that a kindred conciliation has been, and is, taking place between the interests of each citizen and the interests of citizens at large; tending ever towards a state in which the two become merged in one, and in which the feelings answering to them respectively, fall into complete concord.

In the family group, even as we observe it among many inferior vertebrates, we see that the parental sacrifice, now become so moderate in amount as to consist with long-continued parental life, is not accompanied by consciousness of sacrifice; but, contrariwise, is made from a direct desire to make it: the altruistic labors on behalf of young are carried on in satisfaction of parental instincts. If we trace these relations up through the grades of mankind, and observe how largely love rather than obligation prompts the care of children, we see the conciliation of interests to be such that achievement of parental happiness coincides with securing the happiness of offspring: the wish for children among the childless, and the occasional adoption of children, showing how needful for attainment of certain egoistic satisfactions are these altruistic activities. And further evolution, causing along with higher nature diminished fertility, and therefore smaller burdens on parents, may be expected to bring a state in which, far more than now, the pleasures of adult life will consist in raising offspring to perfection while simultaneously furthering the immediate happiness of offspring.

Now though altruism of a social kind, lacking certain elements of parental altruism, can never attain the same level; yet it may be expected to attain a level at which it will be like parental altruism in spontaneity—a level such that ministration to others' happiness will become a daily need—a level such that the lower egoistic satisfactions will be continually subordinated to this higher egoistic satisfaction, not by any effort to subordinate them, but by the preference for this higher egoistic satisfaction whenever it can be obtained.

Let us consider how the development of sympathy, which must advance as fast as conditions permit, will bring about this state.

93. We have seen that during the evolution of life, pleasures and pains have necessarily been the incentives to and deterrents from, actions which the conditions of existence demanded and negatived. An implied truth to be here noted is, that faculties which, under given conditions, yield partly pain and partly pleasure, cannot develop beyond the limit at which they yield a surplus of pleasure: if beyond that limit more pain than pleasure results from exercise of them, their growth must be arrested.

Through sympathy both these forms of feeling are excited. Now a pleasurable consciousness is aroused on witnessing pleasure; now a painful consciousness is aroused on witnessing pain. Hence, if beings around him habitually manifest pleasure and but rarely pain, sympathy yields to its possessor a surplus of pleasure; while, contrariwise, if little pleasure is ordinarily witnessed and much pain, sympathy yields a surplus of pain to its possessor. The average development of sympathy must, therefore, be regulated by the average manifestations of pleasure and pain in others. If the life usually led under given social conditions is such that suffering is daily inflicted, or is daily displayed by associates, sympathy cannot grow: to assume growth of it is to assume that the constitution will modify itself in such way as to increase its pains and therefore depress its energies; and is to ignore the truth that bearing any kind of pain gradually produces insensibility to that pain, or callousness. On the other hand, if the social state is such that manifestations of pleasure predominate, sympathy will increase; since sympathetic pleasures, adding to the totality of pleasures enhancing vitality, conduce to the physical prosperity of the most sympathetic, and since the pleasures of sympathy exceeding its pains in all, lead to an exercise of it which strengthens it.

The first implication is one already more than once indicated. We have seen that along with habitual militancy and under the adapted type of social organization, sympathy cannot develop to any considerable height. The destructive activities carried on against external enemies sear it; the state of feeling maintained causes within the society itself frequent acts of aggression or cruelty; and further, the compulsory cooperation characterizing the militant regime necessarily represses sympathy—exists only on condition of an unsympathetic treatment of some by others.

But even could the militant regime forthwith end, the hindrances to development of sympathy would still be great. Though cessation of war would imply increased adaptation of man to social life, and decrease of sundry evils, yet there would remain much nonadaptation and much consequent unhappiness. In the first place, that form of nature which has generated and still generates wars, though by implication raised to a higher form, would not at once be raised to so high a form that there would cease all injustices and the pains they cause. For a considerable period after predatory activities had ended, the defects of the predatory nature would continue: entailing their slowly diminishing evils. In the second place, the ill-adjustment of the human constitution to the pursuits of industrial life, must long persist, and may be expected to survive in a measure the cessation of wars: the required modes of activity must remain for innumerable generations in some degree displeasurable. And in the third place, deficiencies of self-control such as the improvident show us, as well as those many failures of conduct due to inadequate foresight of consequences, though less marked than now, could not fail still to produce suffering.

Nor would even complete adaptation, if limited to disappearance of the nonadaptations just indicated, remove all sources of those miseries which, to the extent of their manifestation, check the growth of sympathy. For while the rate of multiplication continues so to exceed the rate of mortality as to cause pressure on the means of subsistence, there must continue to result much unhappiness; either from balked affections or from overwork and stinted means. Only as fast as fertility diminishes, which we have seen it must do along with further mental development (*Principles of Biology*, secs. 367–77), can there go on such diminution of the labors required for efficiently supporting self and family, that they will not constitute a displeasurable tax on the energies.

Gradually then, and only gradually, as these various causes of unhappiness become less can sympathy become greater. Life would be intolerable if, while the causes of misery remained as they now are, all men were not only in a high degree sensitive to the pains, bodily and mental, felt by those around and expressed in the faces of those they met, but were unceasingly conscious of the miseries everywhere being suffered as consequences of war, crime, misconduct, misfortune, improvidence, incapacity. But, as the molding and remolding of man and society into mutual fitness progresses, and as the pains caused by unfitness decrease, sympathy can increase in presence of the pleasures that come from fitness. The two changes are indeed so related that each furthers the other. Such growth of sympathy as conditions permit, itself aids in lessening pain and augmenting pleasure; and the greater surplus of pleasure that results makes possible further growth of sympathy.

94. The extent to which sympathy may develop when the hindrances are removed, will be better conceived after observing the agencies through which it is excited, and setting down the reasons for expecting those agencies to become more efficient. Two factors have to be considered—the natural language of feeling in the being sympathized with, and the power of interpreting that language in the being who sympathizes. We may anticipate development of both.

Movements of the body and facial changes are visible effects of feeling which, when the feeling is strong, are uncontrollable. When the feeling is less strong however, be it sensational or emotional, they may be wholly or partially repressed; and there is a habit, more or less constant, of repressing them: this habit being the concomitant of a nature such that it is often undesirable that others should see what is felt. So necessary with our existing characters and conditions are concealments thus prompted, that they have come to form a part of moral duty; and concealment for its own sake is often insisted upon as an element in good manners. All this is caused by the prevalence of feelings at variance with social good—feelings which cannot be shown without producing discords or estrangements. But in proportion as the egoistic desires fall more under control of the altruistic, and there come fewer and slighter impulses of a kind to be reprobated, the need for keeping guard over facial expression and bodily movement will decrease, and these will with increasing clearness convey to spectators the mental state. Nor is this all. Restrained as its use is, this language of the emotions is at present prevented from growing. But as fast as the emotions become such that they may be more candidly displayed, there will go, along with the habit of display, development of the means of display; so that besides the stronger emotions, the more delicate shades and smaller degrees of emotion will visibly exhibit themselves: the emotional language will become at once more copious, more varied, more definite. And obviously sympathy will be proportionately facilitated.

An equally important, if not a more important, advance of kindred nature, is to be anticipated. The vocal signs of sentient states will simultaneously evolve further. Loudness of tone, pitch of tone, quality of tone, and change of tone, are severally marks of feeling; and, combined in different ways and proportions, serve to express different amounts and kinds of feelings. As elsewhere pointed out, cadences are the comments of the emotions on the propositions of the intellect.* Not in excited speech only, but in ordinary speech, we show by ascending and descending intervals, by degrees of

---

* See essay "The Origin and Function of Music."

deviation from the medium tone, as well as by place and strength of emphasis, the kind of sentiency which accompanies the thought expressed. Now the manifestation of feeling by cadence, like its manifestation by visible changes, is at present under restraint; the motives for repression act in the one case as they act in the other. A double effect is produced. This audible language of feeling is not used up to the limit of its existing capacity; and it is to a considerable degree misused, so as to convey other feelings than those which are felt. The result of this disuse and misuse is to check that evolution which normal use would cause. We must infer, then, that as moral adaptation progresses, and there is decreasing need for concealment of the feelings, their vocal signs will develop much further. Though it is not to be supposed that cadences will ever convey emotions as exactly as words convey thoughts, yet it is quite possible that the emotional language of the future may rise as much above our present emotional language, as our intellectual language has already risen above the intellectual language of the lowest races.

A simultaneous increase in the power of interpreting both visible and audible signs of feeling must be taken into account. Among those around we see differences both of ability to perceive such signs and of ability to conceive the implied mental states and their causes: here, a stolidity unimpressed by a slight facial change or altered tone of voice, or else unable to imagine what is felt; and there, a quick observation and a penetrating intuition, making instantly comprehensible the state of mind and its origin. If we suppose both these faculties exalted—both a more delicate perception of the signs and a strengthened constructive imagination—we shall get some idea of the deeper and wider sympathy that will hereafter arise. More vivid representations of the feelings of others, implying ideal excitements of feelings approaching to real excitements, must imply a greater likeness between the feelings of the sympathizer and those of the sympathized with; coming near to identity.

By simultaneous increase of its subjective and objective

factors, sympathy may thus, as the hindrances diminish, rise above that now shown by the sympathetic as much as in them it has risen above that which the callous show.

95. What must be the accompanying evolution of conduct? What must the relations between egoism and altruism become as this form of nature is neared?

A conclusion drawn in the chapter on the relativity of pleasures and pains, and there emphasized as one to be borne in mind, must now be recalled. It was pointed out that, supposing them to be consistent with continuance of life, there are no activities which may not become sources of pleasure, if surrounding conditions require persistence in them. And here it is to be added, as a corollary, that if the conditions require any class of activities to be relatively great, there will arise a relatively great pleasure accompanying that class of activities. What bearing have these general inferences on the special question before us?

That alike for public welfare and private welfare sympathy is essential, we have seen. We have seen that cooperation and the benefits which it brings to each and all, become high in proportion as the altruistic, that is the sympathetic, interests extend. The actions prompted by fellow feeling are thus to be counted among those demanded by social conditions. They are actions which maintenance and further development of social organization tend ever to increase; and therefore actions with which there will be joined an increasing pleasure. From the laws of life it must be concluded that unceasing social discipline will so mold human nature, that eventually sympathetic pleasures will be spontaneously pursued to the fullest extent advantageous to each and all. The scope for altruistic activities will not exceed the desire for altruistic satisfactions.

In natures thus constituted, though the altruistic gratifications must remain in a transfigured sense egoistic, yet they will not be egoistically pursued—will not be pursued from egoistic motives. Though pleasure will be gained by giving pleasure, yet the thought of the sympathetic pleasure to be gained will not occupy consciousness, but only the thought of the pleasure given. To a great extent this is so now. In the truly sympathetic, attention is so absorbed with the proximate end, others' happiness, that there is none given to the prospective self-happiness which may ultimately result. An analogy will make the relation clear.

A miser accumulates money, not deliberately saying to himself—"I shall by doing this get the delight which possession gives." He thinks only of the money and the means of getting it; and he experiences incidentally the pleasure that comes from possession. Owning property is that which he revels in imagining, and not the feeling which owning property will cause. Similarly, one who is sympathetic in the highest sense, is mentally engaged solely in representing pleasure as experienced by another; and pursues it for the benefit of that other, forgetting any participation he will have in it. Subjectively considered, then, the conciliation of egoism and altruism will eventually become such that though the altruistic pleasure, as being a part of the consciousness of one who experiences it, can never be other than egoistic, it will not be consciously egoistic.

Let us now ask what must happen in a society composed of persons constituted in this manner.

96. The opportunities for that postponement of self to others which constitutes altruism as ordinarily conceived, must, in several ways, be more and more limited as the highest state is approached.

Extensive demands on the benevolent, presuppose much unhappiness. Before there can be many and large calls on some for efforts on behalf of others, there must be many others in conditions needing help—in conditions of comparative misery. But, as we have seen above, the development of fellow feeling can go on only as fast as misery decreases. Sympathy can reach its full height only when there have ceased to be frequent occasions for anything like serious self-sacrifice.

Change the point of view, and this truth presents itself

under another aspect. We have already seen that with the progress of adaptation each becomes so constituted that he cannot be helped without in some way arresting a pleasurable activity. There cannot be a beneficial interference between faculty and function when the two are adjusted. Consequently, in proportion as mankind approach complete adjustment of their natures to social needs, there must be fewer and smaller opportunities for giving aid.

Yet again, as was pointed out in the last chapter, the sympathy which prompts efforts for others' welfare must be gained by self-injury on the part of others; and must, therefore, cause aversion to accept benefits derived from their self-injuries. What is to be inferred? While each when occasion offers is ready, anxious even, to surrender egoistic satisfactions; others, similarly natured, cannot but resist the surrender. If anyone, proposing to treat himself more hardly than a disinterested spectator would direct, refrains from appropriating that which is due, others, caring for him if he will not care for himself, must necessarily insist that he shall appropriate it. General altruism then, in its developed form, must inevitably resist individual excesses of altruism. The relation at present familiar to us will be inverted; and instead of each maintaining his own claims, others will maintain his claims for him: not, indeed, by active efforts, which will be needless, but by passively resisting any undue yielding up of them. There is nothing in such behavior which is not even now to be traced in our daily experiences as beginning. In business transactions among honorable men, there is usually a desire on either side that the other shall treat himself fairly. Not unfrequently, there is a refusal to take something regarded as the other's due, but which the other offers to give up. In social intercourse, too, the cases are common in which those who would surrender their shares of pleasure are not permitted by the rest to do so. Further development of sympathy cannot but make this mode of behaving increasingly general and increasingly genuine.

Certain complex restraints on excesses of altruism exist, which, in another way, force back the individual upon a normal egoism. Two may here be noted. In the first place, self-abnegations often repeated imply on the part of the actor a tacit ascription of relative selfishness to others who profit by the self-abnegations. Even with men as they are, there occasionally arises a feeling among those for whom sacrifices are frequently made, that they are being insulted by the assumption that they are ready to receive them; and in the mind of the actor also, there sometimes grows up a recognition of this feeling on their part, and a consequent check on his too great or too frequent surrenders of pleasure. Obviously in more developed natures, this kind of check must act still more promptly. In the second place, when, as the hypothesis implies, altruistic pleasures have reached a greater intensity than they now possess, each person will be debarred from undue pursuit of them by the consciousness that other persons, too, desire them, and that scope for others' enjoyment of them must be left. Even now may be observed among groups of friends, where some competition in amiability is going on, relinquishments of opportunities for self-abnegation that others may have them. "Let her give up the gratification, she will like to do so"; "Let him undertake the trouble, it will please him"; are suggestions which from time to time illustrate this consciousness. The most developed sympathy will care for the sympathetic satisfactions of others as well as for their selfish satisfactions. What may be called a higher equity will refrain from trespassing on the spheres of others' altruistic activities, as a lower equity refrains from trespassing on the spheres of their egoistic activities. And by this checking of what may be called an egoistic altruism, undue sacrifices on the part of each must be prevented.

What spheres, then, will eventually remain for altruism as it is commonly conceived? There are three. One of them must to the last continue large in extent; and the others must progressively diminish, though they do not disappear. The first is that which family-life affords. Always there must be a need for subordination of self-regarding feelings to other-regarding feelings in the rearing of children. Though this will diminish with diminution in the number to be reared, yet it will increase with the greater elaboration and prolongation of the activities on their behalf. But as shown above, there is even now partially effected a conciliation such that those egoistic satisfactions which parenthood yields are achieved through altruistic activities—a conciliation tending ever towards completeness. An important development of family-altruism must be added: the reciprocal care of parents by children during old age—a care becoming lighter and better fulfilled, in which a kindred conciliation may be looked for. Pursuit of social welfare at large must afford hereafter, as it does now, scope for the postponement of selfish interests to unselfish interests, but a continually lessening scope; because as adaptation to the social state progresses, the needs for those regulative actions by which social life is made harmonious become less. And here the amount of altruistic action which each undertakes must inevitably be kept within moderate bounds by others; for if they are similarly altruistic, they will not allow some to pursue public ends to their own considerable detriment that the rest may profit. In the private relations of men, opportunities for self-sacrifice prompted by sympathy, must ever in some degree, though eventually in a small degree, be afforded by accidents, diseases, and misfortunes in general; since, however near to completeness the adaptation of human nature to the conditions of existence at large, physical and social, may become, it can never reach completeness. Flood, fire, and wreck must to the last yield at intervals opportunities for heroic acts; and in the motives to such acts, anxiety for others will be less alloyed with love of admiration than now. Extreme, however, as may be the eagerness for altruistic action on the rare occasions hence arising, the amount falling to the share of each must, for the reasons given, be narrowly limited. But though in the incidents of ordinary life, postponements of self to others in large ways must become very infrequent, daily intercourse will still furnish multitudinous small occasions for the activity of fellow feeling. Always each may continue to further the welfare of others by warding off from them evils they cannot see, and by aiding their actions in ways unknown to them; or, conversely putting it, each may have, as it were, supplementary eyes and ears in other persons, which perceive for him things he cannot perceive himself: so perfecting his life in numerous details, by making its adjustments to environing actions complete.

97. Must it then follow that eventually, with this diminution of the spheres for it, altruism must diminish in total amount? By no means. Such a conclusion implies a misconception.

Naturally, under existing conditions, with suffering widely diffused and so much of effort demanded from the more fortunate in succoring the less fortunate, altruism is understood to mean only self-sacrifice; or, at any rate, a mode of action which, while it brings some pleasure, has an accompaniment of self-surrender that is not pleasurable. But the sympathy which prompts denial of self to please others, is a sympathy which also receives pleasure from their pleasures when they are otherwise originated. The stronger the fellow feeling which excites efforts to make others happy, the stronger is the fellow feeling with their happiness however caused.

In its ultimate form, then, altruism will be the achievement of gratification through sympathy with those gratifications of others which are mainly produced by their activities of all kinds successfully carried on—sympathetic gratification which costs the receiver nothing, but is a gratis addition to his egoistic gratifications. This power of representing in idea the mental states of others, which, during the process of adaptation has had the function of mitigating suffering, must, as the suffering falls to a minimum, come to have almost wholly the function of mutually exalting men's enjoyments by giving everyone a vivid intuition of his neighbor's enjoyments. While pain prevails widely, it is undesirable that each should participate much in the consciousness of others; but with an increasing predominance of pleasure, participation in others' consciousnesses becomes a gain of pleasure to all.

And so there will disappear that apparently permanent opposition between egoism and altruism, implied by the compromise reached in the last chapter. Subjectively looked at, the conciliation will be such that the individual will not have to balance between self-regarding impulses and other-regarding impulses; but, instead, those satisfactions of other-regarding impulses which involve self-sacrifice, becoming rare and much prized, will be so unhesitatingly preferred that the competition of self-regarding impulses with them will scarcely be felt. And the subjective conciliation will also be such that though altruistic pleasure will be attained, yet the motive of action will not consciously be the attainment of altruistic pleasure; but the idea present will be the securing of others' pleasures. Meanwhile, the conciliation objectively considered will be equally complete. Though each, no longer needing to maintain his egoistic claims, will tend rather when occasion offers to surrender them, yet others, similarly natured, will not permit him in any large measure to do this; and that fulfillment of personal desires required for completion of his life will thus be secured to him: though not now egoistic in the ordinary sense, yet the effects of due egoism will be achieved. Nor is this all. As, at an earlier stage, egoistic competition, first reaching a compromise such that each claims no more than his equitable share, afterward rises to a conciliation such that each insists on the taking of equitable shares by others; so, at the latest stage, altruistic competition, first reaching a compromise under which each restrains himself from taking an undue share of altruistic satisfactions, eventually rises to a conciliation under which each takes care that others shall have their opportunities for altruistic satisfactions: the highest altruism being that which ministers not to the egoistic satisfactions of others only, but also to their altruistic satisfactions.

Far off as seems such a state, yet every one of the factors counted on to produce it may already be traced in operation among those of highest natures. What now in them is occasional and feeble, may be expected with further evolution to become habitual and strong; and what now characterizes the exceptionally high may be expected eventually to characterize all. For that which the best human nature is capable of, is within the reach of human nature at large.

98. That these conclusions will meet with any considerable acceptance is improbable. Neither with current ideas nor with current sentiments are they sufficiently congruous.

Such a view will not be agreeable to those who lament the spreading disbelief in eternal damnation; nor to those who follow the apostle of brute force in thinking that because the rule of the strong hand was once good it is good for all time; nor to those whose reverence for one who told them to put up the sword, is shown by using the sword to spread his doctrine among heathens. From the ten thousand priests of the religion of love, who are silent when the nation is moved by the religion of hate, will come no sign of assent; nor from their bishops who, far from urging the extreme precept of the master they pretend to follow, to turn the other cheek when one is smitten, vote for acting on the principle—strike lest ye be struck. Nor will any approval be felt by legislators who, after praying to be forgiven their trespasses as they forgive the trespasses of others, forthwith decide to attack those who have not trespassed against them; and who, after a Queen's Speech has invoked "the blessing of Almighty God" on their councils, immediately provide means for committing political burglary.

But though men who profess Christianity and practice paganism can feel no sympathy with such a view, there are some, classed as antagonists to the current creed, who may not think it absurd to believe that a rationalized version of its ethical principles will eventually be acted upon.

CHAPTER 15

Absolute and Relative Ethics

99.   As applied to ethics, the word "absolute" will by many be supposed to imply principles of right conduct that exist out of relation to life as conditioned on the earth—out of relation to time and place, and independent of the universe as now visible to us—"eternal" principles, as they are called. Those, however, who recall the doctrine set forth in *First Principles*, will hesitate to put this interpretation on the word. Right, as we can think it, necessitates the thought of not-right, or wrong, for its correlative; and hence, to ascribe rightness to the acts of the Power manifested through phenomena, is to assume the possibility that wrong acts may be committed by this Power. But how come there to exist, apart from this Power, conditions of such kind that subordination of its acts to them makes them right and insubordination wrong? How can Unconditioned Being be subject to conditions beyond itself?

If, for example, any one should assert that the Cause of things, conceived in respect of fundamental moral attributes as like ourselves, did right in producing a universe which, in the course of immeasurable time, has given origin to beings capable of pleasure, and would have done wrong in abstaining from the production of such a universe; then, the comment to be made is that, imposing the moral ideas generated in his finite consciousness, upon the Infinite Existence which transcends consciousness, he goes behind that Infinite Existence and prescribes for it principles of action.

As implied in foregoing chapters, right and wrong as conceived by us can exist only in relation to the actions of creatures capable of pleasures and pains; seeing that analysis carries us back to pleasures and pains as the elements out of which the conceptions are framed.

But if the word "absolute," as used above, does not refer to the Unconditioned Being—if the principles of action distinguished as absolute and relative concern the conduct of conditioned beings; in what way are the words to be understood? An explanation of their meanings will be best conveyed by a criticism on the current conceptions of right and wrong.

100. Conversations about the affairs of life habitually imply the belief that every deed named may be placed under the one head or the other. In discussing a political question, both sides take it for granted that some line of action may be chosen which is right, while all other lines of action are wrong. So, too, is it with judgments on the doings of individuals: each of these is approved or disapproved on the assumption that it is definitely classable as good or bad. Even where qualifications are admitted, they are admitted with an implied idea that some such positive characterization is to be made.

Nor is it in popular thought and speech only that we see this. If not wholly and definitely yet partially and by implication, the belief is expressed by moralists. In his *Methods of Ethics* (1st ed., p. 6) Mr. Sidgwick says: "That there is in any given circumstances some one thing which ought to be done and that this can be known, is a fundamental assumption, made not by philosophers only, but by all men who perform any processes of moral reasoning."* In this sentence there is

---

* I do not find this passage in the second edition; but the omission of it appears to have arisen not from any change of view, but because it did not naturally come into the recast form of the argument which the section contains.

specifically asserted only the last of the above propositions; namely, that, in every case, what "ought to be done" "can be known." But though that "which ought to be done" is not distinctly identified with "the right," it may be inferred, in the absence of any indication to the contrary, that Mr. Sidgwick regards the two as identical; and doubtless, in so conceiving the postulates of moral science, he is at one with most, if not all, who have made it a subject of study. At first sight, indeed, nothing seems more obvious than that if actions are to be judged at all, these postulates must be accepted. Nevertheless, they may both be called in question, and I think it may be shown that neither of them is tenable. Instead of admitting that there is in every case a right and a wrong, it may be contended that in multitudinous cases no right, properly so-called, can be alleged, but only a least wrong; and further, it may be contended that in many of these cases where there can be alleged only a least wrong, it is not possible to ascertain with any precision which is the least wrong.

A great part of the perplexities in ethical speculation arise from neglect of this distinction between right and least wrong—between the absolutely right and the relatively right. And many further perplexities are due to the assumption that it can, in some way, be decided in every case which of two courses is morally obligatory.

101. The law of absolute right can take no cognizance of pain, save the cognizance implied by negation. Pain is the correlative of some species of wrong—some kind of divergence from that course of action which perfectly fulfills all requirements. If, as was shown in an early chapter, the conception of good conduct always proves, when analyzed, to be the conception of a conduct which produces a surplus of pleasure somewhere; while, conversely, the conduct conceived as bad proves always to be that which inflicts somewhere a surplus of either positive or negative pain; then the absolutely good, the absolutely right, in conduct, can be that only which produces pure pleasure—pleasure unalloyed with

pain anywhere. By implication, conduct which has any concomitant of pain, or any painful consequence, is partially
wrong; and the highest claim to be made for such conduct is,
that it is the least wrong which, under the conditions, is
possible—the relatively right.

The contents of preceding chapters imply throughout that,
considered from the evolution point of view, the acts of men
during the transition which has been, is still, and long will be,
in progress, must, in most cases, be of the kind here classed as
least wrong. In proportion to the incongruity between the
natures men inherit from the presocial state, and the requirements of social life, must be the amount of pain entailed by
their actions, either on themselves or on others. In so far as
pain is suffered, evil is inflicted; and conduct which inflicts
any evil cannot be absolutely good.

To make clear the distinction here insisted upon between
that perfect conduct which is the subject matter of absolute
ethics, and that imperfect conduct which is the subject matter
of relative ethics, some illustrations must be given.

102. Among the best examples of absolutely right actions to
be named, are those arising where the nature and the requirements have been molded to one another before social
evolution began. Two will here suffice.

Consider the relation of a healthy mother to a healthy infant. Between the two there exists a mutual dependence
which is a source of pleasure to both. In yielding its natural
food to the child, the mother receives gratification; and to the
child there comes the satisfaction of appetite—a satisfaction
which accompanies furtherance of life, growth, and increasing enjoyment. Let the relation be suspended, and on both
sides there is suffering. The mother experiences both bodily
pain and mental pain; and the painful sensation borne by the
child, brings as its results physical mischief and some damage
to the emotional nature. Thus the act is one that is to both
exclusively pleasurable, while abstention entails pain on both;
and it is consequently of the kind we here call absolutely right.

In the parental relations of the father we are furnished with a kindred example. If he is well constituted in body and mind, his boy, eager for play, finds in him a sympathetic response; and their frolics, giving mutual pleasure, not only further the child's physical welfare but strengthen that bond of good feeling between the two which makes subsequent guidance easier. And then if, repudiating the stupidities of early education as at present conceived and unhappily state-enacted, he has rational ideas of mental development, and sees that the secondhand knowledge gained through books should begin to supplement the firsthand knowledge gained by direct observation, only when a good stock of this has been acquired, he will, with active sympathy, aid in that exploration of the surrounding world which his boy pursues with delight; giving and receiving gratification from moment to moment while furthering ultimate welfare. Here, again, are actions of a kind purely pleasurable alike in their immediate and remote effects—actions absolutely right.

The intercourse of adults yields, for the reason assigned, relatively few cases that fall completely within the same category. In their transactions from hour to hour, more or less of deduction from pure gratification is caused on one or other side by imperfect fitness to the requirements. The pleasures men gain by laboring in their vocations and receiving in one form or other returns for their services, usually have the drawback that the labors are in a considerable degree displeasurable. Cases, however, do occur where the energies are so abundant that inaction is irksome; and where the daily work, not too great in duration, is of a kind appropriate to the nature; and where, as a consequence, pleasure rather than pain is a concomitant. When services yielded by such a one are paid for by another similarly adapted to his occupation, the entire transaction is of the kind we are here considering: exchange under agreement between two so constituted, becomes a means of pleasure to both, with no setoff of pain. Bearing in mind the form of nature which social discipline is producing, as shown in the contrast between savage and civilized, the implication is that ultimately men's activities at large will assume this character. Remembering that in the course of organic evolution, the means to enjoyment themselves eventually become sources of enjoyment; and that there is no form of action which may not through the development of appropriate structures become pleasurable; the inference must be that industrial activities carried on through voluntary cooperation, will in time acquire the character of absolute rightness as here conceived. Already, indeed, something like such a state has been reached among certain of those who minister to our æsthetic gratifications. The artist of genius—poet, painter, or musician—is one who obtains the means of living by acts that are directly pleasurable to him, while they yield, immediately or remotely, pleasures to others. Once more, among absolutely right acts may be named certain of those which we class as benevolent. I say certain of them, because such benevolent acts as entail submission to pain, positive or negative, that others may receive pleasure, are, by the definition, excluded. But there are benevolent acts of a kind yielding pleasure solely. Some one who has slipped is saved from falling by a bystander; a hurt is prevented and satisfaction is felt by both. A pedestrian is choosing a dangerous route, or a fellow passenger is about to alight at the wrong station, and, warned against doing so, is saved from evil: each being, as a consequence, gratified. There is a misunderstanding between friends, and one who sees how it has arisen, explains: the result being agreeable to all. Services to those around in the small affairs of life, may be, and often are, of a kind which there is equal pleasure in giving and receiving. Indeed, as was urged in the last chapter, the actions of developed altruism must habitually have this character. And so, in countless ways suggested by these few, men may add to one another's happiness without anywhere producing unhappiness—ways which are therefore absolutely right.

In contrast with these consider the many actions which from hour to hour are gone through, now with an accompaniment of some pain to the actor and now bringing results that are partially painful to others, but which nevertheless are imperative. As implied by antithesis with cases above referred to, the wearisomeness of productive labor as ordinarily pursued, renders it in so far wrong; but then far greater suffering would result, both to the laborer and his family, and therefore far greater wrong would be done, were this wearisomeness not borne. Though the pains which the care of many children entail on a mother, form a considerable setoff from the pleasures secured by them to her children and herself; yet the miseries, immediate and remote, which neglect would entail so far exceed them, that submission to such pains up to the limit of physical ability to bear them, becomes morally imperative as being the least wrong. A servant who fails to fulfill an agreement in respect of work, or who is perpetually breaking crockery, or who pilfers, may have to suffer pain from being discharged; but since the evil is to be borne by all concerned if incapacity or misconduct is tolerated, not in one case only but habitually, must be much greater, such infliction of pain is warranted as a means to preventing greater pain. Withdrawal of custom from a tradesman whose charges are too high, or whose commodities are inferior, or who gives short measure, or who is unpunctual, decreases his welfare, and perhaps injures his belongings; but as saving him from these evils would imply bearing the evils his conduct causes, and as such regard for his well-being would imply disregard of the well-being of some more worthy or more efficient tradesman to whom the custom would else go, and as, chiefly, general adoption of the implied course, having the effect that the inferior would not suffer from their inferiority nor the superior gain by their superiority, would produce universal misery, withdrawal is justified—the act is relatively right.

103. I pass now to the second of the two propositions above enunciated. After recognizing the truth that a large part of human conduct is not absolutely right, but only relatively right, we have to recognize the further truth that in many cases where there is no absolutely right course, but only

courses that are more or less wrong, it is not possible to say which is the least wrong. Recurrence to the instances just given will show this.

There is a point up to which it is relatively right for a parent to carry self-sacrifice for the benefit of offspring; and there is a point beyond which self-sacrifice cannot be pushed without bringing, not only on himself or herself but also on the family, evils greater than those to be prevented by the self-sacrifice. Who shall say where this point is? Depending on the constitutions and needs of those concerned, it is in no two cases the same, and cannot be by anyone more than guessed. The transgressions or shortcomings of a servant vary from the trivial to the grave, and the evils which discharge may bring range through countless degrees from slight to serious. The penalty may be inflicted for a very small offense, and then there is wrong done; or after numerous grave offenses it may not be inflicted, and again there is wrong done. How shall be determined the degree of transgression beyond which to discharge is less wrong than not to discharge? In like manner with the shopkeeper's misdemeanors. No one can sum up either the amount of positive and negative pain which tolerating them involves, or the amount of positive and negative pain involved by not tolerating them; and in medium cases no one can say where the one exceeds the other.

In men's wider relations frequently occur circumstances under which a decision one or other way is imperative, and yet under which not even the most sensitive conscience helped by the clearest judgment, can decide which of the alternatives is relatively right. Two examples will suffice. Here is a merchant who loses by the failure of a man indebted to him. Unless he gets help he himself will fail; and if he fails he will bring disaster not only on his family but on all who have given him credit. Even if by borrowing he is enabled to meet immediate engagements, he is not safe; for the time is one of panic, and others of his debtors by going to the wall may put him in further difficulties. Shall he ask a friend for a loan? On the one hand, is it not wrong forthwith to bring on himself, his family, and those who have business relations with him, the evils of his failure? On the other hand, is it not wrong to hypothecate the property of his friend, and lead him too, with his belongings and dependents, into similar risks? The loan would probably tide him over his difficulty; in which case would it not be unjust to his creditors did he refrain from asking it? Contrariwise, the loan would very possibly fail to stave off his bankruptcy; in which case is not his action in trying to obtain it, practically fraudulent? Though in extreme cases it may be easy to say which course is the least wrong, how is it possible in all those medium cases where even by the keenest man of business the contingencies cannot be calculated? Take, again, the difficulties that not infrequently arise from antagonism between family duties and social duties. Here is a tenant farmer whose political principles prompt him to vote in opposition to his landlord. If, being a Liberal, he votes for a Conservative, not only does he by his act say that he thinks what he does not think, but he may perhaps assist what he regards as bad legislation: his vote may by chance turn the election, and on a Parliamentary division a single member may decide the fate of a measure. Even neglecting, as too improbable, such serious consequences, there is the manifest truth that if all who hold like views with himself, are similarly deterred from electoral expression of them, there must result a different balance of power and a different national policy: making it clear that only by adherence of all to their political principles, can the policy he thinks right be maintained. But now, on the other hand, how can he absolve himself from responsibility for the evils which those depending on him may suffer if he fulfills what appears to be a peremptory public duty? Is not his duty to his children even more peremptory? Does not the family precede the state; and does not the welfare of the state depend on the welfare of the family? May he, then, take a course which, if the threats uttered are carried out, will eject him from his farm; and so cause inability, perhaps temporary perhaps prolonged, to feed his children. The contingent evils are infinitely varied in their ratios. In one case the imperativeness of the public duty is great and the evil that may come on dependents small; in another case the political issue is of trivial moment and the possible injury which the family may suffer is great; and between these extremes there are all gradations. Further, the degrees of probability of each result, public and private, ranging from the nearly certain to the almost impossible. Admitting, then, that it is wrong to act in a way likely to injure the state; and admitting that it is wrong to act in a way likely to injure the family; we have to recognize the fact that in countless cases no one can decide by which of the alternative courses the least wrong is likely to be done.

These instances will sufficiently show that in conduct at large, including men's dealings with themselves, with their families, with their friends, with their debtors and creditors, and with the public, it usually happens that whatever course is taken entails some pain somewhere; forming a deduction from the pleasure achieved, and making the course in so far not absolutely right. Further, they will show that throughout a considerable part of conduct, no guiding principle, no method of estimation, enables us to say whether a proposed course is even relatively right; as causing, proximately and remotely, specially and generally, the greatest surplus of good over evil.

104. And now we are prepared for dealing in a systematic way with the distinction between absolute ethics and relative ethics.

Scientific truths, of whatever order, are reached by eliminating perturbing or conflicting factors, and recognizing only fundamental factors. When, by dealing with fundamental factors in the abstract, not as presented in actual phenomena but as presented in ideal separation, general laws have been ascertained, it becomes possible to draw inferences in concrete cases by taking into account incidental factors. But it is only by first ignoring these and recognizing the essential elements alone, that we can discover the essential truths sought. Take, in illustration, the progress of mechanics from its empirical form to its rational form.

All have occasional experience of the fact that a person

pushed on one side beyond a certain degree, loses his balance and falls. It is observed that a stone flung or an arrow shot, does not proceed in a straight line, but comes to the earth after pursuing a course which deviates more and more from its original course. When trying to break a stick across the knee, it is found that success is easier if the stick is seized at considerable distances from the knee on each side than if seized close to the knee. Daily use of a spear draws attention to the truth that by thrusting its point under a stone and depressing the shaft, the stone may be raised the more readily the further away the hand is towards the end. Here, then, are sundry experiences, eventually grouped into empirical generalizations, which serve to guide conduct in certain simple cases. How does mechanical science evolve from these experiences? To reach a formula expressing the powers of the lever, it supposes a lever which does not, like the stick, admit of being bent, but is absolutely rigid; and it supposes a fulcrum not having a broad surface, like that of one ordinarily used, but a fulcrum without breadth; and it supposes that the weight to be raised bears on a definite point, instead of bearing over a considerable portion of the lever. Similarly with the leaning body, which, passing a certain inclination, overbalances. Before the truth respecting the relations of center of gravity and base can be formulated, it must be assumed that the surface on which the body stands is unyielding; that the edge of the body itself is unyielding; and that its mass, while made to lean more and more, does not change its form—conditions not fulfilled in the cases commonly observed. And so, too, is it with the projectile: determination of its course by deduction from mechanical laws, primarily ignores all deviations caused by its shape and by the resistance of the air. The science of rational mechanics is a science which consists of such ideal truths, and can come into existence only by thus dealing with ideal cases. It remains impossible so long as attention is restricted to concrete cases presenting all the complications of friction, plasticity, and so forth. But now, after disentangling certain fundamental mechanical truths, it becomes possible by their help to guide actions better; and it becomes possible to guide them still better when, as presently happens, the complicating elements from which they have been disentangled are themselves taken into account. At an advanced stage, the modifying effects of friction are allowed for, and the inferences are qualified to the requisite extent. The theory of the pulley is corrected in its application to actual cases by recognizing the rigidity of cordage; the effects of which are formulated. The stabilities of masses, determinable in the abstract by reference to the centers of gravity of the masses in relation to the bases, come to be determined in the concrete by including also their characters in respect of cohesion. The courses of projectiles having been theoretically settled as though they moved through a vacuum, are afterwards settled in more exact correspondence with fact by taking into account atmospheric resistance. And thus we see illustrated the relation between certain absolute truths of mechanical science, and certain relative truths which involve them. We are shown that no scientific establishment of relative truths is possible, until the absolute truths have been formulated independently. We see that mechanical science fitted for dealing with the real, can arise only after ideal mechanical science has arisen.

All this holds of moral science. As by early and rude experiences there were inductively reached, vague but partially true notions respecting the overbalancing of bodies, the motions of missiles, the actions of levers; so by early and rude experiences there were inductively reached, vague but partially true notions respecting the effects of men's behavior on themselves, on one another, and on society: to a certain extent serving in the last case, as in the first, for the guidance of conduct. Moreover, as this rudimentary mechanical knowledge, though still remaining empirical, becomes during early stages of civilization at once more definite and more extensive; so during early stages of civilization these ethical ideas, still retaining their empirical character, increase in precision and multiplicity. But just as we have seen that mechanical knowledge of the empirical sort can evolve into mechanical science, only by first omitting all qualifying circumstances, and generalizing in absolute ways the fundamental laws of forces; so here we have to see that empirical ethics can evolve into rational ethics only by first neglecting all complicating incidents, and formulating the laws of right action apart from the obscuring effects of special conditions. And the final implication is that just as the system of mechanical truths, conceived in ideal separation as absolute, becomes applicable to real mechanical problems in such way that making allowance for all incidental circumstances there can be reached conclusions far nearer to the truth than could otherwise be reached; so, a system of ideal ethical truths, expressing the absolutely right, will be applicable to the questions of our transitional state in such ways that, allowing for the friction of an incomplete life and imperfection of existing natures, we may ascertain with approximate correctness what is the relatively right.

105. In a chapter entitled "Definition of Morality" in *Social Statics*, I contended that the moral law, properly so-called, is the law of the perfect man—is the formula of ideal conduct—is the statement in all cases of that which should be, and cannot recognize in its propositions any elements implying existence of that which should not be. Instancing questions concerning the right course to be taken in cases where wrong has already been done, I alleged that the answers to such questions cannot be given "on purely ethical principles." I argued that—

> No conclusions can lay claim to absolute truth, but such as depend upon truths that are themselves absolute. Before there can be exactness in an inference, there must be exactness in the antecedent propositions. A geometrician requires that the straight lines with which he deals shall be veritably straight: and that his circles, and ellipses, and parabolas shall agree with precise definitions—shall perfectly and invariably answer to specified equations. If you put to him a question in which these conditions are not complied with, he tells you that it cannot be answered. So likewise is it with the philosophical moralist. He treats solely of the *straight* man. He determines the properties of the straight man; describes how the straight man comports himself; shows in what relationship he stands to other straight men; shows how a community of straight men is constituted. Any deviation from

strict rectitude he is obliged wholly to ignore. It cannot be admitted into his premises without vitiating all his conclusions. A problem in which a *crooked* man forms one of the elements is insoluble by him.

Referring to this view, specifically in the first edition of the *Methods of Ethics* but more generally in the second edition, Mr. Sidgwick says:

> Those who take this view adduce the analogy of Geometry to show that Ethics ought to deal with ideally perfect human relations, just as Geometry treats of ideally perfect lines and circles. But the most irregular line has definite spatial relations with which Geometry does not refuse to deal: though of course they are more complex than those of a straight line. So in Astronomy, it would be more convenient for purposes of study if the stars moved in circles, as was once believed: but the fact that they move not in circles but in ellipses, and even in imperfect and perturbed ellipses, does not take them out of the sphere of scientific investigation: by patience and industry we have learnt how to reduce to principles and calculate even these more complicated motions. It is, no doubt, a convenient artifice for purposes of instruction to assume that the planets move in perfect ellipses (or even—at an earlier stage of study—in circles): we thus allow the individual's knowledge to pass through the same gradations in accuracy as that of the race has done. But what we want, as astronomers, to know is the actual motion of the stars and its causes: and similarly as moralists we naturally inquire what ought to be done in the actual world in which we live. [P. 19, 2nd ed.]

Beginning with the first of these two statements, which concerns geometry, I must confess myself surprised to find my propositions called in question; and after full consideration I remain at a loss to understand Mr. Sidgwick's mode of viewing the matter. When, in a sentence preceding those quoted above, I remarked on the impossibility of solving "mathematically a series of problems respecting crooked lines and broken-backed curves," it never occurred to me that I should be met by the direct assertion that "geometry does not refuse to deal" with "the most irregular line." Mr. Sidgwick states that an irregular line, say such as a child makes in scribbling, has "definite spatial relations." What meaning does he here give to the word "definite." If he means that its relations to space at large are definite in the sense that by an infinite intelligence they would be definable; the reply is that to an infinite intelligence all spatial relations would be definable: there could be no indefinite spatial relations—the word "definite" thus ceasing to mark any distinction. If, on the other hand, when saying that an irregular line has "definite spatial relations," he means relations knowable definitely by human intelligence; there still comes the question, how is the word "definite" to be understood? Surely anything distinguished as definite admits of being defined; but how can we define an irregular line? And if we cannot define the irregular line itself, how can we know its "spatial relations" definitely? And how, in the absence of definition, can geometry deal with it? If Mr. Sidgwick means that it can be dealt with by the "method of limits," then the reply is that in such case, not the line itself is dealt with geometrically, but certain definite lines artificially put in quasi-definite relations to it: the indefinite becomes cognizable only through the medium of the hypothetically definite.

Turning to the second illustration, the rejoinder to be made is that in so far as it concerns the relations between the ideal and the real, the analogy drawn does not shake but strengthens my argument. For whether considered under its geometrical or under its dynamical aspect, and whether considered in the necessary order of its development or in the order historically displayed, astronomy shows us throughout, that truths respecting simple, theoretically exact relations, must be ascertained before truths respecting the complex and practically inexact relations that actually exist, can be ascertained. As applied to the interpretation of planetary movements, we see that the theory of cycles and epicycles was based on preexisting knowledge of the circle: the properties of an ideal curve having been learned, a power was acquired of giving some expression to the celestial motions. We see that the Copernican interpretation expressed the facts in terms of circular movements otherwise distributed and combined. We see that Kepler's advance from the conception of circular movements to the conception of elliptic movements, was made possible by comparing the facts as they are with the facts as they would be were the movements circular. We see that the subsequently learned deviations from elliptic movements, were learned only through the presupposition that the movements are elliptical. And we see, lastly, that even now predictions concerning the exact positions of planets, after taking account of perturbations, imply constant references to ellipses that are regarded as their normal or average orbits for the time being. Thus, ascertainment of the actual truths has been made possible only by preascertainment of certain ideal truths. To be convinced that by no other course could the actual truths have been ascertained, it needs only to suppose any one saying that it did not concern him, as an astronomer, to know anything about the properties of circles and ellipses, but that he had to deal with the solar system as it exists, to which end it was his business to observe and tabulate positions and directions and to be guided by the facts as he found them. So, too, is it if we look at the development of dynamical astronomy. The first proposition in Newton's *Principia* deals with the movement of a single body round a single center of force; and the phenomena of central motion are first formulated in a case which is not simply ideal, but in which there is no specification of the force concerned: detachment from the real is the greatest possible. Again, postulating a principle of action conforming to an ideal law, the theory of gravitation deals with the several problems of the solar system in fictitious detachment from the rest; and it makes certain fictitious assumptions, such as that the mass of each body concerned is concentrated in its center of gravity. Only later, after establishing the leading truths by this artifice of disentangling the major factors from the minor factors, is the theory applied to the actual problems in their ascending degrees of complexity; taking in more and more of the minor factors. And if we ask whether the dynamics of the solar system could have been established in any other way, we see that here, too, simple truths holding under ideal conditions, have to be ascertained before real truths existing under complex conditions can be ascertained.

The alleged necessary precedence of absolute ethics over relative ethics is thus, I think, further elucidated. One who has followed the general argument thus far, will not deny that an ideal social being may be conceived as so constituted that his spontaneous activities are congruous with the conditions imposed by the social environment formed by other such beings. In many places, and in various ways, I have argued that conformably with the laws of evolution in general, and conformably with the laws of organization in particular, there has been, and is, in progress, an adaptation of humanity to the social state, changing it in the direction of such as ideal congruity. And the corollary before drawn and here repeated, is that the ultimate man is one in whom this process has gone so far as to produce a correspondence between all the promptings of his nature and all the requirements of his life as carried on in society. If so, it is a necessary implication that there exists an ideal code of conduct formulating the behavior of the completely adapted man in the completely evolved society. Such a code is that here called absolute ethics as distinguished from relative ethics—a code the injunctions of which are alone to be considered as absolutely right in contrast with those that are relatively right or least wrong; and which, as a system of ideal conduct, is to serve as a standard for our guidance in solving, as well as we can, the problems of real conduct.

105a. A clear conception of this matter is so important that I must be excused for bringing in aid of it a further illustration, more obviously appropriate as being furnished by organic science instead of by inorganic science. The relation between morality proper and morality as commonly conceived, is analogous to the relation between physiology and pathology; and the course usually pursued by moralists is much like the course of one who studies pathology without previous study of physiology.

Physiology describes the various functions which, as combined, constitute and maintain life; and in treating of them it assumes that they are severally performed in right ways, in due amounts, and in proper order: it recognizes only healthy functions. If it explains digestion, it supposes that the heart is supplying blood and that the visceral nervous system is stimulating the organs immediately concerned. If it gives a theory of the circulation, it assumes that blood has been produced by the combined actions of the structures devoted to its production, and that it is properly aerated. If the relations between respiration and the vital processes at large are interpreted, it is on the presupposition that the heart goes on sending blood, not only to the lungs and to certain nervous centers, but to the diaphragm and intercostal muscles. Physiology ignores failures in the actions of these several organs. It takes no account of imperfections, it neglects derangements, it does not recognize pain, it knows nothing of vital wrong. It simply formulates that which goes on as a result of complete adaptation of all parts to all needs. That is to say, in relation to the inner actions constituting bodily life, physiological theory has a position like that which ethical theory, under its absolute form as above conceived, has to the outer actions constituting conduct. The moment cognizance is taken of excess of function, or arrest of function, or defect of function, with the resulting evil, physiology passes into pathology. We begin now to take account of wrong actions in the inner life analogous to the wrong actions in the outer life taken account of by ordinary theories of morals.

The antithesis thus drawn, however, is but preliminary. After observing the fact that there is a science of vital actions normally carried on, which ignores abnormal actions; we have more especially to observe that the science of abnormal actions can reach such definiteness as is possible to it, only on condition that the science of normal actions has previously become definite; or rather let us say that pathological science depends for its advances on previous advances made by physiological science. The very conception of disordered action implies a preconception of well-ordered action. Before it can be decided that the heart is beating faster or slower than it should, its healthy rate of beating must be learned; before the pulse can be recognized as too weak or too strong, its proper strength must be known; and so throughout. Even the rudest and most empirical ideas of diseases, presuppose ideas of the healthy states from which they are deviations; and obviously the diagnosis of diseases can become scientific, only as fast as there arises scientific knowledge of organic actions that are undiseased.

Similarly, then, is it with the relation between absolute morality, or the law of perfect right in human conduct, and relative morality which, recognizing wrong in human conduct, has to decide in what way the wrong deviates from the right, and how the right is to be most nearly approached. When, formulating normal conduct in an ideal society, we have reached a science of absolute ethics, we have simultaneously reached a science which, when used to interpret the phenomena of real societies in their transitional states, full of the miseries due to nonadaptation (which we may call pathological states) enables us to form approximately true conclusions respecting the natures of the abnormalities, and the courses which tend most in the direction of the normal.

106. And now let it be observed that the conception of ethics thus set forth, strange as many will think it, is one which really lies latent in the beliefs of moralists at large. Though not definitely acknowledged it is vaguely implied in many of their propositions.

From early times downwards we find in ethical speculations, references to the ideal man, his acts, his feelings, his judgments. When Socrates said that well-doing is the thing to be chiefly studied, and that he achieved it who devoted to the study searching and labor, he made the actions of the superior man his standard, since he gave no other. Plato, in *Minos*, asserts that "the authoritative rescripts or laws are those laid down by the artists or men of knowledge in that department"; and the doctrine contained in *Laches* is that only "the One Wise Man" can estimate the good or evil, or the comparative value of two alternative ends in each individual case": an ideal man is postulated. Aristotle says: "For it is the man whose condition, whether moral or bodily, is in each case perfect who in each case judges rightly, and at once perceives the truth. . . . And herein it is that the perfect man may be said to differ most widely from all others, in that in all such cases he at once perceives the truth, being, as it were, the rule and measure of its application." While observing that the Stoics, like other ancient philosophers, failing to distinguish properly between intellect and feeling, identified wisdom with goodness, we see that they, too, made the perfect man the measure of rectitude. And Epicurus, also, regards the wise man as the only one who can achieve a happy life—"he alone knows how to do the right thing in the right way."

If in modern times, influenced by theological dogmas concerning human sinfulness, and by a theory of divinely prescribed conduct, moralists have not so frequently referred to an ideal, yet various references are traceable. We may see one in the dictum of Kant—"Act only on that maxim whereby thou canst at the same time will that it should become a universal law." For this implies the thought of a society in which the maxim is acted upon by all and universal benefit recognized as the effect: there is a conception of ideal conduct under ideal conditions. And though Mr. Sidgwick, in the quotation above made from him, implies that ethics is concerned with man as he is, rather than with man as he should be; yet, in elsewhere speaking of ethics as dealing with conduct as it should be, rather than with conduct as it is, he postulates ideal conduct and indirectly the ideal man. On his first page, speaking of ethics along with jurisprudence and politics, he says that they are distinguished "by the characteristic that they attempt to determine not the actual but the ideal—what ought to exist, not what does exist."

It requires only that these various conceptions of an ideal conduct and of an ideal humanity, should be made consistent and definite, to bring them into agreement with the conception above set forth. At present such conceptions are habitually vague. The ideal man having been conceived in terms of the current morality, is thereupon erected into a moral standard by which the goodness of actions may be judged; and the reasoning becomes circular. To make the ideal man serve as a standard, he has to be defined in terms of the conditions which his nature fulfills—in terms of those objective requirements which must be met before conduct can be right; and the common defect of these conceptions of the ideal man, is that they suppose him out of relation to such conditions.

All the above references to him, direct or indirect, imply that the ideal man is supposed to live and act under existing social conditions. The tacit inquiry is, not what his actions would be under circumstances altogether changed, but what they would be under present circumstances. And this inquiry is futile for two reasons. The coexistence of a perfect man and an imperfect society is impossible; and could the two coexist, the resulting conduct would not furnish the ethical standard sought. In the first place, given the laws of life as they are, and a man of ideal nature cannot be produced in a society consisting of men having natures remote from the ideal. As well might we expect a child of English type to be born among Negroes, as expect that among the organically immoral, one who is organically moral will arise. Unless it be denied that character results from inherited structure, it must be admitted that since, in any society, each individual descends from a stock which, traced back a few generations, ramifies everywhere through the society, and participates in its average nature, there must, nothwithstanding marked individual diversities, be preserved such community as prevents anyone from reaching an ideal form while the rest remain far below it. In the second place, ideal conduct such as ethical theory is concerned with, is not possible for the ideal man in the midst of men otherwise constituted. An absolutely just or perfectly sympathetic person, could not live and act according to his nature in a tribe of cannibals. Among people who are treacherous and utterly without scruple, entire truthfulness and openness must bring ruin. If all around recognize only the law of the strongest, one whose nature will not allow him to inflict pain on others, must go to the wall. There requires a certain congruity between the conduct of each member of a society and other's conduct. A mode of action entirely alien to the prevailing modes of action, cannot be successfully per-sisted in—must eventuate in death itself, or posterity, or both.

Hence it is manifest that we must consider the ideal man as existing in the ideal social state. On the evolution-hypothesis, the two presuppose one another; and only when they coexist, can there exist that ideal conduct which absolute ethics has to formulate, and which relative ethics has to take as the stan-dard by which to estimate divergencies from right, or degrees of wrong.

CHAPTER 16

The Scope of Ethics

107. $\quad$ At the outset it was shown that as the conduct with which ethics deals, is a part of conduct at large, conduct at large must be understood before this part can be understood. After taking a general view of conduct, not human only but subhuman, and not only as existing but as evolving, we saw that ethics has for its subject matter the most highly evolved conduct as displayed by the most highly evolved being, man—is a specification of those traits which his conduct assumes on reaching its limit of evolution. Conceived thus as comprehending the laws of right living at large, ethics has a wider field than is commonly assigned to it. Beyond the conduct commonly approved or reprobated as right or wrong, it includes all conduct which furthers or hinders, in either direct or indirect ways, the welfare of self or others.

As foregoing chapters in various places imply, the entire field of ethics includes the two great divisions, personal and social. There is a class of actions directed to personal ends, which are to be judged in their relations to personal well-being, considered apart from the well-being of others: though they secondarily affect fellow men these primarily affect the agent himself, and must be classed as intrinsically right or wrong according to their beneficial or detrimental effects on him. There are actions of another class which affect fellow men immediately and remotely, and which, though their results to self are not to be ignored, must be judged as good or bad mainly by their results to others. Actions of this last class fall into two groups. Those of the one group achieve ends in ways that do or do not unduly interfere with the pursuit of ends by others—actions which, because of this difference, we call respectively unjust or just. Those forming the other group are of a kind which influence the states of others without directly interfering with the relations between their labors and the results, in one way or the other—actions which we speak of as beneficent or maleficent. And the conduct which we regard as beneficent is itself subdivisible according as it shows us a self-repression to avoid giving pain, or an expenditure of effort to give pleasure—negative beneficence and positive beneficence.

Each of these divisions and subdivisions has to be considered first as a part of absolute ethics and then as a part of relative ethics. Having seen what its injunctions must be for the ideal man under the implied ideal conditions, we shall be prepared to see how such injunctions are to be most nearly fulfilled by actual men under existing conditions.

108. For reasons already pointed out, a code of perfect personal conduct can never be made definite. Many forms of life, diverging from one another in considerable degrees, may be so carried on in society as entirely to fulfill the conditions to harmonious cooperation. And if various types of men adapted to various types of activities, may thus lead lives that are severally complete after their kinds, no specific statement of the activities universally required for personal well-being is possible.

But though the particular requirements to be fulfilled for perfect individual well-being, must vary along with variations in the material conditions of each society, certain general requirements have to be fulfilled by the individuals of all societies. An average balance between waste and nutrition has universally to be preserved. Normal vitality implies a relation between activity and rest falling within moderate limits of variation. Continuance of the society depends on satisfaction of those primarily personal needs which result in marriage and parenthood. Perfection of individual life hence implies certain modes of action which are approximately alike in all cases, and which therefore become part of the subject matter of ethics.

That it is possible to reduce even this restricted part to scientific definiteness, can scarcely be said. But ethical requirements may here be to such extent affiliated upon physical necessities, as to give them a partially scientific authority. It is clear that between the expenditure of bodily substance in vital activities, and the taking in of materials from which this substance may be renewed, there is a direct relation. It is clear, too, that there is a direct relation between the wasting of tissue by effort, and the need for those cessations of effort during which repair may overtake waste. Nor is it less clear that between the rate of mortality and the rate of multiplication in any society, there is a relation such that the last must reach a certain level before it can balance the first, and prevent disappearance of the society. And it may be inferred that pursuits of other leading ends are, in like manner, determined by certain natural necessities, and from these derive their ethical sanctions. That it will ever be practicable to lay down precise rules for private conduct in conformity with such requirements, may be doubted. But the function of absolute ethics in relation to private conduct will have been discharged, when it has produced the warrant for its requirements as generally expressed; when it has shown the imperativeness of obedience to them; and when it has thus taught the need for deliberately considering whether the conduct fulfills them as well as may be.

Under the ethics of personal conduct considered in relation to existing conditions, have to come all questions concerning the degree in which immediate personal welfare has to be

postponed, either to ultimate personal welfare or to the welfare of others. As now carried on, life hourly sets the claims of
present self against the claims of future self, and hourly brings
individual interests face to face with the interests of other
individuals, taken singly or as associated. In many of such
cases the decisions can be nothing more than compromises;
and ethical science, here necessarily empirical, can do no
more than aid in making compromises that are the least objectionable. To arrive at the best compromise in any case, implies
correct conceptions of the alternative results of this or that
course. And, consequently, in so far as the absolute ethics of
individual conduct can be made definite, it must help us to
decide between conflicting personal requirements, and also
between the needs for asserting self and the needs for subordinating self.

109. From that division of ethics which deals with the right
regulation of private conduct, considered apart from the effects directly produced on others, we pass now to that division of ethics which, considering exclusively the effects of
conduct on others, treats of the right regulation of it with a
view to such effects.

The first set of regulations coming under this head are those
concerning what we distinguish as justice. Individual life is
possible only on condition that each organ is paid for its action
by an equivalent of blood, while the organism as a whole
obtains from the environment assimilable matters that compensate for its efforts; and the mutual dependence of parts in
the social organism, necessitates that, alike for its total life and
the lives of its units, there similarly shall be maintained a due
proportion between returns and labors: the natural relation
between work and welfare shall be preserved intact. Justice,
which formulates the range of conduct and limitations to
conduct hence arising, is at once the most important division
of ethics and the division which admits of the greatest definiteness. That principle of equivalence which meets us when
we seek its roots in the laws of individual life, involves the

idea of *measure;* and on passing to social life, the same principle introduces us to the conception of equity or *equalness,* in the relations of citizens to one another: the elements of the questions arising are *quantitative,* and hence the solutions assume a more scientific form. Though, having to recognize differences among individuals due to age, sex, or other cause, we cannot regard the members of a society as absolutely equal, and therefore cannot deal with problems growing out of their relations with that precision which absolute equality might make possible; yet, considering them as approximately equal in virtue of their common human nature, and dealing with questions of equity on this supposition, we may reach conclusions of a sufficiently definite kind.

This division of ethics considered under its absolute form, has to define the equitable relations among perfect individuals who limit one another's spheres of action by coexisting, and who achieve their ends by cooperation. It has to do much more than this. Beyond justice between man and man, justice between each man and the aggregate of men has to be dealt with by it. The relations between the individual and the state, considered as representing all individuals, have to be deduced—an important and a relatively difficult matter. What is the ethical warrant for governmental authority? To what ends may it be legitimately exercised? How far may it rightly be carried? Up to what point is the citizen bound to recognize the collective decisions of other citizens, and beyond what point may he properly refuse to obey them.

These relations, private and public, considered as maintained under ideal conditions, having been formulated, there come to be dealt with the analogous relations under real conditions—absolute justice being the standard, relative justice has to be determined by considering how near an approach may, under present circumstances, be made to it. As already implied in various places, it is impossible during stages of transition which necessitate ever-changing compromises, to fulfill the dictates of absolute equity; and nothing beyond empirical judgments can be formed of the extent to which they may be, at any given time, fulfilled. While war continues and injustice is done between societies, there cannot be anything like complete justice within each society. Militant organization no less than militant action, is irreconcilable with pure equity; and the inequity implied by it inevitably ramifies throughout all social relations. But there is at every stage in social evolution, a certain range of variation within which it is possible to approach nearer to, or diverge further from, the requirements of absolute equity. Hence these requirements have ever to be kept in view that relative equity may be ascertained.

110. Of the two subdivisions into which beneficence falls, the negative and the positive, neither can be specialized. Under ideal conditions the first of them has but a nominal existence; and the second of them passes largely into a transfigured form admitting of but general definition.

In the conduct of the ideal man among ideal men, that self-regulation which has for its motive to avoid giving pain, practically disappears. No one having feelings which prompt acts that disagreeably affect others, there can exist no code of restraints referring to this division of conduct.

But though negative beneficence is only a nominal part of absolute ethics, it is an actual and considerable part of relative ethics. For while men's natures remain imperfectly adapted to social life, there must continue in them impulses which, causing in some cases the actions we name unjust, cause in other cases the actions we name unkind—unkind now in deed and now in word; and in respect of these modes of behavior which, though not aggressive, give pain, there arise numerous and complicated problems. Pain is sometimes given to others simply by maintaining an equitable claim; pain is at other times given by refusing a request; and again at other times by maintaining an opinion. In these and numerous cases suggested by them, there have to be answered the questions whether, to avoid inflicting pain, personal feelings should be sacrificed, and how far sacrificed. Again, in cases of another class, pain is given not by a passive course but by an active course. How far shall a person who has misbehaved be grieved by showing aversion to him? Shall one whose action is to be reprobated, have the reprobation expressed to him or shall nothing be said? Is it right to annoy by condemning a prejudice which another displays? These and kindred queries have to be answered after taking into account the immediate pain given, the possible benefit caused by giving it, and the possible evil caused by not giving it. In solving problems of this class, the only help absolute ethics gives, is by enforcing the consideration that inflicting more pain than is necessitated by proper self-regard, or by desire for another's benefit, or by the maintenance of a general principle, is unwarranted.

Of positive beneficence under its absolute form nothing more specific can be said than that it must become coextensive with whatever sphere remains for it; aiding to complete the life of each as a recipient of services and to exalt the life of each as a renderer of services. As with a developed humanity the desire for it by everyone will so increase, and the sphere for exercise of it so decrease, as to involve an altruistic competition, analogous to the existing egoistic competition, it may be that absolute ethics will eventually include what we before called a higher equity, prescribing the mutual limitations of altruistic activities.

Under its relative form, positive beneficence presents numerous problems, alike important and difficult, admitting only of empirical solutions. How far is self-sacrifice for another's benefit to be carried in each case?—a question which must be answered differently according to the character of the other, the needs of the other, and the various claims of self and belongings which have to be met. To what extent under given circumstances shall private welfare be subordinated to public welfare?—a question to be answered after considering the importance of the end and the seriousness of the sacrifice. What benefit and what detriment will result from gratuitous aid yielded to another?—a question in each case implying an estimate of probabilities. Is there any unfair treatment of sundry others, involved by more than fair treatment of this one other? Up to what limit may help be given to the existing generation of the inferior, without entailing mischief on future generations of the superior? Evidently to these and many kindred questions included in this division of relative ethics, approximately true answers only can be given.

But though here absolute ethics, by the standard it supplies, does not greatly aid relative ethics, yet, as in other cases, it aids somewhat by keeping before consciousness an ideal conciliation of the various claims involved; and by suggesting the search for such compromise among them, as shall not disregard any, but shall satisfy all to the greatest extent practicable.

APPENDIX TO PART I

The Conciliation

[*While searching for some memoranda, I have discovered the rough draft of a chapter belonging to this work. Whether it was that, when writing out at length the part of the argument it belongs to, I was led to put aside this chapter as having a form unfitting it for incorporation, or whether it was that I had mislaid it, I cannot now remember. The last supposition is, I think, the more probable; since this rough draft contains matter which, had it been before me, I should have embodied.*

Partly because certain of the arguments it contains yield further support to the general conclusion drawn, and partly because such of its arguments as answer to those included in the text are set forth in another way, I have decided here to append this omitted chapter. "The Data of Ethics," as finally elaborated, was based on a manuscript dictated to a shorthand amanuensis, and written out by him in a series of copybooks, one to each chapter: an arrangement which, I suspect, accidentally led to the omission indicated. As, on reading this rough draft, I find that it is fairly coherent and expressed with adequate clearness, I have thought it well to print it just as it stands. In a few places where the shorthand writer failed to interpret his notes, I have supplied, in square brackets, what I suppose were the missing words; and in some other cases I have corrected errors that were obviously due to misunderstanding or to mistranscription.]

317

In the last two chapters have been enunciated the claims of egoism and altruism respectively. Each has been insisted upon so strongly that, taken alone, it would seem to go far toward the repudiation of the other. The usual tendency in ethical speculation is not to recognize in full both factors, as essential to human happiness, but to insist almost exclusively upon the one or the other. Or rather I should say that, in almost all cases, ignoring the egoistic factor, the insistence has been upon the altruistic one.

At first sight it seems that there is some inconsistency in the position here taken. To enunciate the legitimacy of egoism in the way done, possibly caused the reader to think that the higher morality was being denied by the assertion of a system of selfishness. Contrariwise, reading by itself the subsequent chapter, he might, if one who had before appreciated the claims of egoism, be led to suppose that egoism was being ignored, and the tacit assertion made that egoistic grati-fications were to be achieved through fulfillment of altruistic obligations. And finding that each of the chapters to a consid-erable extent seems to conflict with the other, he will incline to allege an incongruity of doctrine. If he does not go farther, he will at any rate be inclined to say that the doctrine implies a necessary incompleteness—implies that there can be no such thing as a life in which all requirements are fully satisfied. That process of evolution set forth in preceding chapters, will ap-pear to be negatived by such incompatibility between the conflicting claims of self and others; so that it cannot end in an entire equilibrium between human nature and its conditions. Taking by itself the chapter on egoism versus altruism, it would seem that for the imperative welfare of the individual, and of those belonging to him, and of those afterwards de-scending from him, there must be such subordination of the claims of others, as from time to time deducts from their welfare or diminishes the total happiness. On the other hand, reading by itself the chapter on altruism versus egoism, it seems to be an inevitable corollary that self-abnegation—that is, the abandonment of a gratification or the submission to a pain due to the craving unsatisfied, is more or less demanded of all, that there may be maintained that social state which, by its prosperity, conduces to the egoistic welfare of each, and that there may be also achieved the character and the capacity which are the means to their egoistic gratifications; and that thus the pursuit of altruistic ends must of necessity entail egoistic deprivations. Or, to put the matter briefly, it seems to be clear that there must be everywhere a certain large percentage of sacrifice—sacrifice of others to self or sacrifice of self to others; and that, in so far as there is sacrifice, there is a submission to pain, positive or negative, and therefore a necessary failure in the working out of [a] nature capable of complete life—that is, complete happiness.

Here there remains to be shown the invalidity of this conclusion. On tracing upwards the process of evolution to a higher stage, we shall see that this conflict between egoism and altruism, which now constitutes the crux in all ethical speculation, is transitional, and is in process of gradual disappearance.

Already in seeking clues for the interpretation of the future, we have gone back to the past; and that we may understand the past have carried our inquiry back to the beginning. In seeking a right interpretation of egoism we set out with life in its earlier stages, and observed the truth that a predominant egoism, through which each achieved the benefits of its own superiority, was the condition not only to the maintenance of life from the beginning, but a condition to the maintenance of each species, and therefore to the evolution of higher species. Similarly, when seeking for an ultimate basis for the claims of altruism, we observed, on going back to its root, that from the beginning altruism has been coessential; in so far that the continued egoism of generation after generation has been made possible only through the altruism which sacrifices, physically and otherwise, a portion of the life of each generation for the next. Here we may with advantage pursue, in seeking the ultimate conciliation of egoism and altruism, the same course. If we similarly go back to the beginning, we shall get a clue to the method by which the conciliation, already in certain directions achieved, will in the future be carried out to the full.

For how is there effected that conciliation of the egoism and altruism, coessential as we have seen, by which each race, and life on the globe as a whole, have been maintained and evolved? How is there achieved that conciliation between the egoism of the parent, which is essential to production and fostering of offspring, and the altruism by which that fostering is effected? The answer is perfectly simple. There has from the beginning been arising, and has arisen more and more to a higher and higher stage, such constitution in each creature, as entailed egoistic gratification in performing the altruistic action.

If we glance afresh at the cases before indicated, in which there is a self-sacrifice of parent for the benefit of offspring, we observe that throughout, this self-sacrifice is made in gratification of a powerful instinct, and is a source of pleasure, and the negation of it an extreme pain. Not to dwell on cases, even low down among invertebrate animals, where, as even with molluscs, great labor is taken in safe laying of ova, or, as in the case of the spider, the ova are carried about and protected till they are hatched—cases which show us even there that this expenditure of labor by which other beings are benefited, is itself done in fulfillment of an instinct which is only to be satisfied by the act, and is therefore in that sense egoistic; we have this relation forced upon us distinctly, when we come to the more highly organized and intelligent creatures. If we ask how it is that there are gone through by a pair of birds, all the labors of nest-building, the denial of activity implied by incubation, the activity of the male in feeding the female while sitting, and the prolonged labors of both in subsequently bringing food to the young; the answer is that all these actions are carried on under the promptings of certain inherited and organized cravings, which make the successive activities sources of gratification. And it needs but to observe the signs of distress consequent on danger to the young to get a measure of the degree of pleasure taken in performing these acts that are directly beneficial to others and at the same time pleasurable to self. Evidently this conciliation between the requirements of egoism and altruism has from the beginning been growing in extent and completeness—necessarily has been doing so—since the higher the type of creature evolved, the more the young becomes dependent upon the parent and the more involved the requirements to be fulfilled in fostering them, and therefore the more continuous and more varied the activities carried on by adults in behalf of the young.

And this conciliation which we see has gone hand-in-hand with evolution, is a conciliation which we see has reached a high degree in the human race. It needs not here to dwell on parental sacrifices as prompted by parental affections. It needs not to dwell on the amount of positive pleasure which the mother derives from daily witnessing that welfare of her offspring which her self-sacrificing efforts achieve; nor does it need to dwell upon the intensity of the unhappiness which from time to time results if illness threatens or death destroys, and if, as a consequence, the mother, no longer called on to make these daily sacrifices, is at the same time defrauded of the pleasures those sacrifices brought. All that needs to be more especially indicated in further insisting on this great fact is that during the evolution of the human race itself there has been a marked further progress in this conciliation; so that whereas during savage life the sacrifices made on the part of both parents are less varied and persistent, they endure for a shorter period, and that among the civilized the labors of both parents, gone through in rearing and education, much more complex, are prolonged over a greater number of years, and the labors gone through in accumulating the means for setting them up in life, and often the injury to health borne in providing them with fortunes, are such as to make it manifest that a large part of the pleasure of daily life is achieved in the process of sacrificing personal ends for the benefit of offspring.

In all which illustrations the one truth to be observed and

carried with us is that there gradually evolves with the evolution of a higher life an organic altruism which, in relation to a
certain limited class of other beings, works to the effect of
making what we call self-sacrifice not a sacrifice in the ordinary sense of the word, but an act which brings more pleasure
than pain—an act which has for its accompaniment an altruistic gratification which outweighs the egoistic gratification lost;
and this, otherwise stated, implies that as the altruistic
gratification is egoistically expressed, egoism and altruism
coalesce.

That which has been in course of achievement in respect of
the limited group of beings constituting a family, in the course
of the evolution of life, and has now, in the human race, been
in very large measure achieved, has been in course of
achievement, and is to a comparatively small extent achieved,
with those larger groups constituting societies. The conciliation between egoism and altruism under their aspects as ordinarily understood, is slowly coming about by analogous conciliation of the egoistic and altruistic gratifications.

Only those whose creed prompts them to believe in the
unalterable badness of human nature, and who, in face of the
evidence which mankind at large furnish, hold that man not
only always has been, but always will be, "desperately
wicked," can refuse to recognize the conspicuous fact that
along with the progress of civilization, there has been growing
up not only that kind of altruism which is shown in decreasing
aggressiveness on fellow-men, but also that kind of altruism
which is shown in actual regard for their welfare. Go back to
the times when blood-feuds were not only chronic between
adjacent tribes but in the later times in which there were
blood-feuds maintained from generation to generation between families of the same tribe, and contrast it with the
present time in which, among civilized peoples, such aggressions as exist, relatively few, are far less violent in kind; and it
cannot be denied that that negative altruism which is shown
in refraining from injuring others, has increased. Contrast the

times in which slavery, existing everywhere, excited even in moralists no repugnance, with modern times when slavery, by the more sympathetically-minded, is characterized as "the sum of all villainies"; and it is undeniable that the extent to which selfish gratification is pursued at the cost of misery to others, is alike less extreme and less widespread. Observe the contrast between savages who torture their captives till they die, or ancient so-called heroes who dragged the dead bodies of slain foes after their chariots, with our own days in which, among the more advanced nations, wounded enemies are cared for, and by-standing nations send out doctors and nurses; and it cannot be questioned that there exists now [more kind feeling] than existed in the less developed human beings. So in the contrast between gladiatorial shows and days when pugilism is forbidden, or between the societies in which seeing animals slay one another is a chief pleasure and societies in which there exist associations and laws for the prevention of such remaining cruelty to animals as exists.

If, from the increase of sympathy shown by the decrease of cruelty, we pass to that which is shown by the establishment of juster social relations, the same thing is shown to us. From the times when the system of internal protection was so little developed that men had to rectify their own grievances by force as well as they might, to the times when there exist guardians of life and property patrolling the streets at all hours, we are shown a gradual rise of that public sentiment expressing regard for the claims of others. Defective as is the administration of law, yet men's properties as well as their lives are far safer than they were in early times; by which there is implied an increase of those feelings which embody them-selves in equitable laws. If we again look at the growth of governmental forms, which have gone on from period to period decreasing the unchecked powers of ruling classes, and extending to lower and lower grades shares of political power, we see both that the institutions so established are more altruistic in the sense that they recognize better the claims of all, and in the sense that they are advocated and carried on grounds of equity and by appeal to men's sense of justice—that is, to the most abstract and latest developed of the altruistic sentiments.

Nor is it otherwise if we consider the altruism which expresses itself in active benevolence. Go back to early societies, and we find little or nothing representing those multitudinous agencies which have grown up during civilization for the care of the sick and aged and the unfortunate. In the rudest forms of society, those who were no longer from one or other cause capable of taking care of themselves, were either killed or left to die. But the moral modification which has resulted from the discipline of social life, as it has gradually passed more and more from the militant to the industrial form, has been accompanied by growth of multitudinous forms of philan- thropic activity—countless societies voluntarily established and carried on, enormous sums of money subscribed, innu- merable people busying themselves with a view to the welfare of those who are not so well off in the world as themselves. That is to say, altruism arising from that same growth of sympathy which checks cruelty and extends justice, has been simultaneously leading to positive exertions for the benefit alike of individuals and of the community at large.

And if we ask what is the attitude of mind in those who are engaged, now in the checking of actions which inflict pain, now in the furtherance of political changes which conduce to more equitable relations, now in the agitations for changing unjust laws, now in the carrying on of organizations for mitigating the pains of less fortunate fellow citizens or increas- ing their pleasures; we see that if [not] in the whole, still in large measure, the prompting cause is an actual satisfaction in the contemplation of the benefits achieved. Large numbers of persons are there who, often postponing in large measure, and sometimes unduly, their private affairs to public affairs, are as eagerly energetic in achieving what they conceive will redound to human welfare at large, or the welfare of particular classes of people, as though they were pursuing their per- sonal ends; and so show us that the gratification of their altruistic feelings has become to them a stimulus approaching in potency to the gratification of their directly egoistic feelings. So that the pursuit of the altruistic pleasure has become a higher order of egoistic pleasure.

It is a paradox daily illustrated, that the belief in irrationalities habitually goes with skepticism of rationalities. Those who are impressed by some statement of a wonder, and accept it on the strength of some emphatic assertion notwithstanding its utter incongruity with all that is known of the course of things, will listen with utter incredulity to inferences drawn by the most cogent reasoning from premises that they do not deny. Incapable of conceiving with any vividness the necessary dependence of conclusions upon premises, where these are at all remote from the simplest matters, they are not affected in their convictions by demonstration, however clear, as they are affected by the manifestation of strong belief in those who make statements to them. And thus while, for example, they see nothing whatever ridiculous in the tradition which ascribes the universe to a greater artificer who was tired after six days' labor, it seems to them quite ridiculous to suppose that there are to come in the future, changes in human nature, and corresponding changes in human society, analogous to, and equally great with, those that have taken place since societies were first formed.

One who, looking at the hour hand of a watch, fails to see it move, and is prompted by his inability to see the movement to say that it does not move, is checked from doing so by his experiences of past occasions when, on looking after an interval, he has seen that movement has taken place; but one can readily imagine that in one who had never had any experiences of watches, and who was told that this hour hand was moving though he could not see it, and that unless familiar with the actions of machinery, it would be of little avail to point out the arrangements of mainspring, balance wheel, pinions, and the like, in such way as to prove to him that although he could not see it, the hour hand must be moving.

And much in the same condition as would be such an one who had never before seen a watch, and who was incredulous as to the movement of the hour hand because it was imperceptible to him, are the great mass of people who habitually look upon human nature and human society as, if not stationary, still, not moving in such way as to be likely to change their places in such great degree as to make them remote from what they now are. They have indeed the opportunity, not paralleled in the hypothetical case just put, of contrasting existing civilized societies with existing savage societies; and they have the opportunity of contrasting the present state of any one civilized society with its preceding state. But strong as is the evidence furnished to them that both the individual human being and the masses of human beings, undergo decided changes, they are so dominated by the daily impression of constancy, as to have either unconsciousness, or no adequate consciousness, of the changes that are, from kindred causes, hereafter to take place. Not denying that there will be changes, their imagination of them is so vague, and their belief in them is so feeble, that, practically, the admission that they may take place amounts to nothing in their general conception of things, and plays no part as a factor in their general thinking. And, most remarkably, this proves to be so not [only] with the commonplace uncultured [and] with those of mere literary culture; but it is to a large extent true of those whose scientific culture should give them clear conceptions of causation—clear conceptions that results will not result without causes, and, conversely, that given the causes the results are inevitable. Even a large proportion of the biological world whose discipline, especially in recent years, might be presumed to give them full faith in the potent working hereafter of causes that have worked so potently heretofore, show no sign that their conceptions of human life and human society are much in advance of those held by other people. Strange to say, naturalists who have accepted in full the general hypothesis of organic evolution, and hold that by direct or indirect adaptation, organisms have perpetually been molded to their respective conditions, and that in the future as the past such moldings to conditions must ever go on, show themselves, like the rest, little regardful of the corollaries which must inevitably follow respecting the future of humanity. And many of them may be numbered among those who, in various ways, are busy in thwarting this process of adaptation as respects men and society.

Hence, not at all among the uneducated class, very little among the class called educated, and in no adequate degree even in the scientific class, is there a belief in the unquestionable truth that altruism in the future will increase as it has increased in the past; and that as, at the present time, there has grown up in the superior types of men, a capacity for receiving much personal pleasure from furthering the welfare of others, and in contemplating such welfare as is produced by other means, so will there in the future grow up a much greater degree, and a much more widespread amount, of such pleasure—so will there in the future come a further identification of altruism with egoism, in the sense that personal gratification will be derived from achieving the gratification of others. So far is it from being true, as might be supposed from the general incredulity, that though there has arisen a considerable moralization of the human being, as a concomitant of civilization, there will be no comparable increase of such moralization in the future, it is true that the moralization will hereafter go on at a much greater rate, because it will no longer be checked by influences hitherto, and at present, in operation. During all the past, and even still, the egoism of warlike activities has been restraining the altruism which grows up under peaceful activities. The need for maintaining adaptation to the militant life, which implies readiness to sacrifice others, has perpetually held in check the progress of adaptation to the industrial life, which, carried on by exchange of services, does not of necessity entail the sacrifice of others to self. And because of these conflicting influences, the growth of altruism has of necessity been slow. What this moral modification due to the adaptation of human beings to peace-

ful social life, might have already achieved in civilized
societies, had it not been for the moral effects that have accompanied the necessary process of compounding and re-
compounding by which great nations have been produced,
we may judge on observing the moral state existing in the few
simple tribes of men who have been so circumstanced as to
carry on peaceful lives. (Here insert examples.)

Judge, then, what might by this time have happened under
the closer mutual dependence and more complex relations
which civilized societies have originated, but for the retarding
causes which have kept sympathies seared; and then judge
what will happen in the future when, by further progress such
as has been going on in the past, we reach eventually a state in
which the great civilized societies reach a condition of permanent peace, and there continues no such extreme check as has
been operating thus far. Not only must we infer that the future
of man and of society will have modifications as great as the
past has shown us, but that it will have much greater. That is
to say, the transformation of altruistic gratifications into egoistic ones, will be carried very much further; and an average
larger share in the happiness of each individual, will depend
on consciousness of the well-being of other individuals.

Doubtless the moral modification of human nature which
has thus to take place hereafter, analogous to that which has
taken place heretofore, will be retarded by other causes than
this primary cause. Not only is the growth of sympathy held
in check by the performance of unsympathetic actions, such
as are necessitated by militant activities, but it is held in check
by the constant presence of pains and unhappinesses, and by
the consciousness that these exist even when they are not
visible. Those in whom the sympathies have become keen, are
of necessity proportionately pained on witnessing sufferings
borne by others, not [only] in those cases where they are the
causes of sufferings, but where the sufferings are caused in
any other way. To those whose fellow feelings were too keenly

alive to the miseries of the great mass of their kind—alive not only to such miseries as they saw but to such miseries as they heard of or read of, and to such miseries as they knew must be existing all around, far and near, life would be made intolerable: the sympathetic pains would submerge not only the sympathetic pleasures but the egoistic pleasures. And therefore life is made tolerable, even to the higher among us at the present time, by a certain perpetual searing of the sympathies, which keeps them down at such level of sensitiveness as that there remains a balance of pleasure in life. Whence it follows that the sympathies can become more and more acute, only as fast as the amount of human misery to be sympathized with becomes less and less; and while this diminution of human misery to be sympathized with, itself must be due in part to the increase of sympathy which prompts actions to mitigate it, it must be due in the main to the decrease of the pressure of population upon the means of subsistence. While the struggle for existence among men has to be carried on with an intensity like that which now exists, the quantity of suffering to be borne by the majority must remain great. This struggle for existence must continue to be thus intense so long as the rate of multiplication continues greatly in excess of the rate of mortality. Only in proportion as the production of new individuals ceases to go on so greatly in excess of the disappearance of individuals by death, can there be a diminution of the pressure upon the means of subsistence, and a diminution of the strain and the accompanying pains that arise more or less to all, and in a greater degree to the inferior. On referring back to the *Principles of Biology*, Part VI, the reader will find grounds for the inference that along with social progress, there must inevitably go a decrease in human fertility, ending in a comparative balance of fertility and mortality, as there comes the time when human evolution approaches its limit of complete adaptation to the social state. And as is here implied, the highest evolution of the sympathies, and consequent reaching of the ultimate altruism, though the progress will go on with comparative rapidity when a peaceful state is once arrived at, will yet only approach its highest degree as this ultimate state is approached.

But one of the chief causes of perplexity in this question, arising from the conflict of egoistic and altruistic requirements, and which is natural to the present condition, is due to the fact that altruism is habitually associated with self-sacrifice. So long as egoism is in excess, and so long as, in consequence of its excess, the counteraction of altruism is shown mainly in checking undue personal gratification, or in assuaging the pains that have been produced by selfishness somewhere or other, it happens, as a matter of course, that the conception of altruism is identified with the conception of abandonment of individual gratification, and self-infliction of more or less pain. This, however, as I have implied, is an erroneous and purely transitional view of the effect of altruism in its ultimate workings out.

Sympathy is the root of every other kind of altruism than that which, from the beginning, originates the parental activities. It is the root of that higher altruism which, apart from the philoprogenitive instinct, produces desire for the happiness of others and reluctance to inflict pain upon them. These two traits are inevitably associated. The same mental faculty which reproduces in the individual consciousness, the feelings that are being displayed by other beings, acts equally to reproduce those states when they are pleasurable or when they are painful. Sympathy, therefore, is a state of the individual, of pleasure or pain, according to the states of the surrounding beings. Consequently it happens, as indicated above, that when there exists around a large proportion of pain, sympathy may entail on its possessor more pain than pleasure, and so is continually kept in check. Contrariwise as, in course of the general evolution of humanity and society, the general increase of sympathy everywhere, and improvement in the social relations consequent upon greater sympathy, it more and more happens that the states of consciousness existing in those around are pleasurable; and in proportion as this happens, the effect of sympathy is to increase the pleasure of the possessor.

Evidently the general corollary from this is that with the increase of sympathy, there arises the double result, that by its increase it tends to decrease the causes of human misery, and in proportion as it decreases the causes of human misery and increases the causes of happiness, it becomes itself the cause of further reflected happiness received by each from others. And the limit towards which this evolution approaches, is one under which, as the amount of pain suffered by those around from individual imperfections and from imperfections of social arrangement and conduct, become relatively small, and simultaneously the growth of sympathy goes on with little check, the sympathy becomes at the same time almost exclusively a source of pleasure received from the happiness of others, and not of pains received from their pains. And as this condition is approached, the function of sympathy is not that of stimulating to self-sacrifice and of entailing upon its possessor positive or negative pain, but its function becomes that of making him a recipient of positive pleasure. The altruism which has to arise, therefore, in future, is not an altruism which is in conflict with egoism, but is an altruism which comes eventually to coincide with egoism in respect of a large range of life; and it becomes instrumental in exalting satisfactions that are egoistic in so far as they are pleasures enjoyed by the individual, though they are altruistic in respect of the origin of these pleasures.

So far then from its being, as is commonly assumed, true that there must go on throughout all the future, a condition in which self-regard is to be continually subjected by the regard for others, it will, contrariwise, be the case, that a regard for others will eventually become so large a source of pleasure, as to compete with in its amount, and indeed overgrow, the pleasure which is derivable from direct egoistic gratification; and the pursuit of this indirect egoistic gratification may so become itself the predominant part of egoism.

Eventually, then, along with the approximately complete adaptation of man to the social state, along with the evolution of a society complete in its adjustments, and along with the ultimate diminution of pressure of population, which must come with the highest type of human life, there will come also a state in which egoism and altruism are so conciliated that the one merges in the other.

To those who look at the creation at large, and the organic creation in particular, from the old point of view of special creation, and who think of the structures and functions of all species as supernaturally given, and therefore fixed by God, there will not only be a repudiation of a conception like this as chimerical, but there will also be an utter imperviousness to all arguments derived from those adaptations of constitution to conditions which the organic creation at large presents, and especially those which present adaptations of the kind here prophesied. But all who take the evolution view, cannot in consistency deny that if we have in lower orders of creatures cases in which the nature is constitutionally so modified that altruistic activities have become one with egoistic activities, there is an irresistible implication that a parallel identification will, under parallel conditions, take place among human beings.

Social insects furnish us with instances completely to the point; and instances showing us, indeed, to what a marvellous degree the life of the individual may be absorbed in subserving the lives of other individuals. Strangely enough, it happens that the typical illustrations taken from the animal creation to enforce on human beings the virtue of activity, are taken from those creatures whose activities are devoted, not to their own special welfare, but to the welfare of the communities they form part of. The ant, which in the Bible is referred to as showing an industry which should shame the sluggard among men, and the busy bee which, in the child's hymn, is named as an example to be followed in making the best of time, are creatures whose activities are not like those commended to the child and the sluggard—activities mainly to be expended in subserving personal well-being; but they are activities which postpone individual well-being so completely to the well-being of the community, that individual life appears to be attended to only just as far as necessary to make possible due attention to the social life. These instances which are given as spurs to egoistic activity, are actually supplied by creatures whose activity is almost wholly altruistic. Throughout the animal kingdom there are found no better examples of energetic industry, than these in which the ends which the activities subserve are altruistic rather than egoistic. And hence we are shown, undeniably, that it is a perfectly possible thing for organisms to become so adjusted to the requirements of their lives, that energy expended for the general welfare may not only be adequate to check energy expended for the individual welfare, but may come to subordinate it so far as to leave individual welfare no greater than is requisite for maintenance of individual life.

And now observe, further, that we are thus shown not only the existence of an almost complete identification of egoism and altruism; but we are also shown that this identification takes place in consequence of the gratification accompanying the altruistic activities having become a gratification that is substantially egoistic. Neither the ant nor the bee can be supposed to have a sense of duty, in the acceptation we give to that word; nor can it be supposed that it is continually undergoing self-sacrifice in the ordinary acceptation of that word. At the very outset of its mature life, the working bee begins that life which, with untiring energy, it pursues to the end— collecting food to feed the growing members of the community, gathering pollen with which to build new cells, and taking only just such food and such rest as are needful to maintain its vigor; and in the absence of those moral instigations existing only in the higher vertebrates, the instigations are in this case simply those resulting from an organization which has become adjusted in the course of evolution to the carrying on a social life. They show us that it is within the possibilities of organization to produce a nature which shall be just as energetic, and even more energetic, in the pursuit of altruistic ends, as is, in other cases, shown in the pursuit of egoistic ends; and they show that in such cases these altruistic ends are pursued in pursuing ends which on their other face are egoistic. For the satisfaction of the needs of the organization, these actions conducive to the welfare of others must be carried on. The seeking for the satisfaction which the organization requires, itself entails the performance of those activities which the welfare of the community requires.

And here we are brought to a special application of that general law, the relativity of pleasure, set forth and illustrated in a preceding chapter. We have but duly to see the far-reaching sequences of this law, to understand, even without such an illustration as that just furnished, that such a relation between the individual and the community is not only possible, but is certain to establish itself if the conditions to its establishment are maintained.

One who once fully grasps the truth that pleasure of every kind is the concomitant of the activity of some nervous structure, inherited from the race or developed by modification in the individual, will see it to be an inevitable corollary that there can be a gratification in altruistic activities just as great as in egoistic activities, if there exists the structure which answers to those activities; and that the evolution of such a structure will inevitably take place, partly by direct and partly by indirect equilibration, where it is to the advantage of the species that it should exist. In proportion as, with the advance of society to a peaceful state, there increases the form of social life which consists in mutual exchange of services—in proportion as it becomes to the advantage of the individual, and to the prosperity of the society, to regard others' claims and fulfill contracts—in proportion as the individual comes to be aided in leading a more complete life, by possessing a nature which begets friendship and kindly offices from all around; in such proportion does there continuously tend to take place both a strengthening of the altruistic emotions directly in the individual, and the increase of those individuals who inherit most largely the altruistic nature. And in proportion as there goes on this individual modification, conducing ever to the prosperity of the society after the peaceful [stage] has been reached, in that same proportion does it also happen that among societies those among whom that modification has gone on most effectually will be those to [survive and grow, so as gradually to replace those societies] in which the individual nature is not so adapted to social requirements. Inevitably, therefore, by this process, the tendency of peaceful conditions is to the continual increase of those faculties, that is, those nervous structures, which have for their spheres of activity, pleasure taken in the welfare of others; and in proportion as this takes place, there is evolved more and more a nature in which the egoistic pursuit of these pleasures, arising from the activity of the altruistic feelings, becomes a source of such altruistic activities as are needful for the general welfare. As certainly as those organized and inherited structures which prompt the activities of the chase, in animals and in men who live by the chase, and which, surviving in civilized men, give them what seems so natural, the pleasure in achieving the success of the chase, are structures which prompt to actions in pursuit of gratification apart from future egoistic ends (for the sportsman may be indifferent to the game he kills); so are there growing up, and will still further grow up with the progress towards a peaceful state, structures which will prompt to altruistic activities, and which will find their gratification in those altruistic activities quite apart from any egoistic motives.

Anyone who looks around and observes the higher types of men and women already existing, will see that even now the evolution of such structures has made considerable progress; and that there is no limit to the progress, save reaching the height at which it completely fulfills requirements.

PART II
THE INDUCTIONS OF ETHICS

CHAPTER 1

The Confusion of Ethical Thought

111. If, in common with other things, human feelings and ideas conform to the general law of evolution, the implication is that the set of conceptions constituting ethics, together with the associated sentiments, arise out of a relatively incoherent and indefinite consciousness; and slowly acquire coherence and definiteness at the same time that the aggregate of them differentiates from the larger aggregate with which it is originally mingled. Long remaining undistinguished, and then but vaguely discernible as something independent, ethics must be expected to acquire a distinct embodiment only when mental evolution has reached a high stage.

Hence the present confusion of ethical thought. Total at the outset, it has necessarily continued great during social progress at large, and, though diminished, must be supposed to be still great in our present semicivilized state. Notions of right and wrong, variously derived and changing with every change in social arrangements and activities, form an assemblage which we may conclude is even now in large measure chaotic.

Let us contemplate some of the chief factors of the ethical

consciousness, and observe the sets of conflicting beliefs and opinions severally resulting from them.

112. Originally, ethics has no existence apart from religion, which holds it in solution. Religion itself, in its earliest form, is undistinguished from ancestor worship. And the propitiations of ancestral ghosts, made for the purpose of avoiding the evils they may inflict and gaining the benefits they may confer, are prompted by prudential considerations like those which guide the ordinary actions of life.

"Come and partake of this! Give us maintenance as you did when living!" calls out the innocent Wood-Veddah to the spirit of his relative, when leaving an offering for him; and then, at another time, he expects this spirit to give him success in the chase. A Zulu dreams that his brother's ghost, scolding him and beating him for not sacrificing, says, "I wish for meat"; and then to the reply, "No, my brother, I have no bullock; do you see any in the cattle pen?" the rejoinder is, "Though there be but one, I demand it." The Australian medicine man, eulogizing the dead hunter and listening to replies from the corpse, announces that should he be sufficiently avenged he has promised that "his spirit would not haunt the tribe, nor cause them fear, nor mislead them into wrong tracks, nor bring sickness amongst them, nor make loud noises in the night." Thus is it generally. Savages ascribe their good or ill fortunes to the doubles of the dead whom they have pleased or angered; and, while offering to them food and drink and clothing, promise conformity to their wishes and beg for their help.*

When from the first stage, in which only the ghosts of fathers and other relatives are propitiated by the members of each family, we pass to the second stage, in which, along with the rise of an established chieftainship, there arises a special fear of the chief's ghost, there results propitiation of this

---

* For further illustrations, see *Principles of Sociology*, secs. 142–43, and *Ecclesiastical Institutions*, sec. 584.

also—offerings, eulogies, prayers, promises. If, as warrior or ruler, a powerful man has excited admiration and dread, the anxiety to be on good terms with his still more powerful double is great, and prompts observance of his commands and interdicts. Of course, after many conquests have made him a king, the expressions of subordination to his deified spirit, regarded as omnipotent and terrible, are more pronounced, and submission to his will becomes imperative: the concomitant idea being that right and wrong consist simply in obedience and disobedience to him.

All religions exemplify these relations of phenomena. Concerning the Tongans, Mariner says that "Several acts acknowledged by all civilized nations as crimes, are under many circumstances considered by them as matters of indifference," unless they involve disrespect to "the gods, nobles, and aged persons." In his description of certain peoples of the Gold Coast, Major Ellis shows that with them the idea of sin is limited to insults offered to the gods, and to the neglect of the gods.

> The most atrocious crimes, committed as between man and man, the gods can view with equanimity. These are man's concerns, and must be rectified or punished by man. But, like the gods of people much farther advanced in civilization, there is nothing that offends them so deeply as to ignore them, or question their power, or laugh at them.

When from these cases, in which the required subordination is shown exclusively in observances expressive of reverence, we pass to cases in which there are commands of the kind called ethical, we find that the propriety of not offending God is the primary reason for fulfilling them. Describing the admonitions given by parents to children among the ancient Mexicans, Zurita instances these:

> Do not poison any one, since you would sin against God in his creature; your crime would be discovered and punished, and . . you would suffer the same death. [P. 138] Do not injure any one, shun adultery and luxury; that is a mean vice which causes the ruin of him

who yields to it, and which offends God. [P. 139] Be modest; humility procures us the favor of God and of the powerful. [P. 141]

Much more pronounced, however, among the Hebrews was the belief that right and wrong are made such simply by the will of God. As Schenkel remarks, "Inasmuch as man owes obedience to God's laws, sin is regarded as rebellion (*Isaiah* i. 2, lix. 13; *Hosea* vii. 13; *Amos* iv. 4)." Conformity to divine injunctions is insisted upon solely because they are divine injunctions, as is shown in *Leviticus* xviii. 4, 5: "Ye shall do my judgments, and keep mine ordinances, to walk therein: I am the Lord your God. Ye shall therefore keep my statutes and my judgments." Such was the view which the Hebrews themselves avowedly entertained. This is proved by their later writings. Bruch remarks that according to the author of the *Book of Wisdom*, "virtue is obedience to the will of God, and where this is expressed in the Law fulfillment of it is required (vi. 5, 19)." And in like manner, Fritzsche says—In *Ecclesiasticus* "the command of God appears as the proper motive of morality."

How little good and bad conduct were associated in thought with the intrinsic natures of right and wrong, and how completely they were associated in thought with obedience and disobedience to Jahveh, we see in the facts that prosperity and increase of population were promised as rewards of allegiance; while there was punishment for such nonethical disobediences as omitting circumcision or numbering the people.

That conformity to injunctions, as well as making sacrifices and singing praises, had in view benefits to be received in return for subordination, other ancient peoples show us. Here are illustrative passages from the *Rig-Veda*.

The unsacrificing Sanakas perished. Contending with the sacrificers the non-sacrificers fled, O Indra, with averted faces. [i. 33, 4–5]

Men fight the fiend, trying to overcome by their deeds him who performs no sacrifices. [vi. 14, 3]

May all other people around us vanish into nothing, but our own offspring remain blessed in this world. [x. 81, 7]

We who are wishing for horses, for booty, for women . . . Indra, the strong one who gives us women. [iv. 17, 16]

A like expected exchange of obligations was shown among the Egyptians when Rameses, invoking Ammon for aid, reminded him of the hecatombs of bulls he had sacrificed to him. And, similarly, it was shown among the early Greeks when Chrises, praying for vengeance, emphasized the claim he had established on Apollo by decorating his temple. Evidently the good and evil which come from enjoined and forbidden actions, are considered as directly caused by God, and not as indirectly due to the constitution of things.

That like conceptions prevailed throughout mediæval Europe everyone knows. With the appeals to saints for aid in battle, with the vows to build chapels to the Virgin by way of compounding for crimes, and with the crusading expeditions and pilgrimages undertaken as means to salvation, there went the idea that divine injunctions are to be obeyed simply because they are divine injunctions; and the accompanying idea was that good and evil are consequences of God's will and not consequences naturally caused. The current idea was well shown in the forms of manumission—"For fear of Almighty God, and for the cure of my soul, I liberate thee" &c. or "For lessening my sins" &c. Even now a kindred conception survives in most men. Not only is it still the popular belief that right and wrong become such by divine fiat, but it is the belief of many theologians and moralists. The speeches of bishops concerning the Deceased Wife's Sisters Bill, sufficiently indicate the attitude of the one; and various books, among others that of the Quaker moralist Jonathan Dymond, show the other. Though there has long been growing a vague recognition of natural sanctions which some actions have and others have not, yet there continues a general belief that moral obligation is supernaturally derived.

113. Various mythologies of ancient peoples, in common with those of some existing savages, describe the battles of the gods: now with one another and now with alien foes. If the

deities of the Scandinavians, the Mongolians, the Indians, the Assyrians, the Greeks, are not all of them successful warriors, yet the supremacy of the gods over other beings, or of one over the rest, is habitually represented as established by conquest. Even the Hebrew deity, characterized as a "man of war," is constantly spoken of as a subduer of enemies, if not personally yet by proxy.

The apotheosized chiefs who become the personages of mythologies (frequently invaders, like the Egyptian gods who came into Egypt from the land of Punt) usually leave behind them wars in progress or unsettled feuds; and fulfillment of their commands, or known wishes, by overcoming enemies, then becomes a duty. Even where there are no bequeathed antagonisms with peoples around, example and precept given by the warrior-king unite in giving divine sanction to the ethics of enmity.

Hence such a fact as that told of the Fijian chief, who was in a state of mental agony because he had displeased his god by not killing enough of the enemy. Hence such representations as are made by Assyrian kings: Shalmaneser II asserting that Asshur "had strongly urged me to conquer and subjugate"; Tiglath Pileser naming Asshur and the great gods as having "ordered an enlarged frontier to" his dominions; Sennacherib describing himself as the instrument of Asshur, and aided by him in battle; Assurbanipal, as fighting in the service of the gods who, he says, are his leaders in war. Of like meaning is the account which the Egyptian king, Rameses II, gives of his transcendent achievements in the field while inspired by the ghost of his deified father. Nor is it otherwise with the carrying on of wars among the Hebrews in pursuance of divine behests; as when it is said—"Whomsoever the Lord our God shall drive out from before us, them will we possess" (*Judges* xi. 24). And among other peoples, in later times, we see the same connection of ideas in the name assumed by Attila— "the scourge of God."

Sanctions for deeds entailed by the conflicts between societies, when not thus arising, inevitably arise from social necessities. Congruity must be established between the conduct found needful for self-preservation and the conduct held to be right. When, throughout a whole community, daily acts are at variance with feelings, these feelings, continually repressed, diminish, and antagonist feelings, continually encouraged, grow; until the average sentiments are adjusted to the average requirements. Whatever injures foes is then thought not only justifiable but praiseworthy, and a part of duty. Success in killing brings admiration above every other achievement; burning of habitations and laying waste of territory become things to be boasted of; while in trophies, going even to the extent of a pyramid of heads of the slain, the conqueror and his followers show that pride which implies the consciousness of great deeds.

These conceptions and feelings, conspicuous in ancient epics and histories, have continued conspicuous during the course of social evolution, and are conspicuous still. If, instead of asking for men's *nominal* code of right and wrong, we seek for their *real* code, we find that in most minds the virtues of the warrior take the first place. Concerning an officer killed in a nefarious war, you may hear the remark—"He died the death of a gentleman." And among civilians, as among soldiers, there is tacit approval of the political brigandage going on in various quarters of the globe; while there are no protests against the massacres euphemistically called "punishments."

114. But though for the defense against, and conquest of, societies, one by another, injurious actions of all kinds have been needful, and have acquired in men's minds that sanction implied by calling them right, such injurious actions have not been needful within each society; but, contrariwise, actions of an opposite kind have been needful. Violent as may frequently be the conduct of tribesmen to one another, combined action of them against other tribes must be impossible in the absence of some mutual trust, consequent on experience of friendliness and fairness. And since a behavior which favors harmonious cooperation within the tribe conduces to its pros-

perity and growth, and therefore to the conquest of other tribes, survival of the fittest among tribes causes the establishment of such behavior as a general trait.

The authority of ruling men gives the ethics of amity collateral support. Dissension being recognized by chiefs as a source of tribal weakness, acts leading to it are reprobated by them; and where the injunctions of deified chiefs are remembered after their deaths, there results a supernatural sanction for actions conducive to harmony, and a supernatural condemnation for actions at variance with it. Hence the origin of what we distinguish as moral codes. Hence the fact that in numerous societies, formed by various races of men, such moral codes agree in forbidding actions which are antisocial in conspicuous degrees.

We find evidence that moral codes thus arising are transmitted from generation to generation, now informally and now formally. Thus "the Karens ascribe all their laws, and instructions, to the elders of preceding generations." According to Schoolcraft, the Dakotas "repeat traditions to the family, with maxims, and tell their children they must live up to them." And then Morgan tells us that among the Iroquois, when mourning for their sachems, "a prominent part of the ceremonial consisted in the repetition of their ancient laws and usages." Whence it is manifest that, sachems being the ruling men, this repetition of their injunctions during their obsequies, amounted to a tacit expression of obedience, and the injunctions became an ethical creed having a quasi-supernatural sanction.

The gravest transgressions, first recognized as such, as their flagitiousness taken for granted, are, in the absence of a systematized code of conduct, not conspicuously denounced by early teachers; any more than by our own priests, the wrongfulness of murder and robbery is much insisted on. Interdicts referring to the less marked deviations from ordinary conduct, and injunctions to behave worthily, are most common. The works of the ancient Indians furnish illustrations; at the same time showing how reaction against extreme egoism leads to enunciation of extreme altruism. Thus, in the later part of that heterogeneous compound, the *Mahabharata,* we read:

> Enjoy thou the prosperity of others,
> Although thyself unprosperous; noble men
> Take pleasure in their neighbor's happiness.

And again in Bharavi's *Kiratarjuniya* it is said:

> The noble-minded dedicate themselves
> To the promotion of the happiness
> Of others—e'en of those who injure them.

So too a passage in the *Cural* runs:

> To exercise benevolence is the whole design of acquiring property.
> He truly lives who knows and discharges the duties of benevolence.
> He who knows them not may be reckoned among the dead.

In the Chinese books we have, besides the injunctions of the Taoists, the moral maxims of Confucius, exemplifying his development of the ethics of amity. Enumerating the five cardinal virtues Confucius says:

> First among these stands *humanity,* that is to say, that universal sympathy which should exist between man and man without distinction of class or race. *Justice,* which gives to each member of the community his due, without favor or affection.

And then in another place he expresses, in a different form, the Christian maxim:

> Do not let a man practice to those beneath him, that which he dislikes in those above him; to those before him, what he dislikes in those behind him; to those on the right hand, that which he dislikes on the left.

Social life in ancient Egypt has produced clear recognition of the essential principles of harmonious cooperation. M. Chabas, as quoted by Renouf and verified by him, says:

> None of the Christian virtues is forgotten in it; piety, charity, gentle-
> ness, self-command in word and action, chastity, the protection of the
> weak, benevolence towards the humble, deference to superiors, re-
> spect for property in its minutest details, . . . all is expressed there, and
> in extremely good language.

And then, according to Kuenen, who gives evidence of the
correspondence, we have the same principles adopted by the
Hebrews, and formulated by Moses into the familiar decalogue; the essentials of which, summed up in the Christian
maxim, serve along with that maxim as standards of conduct
down to our own day.

The broad fact which here chiefly concerns us is that, in one
or other way, communities have habitually established for
themselves, now tacitly and now avowedly, here in rudimentary forms and there in elaborated forms, sets of commands
and restraints conducive to internal amity. And the genesis of
such codes, and partial conformity to them, have been necessary; since, if not in any degree recognized and observed,
there must result social dissolution.

115. As the ethics of enmity and the ethics of amity, thus
arising in each society in response to external and internal
conditions respectively, have to be simultaneously entertained, there is formed an assemblage of utterly inconsistent
sentiments and ideas. Its components can by no possibility be
harmonized, and yet they have to be all accepted and acted
upon. Every day exemplifies the resulting contradictions, and
also exemplifies men's contentment under them.

When, after prayers asking for divine guidance, nearly all
the bishops approve an unwarranted invasion, like that of
Afghanistan, the incident passes without any expression of
surprise; while, conversely, when the Bishop of Durham takes
the chair at a peace meeting, his act is commented upon as
remarkable. When, at a Diocesan Conference, a peer (Lord
Cranbook), opposing international arbitration, says he is "not
quite sure that a state of peace might not be a more dangerous
thing for a nation than war," the assembled priests of the

religion of love make no protest; nor does any general reprobation, clerical or lay, arise when a ruler in the Church, Dr.
Moorhouse, advocating a physical and moral discipline fitting
the English for war, expresses the wish "to make them so that
they would, in fact, like the fox when fastened by the dogs,
die biting," and says that "these were moral qualities to be
encouraged and increased among our people, and he believed
that nothing could suffice for this but the grace of God operating in their hearts." How completely in harmony with the
popular feeling in a land covered with Christian churches and
chapels, is this exhortation of the Bishop of Manchester, we
see in such facts as that people eagerly read accounts of
football matches in which there is an average of a death per
week; that they rush in crowds to buy newspapers which give
detailed reports of a brutal prizefight, but which pass over in a
few lines the proceedings of a peace congress; and that they
are lavish patrons of illustrated papers, half the woodcuts in
which have for their subjects the destruction of life or the
agencies for its destruction.

Still more conspicuous do we find the incongruity between
the nominally accepted ethics of amity and the actually accepted ethics of enmity, when we pass to the Continent. In
France, as elsewhere, the multitudinous appointed agents for
diffusing the injunction to do good to enemies, are practically
dumb in respect of this injunction; and, instead of seeking to
make their people put up the sword, are themselves, under
the direction of these people they have been teaching,
obliged, during their student days, to serve in the army. Not to
achieve any humane end or to enhance the happiness of
mankind, either at home or abroad, do the French submit to
the crushing weight of their military budget; but to wrest back
territories taken from them in punishment for their aggressiveness. And, as we have lately seen, a wave of enthusiasm
very nearly raised to supreme power a soldier who was expected to lead them to a war of revenge.

So is it, too, in Protestant Germany—the land of Luther and
the favorite home of Christian theology. Significant of the

national feeling was that general order to his soldiers issued by the Emperor on ascending the throne, in which, saying that "God's decree places me at the head of the army," and otherwise expressing his submission to "God's will," he ends by swearing "ever to remember that the eyes of my ancestors look down upon me from the other world, and that I shall one day have to render account to them of the glory and honor of the Army." To which add that, in harmony with this oath, pagan alike in sentiment and idea, we have his more recent laudation of dueling clubs: a laudation soon afterwards followed by personal performance of divine service on board his yacht.

How absolute throughout Europe is the contradiction between the codes of conduct adjusted respectively to the needs of internal amity and external enmity, we see in the broad fact that along with several hundred thousand priests who are supposed to preach forgiveness of injuries, there exist immensely larger armies than any on record!

116. But side by side with the ethical conceptions above described, originating in one or other way and having one or other sanction, there has been slowly evolving a different conception—a conception derived wholly from recognition of naturally produced consequences. This gradual rise of a utilitarian ethics has, indeed, been inevitable; since the reasons which led to commands and interdicts by a ruler, living or apotheosized, have habitually been reasons of expediency, more or less visible to all. Though, when once established, such commands and interdicts have been conformed to mainly because obedience to the authority imposing them was a duty, yet there has been very generally some accompanying perception of their fitness.

Even among the uncivilized, or but slightly civilized, we find a nascent utilitarianism. The Malagasy, for example, have

> laws against Adultery, Theft and Murder; . . . there is also a Fine inflicted on a Man, who shall curse another Man's Parents. They never swear profanely, but these things they do, because, *said they,* "it

is convenient and proper; and we could not live by one another, if there were not such laws."

In the later Hebrew writings the beginnings of a utilitarian ethics are visible; for though, as Bruch remarks of the author of *Ecclesiasticus*, "all his ethical rules and precepts in a truly Hebrew way run together in the notion of the fear of God," yet many of his maxims do not originate from divine injunctions. When he advises not to become too dependent, to value a good name, to be cautious in talk, and to be judicious in eating and drinking, he manifestly derives guidance from the results of experience. A fully differentiated system of expediency morals had been reached by some of the Egyptians. Mr. Poole writes:

> Ptah-hotep is wearied with religious services already outworn, and instead of the endless prescriptions of the current religion, he attempts a simple doctrine of morals, founded on the observation of a long life. . . . His proverbs enforce the advantage of virtuous life in the present. The future has no place in the scheme. . . . This moral philosophy of the sages is far above that of the Book of the Dead, inasmuch as it throws aside all that is trivial and teaches alone the necessary duties. But it rests on a basis of . . . expediency. The love of God, and the love of man, are unnoticed as the causes of virtue.

Similarly was it with the later Greeks. In the Platonic Dialogues, and in the *Ethics* of Aristotle, we see morality in large measure separated from theology and placed upon a utilitarian basis.

Coming down to modern days, the divergence of expediency ethics from theological ethics, is well illustrated in Paley, who, in his official character, derived right and wrong from divine commands, and in his unofficial character derived them from observation of consequences. Since his day the last of these views has spread at the expense of the first, and by Bentham and Mill we have utility established as the sole standard of conduct. How completely in this last, conduciveness to human welfare had become the supreme sanction, replacing alleged divine commands, we see in his refusal to call "good" a supreme being whose acts are not sanctioned by "the highest human morality"; and by his statement that "if such a being can sentence me to hell for not so calling him, to hell I will go."

117.   Yet a further origin of moral dictates is to be recognized as having arisen simultaneously. Habits of conformity to rules of conduct have generated sentiments adjusted to such rules. The discipline of social life has produced in men conceptions and emotions which, irrespective of supposed divine commands, and irrespective of observed consequences, issue in certain degrees of liking for conduct favoring social welfare and aversion to conduct at variance with it. Manifestly such a molding of human nature has been furthered by survival of the fittest; since groups of men having feelings least adapted to social requirements must, other things equal, have tended to disappear before groups of men having feelings most adapted to them.

The effects of moral sentiments thus arising are shown among races partially civilized. Cook says: The Otaheitans "have a knowledge of right and wrong from the mere dictates of natural conscience; and involuntarily condemn themselves when they do that to others, which they would condemn others for doing to them." So, too, that moral sentiments were influential during early stages of some civilized races, proof is yielded by ancient Indian books. In the *Mahabharata*, Draupadi complains of the hard lot of her righteous husband, and charges the Deity with injustice; but is answered by Yudhishthira:

> Thou utterest infidel sentiments. I do not act from a desire to gain the recompense of my works. I give what I ought to give . . . Whether reward accrues to me or not, I do to the best of my power what a man should do. . . . It is on duty alone that my thoughts are fixed, and this, too, naturally. The man who seeks to make of righteousness a gainful merchandise, is low. The man who seeks to *milk* righteousness does not obtain its reward. . . . Do not doubt about righteousness: he who does so is on the way to be born a brute.

And similarly, in another of these ancient books, the *Ramayana*, we read:

> Virtue is a service man owes himself, and though there were no Heaven, nor any God to rule the world, it were not less the binding law of life. It is man's privilege to know the Right and follow it.

In like manner, according to Edkins, conscience is regarded among the Chinese as the supreme authority. He says:

> When the evidence of a new religion is presented to them they at once refer it to a moral standard, and give their approval with the utmost readiness, if it passes the test. They do not ask whether it is Divine, but whether it is good.

And elsewhere he remarks that sin, according to the Confucian moral standard, "becomes an act which robs a man of his self-respect, and offends his sense of right," and is not "regarded as a transgression of God's law."

Of modern writers who, asserting the existence of a moral sense, consider the intuitions it yields as guides to conduct, we may distinguish two classes. There are those who, taking a view like that of Confucius just indicated, hold that the *dicta* of conscience are authoritative, irrespective of alleged divine commands; and, indeed, furnish a test by which commands may be known as not divine if they do not withstand it. On the other hand there are those who regard the authority of conscience as second to that of commands which they accept as divine, and as having for its function to prompt obedience to such commands. But the two are at one insofar as they place the *dicta* of conscience above considerations of expediency; and also insofar as they tacitly regard conscience as having a supernatural origin. To which add that while alike in recognizing the moral sentiment as innate, and in accepting the ordinary dogma that human nature is everywhere the same, they are, by implication, alike in supposing that the moral sentiment is identical in all men.

But, as the beginning of this section shows, it is possible to agree with moralists of the intuitive school respecting the existence of a moral sense, while differing from them respecting its origin. I have contended in the foregoing division of this work, and elsewhere, that though there exist feelings of the kind alleged, they are not of supernatural origin but of natural origin; that, being generated by the discipline of the social activities, internal and external, they are not alike in all men, but differ more or less everywhere in proportion as the social activities differ; and that, in virtue of their mode of genesis, they have a coordinate authority with the inductions of utility.

118. Before going further it will be well to sum up these various detailed statements, changing somewhat the order and point of view.

Survival of the fittest insures that the faculties of every species of creature tend to adapt themselves to its mode of life. It must be so with man. From the earliest times groups of men whose feelings and conceptions were congruous with the conditions they lived under, must, other things equal, have spread and replaced those whose feelings and conceptions were incongruous with their conditions.

Recognizing a few exceptions, which special circumstances have made possible, it holds, both of rude tribes and of civilized societies, that they have had continually to carry on external self-defense and internal cooperation—external antagonism and internal friendship. Hence their members have required two different sets of sentiments and ideas, adjusted to these two kinds of activity.

In societies having indigenous religions, the resulting conflict of codes is not overt. As the commands to destroy external enemies and to desist from acts which produce internal dissensions, come either from the living ruler or from the apotheosized ruler; and as, in both cases, the obligation arises not from the natures of the prescribed acts, but from the necessity of obedience; the two, having the same sanction, are not perceived to stand in opposition. But where, as throughout Christendom, the indigenous religion in which the ethics of enmity and the ethics of amity coexisted with like authorities, has been suppressed by an invading religion, which, insisting on the ethics of amity only, reprobates the ethics of enmity, incongruity has resulted. International antagonisms having continued, there has of necessity survived the appropriate ethics of emnity, which, not being included in the nominally accepted creed, has not had the religious sanction. Hence the fact that we have a thin layer of Christianity overlying a thick layer of paganism. The Christianity insists on duties which the paganism does not recognize as such; and the paganism insists on duties which the Christianity forbids. The new and superposed religion, with its system of ethics, has the nominal honor and the professed obedience; while the old and suppressed religion has its system of ethics nominally discredited but practically obeyed. Both are believed in, the last more strongly than the first; and men, now acting on the principles of the one and now on those of the other, according to circumstances, sit down under their contradictory beliefs as well as they may; or, rather, refrain from recognizing the contradictions.

Hence the first of these various confusions of ethical thought. Since, in the general mind, moral injunctions are identified with divine commands, those injunctions only are regarded as moral which harmonize with the nominally accepted religion, Christianity; while those injunctions which belong to the primitive and suppressed religion, authoritative as they may be considered, and eagerly as they are obeyed, are not regarded as moral. There have come to be two classes of duties and virtues, condemned and approved in similar ways, but one of which is associated with ethical conceptions and the other not: the result being that men cannot bring their real and nominal beliefs into harmony.

And then we have the further confusions which arise, not from the conflict of codes, but from the conflict of sanctions. Divine commands are not the authorities whence rules of conduct are derived, say the utilitarians, but their authorities are given by conduciveness to human welfare as ascertained by induction. And then, either with or without recognition of divine commands, we have writers of the moral-sense school making conscience the arbiter; and holding its *dicta* to be authoritative irrespective of calculated consequences. Obviously the essential difference between these two classes of moralists is that the one regards as of no value for guidance the feelings with which acts are regarded, while the other regards these feelings as of supreme value.

Such being the conflict of codes and conflict of sanctions, what must be our first step? We must look at the actual ideas and feelings concerning conduct which men entertain, apart from established nomenclatures and current professions. How needful is such an analysis we shall be further shown while making it; for it will become manifest that the confusion of ethical thought is even greater than we have already seen it to be.

CHAPTER 2

What Ideas and Sentiments Are Ethical?

119. A silent protest has been made by many readers, and probably by most, while reading that section of the foregoing chapter which describes the ethics of enmity. Governed by feelings and ideas which date from their earliest lessons, and have been constantly impressed on them at home and in church, they have formed an almost indissoluble association between a doctrine of right and wrong in general, and those particular commands and interdicts included in the decalogue, which, contemplating the actions of men to one another in the same society, takes no note of their combined actions against men of alien societies. The conception of ethics has, in this way, come to be limited to that which I have distinguished as the ethics of amity; and to speak of the ethics of enmity seems absurd.

Yet, beyond question, men associate ideas of right and wrong with the carrying on of intertribal and international conflicts; and this or that conduct in battle is applauded or condemned no less strongly than this or that conduct in ordinary social life. Are we then to say that there is one kind of right and wrong recognized by ethics and another kind of right and wrong not recognized by ethics? If so, under what title is this second kind of right and wrong to be dealt with?

Evidently men's ideas about conduct are in so unorganized a state, that while one large class of actions has an overtly recognized sanction, another large class of actions has a sanction, equally strong or stronger, which is not overtly recognized.

The existence of these distinct sanctions, of which one is classed as moral and the other not, is still more clearly seen when we contrast the maxims of Christianity with the dogmas of duellists. During centuries throughout Europe, and even still throughout the greater part of it, there has existed, and exists, an imperative "obligation," under certain conditions, to challenge another to fight, and an imperative obligation to accept the challenge—an obligation much more imperative than the obligation to discharge a debt. To either combatant the word "must" is used with as much emphasis as it would be used were he enjoined to tell the truth. The "duty" of the insulted man is to defend his honor; and so wrong is his conduct considered if he does not do this, that he is shunned by his friends as a disgraced man, just as he would be had he committed a theft. Beyond question, then, we see here ideas of right and wrong quite as pronounced, with corresponding sentiments of approbation and reprobation quite as strong, as those which refer to fulfillments and breaches of what are classed as moral injunctions. How, then, can we include the last under ethical science and exclude the first from it?

The need for greatly widening the current conception of ethics is, however, still greater than is thus shown. There are other large classes of actions which excite ideas and feelings undistinguishable in their essential natures from those to which the term ethical is conventionally limited.

120. Among uncivilized and semicivilized peoples, the obligations imposed by custom are peremptory. The universal belief that such things *ought* to be done, is not usually made manifest by the visiting of punishment or reprobation on those who do not conform, because nonconformity is scarcely heard of. How intolerable to the general mind is breach of usages, is shown occasionally when a ruler is deposed and

even killed for disregard of them: a sufficient proof that his act is held wrong. And we sometimes find distinct expressions of moral sentiment on behalf of customs having nothing which we should call moral authority, and even on behalf of customs which we should call profoundly immoral.

I may begin with an instance I have named elsewhere in another connection—the instance furnished by some Mahomedan tribes who consider that one of the worst offenses is smoking: "drinking the shameful," as they term it. Palgrave narrates that while "giving divine honors to a creature," is regarded by the Wahhabees as "the first of the great sins," the second great sin is smoking—a sin in comparison with which murder, adultery, and false witness, are trivial sins. Similarly, by certain Russian sects close to Siberia, smoking is an offense distinguished from all others as being never forgiven: "every crime can be expiated by repentance except this one." In these cases the repugnance felt for an act held by us to be quite harmless, is of the same nature as the repugnance felt for the blackest crimes: the only difference being that it is more intense.

Lichtenstein tells us that when Mulihawang, king of the Matelhapees (a division of the Bechuanas), was told that Europeans are not permitted to have more than one wife, "he said it was perfectly incomprehensible to him how a whole nation could submit voluntarily to such extraordinary laws." Similar was the opinion of the Arab sheikh who, along with his people, received the account of monogamy in England with indignation, and said "the fact is simply *impossible!* How *can* a man be contented with one wife?" Nor is it only men who think thus. Livingstone says of the Makololo women on the shores of the Zambesi, that they were quite shocked to hear that in England a man had only one wife: to have only one was not "respectable." So, too, in Equatorial Africa, according to Reade, "If a man marries, and his wife thinks that he can afford another spouse, she pesters him to marry again; and calls him a 'stingy fellow' if he declines to do so." Similar is the feeling shown by the Araucanian women. "Far from being dissatisfied, or entertaining any jealousy toward the newcomer, she [one of two wives] said that she wished her husband would marry again; for she considered it a great relief to have some one to assist her in her household duties, and in the maintenance of her husband." No notion of immorality, much less criminality, such as we associate with bigamy and polygamy, is here entertained; but, contrariwise, when a woman calls her husband a "stingy fellow" if he does not take a second wife, we have proof that monogamy is reprobated.

Ideas relevant to the relations of the sexes, still more profoundly at variance with our own, are displayed in many places. Books of travel have made readers familiar with the fact that among various races, a traveller entertained by a chief is offered a wife or a daughter as a temporary bedfellow; and the duty of hospitality is held to require this offer. In other cases the loan takes a somewhat different shape. Of the Chinooks we read:

> Among all the tribes, a man will lend his wife or daughter for a fish-hook or a strand of beads. To decline an offer of this sort is, indeed, to disparage the charms of the lady, and therefore give such offense, that although we had occasionally to treat the Indians with rigor, nothing seemed to irritate both sexes more than our refusal to accept the favors of the females.

Still more pronounced is the feeling shown by the members of an Asiatic tribe which Erman visited: "The Chuckchi offer to travelers who chance to visit them, their wives, and also what we should call their daughters' honor, and resent as a deadly affront any refusal of such offers." Here we see that deeds which among ourselves would be classed among the profoundest disgraces, are not only regarded without shame, but declining to participate in them causes indignation: implying a sense of wrong.

As it concerns in another way the relations of the sexes, I may instance next a further contrast between the sentiments entertained by many partially civilized peoples, and those which have arisen along with the advance of civilization. Interdicts on marriages between persons of different ranks, breaches of which have in some cases brought the severest punishment, date back to very early times. Thus, in the *Mahabharata* we read that Draupadi refused the "ambitious Karna," saying, "I wed not with the baseborn." And then, coming down to comparatively modern times, we have the penalties entailed on those who broke the laws against *mésalliances;* as in France during the feudal period, on nobles who married beneath them: they were excluded from tournaments, and their descendants also. But the condemnation thus manifested five centuries ago is not paralleled now. Though a certain amount of reprobation is in some cases shown, in other cases there is approbation; and witness Tennyson's "Miller's Daughter" and Mrs. Browning's "Lady Geraldine's Courtship." Here the different feelings excited, though like in nature to those we call moral, are not concerned with either supposed divine commands or with acts usually classed as moral or immoral.

Returning to the uncivilized races, I may instance the conceptions associated with the division of labor between the sexes. Concerning various tribes of American Indians, North and South, we read that custom, limiting the actions of the men mainly to war and the chase, devolves on the women all the menial and laborious occupations; and these customs have an imperative sanction. Says Falkner concerning the Patagonians: "So rigidly are" the women "obliged to perform their duty, that their husbands cannot help them on any occasion, or in the greatest distress, without incurring the highest ignominy." And these usages are fully approved of by the women themselves; as witness the following extract concerning the Dakotas:

> It is the worst insult one virago can cast upon another in a moment of altercation. "Infamous woman!" will she cry, "I have seen your husband carrying wood into his lodge to make the fire. Where was his squaw, that he should be obliged to make a woman of himself?"

Clearly this indignation is the correlative of a strong moral feeling enlisted on behalf of the prescribed conduct. But if, among ourselves, any women were left, as among the Es-quimaux, "to carry stones [for building houses], almost heavy enough to break their backs," while "the men look on with the greatest insensibility, not stirring a finger to assist them," moral reprobation would be felt. As there are no specific injunctions, divine or human, referring to transactions of these kinds, the strongly contrasted emotions which they excite in ourselves and in these uncivilized peoples, must be ascribed to unlikenesses of customs—unlikenesses, however, which are themselves significant of innate emotional un-likenesses.

As further illustrating in a variety of ways these differences of feelings akin in nature to those we call moral, though not ordinarily classed as such, I may, without commenting upon each, here append a series of them.

> The Caffers despise the Hottentots, Bushmen, Malays, and other people of color, on account of their not being circumcised. On this account, they regard them as boys, and will not allow them to sit in their company, or to eat with them.
>
> A Mayoruna, who had been baptized, when at the point of death was very unhappy . . . because, dying as a Christian, instead of furnishing a meal to his relations, he would be eaten up by worms.
>
> The Bambara washerwomen . . . were stark naked, yet they man-ifested no shame at being seen in this state by the men composing our caravan.

And a kindred statement is made concerning the Waka-virondo by Thomson, who describes their women as never-theless altogether modest, and, remarking that "morality has nothing to do with clothes," says of these people that "they are the most moral of all the tribes of this region, and they are simply angels of purity beside the decently dressed Masai." "I found that the married men," among the Hassanyeh Arabs, says Petherick,

> felt themselves highly flattered by any attentions paid to their better halves during their free-and-easy days. [Their marriages are for three or four days in the week only.] They seem to take such attentions as evidence that their wives are attractive.

Among the Khonds, so far as constancy to a husband from being required in a wife, that her pretensions do not, in the least, suffer diminution in the eyes of either sex when fines are levied on her convicted lovers; while on the other hand, infidelity on the part of a married man is held to be highly dishonorable, and is often punished by deprivation of many social privileges.

I have reserved for the last, two remarkable cases in which feelings like those which we class as moral, are definitely expressed in ways to us very surprising. The first concerns the Tahitians, who were described by Cook as without shame in respect of actions which among ourselves especially excite it, and as feeling shame in respect of actions which among ourselves excite none. These people were extremely averse to our custom of eating in society. "They eat alone, they said, because it was right." The other instance, equally anomalous, is even more startling. In Vate "it is considered a disgrace to the family of an aged chief if he is not buried alive." A like usage and accompanying feeling existed in Fiji.

A son said, when about to bury his mother alive, that it was from love to his mother that he had done so; that, in consequence of the same love, they were now going to bury her, and that none but themselves could or ought to do so sacred an office! . . . she was their mother, and they were her children, and they ought to put her to death.

The belief being that people commence life in the next world at the stage they have reached when they leave this world; and that hence postponement of death till old age entails a subsequent miserable existence.

Thus we have abundant proof that with acts which do violence to our moral sentiments, there are associated, in the minds of other races, feelings and ideas not only warranting them but enforcing them. They are fulfilled with a sense of obligation; and nonfulfillment of them, regarded as breach of duty, brings condemnation and resulting self-reproach.

121. Everywhere during social progress custom passes into law. Practically speaking, custom *is* law in undeveloped

societies. "The old Innuits did so, and therefore we must," say the existing Innuits (Esquimaux); and other uncivilized peoples similarly express the constraint they are under. In subsequent stages, customs become the acknowledged bases of laws. It is true that afterwards the body of laws is made up in part of alleged divine commands—the *themistes* of the Greeks, for example; but in reality these, supposed to come from one who was originally an apotheosized ruler, usually enforce existing customs. *Leviticus* shows us a whole body of practices, many of them of kinds which would be now regarded as neither religious nor moral, thus acquiring authority. Whether inherited from the undistinguished forefathers of the tribes, or ascribed to the will of a deceased king, customs embody the rule of the dead over the living; as do also the laws into which they harden.

Of course, therefore, if ideas of duty and feelings of obligation cluster round customs, they cluster round the derived laws. The sentiment of "ought" comes to be associated with a legal injunction, as with an injunction traced to the general authority of ancestors or the special authority of a deified ancestor. And not only does there hence arise a consciousness that obedience to each particular law is right and disobedience to it wrong, but eventually there arises a consciousness that obedience to law in general is right and disobedience to it wrong. Especially is this the case where the living ruler has a divine or semidivine character; as witness the following statement concerning the ancient Peruvians: "The most common punishment was death, for they said that a culprit was not punished for the delinquencies he had committed, but for having broken the commandment of the Ynea, who was respected as God." And this conception, reminding us of religious conceptions anciently current and still current, is practically paralleled by the conceptions still expressed by jurists and accepted by most citizens. For though a distinction is commonly made between legal obligation and moral obligation, in those cases where the law is of a kind in respect of which ethics gives no direct verdict; yet the obligation to obey has come to be, if not nominally yet practically, a moral obligation. The words habitually used imply this. It is held "right" to obey the law and "wrong" to disobey it. Conformity and nonconformity bring approbation and reprobation, just as though the legal injunction were a moral injunction. A man who has broken the law, even though it be in a matter of no ethical significance—say a householder who has refused to fill up the census paper or a peddler who has not taken out a license—feels, when he is brought before the magistrates, that he is regarded not only by them but by spectators as morally blameworthy. The feeling shown is quite as strong as it would be were he convicted of aggressing on his neighbors by nuisances—perpetual noises or pestilent odors—which are moral offenses properly so called. That is to say, law is upheld by a sentiment indistinguishable from moral sentiment. Moreover, in some cases where the two conflict, the sentiment which upholds the legal *dictum* overrides the sentiment which upholds the moral *dictum;* as in the case of the peddler above named. His act in selling without a license is morally justifiable, and forbidding him to sell without a license is morally unjustifiable—is an interference with his due liberty, which is ethically unwarranted. Yet the factitious moral sentiment enlisted on behalf of legal authority, triumphs over the natural moral sentiment enlisted on behalf of rightful freedom.

How strong is the artificial sanction acquired by a constituted authority, is seen very strikingly in the doings of Joint Stock associations. If the directors of a company formed to carry out a specified undertaking, decide to extend their activities so as to include undertakings not originally specified, and even undertakings wholly unallied to those originally specified; and if they bring before the proprietary their proposals for doing this; it is held that if a majority (at one time a simple majority, but now two-thirds) approve the proposal, the proprietary at large is bound by the decision. Should a few protest against being committed to such new undertakings, they are frowned upon and pooh-poohed as unreasonable obstructions: moral reprobation is vented against such resistance to the ruling agent and its supporters. Nevertheless, the moral reprobation should be inverted. As a question of pure equity, the incorporated body cannot enter on any businesses not specified or implied in the deed of incorporation. Those who break the original contract by entering on unspecified businesses, are unjustified; while those who stand by the original contract, however few in number, are justified. Yet so strong is the quasi-moral sanction associated with the acts of a constituted authority, that its ethically wrong course is thought right, and insistence on regard for the ethically right course is thought wrong!

122. How then are ethical ideas and sentiments to be defined? How, indeed, are they to be conceived in any consistent way? Let us recapitulate.

Throughout the past, and down to present days in most minds, conceptions of right and wrong have been directly associated with supposed divine injunctions. Acts have been classed as good or bad, not because of their intrinsic natures but because of their extrinsic derivations; and virtue has consisted in obedience. Under certain circumstances, we find conduct regarded as praiseworthy or blameworthy according as it does or does not inflict suffering or death upon fellow beings; while, under other circumstances, we find the praise or blame given according as it does or does not conduce to the welfare of fellow beings. Then there is the opposition between hedonism and asceticism: by some approbation is felt for deeds which apparently conduce to the happiness of self or others or both; while, contrariwise, others look with reprobation upon a way of living which makes happiness an end. By this class the perceptions of good and evil conduct, along with love of the one and hatred of the other, are traced to a moral sense; and ethics becomes the interrogation of, and obedience to, conscience. Contrariwise, by that class such guidance is ridiculed; and calculations of consequences, irrespective of sentiment of right or theory of right, occupy the ethical sphere. Universally in early stages, and to a considerable degree in late stages, the idea of *ought* is associated with conformity to established customs, irrespective of their natures; and when established customs grow into laws, the idea of *ought* comes to be associated with obedience to laws: no matter whether considered intrinsically good or intrinsically bad.

Clearly, therefore, the conceptions of *right, obligation, duty,* and the sentiments associated with those conceptions, have a far wider range than the conduct ordinarily conceived as the subject matter of moral science. In different places and under different circumstances, substantially the same ideas and feelings are joined with classes of actions of totally opposite kinds, and also with classes of actions of which moral science, as ordinarily conceived, takes no cognizance. Hence, if we are to treat the subject scientifically, we must disregard the limits of conventional ethics, and consider what are the intrinsic natures of ethical ideas and sentiments.

123. A trait common to all forms of sentiments and ideas to be classed as ethical, is the consciousness of *authority.* The nature of the authority is inconstant. It may be that of an apotheosized ruler or other deity supposed to give commands. It may be that of ancestors who have bequeathed usages, with or without injunctions to follow them. It may be that of a living ruler who makes laws, or a military commander who issues orders. It may be that of an aggregate public opinion, either expressed through a government or otherwise expressed. It may be that of an imagined utility which every one is bound to further. Or it may be that of an internal monitor distinguished as conscience.

Along with the element of authority, at once intellectually recognized and emotionally responded to, there goes the element, more or less definite, of *coercion.* The consciousness of *ought* which the recognition of authority implies, is joined with the consciousness of *must*, which the recognition of force implies. Be it the power of a god, of a king, of a chief soldier, of a popular government, of an inherited custom, of an unorganized social feeling, there is always present the conception of a power. Even when the injunction is that of an internal monitor, the conception of a power is not absent; since the expectation of the penalty of self-reproach, which disobedience may entail, is vaguely recognized as coercive.

A further component of the ethical consciousness, and often the largest component, is the represented *opinion* of other individuals, who also, in one sense, constitute an authority and exercise a coercion. This, either as actually implied in others' behavior, or as imagined if they are not present, commonly serves more than anything else to restrain or impel. How large a component this is, we see in a child who blushes when wrongly suspected of a transgression, as much as when rightly suspected; and probably most have had proof that, when guiltless, the feeling produced by the conceived reprobation of others is scarcely distinguishable from the feeling which would be produced by such reprobation if guilty. That an imagined public opinion is the chief element of consciousness in cases where the acts ascribed or committed are intrinsically wrong, is shown when this imagined or expressed opinion refers to acts which are not intrinsically wrong. The emotion of shame ordinarily accompanying some gross breach of social convention which is morally indifferent, or even morally praiseworthy (say wheeling home the barrow of a costermonger who has lamed himself), may be quite as strong as the emotion of shame which follows the proved utterance of an unwarranted libel—an act intrinsically wrong. In the majority of people the feeling of *ought not* will be more peremptory in the first case than in the last.

If, now, we look at the matter apart from conventional classifications, we see that where the consciousnesses of authority, of coercion, and of public opinion, combined in different proportions, result in an idea and a feeling of obligation, we must class these as ethical irrespective of the kind of action to which they refer. If the associated conceptions of right are similar, and the prompting emotions similar, we must consider the mental states as of the same nature, though they are enlisted on behalf of acts radically opposed. Or rather, let us say that, with the exception of an idea and a sentiment incidentally referred to, we must class them as forming a body of thought and feeling which may be called proethical; and which, with the mass of mankind, stands in place of the ethical properly so called.

124. For now let us observe that the ethical sentiment and idea properly so called, are independent of the ideas and sentiments above described as derived from external authorities, and coercions, and approbations—religious, political, or social. The true moral consciousness which we name conscience, does not refer to those extrinsic results of conduct which take the shape of praise or blame, reward or punishment, externally awarded; but it refers to the intrinsic results of conduct which, in part and by some intellectually perceived, are mainly and by most, intuitively felt. The moral consciousness proper does not contemplate obligations as artificially imposed by an external power; nor is it chiefly occupied with estimates of the amounts of pleasure and pain which given actions may produce, though these may be clearly or dimly perceived; but it is chiefly occupied with recognition of, and regard for, those *conditions* by fulfillment of which happiness is achieved or misery avoided. The sentiment enlisted on behalf of these conditions is often in harmony with the proethical sentiment compounded as above described, though from time to time in conflict with it; but whether in harmony or in conflict, it is vaguely or distinctly recognized as the rightful ruler: responding, as it does, to consequences which are not artificial and variable, but to consequences which are natural and permanent.

It should be remarked that along with established supremacy of this ethical sentiment proper, the feeling of obligation, though continuing to exist in the background of consciousness, ceases to occupy its foreground; since the right actions are habitually performed spontaneously or from liking. Though, while the moral nature is imperfectly developed, there may often arise conformity to the ethical sentiment under a sense of compulsion by it; and though, in other cases, nonconformity to it may cause subsequent self-reproach (as instance a remembered lack of gratitude, which may be a source of pain without there being any thought of extrinsic penalty); yet with a moral nature completely balanced, neither of these feelings will arise, because that which is done is done in satisfaction of the appropriate desire.

And now having, mainly for the purpose of making the statement complete, contemplated the ethical sentiment proper, as distinguished from the proethical sentiment, we may for the present practically dismiss it from our thoughts, and consider only the phenomena presented by the proethical sentiment under its various forms. For throughout the remaining chapters of this division, treating inductively of ideas and feelings about conduct displayed by mankind at large we shall be concerned almost exclusively with the proethical sentiment: the ethical sentiment proper being, in the great mass of cases, scarcely discernible.

Before entering on the task indicated, let me add that a good deal which approaches to repetition will be found in the immediately succeeding pages—not repetition in so far as the evidence given is concerned, but in so far as the cardinal ideas are concerned. In the preliminary discussion to which this chapter and the preceding one have been devoted, it has been necessary to state in brief some of the leading conceptions which a general inspection of the phenomena suggests. These conceptions have now to be set forth in full, along with the masses of facts which give birth to them. But while it seems well to apologize beforehand for the recurrence, in elaborated forms, of ideas already expressed in small space, I do not altogether regret having to elaborate the ideas; since there will be afforded occasion for further emphasizing conclusions which can scarcely be too much dwelt upon.

CHAPTER 3

Aggression

125. Under this title, accepted in its full meaning, may be ranged many kinds of acts—acts so many and various that they cannot be dealt with in one chapter. Here I propose to restrict the application of the title to acts inflicting bodily injury on others to the extent of killing or wounding them—acts of kinds which we class as destructive.

Even of these acts, which we may consider as completely or partially homicidal, there are sundry kinds not comprehended under aggression as ordinarily understood. I refer to those which do not imply antagonism or conflict.

The first of them to be named is infanticide. Far from being regarded as a crime, child-murder has been, throughout the world in early times, and in various parts of the world still is, regarded as not even an offense: occasionally, indeed, as a duty. We have that infanticide which is dictated by desire to preserve the lives of adults; for in a tribe which is ever on the border of starvation, addition of some to its number may prove fatal to others. Female infanticide, too, is often dictated by thought of tribal welfare: the established policy is to kill girls, who, while not useful for purposes of war and the chase, will, if in excess, injuriously tax the food supplies. Then, again, we have the child-murder committed in a fit of passion.

371

Among savages, and even among the semicivilized, this is considered an indifferent matter: the power of life and death over children being, in early stages, taken for granted. Once more we have the sacrifice of children to propitiate cannibal chiefs, living or dead. Regarded as an obligation, this may be classed as prompted by a proethical sentiment.

Turning to the socially sanctioned homicides of which the victims are adults, we may set down first those which in many places occur at funerals; as instance Indian suttees until recent times. On much larger scales are the immolations during the obsequies of chiefs and kings. The killing of wives to accompany their dead husbands to the other world, and the killing of male attendants to serve them in the other world (sometimes also of friends) are forms of wholesale slaughter which have occurred in many countries, and still occur in parts of Africa. And with these may be joined such slaughters as those which are common in Dahomey, where a man is killed that his double may carry a message from the king to a deceased ancestor. Homicides of this class have also a kind of proethical warrant; since they are instigated by reverence for custom and by the obligation of loyalty.

Lastly we have the homicides prompted by beliefs classed as religious. With or without the ascription of divine cannibalism, the sacrifices of victims to deities have prevailed widely among various races in early times—Phoenicians, Scythians, Greeks, Romans, Assyrians, Hebrews &c.— carried, in some places, to great extremes; as in Ancient Mexico, where thousands of human victims annually were slain on altars, and where wars were made on the plea that the gods were hungry. And to these religious homicides which, in early stages, ministered to the supposed appetites of the gods, must be added the religious homicides which, in comparatively modern times, have been committed, alike by Catholics and Protestants, to appease the supposed wrath of their God against misbelievers.

Under that theory which regards the rightness of acts as constituted by fulfillment of divine injunctions, these religious homicides, in common with sundry of those above described, were prompted by one of the motives we class as proethical.

126. From these aggressions, taking the form of homicides, which are not consequent on personal or tribal antagonisms, let us pass to those of which bloodthirstiness is the cause, with or without enmity, personal or tribal.

I will begin with an instance which I have named elsewhere—that of the Fijians, among whom murder was thought honorable. Credence to this statement, which otherwise one would be inclined to withhold, is justified by knowledge of kindred statements respecting other peoples. Livingstone tells us that a Bushman

> sat by the fire relating his early adventures: among these was killing five other Bushmen. "Two," said he, counting on his fingers, "were females, one a male, and the other two calves." "What a villain you are to boast of killing women and children of your own nation! What will God say when you appear before him?" "He will say," replied he, "that I was a very clever fellow." . . . I discovered that, though he was employing the word which is used among the Bakwains when speaking of the Deity, he had only the idea of a chief, and was all the time referring to Sekomi.

Still more astounding is the state of things, and the kind of sentiment, described by Wilson and Felkin in their account of Uganda. Here is an illustrative incident.

> A young page of Mtesa's [king of Uganda], son of a subordinate chief, was frequently employed to bring me messages from the palace, and one morning came down to my house, and informed me with great glee that he had just killed his father. I inquired why he had done this, and he said that he was tired of being merely a servant, and wished to become a chief, and said so to Mtesa, who replied, "Oh, kill your father, and you will become a chief"; and the boy did so.

That, among peoples who lead lives of aggression, it is a virtue to be a destroyer and a vice to be peaceful, sundry cases prove.

The name of "harami"—brigand—is still honorable among the
Hejazi Bedouins. . . . He, on the other hand, who is lucky enough, as
we should express it, to die in his bed, is called "fatis" (carrion, the
corps crévé of the Klephts); his weeping mother will exclaim, "O that
my son had perished of a cut-throat!" and her attendant crones will
suggest, with deference, that such evil came of the will of Allah.

How profound may become the belief in the virtue of manslaughter, is made clear by the Kukis, whose paradise is "the
heritage of the man who has killed the largest number of his
enemies in life, the people killed by him attending on him as
his slaves."

With this supposed divine approval of manslaying, we may
join the social approval manifested in other cases. Among the
Pathans, one of the tribes on the northwest frontier of the
Punjab, "there is hardly a man whose hands are unstained,"
and "each person counts up his murders." That, under wild
social conditions, a sentiment of this kind readily arises, was
shown in California during the gold period. Murderers "continued to notch the number of their victims on neatly kept
hilts of pistols or knives."

127. If from the implied or expressed belief in the honorableness of private homicide, illustrated by some still-extant
savages, we turn to the belief in the honorableness of that
public and wholesale homicide for which the occasions are
given by real or pretended intertribal or international injuries,
ancient records of barbarous and semicivilized peoples furnish illustrations in abundance.

Among the gods of the primitive Indians, Indra is lauded in
the *Rig-Veda* as the devastating warrior, and Agni, too, "was
born, the slayer of the enemy," and the "destroyer of cities."
Emulating their gods, the warriors of the *Rig-Veda* and the
Mahabharata glory in conquests. Propitiating Indra with deep
libations, the hero prays: "Let us share the wealth of him
whom thou hast slain; bring us to the household of him who
is hard to vanquish." And then with such prayers, common

to militant peoples, may be joined passages from the *Mahabharata* recommending atrocities.

> Let a man inspire his enemy with confidence for some real reason, and then smite him at the proper time, when his foot has slipped a little.
>
> Without cutting into an enemy's marrow, without doing something dreadful, without smiting like a killer of fish, a man does not attain great prosperity.
>
> A son, a brother, a father, or a friend, who present any obstacle to one's interests are to be slain.

After these early Aryans, look now at some of the early Semites. Still more extreme in the implied praiseworthiness of sanguinary deeds, are they shown to have been by their records. Assyrian kings glorify themselves in inscriptions describing wholesale slaughters and the most savage cruelties. Sennacherib, driving his chariot through "deep pools of blood," boasts—"with blood and flesh its wheels were clogged"; Assurbanipal says of the conquered—"their tongues I pulled out," "the limbs cut off I caused to be eaten by dogs, bears, eagles, vultures, birds of heaven"; Tiglath-Pileser's account of the slain Muskayans is that "their carcases covered the valleys and the tops of the mountains"; in an inscription of Assur-natsir-pal come the words—"I am a weapon that spares not," the revolted nobles "I flayed, with their skins I covered the pyramid," "their young men and maidens I burned as a holocaust"; and of his enemies Shalmaneser II says—"with their blood I dyed the mountains like wool." Evidently the expectation was that men of after times would admire these merciless destructions, and this implies belief in their righteousness; for we cannot assume that these Assyrian kings intentionally made themselves eternally infamous.

Omitting evidence furnished in plenty by the histories of the Egyptians, Persians, Greeks, Macedonians, Romans, we find kindred thoughts and feelings betrayed by the peoples of northern Europe. The Gauls of early days, galloping home with the heads of their enemies slung to their saddles, displayed them on stakes or preserved them in chests. According to Cæsar, the Suevi and Germans generally "esteem it their greatest praise . . . that the lands about their territories lie unoccupied to a very great extent." And the fact that the Norse paradise was conceived as a place for daily combats, sufficiently shows how dominant was the belief in the virtue of successful aggression. That throughout the Middle Ages successful aggression was thought the one thing worth living for, needs no proof. History, which is little more than the Newgate Calendar of nations, describing political burglaries and their results, yields illustrations on every page: "arms and the man" supply the universal theme. No better way of showing the dominant sentiment down to comparatively recent times, can be found than that of quoting the mottoes of nobles, of which here are some English ones. Earl of Rosslyn—"Fight"; Baron Hawke—"Strike"; Earl of Sefton—"To conquer is to live"; the Marquis of Downshire—"By God and my sword I will obtain"; the Earl of Carysfort—"This hand is hostile"; Count Magawley—"The red hand to victory"; the Duke of Athole—"Forth, fortune, and fill the fetters." And the general spirit is well shown by lines illustrating the motto of the Middleton family:

> My sword, my spear, my shaggy shield,
> These make me lord of all below,
> And he who fears the lance to wield
> Beneath my shaggy shield must bow,
> His lands, his vineyards must resign,
> For all that cowards have is mine.

Mottoes being the expressions of feelings held above all others worthy, and tacitly assuming the existence of like feelings in others, those quoted imply the social sanction given to aggressiveness; and we need but recall the religious ceremonies on the initiation of a knight, to see that his militant course of life was supposed to have a divine sanction also. War, even unprovoked war, was supported by a proethical sentiment.

Nor is it essentially otherwise even now. Thinly veiled by conventional respect for the professed religious creed, the old spirit continually discloses itself. Much more feeling than is excited by a hymn, is excited by the song—"The Hardy Norseman"; and pride in the doing of the "seawolves" who "conquered Normandy," shown by the line—"Oh, ne'er should we forget our sires," is habitually sympathized in. No reading is more popular than narratives of battles; and the epithet "great," as applied to Alexander, Karl, Peter, Frederick, Napoleon, is applied notwithstanding all the atrocities they committed. Occasionally, indeed, we meet with overt expression of this sentiment. Lord Wolseley says of the soldier: "He must believe that his duties are the noblest that fall to man's lot. He must be taught to despise all those of civil life": a sentiment which is not limited to the "duties" of the soldier as a defender of his country, which in our day he never performs, but is extended to his "duties" as an invader of other countries, and especially those of weak peoples: the appetite for aggression transforms baseness into nobility. When, in the Hindoo epic, the god Indra is described as conquering a woman, we are astonished to find a victory which we should consider so cowardly lauded by the poet; and when, on the walls of Karnak, we see Rameses represented as a giant holding by the hair half-a-dozen dwarfs, and cutting off all their heads with one sweep of his sword, we think it strange that he should have thought to glorify himself by depicting an easy triumph of strong over weak. But when with arms of precision, with shells, with rockets, with far-reaching cannon, peoples possessed only of feeble weapons are conquered with as great facility as a man conquers a child, there comes applause in our journals, with titles and rewards to the leaders! The "duties" of the soldier so performed are called "noble"; while, held up in contrast with them, those of the peaceful citizen are called despicable!

Beyond question, then, the sentiment which rejoices in personal superiority, and, not asking for equitable cause, is ready, under an authority it willingly accepts, to slaughter so-called enemies, is still dominant. The social sanction, and the reflected inner sanction due to it, constitute a proethical sentiment which, in international relations, remains supreme.

128. The ethics of enmity thus illustrated, very little qualified in some tribes of savages, especially cannibals, qualified in but a moderate degree in ancient semicivilized societies, and continuing predominant during the development of civilized societies, has been qualified more and more by the ethics of amity as the internal social life has disciplined men in cooperation: the relative prosperities of nations, while in part determined by their powers of conquest, having been all along in part determined by the extents to which, in daily intercourse, the aggressiveness of their members has been restrained.

Such peoples as have produced literatures show us, in relatively early days, the rise of an ethics of amity, set in opposition to the ethics of enmity. Proceeding, as the expressions of it do, from the mouths of poets and sages, we may not measure by them the beliefs which then prevailed; any more than we may now measure the prevailing beliefs by the injunctions to forgive enemies, perpetually uttered by our priests. But even the occasional enunciation of altruistic sentiments, occurring in ancient societies after there had been long-established states of relatively peaceful life, is significant. And it is interesting to observe, too, how, after the absolute selfishness of the antagonistic activities, a violent reaction led to the preaching of absolute unselfishness. Thus while of that vast compilation which constitutes the *Mahabharata*, the older parts are saguinary in sentiment, the latter parts contain condemnations of needless warfare. It is said that fighting is the worst means of gaining victory, and that a king should extend his conquests without fighting. And there are much more pronounced reprobations of aggressive action, as this:

> Treat others as thou would'st thyself be treated.
> Do nothing to thy neighbor, which hereafter
> Thou would'st not have thy neighbor do to thee.
> A man obtains a rule of action by looking on his neighbor as himself.

And then in the writings of an Indian moralist, said by Sir William Jones to date three centuries B.C., we read the extreme statement: "A good man who thinks only of benefiting his enemy has no feelings of hostility towards him even at the moment of being destroyed by him." Similarly among the Persians, we find Sadi writing—"Show kindness even to thy foes"; and again—"The men of God's true faith, I've heard, grieve not the hearts e'en of their foes." In like manner among the Chinese, the teaching of Lao-Tsze was that

> Peace is his highest aim. . . . he who rejoices at the destruction of human life is not fit to be entrusted with power in the world. He who has been instrumental in killing many people should move on over them with bitter tears.

Confucius said: "In carrying on your government, why should you use killing at all? Let your *evinced* desires be for what is good, and the people will be good." Mencius held that "he who has no pleasure in killing men can" unite the empire; and of the warlike he said that:

> When contentions about territory are the ground on which they fight, they slaughter men, till the fields are filled with them. When some struggle for a city is the ground on which they fight, they slaughter men till the city is filled with them. . . . Death is not enough for such a crime.

Early as was his time, Mencius evidently entertained higher sentiments than do "the western barbarians" at the present time. The characterization which has been given to slavery—

"the sum of all villainies"—would probably have been given by him to aggressive war.

In section 573 of *The Principles of Sociology*, as also in section 437, instances are given of various tribes which, nonaggressive externally are also nonaggressive internally—tribes in which crimes of violence are so rare that scarcely any control is needed. There may be added a few other examples. There are the aborigines of Sumatra, a simple people who, thrust into the interior by the Malays, are described by Marsden as "mild, peaceable, and forbearing"—that is nonaggressive. There are the Thârus, inhabiting a retired strip of forest at the foot of the Himalayas, which affords them a refuge from invaders, and who are described as "a peaceful and good-natured race." Further, we have a specially relevant testimony given by different authorities respecting the Iroquois. In his work, *The League of the Iroquois*, Morgan says: "It was the boast of the Iroquois that the great object of their confederacy was peace—to break up the spirit of perpetual warfare, which had wasted the red race from age to age." And then clear indication of the results is contained in the following statement made by the same writer: "Crimes and offenses were so unfrequent under their social system, that the Iroquois can scarcely be said to have had a criminal code."

Here, however, the truth which it specially concerns us to note is that during states of hostility which make aggression habitual, it acquires a social sanction, and in some cases a divine sanction: there is a proethical sentiment enlisted on its behalf. Contrariwise, in the cases just referred to, aggressiveness meets with reprobation. An ethical sentiment, rightly so-called, produces repugnance to it.

Nor was it otherwise with the Hebrews. After the chronic antagonisms of nomadic life had been brought to an end by their captivity, and after their subsequent wars of conquest had ended in a comparatively peaceful state, the expression of altruistic sentiments became marked; until, in *Leviticus*, we see emerging the principle, often regarded as exclusively Christian—"Thou shalt love thy neighbor as thyself"—a principle, however, which appears to have been limited to "the congregation of the children of Israel." And then in later days by the Essenes, as well as by Christ and his apostles, the ethics of amity, extended so as to include enemies, was carried even to the extreme of turning the cheek to the smiter.

129. Into what general induction may these facts be grouped? Taken in the mass, the evidence shows, as we might expect, that in proportion as intertribal and international antagonisms are great and constant, the ideas and feelings belonging to the ethics of enmity predominate; and, conflicting as they do with the ideas and feelings belonging to the ethics of amity, proper to the internal life of a society, they in greater or less degrees suppress these, and fill with aggressions the conduct of man to man.

Miscellaneous kinds of homicide, such as were noted at the outset—infanticide, killing for cannibalism, immolations at funerals, sacrifices to the gods—are characteristic of societies in which warfare is habitual. Those most atrocious of man-eaters, the Fijians, among whom every one carried his life in his hand, implied their ingrained militancy by their conception of the other world, where their gods "make war, and kill and eat each another," and bear such names as "the murderer," "fresh from the cutting up or slaughter," &c.; where a chief arriving after death, boasts that he has "destroyed many towns, and slain many in war"; and where "men who have not slain an enemy" suffer "the most degrading of all punishments." The Bushmen, exhibiting pride in private murder, pass their lives in ceaseless antagonism with men and beasts around—aggressing and aggressed upon. So, too, the Bedouin tribes instanced as thinking any death save one suffered in combat disgraceful, commit never-ending aggressions. And the Waganda, the king of whom suggested to his page the parricide gladly carried out by him, are soldiers noted for "their warlike character, which tinges the whole of their life and government."

If, from the relations as illustrated in these extreme cases, we pass to the relations as illustrated in developing societies, we see that with decrease of external aggressiveness there goes decrease of internal aggressiveness. During the Merovingian period, along with chronic militant activities on large and small scales, occurring even to the extent of wars between towns, perpetual violence characterized the relations of individuals: kings murdered their queens, royal fathers were murdered by their sons, princely brothers murdered brothers, while bloodshed and cruelty prevailed everywhere. In the next period the conquests of Charlemagne were accompanied by atrocities large and small. He beheaded 4,000 Saxons in one day, and inflicted death on those who refused baptism or ate flesh during Lent. Similarly throughout the feudal ages, recurring international fights were accompanied by perpetual fights among nobles; the chroniclers describe little else than crimes; and the slaughtering of serfs by knights was passed over as a thing not calling for reproach. But as the course of ages and the consolidation of kingdoms brought diminution of a diffused warfare, and as, by consequence, industrial activities, with resulting internal cooperation, filled larger spaces in men's lives, the more unscrupulous forms of aggressiveness came to be reprobated, while approbation was given to conduct characterized by regard for others. And though modern times have seen great wars, yet, since the militant activities have not been all-pervading as in earlier times, the sentiments appropriate to peaceful activities have not been so universally repressed. Moreover, as we elsewhere saw (*Principles of Sociology,* sec. 573), the brutality of citizens to one another has from time to time increased along with renewed militancy and decreased along with cessation of it; while there have been concomitant modifications in the ethical standard.

CHAPTER 4

Robbery

130. Between physically injuring another, partially or to the death, and injuring him either by taking possession of his body and labor, or of his property, the kinship in nature is obvious. Both direct and indirect injuries are comprehended under the title "Aggression"; and the second, like the first, might, without undue straining of words, have been brought within the limits of the last chapter. But, as before implied, it has seemed more convenient to separate the aggression which nearly always has bloodshed for its concomitant, from the aggression which is commonly bloodless. Here we have to deal with this last.

The extreme form of this last aggression is that which ends in capturing a man and enslaving him. Though to class this under the head of robbery is to do some violence to the name, yet we may reasonably say that to take a man from himself, and use his powers for other purposes than his own, is robbery in the highest degree. Instead of depriving him of some product of past labor voluntarily undertaken, it deprives him of the products of future labors which he is compelled to undertake. At any rate, whether rightly to be called robbery or not, it is to be classed as an aggression, if not so grave as that of inflicting death, yet next to it in gravity.

It is needless here to furnish proofs that this kind of aggression has been, from very early stages of human progress, a concomitant of militancy. Eating the vanquished or turning them into bondsmen, commonly became alternatives where intertribal conflicts were perpetual. From the incidental making of captives there has frequently grown up the intentional making of captives. An established policy has dictated invasions to procure workers or victims. But whether with or without intention, this robbery in the highest degree has been, throughout, a concomitant of habitual war; could not, indeed, have arisen to any extent without war.

A closely allied form of robbery—somewhat earlier, since we find it in rude tribes which do not make slaves—is the stealing of women. Of course, along with victory over combatants there has gone appropriation of the noncombatants belonging to them; and women have consequently been in all early stages among the prizes of conquerors. In books treating of primitive marriage, like that of Mr. McLennan, there will be found evidence that the stealing of women not unfrequently becomes the normal process by which the numbers of a tribe are maintained. It is found best to avoid the cost of rearing them, and to obtain by fighting or theft the requisite number from other tribes. Becoming a traditional policy, this custom often acquires a strong sanction; and is supposed by some to have originated the interdict against marriage with those of the same clan. But, however this may be, we habitually find women regarded as the most valued spoils of victory; and often, where the men are killed, the women are preserved to become mothers. It was so with the Caribs in their cannibal days; and it was so with the Hebrews, as shown in *Numbers* xxxi. 17–18, where we read that, after a successful war, all the wives and the males among the children were ordered by Moses to be killed, while the virgins were reserved for the use of the captors. (See also *Deuteronomy* xxi.)

Now the truth here to be observed is that in societies which have not risen to high stages, the ethical sentiment, or rather the proethical sentiment, makes no protest against robberies of these kind; but, contrariwise, gives countenance to them. The cruel treatment of prisoners delineated in Egyptian and Assyrian wall paintings and wall-sculptures, implies, what the records tell, that there was a social sanction for their subsequent bondage. Similarly, we do not see in the literature of the Greeks, any more than in the literature of the Hebrews, that the holding of men in slavery called forth moral reprobation. It was the same with the capture of women and the making wives of them, or more frequently concubines: this was creditable rather than discreditable. With the social sanction for the stealing of women by the early Aryans, as narrated in the *Mahabharata*, there was also a divine sanction; and it is manifest that among the Hebrews there was social if not divine sanction for the taking of the virgins of Jabesh Gilead for wives, and also for the stealing of the "daughters of Shiloh" (*Judges* xxi).

Under this head it needs only to add that modern progress with its prolonged discipline of internal amity, as opposed to that of external enmity, has been accompanied by disappearance of these grossest forms of robbery. The ethical sentiment, rightly so-called, has been developed to the extent needful for suppressing them.

131. Success in war being honorable, all accompaniments and signs of such success become honorable. Hence, along with the enslaving of captives if they are not eaten, and along with the appropriation of their women as concubines or wives, there goes the seizing of their property. A natural sequence is that not only during war but at other times, robbery of enemies, and by implication of strangers, who are ordinarily classed as enemies, is distinguished from robbery of fellow tribesmen: the first being called good even when the last is called bad.

Among the Comanches "a young man is not thought worthy to be counted in the list of warriors, till he has returned from some successful plundering expedition, . . . the greatest thieves are . . the most respectable members of society." A

Patagonian is considered "as indifferently capable of supporting a wife unless he is an adept in the art of stealing from a
stranger." Livingstone says of the East Africans:

> In tribes which have been accustomed to cattle-stealing, the act is
> not considered immoral, in the way that theft is. Before I knew the
> language well, I said to a chief, "You stole the cattle of so and so." "No,
> I did not steal them," was the reply, "I only *lifted* them." The word
> *"gapa"* is identical with the Highland term for the same deed.

Concerning the Kalmucks the account of Pallas is that they are
addicted to theft and robbery on a large scale, but not of
people of their own tribe. And Atkinson asserts the like of the
Kirghiz: "Thieving of this kind [stealing horses or camels from
one of the same tribe] is instantly punished among the Kirghiz; but a baranta, like the sacking of a town, is honorable
plunder." Hence doubtless arises that contrast, seeming to us
so strange, between the treatment which robber-tribes, such
as Bedouins, show to strangers under their roofs and the
opposite treatment they show to them after they have de-
parted. Says Atkinson: "My host [a Kirghiz chief] said
Koubaldos [another Kirghiz chief to whom I was going] would
not molest us at his *aoul*, but that some of his bands would be
set on our track and try to plunder us on our march." Perhaps
it is among the Turkomans that we find the most marked
illustrations of the way in which predatory tribes come to
regard theft as honorable. By the people of Merv, raids "even
among members of the same tribe are not, or were not until
lately, looked upon in the light of robberies"; but the raids
must be on a respectable scale. "It is curious that, while
red-handed murder and robbery were a recognized means of
existence among the Tekkés, thievery, in the sense of stealing
from the person, or filching an article from a stall of the bazaar,
was despised." And Mr. O'Donovan subsequently relates that
when urging on the Merv Council the cessation of marauding
expeditions, a member "with angry astonishment" asked
"how in the name of Allah they were going to live if raids were
not to be made"! To all which evidence we may add the facts

that "the Pathan mother often prays that her son may be a successful robber," that according to Rowney the like is done by the Afridi mother, and the further fact that among the Turkomans a celebrated robber becomes a saint, and pilgrimages are made to his tomb to sacrifice and pray.

While, in most of these cases, a marked distinction is recognized between robbery outside the tribe and robbery within the tribe, in other cases the last as well as the first is deemed not only legitimate but praiseworthy. Dalton says of the Kukis: "The accomplishment most esteemed amongst them was dexterity in thieving." Similarly, according to Gilmour, "In Mongolia known thieves are treated as respectable members of society. As long as they manage well and are successful, little or no odium seems to attach to them." Of another Asiatic tribe we read: "They [Angamis] are expert thieves and glory in the art, for among them, as with the Spartans of old, theft is only dishonorable and obnoxious to punishment when discovered in the act of being committed." From America may be instanced the case of the Chinooks, by whom "cunning theft is regarded as honorable; but they despise and often punish the inexpert thief." A case in Africa is furnished by the Waganda, warlike and bloodthirsty, among whom "the distinctions between *meum* and *tuum* are very ill-defined; and indeed all sin is only relative, the crime consisting in being detected." And then, passing to Polynesia, we find that among the Fijians "success, without discovery, is deemed quite enough to make thieving virtuous, and a participation in the ill-gotten gain honorable." So that in these instances skill or courage sanctifies any invasion of property rights.

132. Evidence yielded by the historic races proves that along with a less active life of external enmity and a more active life of internal amity, there goes a change of ethical ideas and sentiments, allied to that noted in the last chapter.

The *Rig-Veda* describes the thievish acts of the gods. Vishnu "stole the cooked mess" at the libations of Indra. When

Tvashtri began to perform a soma-sacrifice in honor of his son who had been slain by Indra, and refused, on the ground of his homicide, to allow the latter to assist at the ceremony, then "Indra interrupted the celebration, and drank off the soma by force."

The moral principle thus exemplified by the gods is paralleled by the moral principle recommended for men: "Even if he were to covet the property of other people, he is bound as a Kshatriya to take it by force of arms, and never to beg for it." But the Indian literature of later ages, displaying the results of settled life, inculcates opposite principles.

Passing over illustrative facts furnished by other ancient historic peoples, it will suffice if we glance at the facts which mediæval and modern histories furnish. Dasent tells us of the Norsemen that "Robbery and piracy in a good straightforward wholesale way were honored and respected." Similarly with the primitive Germans. Describing them, Cæsar says:

> Robberies which are committed beyond the boundaries of each state bear no infamy. . . . And when any of their chiefs has said in an assembly "that he will be their leader, let those who are willing to follow, give in their names"; they who approve of both the enterprise and the man arise and promise their assistance, and are applauded by the people; such of them as have not followed him are considered deserters and traitors, and confidence in all matters is afterward refused them.

Not to attempt the impossible task of tracing through some ten centuries the relation between the perpetual wars, large and small, public and private, and the plundering of men by one another, wholesale and retail, it will suffice to single out special periods. Of France in the early feudal period, Ste. Palaye says: "Our old writers denounce the avarice, greed, deceit, perjury, pillage, theft, and brigandage, and other excesses of an unbridled soldiery, equally devoid of principles, morals, and sentiments." During the Hundred Years War a regime of robbery became universal. Among the nobles the desire for plunder was the motive for fighting. Everywhere there was brigandage on a large scale, as well as on a small scale. In addition to multitudinous scattered highwaymen there were organized companies of robbers who had their fortresses, lived luxuriously on the spoils of the surrounding country, kidnapped children for pages and women for concubines, and sold at high prices safe-conducts to travelers. And then, along with all these plunderings on land, there was habitual piracy at sea. Not only states, but towns and individuals equipped vessels for buccaneering; and there were established refuges for marine freebooters. Take, again, the evidence furnished by the Thirty Years War in Germany. Universal marauding became the established system. Soldiers were brigands. Not only did they plunder the people everywhere, but they used "thousandfold torments" to make them disclose the places where they had hidden their goods; and the peasants had to "till their fields armed to the teeth" against their fellow countrymen. Meanwhile the soldiers were themselves cheated by their officers, small and great, who some of them made large fortunes by their accumulated embezzlements, at the same time that the princes robbed the nation by debasing the coinage.

Involved and obscure as the evidence is, no one can fail to recognize the broad fact that with progress towards a state in which war is less frequent, and does not, as of old, implicate almost everyone, there has been a decrease of dishonesty, and a higher appreciation of honesty; to the extent that now robbery of a stranger has come to be as much a crime as robbery of a fellow citizen. It is true that there are still thefts. It is true that there are still multitudinous frauds. But the thefts are not so numerous, and the frauds are not of such gross kinds as they were. From the days when kings frequently tricked their creditors and shopkeepers boasted of their ability to pass bad money, as Defoe tells us, we have somewhat advanced in the respect for *meum* and *tuum*. Nay, as shown by Pike's *History of Crime*, the contrast is marked even between the amount of transgression against property during the war period ending in 1815 and the recent amount of such transgression.

133. But of the relationship alleged, the clearest proofs are furnished by contrasts between the warlike uncivilized tribes instanced above, and the peaceful uncivilized tribes. Here are traits presented by some of these last.

Not only, according to Hartshorne, is the harmless Wood-Veddah perfectly honest, but he cannot conceive it possible that a man should "take that which does not belong to him." Of the Esquimaux, among whom war is unknown, we read that "they are uniformly described as most scrupulously honest"; and any such qualification of this statement as is made by Bancroft, refers to Esquimaux demoralized by contact with white traders. Of the Fuegians we learn from Darwin that "if any present was designed for one canoe, and it fell near another, it was invariably given to the right owner." And Snow says they were very honorable in their commercial dealings with him. Concerning certain of the Papuans on the southern coast of New Guinea, who are described as too independent for combined action in war, we read that "in their bargaining the natives have generally been very honest, far more so than our own people." And concerning others of this race, Kops tells us that the natives of Dory give evidence "of an inclination to right and justice, and strong moral principles. Theft is considered by them as a very grave offense, and is of very rare occurrence." A like character is ascribed by Kolff to the aborigines of Lette. In *The Principles of Sociology*, sections 437 and 574, I have given testimonies respecting the honesty of the peaceful Todas, Santáls, Lepchas, Bodo and Dhimáls, Hos, Chakmás, Jakuns. Here I add some further testimonies. Consul Baker tells us of the aborigines of Vera Cruz, now a subject race averse to military service, that "the Indian is honest, and seldom yields to even the greatest temptation to steal." In his description of a race inhabiting a "long strip of swamp and forest" at "the foot of the Himalayas," Mr. Nesfield says that "their honesty is vouched for by a hundred stories"; "such at least is the character of the Tharu, so long as he remains in the safe seclusion of his solitary wilds," where he is free from hostilities. And then, with the fact stated by Morgan concerning the Iroquois, that "theft, the most despicable of human crimes, was scarcely known among them," we have to join the fact that their league had been formed for the preservation of peace among its component peoples and had succeeded in its purpose for many generations.

CHAPTER 5

Revenge

134. Among intelligent creatures the struggle for existence entails aggressions. Where these are not the destructive aggressions of carnivorous creatures on their prey, they are the aggressions, not necessarily destructive but commonly violent, of creatures competing with one another for food. Animals severally impelled by hunger are inevitably led into antagonisms by endeavors severally to seize whatever food they can; and injuries, more or less decided, are usual concomitants.

Aggression leads to counteraggression. Where both creatures have powers of offense, they are likely both to use them; especially where their powers of offense are approximately equal, that is, where they are creatures of the same species: such creatures being also those commonly brought into competition. That results of this kind are inevitable, will be manifest on remembering that among members of the same species, those individuals which have not, in any considerable degree, resented aggressions, must have ever tended to disappear, and to have left behind those which have with some effect made counteraggressions. Fights, therefore, not only of predatory animals with prey but of animals of the same kind with one another, have been unavoidable from the first and have continued to the last.

Every fight is a succession of retaliations—bite being given for bite, and blow for blow. Usually these follow one another in quick succession, but not always. There is a postponed retaliation; and a postponed retaliation is what we call revenge. It may be postponed for so short a time as to be merely a recommencement of the fight, or it may be postponed for days, or it may be postponed for years. And hence the retaliation which constitutes what we call revenge, diverges insensibly from the retaliations which characterize a conflict.

But the practice, alike of immediate revenge and of postponed revenge, establishes itself as in some measure a check upon aggression; since the motive to aggress is checked by the consciousness that a counteraggression will come: if not at once then after a time.

135. Among human beings in early stages, there hence arises not only the practice of revenge but a belief that revenge is imperative—that revenge is a duty. Here, from Sir George Grey's account of the Australians, we have a graphic picture of the sentiment and its results:

> The holiest duty a native is called on to perform is that of avenging the death of his nearest relation, for it is his peculiar duty to do so: until he has fulfilled this task, he is constantly taunted by the old women; his wives, if he be married, would soon quit him; if he is unmarried, not a single young woman would speak to him; his mother would constantly cry, and lament she should ever have given birth to so degenerate a son; his father would treat him with contempt, and reproaches would constantly be sounded in his ear.

Of illustrations from North America that furnished by the Sioux may be named. Burton says: "The obstinate revengefulness of their vendetta is proverbial; they hate with the 'hate of Hell'; and, like the Highlanders of old, if the author of an injury escape them, they vent their rage upon the innocent, because he is of the same clan or color." From South America a case given by Schomburgk may be quoted: "My revenge is not yet satisfied, there still lives a member of the hated family," said a Guiana native, whose relative he suspected to have been poisoned. Here, again, is an instance from Williams' account of the Fijians.

> At that hour of death, he never forgets an enemy, and at that time he never forgives one. The dying man mentions his foe, that his children may perpetuate his hatred—it may be against his own son—and kill him at the first opportunity.

And then Thomson tells us of the New Zealanders that "not to avenge the dead, according to native law, indicates the most craven spirit." Passing to Asia I may quote Macrae's account of the Kukis.

> Like all savage people, the Kukis are of a most vindictive disposition; blood must always be shed for blood. . . . If a man should happen to be killed by an accidental fall from a tree, all his relations assemble . . . and reduce it to chips.

In Petherick, we read that the shedding of blood is "an offense with Arabs that neither time nor contrition can obliterate, thirst for revenge descending from father to son, and even through successive generations." So too of the East Africans Burton writes:

> Revenge is a ruling passion, as the many rancorous fratricidal wars that have prevailed between kindred clans, even for a generation, prove. Retaliation and vengeance are, in fact, their great agents of moral control.

In all these cases we see that either avowedly or tacitly revenge is considered a moral obligation.

The early stages of various existing people yield equally clear evidence. In his *Japan in Days of Yore*, Mr. Dening translates the life of Musashi, published by the Momtusho (Education Department), narrating a prolonged vendetta full of combats and murders; and, in partial sympathy with the Japanese educationists, remarks that his hero's acts of undying revenge, displayed "so many of the nobler aspects of human nature" and are "calculated to inspire confidence in humanity." A kindred spirit is shown in the early Indian literature. The gods are revengeful. As described in the *Rig-Veda*, "Agni swallows his enemies, tears their skin, minces their members, and throws them before the wolves to be eaten by them, or by the shrieking vultures." And the ascribed character of the gods is participated in by their devotees, as instance the invocation:

> Indra and Soma, burn the Rakshas, destroy them, throw them down, ye two Bulls, the people that grow in darkness. Hew down the madmen, suffocate them, kill them, hurl them away, and slay the voracious. Indra and Soma, up together against the cursing demon! May he burn and hiss like an oblation in the fire! Put your everlasting hatred on the villain.

The narrative of the "ferocious and deadly struggle" carried on "with all the frenzied wrath of demons," as Wheeler says, is full of vows of revenge—a revenge extending to horrible treatment of enemies' remains. Nor do we find a different sentiment displayed among the Hebrews, whether in the ascribed actions of Jahveh or the actions of his worshippers. The command to "blot out the remembrance of Amalek from under heaven" (*Deuteronomy* xxv. 19), and the fulfillment of this command by Saul and Samuel, to the extent of destroying not only the Amalekites but all their cattle, is a typical example of the implied divine revenge—a sample variously paralleled in other cases. And with this sanctification of revenge we see that the acts and feelings of the Hebrews themselves harmonized. The wreaking of vengeance was bequeathed as a duty; as when David, after enjoining Solomon to walk in the ways of the Lord, told him not to spare the son of a man who had cursed him (and who had been forgiven on oath), saying "but his hoar head bring thou down to the grave with blood" (1 *Kings* ii. 9).

It is superfluous to illustrate in detail the kindred sentiments and ideas of European peoples throughout mediæval
times. Most of the political and private incidents narrated
exhibit them. To inflict vengeance was among them, as now
among savages, considered an obligation; and when, occasionally, the spirit flagged in men it was kept alive by women,
as in the Merovingian period by Fredegonde and Brunehaut.
Then in later centuries there were chronic family feuds between nobles everywhere, transmitted from generation to
generation. And the spirit was still active down to the time of
the Abbé Brantôme, who, in his will, enjoins a nephew to
execute vengeance on his behalf should he be injured when
too old to avenge himself. Nay, the vendetta, once so general,
is even now not extinct in the East of Europe.

Though, throughout the modern civilized world, not perturbed everywhere and always by conflicts, life does not
furnish such multitudinous examples of like meaning, yet
survival of the ethics of enmity, in so far as it enjoins revenge,
is sufficiently manifest. Duels almost daily occurring somewhere or other on the Continent, exhibit the conceived obligation under its private form; and under its public form we have
before us a striking example in the persistent desire which the
French cherish to punish the Germans for defeating them—a
desire of which the strength has lately (August 1891) been
shown by the remarkable fact that while professedly en-
thusiastic advocates of liberty and upholders of free institutions, they have been lauding "the noble Russian people" and
the despotic Czar who holds them in bondage; and all because
they hope thus to be aided in their wished-for fight with
Germany. Clearly the appropriate expression of their feeling
is—Not that we love freedom less but that we love revenge
more.

136. But, while societies have been in course of growth and
consolidation, there have been occasional expressions of ideas
and sentiments opposite to these—occasional expressions
which, as they are associated with the arrival at more settled

social states, may be fairly regarded as consequent upon a diminution of warlike activities.

Various illustrations are furnished by the literature of Hindostan. In the code of Manu we read:

> Wound not another, though by him provoked,
> Do no one injury by thought or deed,
> Utter no word to pain thy fellow creatures.

And again, in another place, there is the exhortation—

> Treat no one with disdain, with patience bear
> Reviling language; with an angry man
> Be never angry; blessings give for curses.

Of like spirit is the following from the *Cural:* "To do no evil even to enemies will be called the chief of virtues." So, too, among some of the Persians. In their literature of the seventh century we find the passage—"Think not that the valor of a man consists only in courage and force; if you can rise above wrath and forgive, you are of a value inestimable." At a later date, namely in a story of Sadi, there occurs the injunction:

> Hast thou been injured? suffer it and clear
> Thyself from guilt in pardoning others' sin.

And still more extreme is the doctrine we find in Hafiz, as translated by Sir William Jones:

> Learn from yon orient shell to love thy foe,
> And store with pearls the hand, that brings thee woe,
> Free, like you rock, from base vindictive pride,
> Imblaze with gems the wrist, that rends thy side.

Nor are the writings of the Chinese sages without kindred utterances of sentiment. Lao-Tsze says, "Recompense injury with kindness." So also according to Mencius, "A benevolent man does not lay up anger, nor cherish resentment against his brother, but only regards him with affection and love." While

Confucius, in conformity with his doctrine of the mean, expresses a less extreme view:

> "What do you say concerning the principle that injury should be recompensed with kindness?" The Master said, "With what then will you recompense kindness? Recompense injury with justice, and recompense kindness with kindness."

In the later stages of Hebrew civilization, we similarly find the social and divine sanctions for revenge occasionally qualified—a mingling of opposed ideas and sentiments. While, in *Ecclesiasticus* xxx. 6, a father is regarded as happy who leaves "an avenger against his enemies," yet in chapter x. 6 there is an injunction to "bear not hatred" for wrong received—an injunction containing in germ the ethical principle which, centuries later, took shape in Christianity.

137. Proofs that decline of vindictiveness and growth of forgiveness are associated with decrease of militancy and increase of peaceful cooperation, cannot be clearly disentangled from the facts; since the two kinds of life have nearly everywhere, and at all times, been associated in one or other proportion. But to such general evidence as the foregoing quotations furnish, may be added some evidence furnished by existing societies.

There is the fact that throughout the chief nations of Europe, the family vendetta has disappeared during a period in which the conflicts of nations have become less constant, and the peaceful exchange of services within each nation more active: a contrast between ancient and modern which asserted itself soonest where the industrial type was earliest developed, namely, among ourselves.

Again, there is the fact that in our own society, with its comparatively small number of soldiers and a militancy less predominant than that of continental societies with their vast armies and warlike attitudes, there has been a suppression of the revenge for private insults, while this with them continues; and so far has the vindictive spirit declined that an injured man who shows persistent animosity towards one who has injured him, is reprobated rather than applauded: forgiveness is, at any rate by many, tacitly approved.

But if we seek a case in which the virtue supposed to be especially Christian is practiced, we must seek it among the non-Christians. Certain peaceful tribes of the Indian hills are characterized by it, as witness this account of the Lepchas:

> They are wonderfully honest, theft being scarcely known among them; they rarely quarrel among themselves. . . . They are singularly forgiving of injuries, when time is given them, after hasty loss of temper. Although they were ready enough to lodge complaints before the magistrate against one another in cases of assault and other offenses, they rarely prosecuted to a decision, generally preferring to submit to arbitration, or making mutual amends and concessions. They are averse to soldiering, and cannot be induced to enlist in our army even for local service in the Hills.

Thus we get both positive and negative evidence that the revengefulness within each society is proportionate to the habitual conflict with other societies; and that while, at the one extreme, there is a moral sanction for revenge, at the other extreme there is a moral sanction for forgiveness.

CHAPTER 6

Justice

138. $\mathbf{P}$erhaps the soul of goodness in things evil is by nothing better exemplified than by the good thing, justice, which, in a rudimentary form, exists within the evil thing revenge. Meeting aggression by counteraggression is, in the first place, an endeavor to avoid being suppressed by the aggressor, and to maintain that ability to carry on life which justice implies; and it is, in the second place, an endeavor to enforce justice by establishing an equality with the aggressor: inflicting injuries as great as have been received.

This rude process of balancing claims usually fails to establish equilibrium. Revenge, habitually carried not as far only as suffices to compensate for injuries received but, if possible, farther, evokes re-revenge, which also, if possible, is carried to excess; and so there results chronic wars between tribes and chronic antagonisms between families and between individuals. These commonly continue from generation to generation.

But occasionally there is shown a tendency towards establishment of an equilibrium, by bringing aggression and counteraggression to a definite balance, achieved by measure. Let us look at the evidence.

139. Men of various rude types, as the Australians, constantly show the idea, tacitly asserted and acted upon, that

the loss of a life in one tribe must be compensated by the infliction of a death in another tribe; some member of which is known, or supposed, to have caused the said loss of life. And since deaths from disease and old age are, among others, ascribed to the machinations of foes—since equivalent deaths must be inflicted for these also, there have to be frequent balancing of losses. (It seems clear, however, that these re-venges and re-revenges cannot be always carried out as al-leged. For if not only deaths by violence but deaths by disease entail them the two tribes must soon disappear by mutual extirpation.) Races much more advanced in some cases carry out, not this secret balancing of mortality accounts between tribes, but an overt balancing. This is the case with the Suma-trans, among whom the differences are squared by money payments.

This maintenance of intertribal justice, prompted in part by consciousness of that corporate injury which loss of a member of the tribe entails, and requiring the infliction of an equiva-lent corporate injury on the offending tribe, has the trait that it is indifferent what member of the offending tribe is killed in compensation: whether it be the guilty man or some innocent man matters not. This conception of intertribal justice is re-peated in the conception of inter-family justice. Those early types of social organization in which the family is the unit of composition, show us that in each family there arises an idea allied to the idea of nationality; and there results an allied system of reprisals for the balancing of injuries. The Philip-pine Islands supply evidence. "In the province of La Isabela, the Negrito and Igorrote tribes keep a regular *Dr.* and *Cr.* account of heads." A further interesting illustration is yielded by the Quianganes of Luzon. From an account of them given by Prof. F. Blumentritt, here is a translated passage:

> Blood vengeance is a sacred law with the Quianganes. If one plebeian is killed by another, the matter is settled in a simple manner by killing the murderer or some one of his family who is likewise a plebeian. But if a prominent man or noble is killed by a plebeian, vengeance on the

murderer, a mere plebeian, is not enough; the victim of the sin-offering must be an equivalent in rank. Another nobleman must fall for the murdered noble, for their doctrine is—What kind of an equivalent is it to kill some one who is no better than a dog? Hence the family of the slain noble looks around to see if it cannot find a relative of the murderer to wreak vengeance upon, who is also a noble; while the murderer himself is ignored. If no noble can be found among his relatives, the family of the murdered man wait patiently till some one of them is received into the noble's caste; then the vendetta is prosecuted, although many years may have elapsed. When the blood-feud is satisfied a reconciliation of the contending factions takes place. In all the feuds the heads of the murdered champions are cut off and taken home, and the head-hunters celebrate the affair festally. The skulls are fixed to the front of the house.

Here the need for inflicting an injury of like amount, and so equalizing the losses, is evidently the dominant need. The Semitic peoples in general furnish kindred facts. Burckhardt writes:

> It is a received law among all the Arabs, that whoever sheds the blood of a man, owes blood on that account to the family of the slain person. . . . The lineal descendants of all those who were entitled to revenge at the moment of the man-slaughter, inherit this right from their parents.

And respecting this system of administering rude justice by the balancing of deaths between families, Burckhardt remarks: "I am inclined to believe that this salutary institution has contributed, in a greater degree than any other circumstance, to prevent the warlike tribes of Arabia from exterminating one another . . . the terrible 'blood-revenge' renders the most inveterate war nearly bloodless." The evident implication being that dread of this persistent revenge, makes members of different families and tribes fearful of killing one another. That with the feelings and practices of existing Semites, those of ancient Semites agreed, there is good reason to believe. The authorization of blood-revenge between families, is implied in 1 *Kings* ii. 31, 33, as well as elsewhere. How, among European peoples in early times, kindred conceptions led to kindred usages, need not be shown in detail. The fact that when the system of taking life for life was replaced by the system of compensations, these were adjusted to ranks, so that the murder of a person more valuable to the group he belonged to was compounded for by a larger fine payable to it, shows how dominant was the idea of group injury, and how dominant was the idea of equivalence.

140. But these ideas of family injury and family guilt have all along been accompanied by ideas of individual injury and individual guilt: here very distinct and there less distinct.

They are very distinct among some peoples in early social stages, as is shown by the account which Im Thurn gives of the Guiana tribes.

> In the absence of anything corresponding to police regulations, their mutual relations in everyday life are very well-ordered by the traditional respect which each individual feels for the rights of the others, and by their dread of adverse public opinion should they act contrary to such traditions. . . . The smallest injury done by one Indian to another, even if unintentional, must be atoned by suffering a similar injury.

And that among the Hebrews there was a balancing of individual injuries is a fact more frequently referred to than is the fact that there was a balancing of family injuries; as witness the familiar "eye for eye, tooth for tooth, hand for hand, foot for foot" prescribed in *Deuteronomy* xix.

The decline of family responsibility and growth of individual responsibility, seem to be concomitants of the change in social organization from the type in which the family is the unit of composition to the type in which the individual is the unit of composition. For, evidently, as fast as the family organization dissolves, there cease to be any groups which can be held responsible to one another for injuries inflicted by their members; and as fast as this happens the responsibility must fall on the members themselves. Thus it naturally happens that along with social evolution, there emerges from that unjust form of retaliation, in which the groups more than their component men are answerable, that just form in which the men themselves are answerable: the guilty person takes the consequences of his acts, and does not leave them to be borne by other persons.

An instructive contrast in the literature of the Hebrews supports this conclusion. In the earlier writings, God is represented as punishing not only those who have sinned against him, but their posterity for generations. In the later writings, however, there occurs the prophecy of a time when this shall no longer be. Here is a passage from *Jeremiah* xxxi. 29, 30: "In those days they shall say no more, The fathers have eaten a sour grape, and the children's teeth are set on edge. But every one shall die for his own iniquity: every man that eateth the sour grape, his teeth shall be set on edge."

That in European peoples growth of this factor in the conception of justice has gone along with the lapsing of group organization and the rise of individual citizenship, is clear. And it is interesting to observe how strange now seem to us the old idea and sentiment, when we come in contact with them, as in China, where the group organization lingers, and it is thought sufficient if, in compensation for one of our people who has been murdered, a victim is delivered up: no matter whether the victim be the guilty man or not.

141. But while, in the more advanced social stages, maintenance of the relation between conduct and consequence comes to be recognized as required by justice; in early social stages the idea of equality is that which chiefly obtains recognition, under the form of an infliction of equivalent injuries. It could scarcely be otherwise. During times of unceasing strife, with entailed wounds and deaths, this is the only equality admitting of distinct maintenance. Evidently, however, from this practice of balancing deaths and mutilations, there tends to arise one component in the conception of equity.

We may see, too, that the activities of militant life themselves afford scope for some further development of the idea;

and occasionally there grow up usages requiring some maintenance of equality, even in the midst of conflict. Speaking of
certain early wars recorded in the Indian books, Wheeler
remarks that

> The sentiment of honor which undoubtedly prevailed amongst the
> ancient Kshatriyas made them regard an attack upon a sleeping
> enemy as a heinous crime. . . . Aswattháma even whilst bent upon
> being revenged on the murderer of his father, awoke his sleeping
> enemy before slaying him.

And various histories yield occasional signs of the belief that
under certain circumstances—especially in personal combats—foes should be placed under something like equal conditions before they are attacked; though, very generally, the
aim has been the reverse—to attack them under every disadvantage.

That all along the idea of likeness of treatment has entered
into human relations at large, but chiefly among members of
the same society, is manifest. But any considerable development of it has been inconsistent with militant life and militant
organization. While war, even when retaliatory, has necessarily been a discipline in injustice, by inflicting wounds and
death upon individuals who have mostly been guiltless of
aggression, it has, at the same time, necessitated within each
society a type of organization which has disregarded the requirements of justice; alike by the coercive arrangements
within its fighting part, by the tyranny over slaves and serfs
forming its industrial part, and by the subjection of women.
Hence the broad fact that throughout civilization the relations
of citizens have become relatively equitable only as fast as
militancy has become less predominant; and that only along
with this change has the sentiment of justice become more
pronounced.

As yielding converse evidence I must again refer to the
habits and sentiments which accompany entire peacefulness.
Already in the last chapter but one I have named some
peoples whose unaggressiveness towards other peoples is

accompanied by unaggressiveness among themselves; and of course this trait is in part ascribable to that regard for others' claims which justice implies. Already, too, in the last chapter, I have quoted various travelers in proof of the great honesty characterizing tribes of this same class: and of course their honesty may be taken as, in a considerable degree, proof of the prevailing sentiment of justice. Here, to this indirect evidence, I may add evidence of a more direct kind, furnished by the treatment of women and children among them. In *The Principles of Sociology,* sections 324, 327, I have drawn a contrast between the low *status* of women among militant savages, as well as the militant semicivilized, and the high *status* of women among these uncultured but unmilitant peoples; showing that by the Todas, low as they are in sundry respects, the women are relieved from all hard work, and "do not even step out of doors to fetch water or wood"; that the wives of the Bodo and Dhimáls "are free from all outdoor work whatever"; that among the Hos a wife "receives the fullest consideration due to her sex"; and that among the "industrious, honest, and peace-loving Pueblos," no girl is forced to marry against her will, and "the usual order of courtship is reversed"—facts all of them showing a recognition of that equality of claims which is an essential element in the idea of justice. And here I may add an instance not before mentioned, furnished by the Manansas, who occupy a hill country in which they have taken refuge from the invading Bamangwatos and Makololo. Said one of them to Holub, "We want not the blood of the beasts, much less do we thirst for the blood of men"; and hence they are regarded with great contempt by the more powerful tribes. Holub, however, testifying to their honesty and fidelity, says that "nothing worse seems to be alleged against them than their habitual courtesy and good-nature"; and he adds, "They treat their women in a way that offers a very favorable contrast to either the Bechuanas or the Matabele": that is, they are relatively just to them. Similarly, in *The Principles of Sociology,* sections 330–32, I have shown how much the way in which children are treated by warlike peoples who exercise over them the powers of life and death, and behave to boys far better than to girls, differs from the way in which they are treated by these unwarlike peoples, whose conduct to them is both kind and equal; girls are dealt with as fairly as boys.

To these indications that the sentiment of justice is marked where the habits are peaceful, something should be added respecting the overt expression of it. Little that is definite can be expected from the uncultured, since both the sentiment and the idea are complex. We may, however, infer that in a Wood-Veddah who cannot conceive that a man should take that which is not his own, there exists a sufficiently clear, if not a formulated, idea of justice; and we may fairly say that this idea is implied in the peaceful Thârus who, when they fly to the hills for refuge, "always leave any arrears of rent that may be due tied up in a rag to the lintel of their deserted house." Nor can we doubt that both the sentiment and idea, from which result regard for other men's claims, must be dominant in the Hos, of whom we read that one suspected of theft is not unlikely to commit suicide, as also in the Let-htas, an aboriginal hill tribe in Burma, described as ideally good, among whom one accused by several of an evil act "retires to some secluded spot, there digs his grave and strangles himself." But it is only when we pass to peoples who have risen to a state of culture high enough to evolve literatures, that we get definite evidence concerning the conception of justice which has arisen, and among these we meet with a very significant fact.

For throughout ancient societies at large, militant in their activities, in their types of structure, and in the universally established system of *status* of compulsory cooperation, justice is not differentiated in thought from altruism in general. In the literatures of the Chinese, the Persians, the Ancient Indians, the Egyptians, the Hebrews, justice is in the main confounded with generosity and humanity. The maxim commonly supposed to be especially Christian, but which, as we have seen, was in kindred forms enunciated among various peoples in pre-Christian days, shows us this. "Do unto others as ye would that they should do unto you," is an injunction which merges generosity and justice in one. In the first place, it makes no distinction between that which you are called upon to do to another on grounds of equity, and that which you are called upon to do to him on grounds of kindness; and, in the second place, it includes no recognition, overt or tacit, of those claims of the doer which we call "rights." In the consciousness of justice properly so-called, there is included an egoistic as well as an altruistic element—a consciousness of the claim of self and a sympathetic consciousness of the claims of others. Perception and assertion of this claim of self, cannot develop in a society organized for warfare, and carried on by compulsory cooperation. Universal paralysis would ensue if each man were free, within the limits prescribed by equity, to do as he liked. Under a despotic rule there is scope for any amount of generosity but for only a limited amount of justice. The sentiment and the idea can grow only as fast as the external antagonisms of societies decrease and the internal harmonious cooperations of their members increase.

CHAPTER 7

Generosity

142.   To bring into intelligible order the kinds of conduct
ordinarily grouped under the name generosity is difficult; partly because much which passes under the name is
not really prompted by generous feeling, and partly because
generosity rightly so-called is complex in nature and its composition variable.

Generosity is a double-rooted sentiment: one of its roots
being very ancient and the other very modern. Its ancient
root is the philoprogenitive instinct, which, as manifested
throughout a large part of the animal kingdom, leads to the
sacrifice of self for the benefit of offspring. This form of
generosity coexists in many creatures with absolute disregard
of the welfare of all save offspring: conspicuously so in the
Carnivora and less conspicuously so in the *Herbivora*. The
relatively modern root of generosity is sympathy, which is
shown by some of the higher gregarious creatures, as the dog,
in considerable degrees. This trait is more variously and
largely displayed by human beings, and especially by certain
higher types of them. The earlier factor in the sentiment is
personal and narrow, while the later is impersonal and broad.

In mankind, generosity ordinarily combines the two. The
love of the helpless, which constitutes the essential part of the

philoprogenitive instinct, is, nearly always, associated with fellow feeling: the parent sympathizes with the pleasures and pains of the child. Conversely, the feeling which prompts a generous act of one adult to another, commonly includes an element derived from the early instinct. The individual aided is conceived in a distinct or vague way as an object of pity; and pity is a sentiment closely allied to the parental, since it is drawn out towards some being relatively helpless or unfortunate or suffering.

To this mixed nature of the sentiment as commonly displayed, is due the confusion in its manifestations among races in different stages; and to it must consequently be ascribed the perplexities which stand in the way of satisfactory inductions.

143. As a preliminary it should be further remarked that the sentiment of generosity, even in its developed form, is simpler than the sentiment of justice; and hence is earlier manifested. The one results from mental representations of the pleasures or pains of another or others—is shown in acts instigated by the feelings which these mental representations arouse. But the other implies representations, not simply of pains or pleasures, but also, and chiefly, representations of the *conditions* which are required for, or are conducive to, the avoidance of pains or procuring of pleasures. Hence it includes a set of mental actions superposed on the mental actions constituting generosity.

Recognition of this truth makes comprehensible the order of their succession in the course of civilization. And this order will be rendered still more comprehensible if we remember that generosity, among people of low intelligence, often results from inability to represent to themselves distinctly the consequences of the sacrifices they make—they are improvident.

144. First to be dealt with is that pseudo-generosity mainly composed of other feelings than benevolent ones. The wish for the welfare of another is, indeed, rarely without alloy:

there are mostly present other motives—chiefly the desire for applause. But to the lowest of the actions apparently caused by generosity, these other motives form the predominant or sole prompters instead of the subordinate prompters.

The display of hospitality among uncivilized and barbarous peoples furnishes striking examples. Of the Bedouin "at once rapacious and profuse," and who is scrupulously hospitable, Palgrave says: "He has in general but little to offer, and for that very little he not unfrequently promises himself an ample retribution, by plundering his last night's guest when a few hours distant on his morning journey." Similarly of the Kirghiz, we are told by Atkinson that a chief who does not molest travelers while with him, sends his followers to rob them on their march. In East Africa, too, a chief of Urori "will entertain his guests hospitably as long as they remain in his village, but he will plunder them the moment they leave it." Still more startling are the apparent incongruities of conduct among the Fijians. "The same native who within a few yards of his house would murder a coming or departing guest for sake of a knife or a hatchet, will defend him at the risk of his own life as soon as he has passed his threshold." And then how little relation there is between generosity rightly so-called and hospitality in such cases, is further shown by the statement of Jackson that the Europeans who have lived long among Fijians have become hospitable: "a practice which they have adopted through the example of these savages."

Among the uncivilized at large, of whatever type, hospitality of a less treacherous kind, prompted apparently by usage the origin of which is difficult to understand, is constantly displayed. " 'Custom' enjoins the exercise of hospitality on every Aino. They receive all strangers as they received me, giving them of their best, placing them in the most honorable place, bestowing gifts upon them, and, when they depart, furnishing them with cakes of boiled millet." We read that among the Australians, the laws of hospitality require that strangers should be perfectly unmolested during their sojourn. Jackson says that according to the rules of Samoan hospitality, strangers are well treated, receiving the best of everything. According to Lichtenstein "the Caffres are hospitable"; and that "the hospitality of the Africans has been noticed by almost every traveler who has been much among them" is remarked by Winterbottom. Of the tribes inhabiting North America Morgan says: "One of the most attractive features of Indian society was the spirit of hospitality by which it was pervaded. Perhaps no people ever carried this principle to the same degree of universality, as did the Iroquois." So, too, Angas tells us of the New Zealanders that they are very hospitable to strangers.

By this last people we are shown in how large a measure the love of applause is a factor in apparent generosity. The New Zealanders, writes Thomson, have a great admiration of profuseness, and desire to be considered liberal at their feasts; and elsewhere he says that by them "heaping up riches, unless to squander, was disgraceful." To an allied feeling may be ascribed the trait presented by the people of St. Augustine Island, among whom the dead were judged and sent to happiness or misery according to their "goodness" or "badness"; and "*goodness* meant one whose friends had given a grand funeral feast, and *badness* a person whose stingy friends provided nothing at all." To this peremptory desire for approval is in some cases due an expenditure, on the occasion of a death or a marriage, so great that the family is impoverished by it for years; and in one case, if not in more cases, female infanticide is committed with the view of avoiding the ruinous expense which a daughter's marriage entails.

To the prompters of pseudo-generosity thus disclosed, may be added another disclosed by the habits of civilized settlers in remote regions. Leading solitary lives as such men do, the arrival of a stranger brings an immense relief from monotony, and gratifies the craving for social intercourse. Hence it happens that travelers and sportsmen are not only welcomed but even pressed to stay.

Manifestly, then, the sentiment which in many cases instigates hospitality to visitors and feasts to friends, is a proethical sentiment. There goes with it little, or none, of the ethical sentiment proper.

145. We find, however, among some of the most uncivilized peoples, displays of a generosity which is manifestly genuine—sometimes, indeed, find displays of it greater than among the civilized.

Burchell tells us even of the Bushmen that towards one another they "exercise the virtues of hospitality and generosity; often in an extraordinary degree." So, too, he says that the Hottentots are very hospitable among themselves, and often to people of other tribes; and Kolben expresses the belief that "In Munificence and Hospitality the *Hottentots,* perhaps, go beyond all the other Nations upon Earth." Of the East Africans, again, Livingstone says: "The real politeness with which food is given by nearly all the interior tribes, who have not had much intercourse with Europeans, makes it a pleasure to accept." Though, in the following extract concerning the people of Loango, there is proof that love of approbation is a strong prompter to generous actions, yet there seems evidence that there is mingled with it a true sentiment of generosity.

> They are always ready to share the little they have with those whom they know to be in need. If they have been fortunate in hunting and fishing, or have procured something rare, they immediately run and tell their friends and neighbors, taking to each his share. They would choose to stint themselves rather than not give them this proof of their friendship. . . . They call the Europeans *close fists,* because they give nothing for nothing.

Other races, some lower and some higher, yield like facts. We read that the Australian natives who have been successful in hunting always, and without any remark, supply those of their number who have been unsuccessful with a share of their meal. The account given by Vancouver of the Sandwich Islanders, shows that, in their generosity towards strangers, they were like most uncivilized peoples before bad treatment by Europeans had demoralized them. He says: "Our reception and entertainment here [at Hawaii] by these unlettered people, who in general have been distinguished by the appellation of savages, was such as, I believe, is seldom equalled by the most civilized nations of Europe." Brett describes the Guiana tribes as "passionately fond of their children; hospitable to every one; and, among themselves, generous to a fault." These instances I may reinforce by one from a remote region. Bogle stayed while in Tibet with the Lama's family—that is, with his relations, at whose hands he received much kindness. When he offered them presents they refused to accept them, saying, "You . . . are come from a far country; it is our business to render your stay agreeable; why should you make us presents?"

146. Various of the uncivilized display generosity in other ways than by hospitality, and in ways which exhibit the sentiment more clearly detached from other sentiments. Illustrations are furnished by that very inferior race, the Australians. They were always willing to show Mr. Eyre where water was to be had, and, even unsolicited, would help his men to dig for it. Their kindness in this respect seems the more remarkable on remembering how difficult it was for them to find a proper supply for themselves. Sturt tells us that a friendly native has been known to interpose, at great personal risk, on behalf of travelers whom a hostile tribe was about to attack. With an adjacent race it was the same. During troubled times in Tasmania, the lives of white people were in several instances "saved by the native women, who would often steal away from the tribe, and give notice of an intended attack." Under another form, much generosity of feeling is shown by the Tongans. Mariner writes of them that

> They never exult in any feats of bravery they may have performed, but, on the contrary, take every opportunity of praising their adversaries; and this a man will do, although his adversary may be plainly a coward, and will make an excuse for him, such as the unfavorableness of the opportunity, or great fatigue, or ill state of health, or badness of his ground, &c.

These, and many kindred facts, make it clear that the name "savages," as applied to the uncivilized, misleads us; and they suggest that the name might with greater propriety be applied to many among ourselves and our European neighbors.

147. If, as we see, under the form of hospitality enforced by custom, in which it is largely simulated, or under forms in which it is more manifestly genuine, generosity is widely prevalent among peoples who have not emerged from low stages of culture; we need not be surprised to find expressions of generous sentiments, and injunctions to perform generous actions, in the early literatures of races which have risen to higher stages. The ancient Indian books furnish examples. Here, from the *Rig-Veda,* is an extract exhibiting the interested or nonsympathetic prompting of generosity: "The givers of largesses abide high in the sky; the givers of horses live with the sun; the givers of gold enjoy immortality; the givers of raiment prolong their lives." Similarly *Rig-Veda* X. 107, eulogizes liberality to priests.

> I regard as the king of men him who first presented a gift. . . . The wise man makes largesse, giving his breastplate. Bountiful men neither die nor fall into calamity; they suffer neither wrong nor pain. Their liberality confers on them this whole world as well as heaven.

In the Code of Manu, too, we read that strangers are to be allowed to sojourn and be well entertained. He must eat before the householder (iii. 105). "The honoring of a guest confers wealth, reputation, life, and heaven" (iii. 106; iv. 29) and delivers from guilt (iii. 98). And kindred reasons for hospitality are given by Apastamba: The reception of guests is rewarded by "immunity from misfortunes, and heavenly bliss" (ii. 3, 6, 6). "He who entertains guests for one night obtains earthly happiness, a second night gains the middle air, a third heavenly bliss, a fourth the world of unsurpassable bliss; many nights procure endless worlds" (ii. 3, 7, 16). The literature of the Persians contains kindred thoughts. In the *Shâyast,* the clothing of the soul in the next world is said to be formed "out of almsgivings." Passages in the *Gulistan* enjoin liberality while reprobating asceticism: "The liberal man who eats and bestows, is better than the religious man who fasts and hoards. Whosoever hath forsaken luxury to gain the approbation of mankind, hath fallen from lawful into unlawful voluptuousness." And in the same work we have a more positive injunction to be generous, but still associated with self-interest as a motive: "Do good, and do not speak of it, and assuredly thy kindness will be recompensed to thee."

Passing to China we find in Confucius various kindred injunctions; dissociated, too, from promptings of lower motives. Here are examples:

> Now the man of perfect virtue, wishing to be established himself, seeks also to establish others; wishing to be enlarged himself, he seeks also to enlarge others.
>
> The Master said, "Though a man have abilities as admirable as those of the duke of Chow, yet if he be proud and niggardly, those other things are really not worth being looked at."
>
> When any of his [Confucius's] friends died, if he had no relations who could be depended on for the necessary offices, he would say, "I will bury him."

That in the sacred books of the Hebrews are to be found kindred admonitions, here joined with promises of supernatural rewards and there without such promises, needs no saying. It should be added, however, that we are not enabled by these quoted passages to compare the characters displayed by Indians, Persians, Chinese, or Hebrews, with the characters described in the foregoing accounts travelers give us of the uncivilized; for these passages come from the writings of exceptional men—poets and sages. But though violent reaction against an all-pervading selfishness may mostly be the cause of exaggerated expressions of generosity, we must admit that the possibility of such exaggerated expressions goes for something.

148. Concerning generosity among European peoples, as exhibited in history at successive stages of their progress, no

very definite statements can be made. We have evidence that in early days there existed much the same feelings and practices as those now existing among savages—practices simulating generosity. Tacitus says of the primitive Germans: "No nation indulges more profusely in entertainments and hospitality. To exclude any human being from their roof is thought impious." And these usages and ideas went, as we know, along with utter lack of sympathy: they implied the generosity of display sanctified by tradition.

Throughout the Middle Ages and down to comparatively recent times, we see, along with a decreasing generosity of display, little more than the generosity prompted by hope of buying divine favor. The motive has been all along expressed in the saying, "He that hath pity upon the poor lendeth to the Lord" (*Proverbs* xix. 17); and the Lord is expected to pay good interest. Christianity, even in its initial form, represents the giving of alms as a means of salvation; and throughout many centuries of Christian history the giving of alms had little other motive. Just as they built chapels to compound for crimes and manumitted slaves to make peace with God; so, beyond a desire for the applause which followed largesse, the only motive of the rich for performing kind actions was an other-worldly motive—a dread of hell and wish for heaven. As Mr. Lecky remarks, "Men gave money to the poor, simply and exclusively for their own spiritual benefit, and the welfare of the sufferer was altogether foreign to their thoughts." How utterly alien to generosity, rightly so-called, was the feeling at work, is shown by the unblushing, and indeed self-satisfied, avowal made by Sir Thomas Browne in the passage which Mr. Lecky quotes from him—"I give no alms to satisfy the hunger of my brother, but to fulfill and accomplish the will and command of my God."

In modern days, however, we may recognize a growing proportion of true generosity—the ethical sentiment as distinguished from the proethical sentiment. Though there is still in predominant amount that transcendental self-seeking which does good here merely to get happiness hereafter—

though there are even multitudes who, in the spirit of Sir Thomas Browne, feel no shame in the avowal that their kindnesses to others are prompted by the wish to please God more than by the wish to further human welfare; yet there are many who, in conferring benefits, are prompted mainly, and others who are prompted wholly, by fellow feeling with those whom they aid. And beyond the manifestations of this sentiment of true generosity in private actions, there are occasionally manifestations of it in public actions; as when the nation made a sacrifice of twenty millions of money that the West Indian slaves might be emancipated.

That this development of true generosity has been consequent on increase of sympathy, and that sympathy has gained scope for exercise and growth with the advance to an orderly and amicable social life, scarcely needs saying.

149. For reasons given at the outset, it is difficult to bring the various manifestations of pseudo-generosity and generosity proper, into generalizations of a definite kind. And the impediment due to the complexity and variable composition of the emotion prompting generous acts, is made greater by the inconsistency of the traits which men, and especially the lower types of men, present. Unbalanced as their natures are, they act in quite opposite ways according to the impulse which is for the moment in possession of consciousness. Angas tells us that "infanticide is frequent among the New Zealanders." Yet "both parents are almost idolatrously fond of their children"; and while Cook described them as "implacable towards their enemies," Thomson observed that they were kind to their slaves. Other instances are furnished by the Negro races. Reade says that in parts of equatorial Africa where there is the greatest treachery, there are also strong marks of affectionate friendship. Concerning the East Africans Burton writes: "When childhood is passed, the father and son become natural enemies, after the manner of wild beasts. Yet they are a sociable race, and the sudden loss of relatives sometimes leads from grief to hypochondria and

insanity." Lacking those higher emotions which serve to coordinate the lower, these last severally determine the actions now this way and now that, according to the incidents of the moment. Hence only by comparison of extremes are we likely to discover any significant relations of facts.

In the accounts of those most ferocious savages, the cannibal Fijians, who worship cannibal gods—savages whose titles of honor are "the waster of" such a coast, "the depopulator of" such an island, and who committed atrocities which Williams said "I *dare* not record here," no mention is made of any generosity save that which results from display. Among the predatory red men of North America, the Dakotas may be singled out as those who, in the greatest degree, show the aggressiveness and revengefulness fostered by a life of chronic war—men by whom prisoners, especially aged ones, are handed over to the squaws to torture for their amusement. Here generosity is referred to only to note its absence: the Dakota is ungenerous, says Burton—never gives except to get more in return. Similarly of the Nagas, ever fighting, village with village as well as with neighboring races, carrying blood feuds to extremes, dreaded as robbers and murderers, and always mutilating their dead enemies, we read that "they are totally devoid of a spark of generosity, and will not give the most trifling articles without receiving remuneration."

Of the converse connection of traits the evidence is usually not clear, for the reason that the generosity ascribed to tribes which do not carry on perpetual hostilities is mostly of the kind shown in hospitality, which is always open to the interpretation of being due in part, if not wholly, to usage or love of display. Thus Colquhoun, who talks of the "hospitable aborigines" and says "it is quite refreshing to turn from the Christian Anamites to the less repulsive, if heathen, hill-tribes" (the Steins who inhabit "fever-stricken haunts," where they can lead peaceful lives), says that "amongst them a stranger is certain of a welcome; the fatted pig or fowl is at once killed, the loving cup produced." Similarly in his earlier work, *Across Chrysê*, Mr. Colquhoun, speaking of indigenous peoples here and there islanded among the conquering Tartars, speaks of them as "very pleasant in their ways, kind and hospitable"; and afterward he quotes the impressions of a resident French missionary, who spoke of the peaceful native inhabitants as "simple, hospitable, honest," having "le bon coeur," while of the governing Chinese, and especially the military mandarins, his verdict was—"être mandarin, c'est être voleur, brigand!" Of like meaning is the contrast drawn by the Abbé Favre in his *Account of the Wild Tribes of the Malayan Peninsula.* On the one hand he describes the conquering race, the Malays, as being full of predatory vices, lying, cheating, plundering—"no man can entrust them with anything"; and, so far from being hospitable, using every means to fleece the traveler. On the other hand of the aboriginal peoples, who "fled to the fastnesses of the interior, where they have since continued in a savage state," he tells us that their disputes are settled "without fighting or malice," that they are "entirely inoffensive," and "generally kind, affable, inclined to gratitude and to beneficence," "liberal and generous." Briefly contrasting the two, he says—"The actions of Malays generally show low sentiments and a sordid feeling; but the Jakuns are naturally proud and generous"; and then he asks, "Whence then comes so remarkable a difference?" As a cause he comments on the "plundering and bloody actions" of the piratical Malays; while the Jakuns have been led into quiet lives in their fastnesses. Let me add, lastly, the case of the peaceful and "simple Arafuras," of whom the French resident, M. Bik, says: "They have a very excusable ambition to gain the name of rich men, by paying the debts of their poorer fellow villagers. . . . Thus the only use they make of their riches is to employ it in settling differences."

CHAPTER 8

Humanity

150.   The division between the subject matter of this chapter and that of the last chapter, is in large measure artificial, and defensible only for convenience' sake. Kindness, pity, mercy, which we here group under the general head of humanity, are closely allied to generosity; though less liable than it to be simulated by lower feelings. They are all altruistic sentiments, and have for their common root, sympathy. Hence we may expect to find, as we shall find, that in respect of their relations to other traits of nature, and to type of social life, much the same may be said of them as may be said of generosity.

It may also be said of them, as of generosity, that while in their developed forms they are mainly prompted by mental representations of the pains or pleasures of other beings, they usually contain to the last, as they contain in chief measure at first, the parental feeling—the feeling which is excited by the consciousness of relative incapacity or helplessness—the pleasure felt in taking care of something which tacitly appeals for aid. And the mixed nature of these sentiments hence resulting, adds, as in the case of generosity, to the difficulty of generalizing.

A further difficulty, which is indeed a sequence of the last, results from the incongruous emotions which many types of men, and especially inferior types, display. Thus, while Moffat says "the Bushmen will kill their children without remorse," and while Lichtenstein tells us that no other savages betray "so high a degree of brutal ferocity"; Moffat, speaking of their attentions to him when he was ill, says: "I was deeply affected by the sympathy of these poor Bushmen, to whom we were utter strangers." Agreeing with Burchell, Kolben describes the Hottentots as friendly, liberal, benevolent; and yet, from Kolben, as from Sparrman, we learn that they frequently bury infants alive, and leave their aged to die in solitary places. It is so, too, with the Australians. While they abandon their aged to perish, and often destroy their infants, they are represented as fond and indulgent parents, and as often showing kind feelings to travelers. More strange still is the contrast exhibited in Borneo, where, according to Boyle, a Dyak has often been seen rushing "through a captured village, clasping in his arms a young child as tenderly as possible, without relaxing his grasp of its father's gory head."

In face of such facts it seems unlikely that our inductions concerning the relations of humane feeling to type of man, and to social type, can be more than rudely approximate.

151. We may fitly begin with illustrations of entire lack of sympathy, now taking the negative shape of simple indifference to others' suffering, and now taking the positive shape of delight in their suffering. Of the Karens Mason says: "I have stood over an old woman dying alone in a miserable shed, and tried in vain to induce her children and grandchildren, close by, to come to help her." The lack of feeling shown by the Honduras people in Herrera's day, he illustrates by the refusal of a wife to kill a hen for her sick husband, because, as she said, "her husband would die, and then she should lose him and the hen too." Various Negro races furnish kindred examples. While, concerning the natives of Loando, Monteiro says that "the Negro is not cruelly inclined" [not actively cruel], yet "he has not the slightest idea

of mercy, pity, or compassion": "A fellow creature, or animal, writhing in pain or torture, is to him a sight highly provocative of merriment and enjoyment." Duncan and Burton agree in saying that the Dahomans, who "are void either of sympathy or gratitude, even in their own families," are "in point of parental affection, inferior to brutes." And then the Ashantis show us this indifference formulated as a principle of conduct. Two of their proverbs, as rendered by Burton, run thus: "If another suffers pain, *(to you)* a piece of wood suffers." "The distress of others is no concern of yours; do not trouble yourself about it."

Passing from negative to positive cruelty, we find in the Damaras illustrations of both. Baines says of them: "Everybody knows that in other tribes the aged and helpless are left to perish, but that a mother should refuse to pull a few bundles of grass to close up a sleeping hut for her sick daughter. . . . is almost beyond belief." And, according to Galton, a sick man "is pushed out of his hut by his relations away from the fire into the cold; they do all they can to expedite his death." So with the negative inhumanity of the Dahomans above named may be joined their positive inhumanity; shown, for instance, in the "annual customs" at which numbers of victims are slaughtered to supply a dead king "with fresh attendants in the shadowy world," and again shown by decorating their buildings with great numbers of human skulls, which they make war to obtain. Of kindred testimonies Holub yields one concerning the Marutse, asserting that "a brutal cruelty is one of the predominant failings of these people"; and another is yielded by Lord Wolseley, who says that "the love of bloodshed and of watching human bodily suffering in any shape is a real natural pleasure to the Negroes of West Africa."

To these cases of positive inhumanity, may be added those displayed by the predatory tribes of North America who, while they discipline their young men by subjecting them to tortures, also torture their enemies. "Wolves of women borne," as the Prairie Indians are called, hand over "an old man or woman" for torture, "to the squaws and papooses, pour les amuser." Burton who tells us this, says of the Yutahs that they are "as cruel as their limited intellects allow them to be." From another authority we learn that the squaws among the Comanches are crueler than the men, and delight in torturing the male prisoners.

152. How often misused words generate misleading thoughts! Savage, originally meaning rude, wild, uncultured, was consequently applied to aboriginal peoples. Behaving treacherously and cruelly to voyagers, as some of them did in retaliation, this trait was regarded as a universal trait; and "savage" came to mean ferocious. Hence the baseless belief that savageness in this sense, characterizes the uncivilized in contrast with the civilized. But the inhumanity which has been shown by the races classed as civilized, is certainly not less, and has often been greater, than that shown by the races classed as uncivilized.

Passing over the multitudinous cruelties which stain the annals of ancient Eastern nations, of whom the Assyrians may be named as a sample; merely naming the doings of the admired Homeric Greeks—liars, thieves, and murderers, as Grote shows—whose heroes revelled in atrocities; and not dwelling on the brutalities of the Spartans or the callousness, if nothing more, of other later Greeks; we may turn to the Romans, whose ruthless civilization, lauded by admirers of conquests, entailed on Europe centuries of misery. Twenty generations of predatory wars, developed a nature of which the savagery has rarely been equalled by that of the worst barbarian races known to us. Though the torture of captives has been practiced by the North American Indians, they have not been in the habit of torturing their slaves. Though there were subject tribes among the Fijians who were liable to be used for cannibal feasts, yet the Fijians did not go to the length of killing hundreds of his fellow slaves along with one who had murdered his master. And if very often the uncivilized reduce to bondage such of the conquered as are not slain, they do not form them into herds, make them work like beasts, and deny them all human privileges; nor do they use any of them to gratify their appetites for bloodshed by combats in arenas—appetites so rampant in Rome that the need for satisfying them was bracketed with the need for satisfying bodily hunger. Using the word "savage" in its modern acceptation, we may fairly say that, leaving the Fijians out of the comparison, the white savages of Rome outdid all which the dark savages elsewhere have done.

Were it not that men are blinded by the theological bias and the bias of patriotism, it would be clear to them that throughout Christian Europe also, during the greater part of its history, the inhumanity fostered by the wars between societies, as well as by the feuds within each society, has been carried to extremes beyond those reached by inferior peoples whom we think of as ferocious. Though the atrocities committed by such semicivilized races as the Mexicans and Central Americans, such as skinning victims alive and tearing out their palpitating hearts, may not have been paralleled in Europe; yet Europeans, loudly professing a religion of love, have far exceeded them in the ingenuity of their multitudinous appliances for the infliction of prolonged agonies on heretics, on witches, and on political offenders. And even now, though at home the discipline of a peaceful social life has nearly extinguished such inhumanities, yet by our people abroad there are still perpetrated inhuman deeds, if not of these kinds, yet of other kinds. The doings of Australian settlers to the natives, of "beachcombers" and kidnappers in the Pacific, do but exemplify in vivid ways the barbarous conduct of European invaders to native races—races which, when they retaliate, are condemned as "savage."

153. While men of some varieties appear to be devoid of sympathy, and the moral traits which it originates, there are men of other varieties who, inferior to ourselves as they may be in respect of culture, are our equals, and some of them our superiors, in respect of humanity. Here, in the briefest way, I

string together the testimonies of travelers, whose names will be found in the references.

The Veddahs are "in general gentle and affectionate"; "widows are always supported by the community." Tannese—"The sick are kindly attended to the last." In New Guinea some tribes of Papuans have shown great humanity to Europeans placed at their mercy. Dyaks—"Humane to a degree which well might shame ourselves." Malagasy—"Treat one another with more humanity than we do." Esquimaux— "As between themselves, there can be no people exceeding them in this virtue—kindness of heart." Iroquois—"Kindness to the orphan, hospitality to all, and a common brotherhood" were enjoined. Chippewas—before the white man came, there was more "charity practiced towards one another; and the widow and orphan were never allowed to live in poverty and want." Araucanians—No indigent person is to be found . . . the "most incapable of subsisting themselves are decently clothed:" "generous and humane towards the vanquished." Mandingos—"It is impossible for me to forget the disinterested charity, and tender solicitude, with which many of these poor heathens . . . sympathized with me in my sufferings." And Kolff, speaking of the "continued kindness" of the inhabitants of Luan, says—"I never met with more harmony, contentment and toleration, more readiness to afford mutual assistance, more domestic peace and happiness, nor more humanity and hospitality."

Though, as in the case of the Bushmen, characterized by Moffat in the first section of this chapter, humane actions on some occasions are associated with brutal actions on other occasions, yet in some of the peoples here instanced—the Veddahs, the Esquimaux, and the inhabitants of Luan—there is no such alloy.

154. In the literatures of ancient Eastern peoples, there are numerous expressions of humane sentiments and exhortations to humane actions—utterances of poets and sages, which, though they probably indicate in but small measure

the prevailing sentiments, may be taken as in some measure significant of advance consequent on settled social life. Among the early Indian books, the *Mahabharata* contains the following:

> To injure none by thought or word or deed,
> To give to others, and be kind to all—
> This is the constant duty of the good.

And in the same book, the princess Savitri, urging Yama, the god of death, to give back the soul of her husband which he was carrying away, tells the god how noble is the quality of mercy. She argues that to give is more divine than to take; to preserve is mightier than to destroy. The sacred book of the Persians, the *Zend-Avesta*, appears to have its humane precepts in some measure prompted by the doctrine of metempsychosis—kind treatment of animals being insisted upon partly for that reason; but Sadi, in the *Gulistan*, has definite injunctions of a relevant kind:

> Show mercy to the weak peasant . . . it is criminal to crush the poor
> and defenceless subjects with the arm of power. . . . Thou who art
> indifferent to the sufferings of others deservest not to be called a man.

Charitable conduct was insisted upon among the Egyptians too. According to Birch and Duncker, it was enjoined "to give bread to the hungry, water to the thirsty, clothes to the naked, and shelter to the wanderer"; and the memoirs in the tombs "portray just and charitable lives, protection of the widow and the needy, care for the people in times of famine." Similarly, the books of the Chinese sages agree in emphasizing the virtues which flow from fellow-feeling. According to Legge, Lâo-tsze "seems to condemn the infliction of capital punishment; and he deplores the practice of war." In a like spirit Confucius says that "benevolence is the characteristic element of humanity." And Mencius too, while alleging that the "feeling of commiseration is essential to man," remarks that "so is the superior man affected towards animals, that, having seen them alive, he cannot bear to see them die." To all which has of course to be added the evidence furnished by the sacred books of the Hebrews, in the later of which there are injunctions to show kindness and mercy, not to men only but to animals— injunctions which the European peoples who avowedly accepted them, along with the still more humane doctrine of Jesus, did so little throughout many centuries to practice, even in small measure.

155. Amid perturbing causes and conflicting testimonies, no general conclusions seem trustworthy save those reached by putting side by side the extreme cases. Comparisons so made justify anticipation.

Of the Karens, instanced above as absolutely heartless, it is said that "every tribe is antagonistic to each other," and there is almost continual war. So too is it with another Indian race, the Afridis. The intensity of the fighting propensity among them is such that "an Afridi generally has a blood feud with nine out of ten of his own relations"; and their lack of all humane sentiment is implied by the statement that "ruthless, cowardly robbery, cold-blooded, treacherous murder, are to an Afridi the salt of life." Then we have the case of the Dahomans, above shown to be utterly void of sympathy, even with their own offspring, and whose absolutely militant social state is so exceptionally indicated by their army of Amazons. The wildest tribes of the North American Indians, too, the Dakotas and the Comanches, whose inhumanity is shown by torturing their prisoners, are tribes of warriors carrying on chronic feuds and perpetual wars.

Of the converse relation, the most marked cases above instanced are those exhibited by certain absolutely peaceful peoples—the Esquimaux, the inhabitants of Luan, the Veddahs. Among such, free as they are from those passions which intertribal enmities exercise and increase, we find an unusual display of that fellow-feeling which results in kindly behavior and benevolent actions.

And here, along with this contrast, may be joined a contrast of kindred nature, between the absence and presence of a trait allied to humane feeling—I mean gratitude; for of gratitude, as of humanity, the ultimate root is sympathy. Of the fighting and destructive Fijians Williams says:

> Ingratitude deeply and disgracefully stains the character of the Fijian heathen. . . . If one of them, when sick, obtained medicine from me, he thought me bound to give him food; the reception of food he considered as giving him a claim on me for covering; and, that being secured, he deemed himself at liberty to beg anything he wanted, and abuse me if I refused his unreasonable request.

On the other hand, what do we read about the Veddahs, living always in peace? Mr. Atherton describes them as "very grateful for attention or assistance"; and, as quoted by Pridham, Mr. Bennett says that after having given some Veddahs presents and done them a service,

> a couple of elephants' tusks, nearly six feet in length, found their way into his front verandah at night, but the Veddahs who had brought them never gave him an opportunity to reward them. "What a lesson in gratitude and delicacy," he observes, "even a Veddah may teach!"

Truly, indeed, they may teach this, by making in so unobtrusive a way, and with great labor, a return greater in value than the obligation; and they may teach more—may teach that where there have not been preached the Christian virtues, these may be shown in a higher degree than where they are ostentatiously professed and perpetually enjoined.

CHAPTER 9

Veracity

156. **C**omplete truthfulness is one of the rarest of virtues. Even those who regard themselves as absolutely truthful are daily guilty of overstatements and understatements. Exaggeration is almost universal. The perpetual use of the word "very," where the occasion does not call for it, shows how widely diffused and confirmed is the habit of misrepresentation. And this habit sometimes goes along with the loudest denunciations of falsehood. After much vehement talk about "the veracities," will come utterly unveracious accounts of things and people—accounts made unveracious by the use of emphatic words where ordinary words alone are warranted: pictures of which the outlines are correct but the lights and shades and colors are doubly and trebly as strong as they should be.

Here, among the countless deviations of statement from fact, we are concerned only with those in which form is wrong as well as color—those in which the statement is not merely a perversion of the fact but, practically, an inversion of it. Chiefly, too, we have to deal with cases in which personal interests of one or other kind are the prompters to falsehood—now the desire to inflict injury, as by false witness; now the desire to gain a material advantage; now the desire to escape a punishment or other threatened evil; now the desire to get favor by saying that which pleases. For in mankind at large, the love of truth for truth's sake, irrespective of ends, is but little exemplified.

Here let us contemplate some of the illustrations of veracity and unveracity—chiefly unveracity—furnished by various human races.

157. The members of wild tribes in different parts of the world, who, as hunters or as nomads, are more or less hostile to their neighbors, are nearly always reprobated by travelers for their untruthfulness; as are also the members of larger societies consolidated by conquest under despotic rulers.

Says Burton of the Dakotas—"The Indian, like other savages, never tells the truth." Of the Mishmis, Griffith writes— "They have so little regard for truth, that one cannot rely much on what they say." And a general remark, *à propos* of the Kirghiz, is to the same effect. "Truth, throughout Central Asia, is subservient to the powerful, and the ruler who governs leniently commands but little respect."

Of the settled societies, the first to be named is the Fijian. Williams tells us that

> Among the Fijians the propensity to lie is so strong, that they seem to have no wish to deny its existence. . . . Adroitness in lying is attained by the constant use made of it to conceal the schemes and plots of the Chiefs, to whom a ready and clever liar is a valuable acquisition. . . . "A Fijian truth" has been regarded as a synonym for a lie.

Of kindred nature, under kindred conditions, is the trait displayed by the people of Uganda.

> In common with all savage tribes, truth is held in very low estimation, and it is never considered wrong to tell lies; indeed, a successful liar is considered a smart, clever fellow, and rather admired.

So, too, was it among the ancient semicivilized peoples of Central America. De Laet says of certain of them, living under a despotic and bloody regime—"they are liars, like most of the Indians." And concerning the modern Indians, who may be supposed to have preserved more or less the character of their progenitors, Dunlop writes:

> I never have found any native of Central America, who would admit that there could be any vice in lying; and when one has succeeded in cheating another, however gross and infamous the fraud may be, the natives will only remark, *"Que hombre vivo"* (What a clever fellow).

A like fact is given by Mr. Foreman in his work on the Philippine Islands. He says the natives do not "appear to regard lying as a sin, but rather as a legitimate, though cunning, convenience."

158. The literatures of ancient semicivilized peoples yield evidence of stages during which truth was little esteemed, or rather, during which lying was tacitly or openly applauded. As we saw in a recent chapter (section 127) deception, joined with atrocity, was occasionally inculcated in the early Indian literature as a means to personal advancement. We have proof in the Bible that, apart from the lying which constituted false witness, and was to the injury of a neighbor, there was among the Hebrews but little reprobation of lying. Indeed it would be remarkable were it otherwise, considering that Jahveh set the example; as when, to ruin Ahab, he commissioned "a lying spirit" (1 *Kings*, xxii. 22) to deceive his prophets; or as when, according to *Ezekiel*, xiv. 9, he threatened to use deceptions as a means of vengeance.

> If the prophet be deceived when he hath spoken a thing, I the Lord have deceived that prophet, and I will stretch out my hand upon him, and will destroy him from the midst of my people Israel.

Evidently from a race-character which evolved such a conception of a deity's principles, there naturally came no great regard for veracity. This we see in sundry cases; as when Isaac said Rebecca was not his wife but his sister, and nevertheless received the same year a bountiful harvest: "the Lord blessed him" (*Gen*. xxvi, 12); or as when Rebecca induced Jacob to tell a lie to his father and defraud Esau—a lie not condemned but shortly followed by a divine promise of prosperity; or as when Jeremiah tells a falsehood at the king's suggestion. Still we must not overlook the fact that in the writings of the Hebrew prophets, as also in parts of the New Testament, lying is strongly reprobated. Averaging the evidence, we may infer that along with the settled life of the Hebrews there had grown up among them an increased truthfulness.

Much regard for veracity was hardly to be expected among the Greeks. In the *Iliad* the gods are represented not only as deceiving men but as deceiving one another. The chiefs "do not hesitate at all manner of lying." Pallas Athene is described as loving Ulysses because he is so deceitful; and, in the words of Mahaffy, the Homeric society is full of "guile and falsehood."* Nor was it widely otherwise in later days. The trait alleged of the Cretans—"always liars"—though it may have been more marked in them than in Greeks at large, did not constitute an essential difference. Mahaffy describes Greek conduct in the Attic ages as characterized by "treachery" and "selfish knavery," and says that Darius thought a Greek who kept his word a notable exception.

Evidence of the relation between chronic hostilities and

---

* Marvelous are the effects of educational bias. Familiarity with the doings of these people, guilty of so many "atrocities," characterized by such "revolting cruelty of manners," as Grote says, who were liars through all grades from their gods down to their slaves, and whose religion was made up of gross and brutal superstitions, distinguishes one of our leading statesmen; and, joined to familiarity with the doings of other Greeks, it is thought by him to furnish the best possible preparation for life of the highest kind. In a speech at Eton, reported in *The Times*, of 16 March, 1891, Mr. Gladstone said—"If the purpose of education is to fit the human mind for the efficient performance of the greatest functions, the ancient culture, and, above all, Greek culture, is by far the best, the most lasting, and the most elastic instrument that can possibly be applied to it." Other questions aside, one might ask with puzzled curiosity which of Mr. Gladstone's creeds, as a statesman, it is which we must ascribe to the influence of Greek culture—whether the creed with which he set out as a Tory when fresh from Oxford, or the extreme radical creed which he has adopted of late years?

utter disregard of truth, is furnished throughout the history of Europe. In the Merovingian period—"the era of blood"—oaths taken by rulers, even with their hands on the altar, were forthwith broken; and Salvian writes—"If a Frank forswear himself, where's the wonder, when he thinks perjury but a form of speech, not of crime?" After perpetual wars during the two hundred years of the Carolingian period, with Arabs, Saracens, Aquitanians, Saxons, Lombards, Slavs, Avars, Normans, came the early feudal period, of which H. Martin says:

> The tenth [century] may pass for the era of fraud and deceit. At no other epoch of our history does the moral sense appear to have been so completely effaced from the human soul as in that first period of feudalism.

And then, as an accompaniment and consequence of the internal conflicts which ended in the establishment of the French monarchy, there was a still-continued treachery: the aristocracy in their relations with one another "were without truth, loyalty, or disinterestedness . . . Neither life nor character was safe in their hands." Though Mr. Lecky ascribes the mediæval "indifference to truth" to other causes than chronic militancy, yet he furnishes a sentence which indirectly yields support to the induction here made, and is the more to be valued because it is not intended to yield such support. He remarks that "where the industrial spirit has not penetrated, truthfulness rarely occupies in the popular mind the same prominent position in the catalogue of virtues" as it does among those "educated in the habits of industrial life."

Nor do we fail to see at the present time, in the contrasts between the Eastern and Western nations of Europe, a like relation of phenomena.

159. Reflection shows, however, that this relation is not a direct one. There is no immediate connection between blood-thirstiness and the telling of lies. Nor because a man is kind-hearted does it follow that he is truthful. If, as above implied, a

life of amity is conducive to veracity, while a life of enmity fosters unveracity, the dependencies must be indirect. After glancing at some further facts, we shall understand better in what ways these traits of life and character are usually associated.

In respect of veracity, as in respect of other virtues, I have again to instance various aboriginal peoples who have been thrust by invading races into undesirable habitats; and have there been left either in absolute tranquillity or free from chronic hostilities with their neighbors. Saying of the Kois that they all seem to suffer from chronic fever (which sufficiently shows why they are left unmolested in their malarious wilds) Morris tells us that "They are noted for truthfulness, and are quite an example in this respect to the civilized and more cultivated inhabitants of the plains." According to Shortt, in his *Hill Ranges of Southern India,*

> A pleasing feature in their [Sowrahs] character is their complete truthfulness. They do not know how to tell a lie. They are not sufficiently civilized to be able to invent.

I may remark in passing that I have heard other Anglo-Indians assign lack of intelligence as the cause of this good trait—a not very respectable endeavor to save the credit of the higher races. Considering that small children tell lies, and that lies are told, if not in speech yet in acts, by dogs, considerable hardihood is shown in ascribing the truthfulness of these and kindred peoples to stupidity. In his *Highlands of Central India,* Forsyth writes: "The aborigine is the most truthful of beings, and rarely denies either a money obligation or a crime really chargeable against him." Describing the Râmósîs, Sinclair alleges that

> They are as great liars as the most civilized races, differing in this from the Hill tribes proper, and from the Parwâris, of whom I once knew a Brâhman to say: "The Kunabîs, if they have made a promise, will keep it, but a Mahâr [Parwari] is such a fool that he will tell the truth without any reason at all."

And this opinion expressed by the Brahman, well illustrates the way in which their more civilized neighbors corrupt these veracious aborigines; for while Sherwill, writing of another tribe, says "The truth is by a Sonthal held sacred, offering in this respect a bright example to their lying neighbors the Bengalis," it is remarked of them by Man that "Evil communications are exercising their baneful influences over them, and soon, I fear, the proverbial veracity of the Sonthal will cease to become a byword."

In *The Principles of Sociology*, vol. ii, sections 437 and 574, I gave the names of others of these Indian hill-tribes noted for veracity—the Bodo and Dhimáls, the Carnatic aborigines, the Todas, the Hos; and here I may add one more, the Puluyans, whose refuge is "hemmed in on all sides by mountains, woods, backwaters, swamps, and the sea," and who "are sometimes distinguished by a rare character for truth and honor, which their superiors in the caste scale might well emulate." So too is it in a neighboring land, Ceylon. Wood-Veddahs are described as "proverbially truthful and honest." From other regions there comes kindred evidence. Of some Northern Asiatic peoples, who are apparently without any organization for offense or defense, we read: "To the credit of the Ostiaks and Samoiedes it must be said, that they are eminently distinguished for integrity and truthfulness."

But now we have to note facts which make us pause. There are instances of truthfulness among peoples who are but partially peaceful, and among others who are anything but peaceful. Though characterized as "mild, quiet, and timid," the Hottentots have not infrequent wars about territories; and yet, in agreement with Barrow, Kolben says the Word of a Hottentot "is sacred: and there is hardly any thing upon earth they look upon as a fouler crime than breach of engagement." Morgan, writing of the Iroquois, states that "the love of truth was another marked trait of the Indian character." And yet, though the Iroquois league was formed avowedly for the preservation of peace, and achieved this end in respect of its component nations, these nations carried on hostilities with their neighbors. The Patagonian tribes have frequent fights with one another, as well as with the aggressive Spaniards; and yet Snow says—"A lie with them is held in detestation." The Khonds, too, who believe that truthfulness is one of the most sacred duties imposed by the gods, have "sanguinary conflicts" between tribes respecting their lands. And of the Kolis, inhabiting the highlands of the Dekhan, we read that though "manly, simple, and truthful," they are "great plunderers" and guilty of "unrelenting cruelty."

What is there in common between these truthful and pacific tribes and these truthful tribes which are more or less warlike? The common trait is that they are not subject to coercive rule. That this is so with tribes which are peaceful, I have shown elsewhere (*Principles of Sociology*, ii, sections 573–74); and here we come upon the significant fact that it is so, too, with truthful tribes which are not peaceful. The Hottentots are governed by an assembly deciding by a majority, and the head men have but little authority. The Iroquois were under the control of a council of fifty elected sachems, who could be deposed by their tribes; and military expeditions, led by chiefs chosen for merit, were left to private enterprise and voluntary service. Among the Patagonians there was but feeble government: followers deserting their chiefs if dissatisfied. Writing of the Khonds' "system of society" Macpherson says— "The spirit of equality pervades its whole constitution, society is governed by the moral influence of its natural heads alone, to the entire exclusion of the principle of coercive authority."

160. In the remarks of sundry travelers, we find evidence that it is the presence or absence of despotic rule which leads to prevalent falsehood or prevalent truth.

Reference to the *Reports on the Discovery of Peru* of Xeres and Pizarro (pp. 68–69, 85–86, 114–20), makes it manifest that the general untruthfulness described was due to the intimidation the Indians were subject to. So, too, respecting the Mexicans, the Franciscan testimony was—"They are liars, but to those who treat them well they speak the truth readily." A clear conception of the relation between mendacity and fear was given to Livingstone by his experiences. Speaking of the falsehood of the East Africans he says,

> But great as this failing is among the free, it is much more annoying among the slaves. One can scarcely induce a slave to translate anything truly: he is so intent on thinking of what will please.

And he further remarks that "untruthfulness is a sort of refuge for the weak and oppressed."

A glance over civilized communities at once furnishes verification. Of European peoples, those subject to the most absolute rule, running down from their autocrats through all grades, are the Russians; and their extreme untruthfulness is notorious. Among the Egyptians, long subject to a despotism administered by despotic officials, a man prides himself on successful lying, and will even ascribe a defect in his work to failure in deceiving some one. Then we have the case of the Hindus, who, in their early days irresponsibly governed, afterwards subject for a long period to the brutal rule of the Mahometans, and since that time to the scarcely-less brutal rule of the Christians, are so utterly untruthful that oaths in Courts of Justice are of no avail, and lying is confessed to without shame. Histories tell like tales of a mendacity which, beginning with the ruled, infects the rulers. Writing of the later feudal period in France, Michelet says: "It is curious to trace from year to year the lies and tergiversations of the royal false coiner": but nowadays political deceptions in France, though still practiced, are nothing like so gross. Nor has it been otherwise among ourselves. If with the "universal and loathsome treachery of which every statesman of every party was continually guilty," during Elizabeth's reign, while monarchical power was still but little qualified, we contrast the veracity of statesmen in recent days, we see a kindred instance of the relations between the untruthfulness which accompanies tyranny and the truthfulness which arises along with increase of liberty.

Hence such connections as we trace between mendacity and a life of external enmity, and between veracity and a life of internal amity, are not due to any direct relations between violence and lying and between peacefulness and truth-telling; but are due to the coercive social structure which chronic external enmity develops, and to the noncoercive social structure developed by a life of internal amity. To which it should be added that under the one set of conditions there is little or no ethical, or rather proethical, reprobation of lying; while under the other set of conditions the proethical reprobation of lying, and in considerable measure the ethical reprobation, become strong.

CHAPTER 10

Obedience

161. Under the one name "obedience" are grouped two kinds of conduct, which have widely different sanctions: the one sanction being permanent and the other temporary. Filial obedience and political obedience being thus bracketed, the idea of virtuousness is associated with both; and almost everyone thinks that a submission which is praiseworthy in the one case, is praiseworthy in the other also.

Here we have to recognize the truth that while due subordination of child to parent originates in a permanent order of Nature, and is unconditionally good, the subordination of citizen to government is appropriate to a process which is transitional, and is but conditionally good.

It is true that in societies which have had a genesis of the kind erroneously supposed by Sir Henry Maine to be universal, the two kinds of obedience have a common root: the patriarchal group grows out of the family, and, by insensible steps, the subjection of children to parents passes into the subjection of adult sons to their father, and the subjection of family groups to the father of the father or patriarch. It is true, also, that by union of many patriarchal groups there is produced an organization in which a supreme patriarch is the political head. But in developed societies, such as those of modern days, these primitive relationships have wholly disappeared, and the two kinds of obedience have become quite distinct. Nevertheless, being in large measure prompted by the same sentiment, the two commonly vary together.

In contemplating the facts, we will first take those which concern the subordination of child to father, and then those which concern the subordination of citizen to government.

162. The earliest social stages are characterized not only by absence of chiefs, and therefore absence of the sentiment which causes political submission, but they are often characterized by such small submission of sons as renders the human family group near akin to the brutal family group—a group in which parental responsibility on the one side, and filial subjection on the other, soon cease.

The American races yield instances. The Araucanians "never punish their male children, considering chastisement degrading, and calculated to render the future man pusillanimous and unfit for the duties of a warrior." Among the Arawaks affection seems to prompt this lenient treatment: a father "will bear any insult or inconvenience from his child tamely, rather than administer personal correction." And then of a Dakota boy we read that "at ten or twelve, he openly rebels against all domestic rule, and does not hesitate to strike his father: the parent then goes off rubbing his hurt, and boasting to his neighbors of the brave boy whom he has begotten." Some Old World races supply kindred illustrations. Of the East Africans, Burton says: "When childhood is past, the father and son become natural enemies, after the manner of wild beasts." So, too, when, writing about the Bedouin character, and commenting on "the daily quarrels between parents and children," Burckhardt tells us that "instead of teaching the boy civil manners, the father desires him to beat and pelt the strangers who come to the tent," to cultivate his high spirit: adding elsewhere that "the young man, as soon as it is in his power, emancipates himself from the father's authority . . . whenever he can become master of a tent himself . . . he listens to no advice, nor obeys any earthly command but that of his own will." Associated with insubordination to parents, we sometimes have cruelty shown to them in age. A Chippewayan old man "is neglected, and treated with great disrespect, even by his own children"; and the Kamtschadales "did not even consider it a violation of filial duty to kill them [their parents] when they became burdensome."

Towards mothers, more especially, is disregard shown: their relatively low position as slaves to men, prompting contempt for them. By the Dakotas "the son is taught to make his mother toil for him." In Fiji "one of the first lessons taught the infant is to strike its mother, a neglect of which would beget a fear lest the child should grow up to be a coward." When a young Hottentot has been admitted into the society of men

> He may insult his mother when he will with impunity. He may cudgel her, if he pleases, only for his humor, without any danger of being called to an account for it. Such actions are esteemed as tokens of a manly temper and bravery.

Concerning the Zulu boys Thompson writes: "It is a melancholy fact, that when they have arrived at a very early age, should their mothers attempt to chastise them, such is the law, that these lads are at the moment allowed to kill their mothers." And Mason says of the Karens:

> Occasionally, when the mother gives annoyance to her children by reproving them; one will say: "My mother talks excessively. I shall not be happy till she dies. I will sell her, though I do not get more than a gong or five rupees for her." And he sells her.

So far as these instances go, they associate lack of obedience of children to parents with a low type of social organization. This, however, is not a uniform relation, as we see in the case of the Esquimaux, among whom "the affection of the parents for their children is very great, and disobedience on the part of the latter is rare. The parents never inflict physical chastisement upon the children." The fact would appear to be that in the lowest social groups, we may have either filial obedience or filial disobedience; but that if the groups are of kinds which lead lives of antagonism, then, in the absence of filial obedience, there does not arise that cohesion required for social organization.

163. This is implied by the converse connection which we see displayed among various types of men.

If, with the wandering Semites above named, we contrast the Semites who, though at first wandering, became settled and politically organized, we see little filial subordination in the one and much in the other. Among the Hebrews the head of the family exercised capital jurisdiction (*Genesis* xxxviii. 24). In the decalogue (*Exodus* xx. 12) honoring parents comes next to obeying God. In *Leviticus* xx. 9, punishment is threatened for cursing father or mother, just as it is for blasphemy; and in *Deuteronomy* xxi. 18–21, it is ordered that a rebellious son shall be publicly stoned to death. Of another branch of the race, which assumed the coercive type of social organization—the Assyrians—we read that "a father was supreme in his household . . . If the son or daughter disowned his father he was sold as a slave, and if he disowned his mother he was outlawed."

By the Hindus, filial piety, vividly shown by sacrifices of food to deceased father, grandfather, great-grandfather, &c., was in early times vividly shown, too, during life.

> The father of Nakiketas had offered what is called an All-sacrifice, which requires a man to give away all that he possesses. His son, hearing of his father's vow, asks him, whether he does or does not mean to fulfill his vow without reserve. At first the father hesitates; at last, becoming angry, he says: "Yes, I shall give thee also unto death." The father, having once said so, was bound to fulfill his vow, and to sacrifice his son to death. The son is quite willing to go, in order to redeem his father's rash promise.

No less conspicuously has this connection been exhibited in China, where it has continued from the earliest recorded days down to our own. With the established worship of ancestors, by whom are supposed to be consumed the periodical offerings of food, &c., made to them, there has all along gone the absolute subordination of children to living parents. Says Confucius—"Filial piety and fraternal submission!—are they not the root of all benevolent actions?" An old Chinese saying runs—"Among the hundred virtues, filial piety is the chief"; and a sacred edict of 1670 says filial piety is "the first and greatest of the commandments in China." It was the same in another large society of which the continuity goes back beyond our chronology: I mean that of the Egyptians. According to Ptah-hotep, "The secret of moral duty is obedience; filial obedience is its root." Nor was it otherwise with the society which, beginning as a small cluster of clans, spread and spread till it overran all Europe, with parts of Asia and Africa. The subjection of sons to fathers in early Roman days, and long afterwards, was absolute—less qualified indeed, than in China; for though down to the present time Chinese parents have the right of infanticide, and may sell their children as servants or slaves; and though, by implication, adult sons can do nothing without parental approval, or own property not subject to parental confiscation; yet we do not read that the Chinese have exercised the power of life and death over adult children, as did the Romans. Of course with the establishment of this absolute parental power went the assumption that filial submission should be absolute. And if, throughout subsequent European history, a father's authority and a child's subjection have been less extreme; yet, up to comparatively modern times, they have been very decided.

By various types of men we are thus shown that filial obedience has constantly accompanied social growth and consolidation: if not throughout, yet during its earlier stages.

164. The height to which political obedience rises is determined, in chief measure, by the existence of favorable conditions. If the physical characters of the habitat are such as to

negative large aggregations of men—as they do in wide tracts which are barren, leading to nomadic life, or as they do where mountain chains cut off group from group—the tendency seems rather to be for the filial sentiment to develop no further than the patriarchal; and along with this restricted growth there may go resistance to a wider rule. The Khonds exemplify this:

> For the head of a family all the tribes have the greatest respect, it being a proverb with them that "A man's father is his God on earth." The social organization among them is indeed strictly patriarchal, the father of a family being its absolute ruler in every case. Disobedience to him under any circumstances is regarded as a crime.

This trait is possessed by another mountain people, the Bhils, who, along with a certain amount of submission to general chiefs, show an extreme allegiance to their family chiefs or patriarchs, called Turwees.

> So wonderful is the influence of the chief over this infatuated people, that in no situation, however desperate, can they be induced to betray him. . . . To kill another when their Turwee desires, or to suffer death themselves, appears to them equally a matter of indifference.

From filial obedience, thus widening in range, may in time develop a settled political obedience, where physical circumstances favor it; and especially where there arises combined action in war. Pallas tells us that the Kalmucks manifest much "attachment towards their legitimate rulers"; and that they honor and obey their parents. Among the Sgaus, a division of the Karens (apparently unlike the other divisions), "The elders say: 'O children and grandchildren! respect and reverence your mother and father.' . . . 'O, children and grandchildren! obey the orders of kings, for kings in former times obeyed the commands of God.' " But it is in the larger societies of primitive types that the two kinds of obedience are most closely associated. In China where, as before shown, filial obedience is extreme, we see them jointly insisted upon;

as implied by Tsze-hea when he lauded a man "if, in serving his parents, he can exert his utmost strength, if, in serving his prince, he can devote his life"; and as implied in the conduct of Confucius, already quoted as enjoining filial obedience, who when "passing the vacant place of the prince, his countenance appeared to change, and his legs to bend under him, and his words came as if he hardly had breath to utter them." After recognizing in China occasional dissent, as of Mencius, who in one place suggests rebellion, we may pass to Persia. Here, too, there were solitary expressions of independence, as by the Darwesh who said that "kings are for the protection of their subjects, not subjects for the service of kings"; but, in general, political obedience was urged, for reasons of prudence if for no other. One of their vazirs said:

Opinions differing from the king, to have
'Tis your own hands in your own blood to lave.
Should he affirm the day to be the night,
Say you behold the moon and Pleiads' light.

And Sadi enjoins the attitude of submission as a part of duty: instance the sentence: "Whosoever possesseth the qualities of righteousness placeth his head on the threshold of obedience." Among the Ancient Indians, instanced above as carrying to an extreme the submission of son to father, political submission was strongly insisted on; as in the Code of Manu, where it is held wrong to treat even a child-king "as if he were a mortal; he is a great divinity in human shape." Then in Egypt, along with that exhortation to obey parents quoted from Ptah-hotep, may be named his approval of wider obedience: "If thou abasest thyself in obeying a superior, thy conduct is entirely good before God." Commenting on the groveling prostrations represented in their sculptures and paintings, Duncker remarks that the Egyptians "worshipped their kings as the deities of the land." Indeed, in the inscriptions on the tombs of officials, the deeds implying such worship are specified as proofs of their virtue. Nor was it otherwise with the Hebrews. While, in their decalogue, religious obedience and filial obedience are closely coupled, there was elsewhere joined with these political obedience; as in *Proverbs* xvi. 10, where it is said: "A divine sentence is in the lips of the king; his mouth transgresseth not."

Throughout European history a like relationship is traceable. Along with the theory and practice of absolute subjection of child to parent, there went the theory and practice of absolute subjection to the chief man of the group—now to the local head, while the groups were small and incoherent, and now to the central head, when they became large and consolidated. Less definite forms of rule having been replaced by feudalism, there first came fealty to the feudal lord, and then, with advancing political integration, there came loyalty to the king. In the old French epic the one inexpiable crime is the treason of a vassal; the noblest virtue is a vassal's fidelity. In our own country the extreme loyalty of the highlanders to the chiefs of their clans, and subsequently to the Stuarts as their kings, exemplifies the dominance of the sentiment; while the English nobility have, among other ways of showing this feeling, shown it in sundry of their mottoes; as instance—Paulet and others, "Aimez loyaulté"; Earl Grey and others, "De bon vouloir servir le roy"; Earl of Lindsay, "Loyalty binds me"; Baron Mowbray, "I will be loyal during my life"; Earl of Rosse, "For God and the King"; Adair, "Loyal to the death."

And here let us note how the frequency with which loyalty is thus expressed as the highest of sentiments, reminds us of the frequency with which aggressiveness has been, by other nobles, chosen as the sentiment most worthy to be professed.

165. The significance of this association lies in the fact that they are both accompaniments of chronic militancy. When we remember that first of all the chief, and in later days the king, and later still the emperor, is primarily the supreme commander; and that his headship in peace is but a sequence of his headship in war; it is clear that at the outset political obedience is identical with military obedience. Further, it needs but to consider that for success in war absolute subor-

dination to the commander-in-chief is essential, and that absolute subordination to him as king is a concomitant, to see that while the militancy remains active, the two remain one.

Additional evidence of this relationship is yielded by a few cases in which political obedience is carried to an extreme exceeding obedience of all other kinds. The first to be named is afforded by a people who have passed away—the warlike and cannibal Mexicans, who invaded their neighbors to get victims to satisfy their hungry gods. Montezuma II, says Herrera, "caused himself to be so highly respected, that it almost came to be adoration. No commoner was to look him in the face, and if one did, he died for it." According to Peter of Ghent, "the worst feature in the character of the Indians is their submissiveness"; and then Herrera, illustrating their loyalty, names a man who would not betray his lord, but rather than do so allowed himself to be "torn piecemeal" by dogs. Among existing peoples, a striking example is furnished by the cannibal Fijians. These ferocious savages, revelling in war and destruction, are described by Erskine as intensely loyal. So obedient are they to their chiefs, says Jackson, that they have been known to eat pumice-stone when commanded to do so; and Williams says that a condemned man stands unbound to be killed, himself declaring, "Whatever the king says, must be done." Of the bloody Dahomans, too, with their Amazon army, we are told by one traveler that "before the king all are slaves alike," and by another that "they reverence him with a mixture of love and fear, little short of adoration": "parents are held to have no right or claim to their children, who, like everything else, belong to the king." So that political subordination submerges all other kinds of subordination.

Nor is it only by these extreme cases, and by the extreme converse cases, that this connection is shown. It is shown also by the intermediate cases: instance the various peoples of Europe. In Russia militancy and its appliances subordinate the entire national life; and among Europeans the Russians display the most abject obedience: gaining, thereby, the applause of Mr. Carlyle. Loyal to the point of worship, they submit unresistingly to the dictation of all state officials down to the lowest. On the other hand, we are ourselves the people among whom militancy and its appliances occupy the smallest space in the national life, and among whom there is least political subjection. The government has come to be a servant instead of a master. Citizens severely criticize their princes; discuss the propriety of abolishing one division of the legislature; and expel from power ministers who do not please them.

Nor is it otherwise when we compare earlier and later stages of the same nation. By these, too, we are shown that as fast as the life of internal amity outgrows the life of external enmity, the sentiment of obedience declines. Though submissive loyality to the living German Kaiser is great, yet it is not so great as was the submissive loyalty to his conquering ancestor, Frederick II, when Forster wrote: "What chiefly disgusted me was the deification of the king." If, notwithstanding the nominally free form of their government, the mass of the French people let their liberties be trampled upon to an extent which the English delegates to a Trades-Union Congress in Paris said is "a disgrace to, and an anomaly in, a Republican nation"; yet their willing subordination is not so great as it was at the time when war had raised the French monarchy to its zenith. In our own case, too, while there is a marked contrast between the amount of war, internal and external, in early days, and the complete internal peace, joined with long external peace, which recent times have known; there is a contrast no less marked between the great loyalty shown in early days and the moderate loyalty, largely nominal, shown at present.

It remains only to add that, along with the decline of political subordination there has gone a decline of filial subordination. The harsh rule of parents and humble submission of children in past centuries, have, in our times, been exchanged for a very moderate exercise of parental authority and a filial subjection which, far less conspicuous during youth than it used to be, almost ceases when the age for marriage arrives.

166. Thus, akin though they are in the sentiment prompting them, and in the main varying together, the two kinds of obedience, filial and political, have different sanctions. The one is bound up with the laws of life, while the other is dependent on the needs of the social state, and changes as they change.

For the obedience of child to parent there is the warrant arising from relatively imperfect development, and there is the warrant arising from the obligation to make some return for benefits received. These are obviously permanent; and though, with the advance from lower to higher types of man and society, filial subjection decreases, yet some degree of it must ever remain, and must continue to be prompted by an ethical sentiment properly so-called.

On the other hand, political obedience, nonexistent in groups of primitive men, comes into existence during the political integrations effected by war—during the growth and organization of large societies formed by successive conquests. The development of political obedience in such societies is a necessity; since, without it, there cannot be carried on the combined actions by which subjugations and consolidations are brought about.

The implication is that the sentiment of political obedience, having but a transitional function, must decrease in amount as the function decreases in needfulness. Along with decline of that system of *status* characterizing the militant type of organization, and rise of that system of contrast characterizing the industrial type, the need for subjection becomes gradually less. The change of sentiment accompanying this change from compulsory cooperation to voluntary cooperation, while it modifies the relations of citizens to one another, modifies also their relations to their government: to this the same degree of obedience is neither required nor felt. Humble submission ceases to be a virtue; and in place of it there comes the virtue of independence.

Decline of political obedience and waning belief in the duty

of it, go along with increasing subordination to ethical principles, a clearer recognition of the supremacy of these, and a
determination to abide by them rather than by legislative
dictates. More and more the proethical sentiments prompting
obedience to government, come into conflict with the ethical
sentiment prompting obedience to conscience. More and
more this last causes unconformity to laws which are at variance with equity. And more and more it comes to be felt that
legal coercion is warranted only insofar as law is an enforcer of
justice.

That political obedience is thus a purely transitional virtue,
cannot be perceived while the need for political subordination
remains great; and while it remains great the unlimited
authority of the ruling power (if not a man then a majority)
will continue to be asserted. But if from past changes we are to
infer future changes, we may conclude that in an advanced
state, the sphere of political obedience will have comparatively narrow limits; and that beyond those limits the
submission of citizen to government will no more be regarded
as meritorious than is now the cringing of a slave to a master.

CHAPTER 11

Industry

167. If we are to understand the origins and variations of the sentiments, ethical and proethical, which have been entertained in different times and places concerning industry and the absence of industry, we must first note certain fundamental distinctions between classes of human activities, and between their relations to the social state.

Industry, as we now understand it, scarcely exists among primitive men—scarcely, indeed, *can* exist before the pastoral and agricultural states have been established. Living on wild products, savages of early types have to expend their energies primarily in gathering and catching these: the obtainment of some, like fruits and roots, being easy and safe, and the obtainment of others, such as beasts of which some are swift and some are large, being difficult and dangerous. After these the remaining activities, more difficult and dangerous than those the chase implies, are implied by warfare with fellow men. Hence the occupations of the utterly uncivilized may be roughly divided into those which demand strength, courage, and skill, in large measure, and those which demand them in but small measure or not at all. And since in most cases the preservation of the tribe is mainly determined by its success in war and the chase, it results that the strength, courage, or skill shown in these, come to be honored both for themselves and for their value to the tribe. Conversely, since the digging up of roots, the gathering of wild fruits, and the collecting of shell-fish, do not call for strength, courage, and skill, and do not conspicuously further tribal preservation, these occupations come to be little honored or relatively despised. An implication strengthens the contrast. While the stronger sex is called on to devote itself to the one, the other is left to the weaker sex: sometimes aided by conquered men, or slaves. Hence arises a further reason why, in primitive societies, honor is given to the predatory activities while the peaceful activities are held in dishonor. Industry, therefore, or that which at first represents it, is not unnaturally condemned by the proethical sentiment.

The only kinds of activity to be classed as industrial which the warriors of the tribe may enter upon, are those necessitated by the making of weapons and the erection of wigwams or huts: the one, closely associated with war and the chase, demanding also the exercise of skill; and the other demanding both skill and strength—not the moderate strength shown in monotonous labor, but the great strength which has to be suddenly exerted. And these apparent exceptions furnish a verification; for they further show that the occupations held in contempt are those which, demanding relatively little power, physical or intellectual, can be carried on by the inferior.

The contrast thus initiated between the sentiments with which these classes of occupations are regarded, has persisted with but small, though increasing, qualification, throughout the course of human progress; and it has thus persisted because the causes have in the main persisted. While the self-preservation of societies has most conspicuously depended on the activities implied by successful war, such activities have been held in honor; and, by implication, industrial activities have been held contemptible. Only during recent times—only now that national welfare is becoming more and more dependent on superior powers of production, and such superior powers of production are becoming more and more dependent on the higher mental faculties, are other occupations than militant ones rising into respectability; while simultaneously respectability is being acknowledged in the accompanying capacity for persistent and monotonous application.

Carrying this clue with us, we shall be able now to understand better the ethics of labor, as changing from people to people and from age to age.

168. The North American Indians furnish the simplest and clearest illustrations of predatory habits and associated sentiments. Schoolcraft says of the Chippewas:

> They have regarded the use of the bow and arrow, the war club and spear, as the noblest employments of man. . . . To hunt well and to fight well, are the first and the last themes of their hopes and praises of the living and the dead. . . . They have ever looked upon agricultural and mechanical labors as degrading.

Of the Snake Indian, Lewis and Clarke write: "He would consider himself degraded by being compelled to walk any distance." Of kindred nature is Burton's account of the Dakotas: "The warrior, considering the chase as an ample share of the labor curse, is so lazy that he will not rise to saddle or unsaddle his pony. . . . Like a wild beast he cannot be broken to work: he would rather die than employ himself in honest industry." By the more civilized Iroquois, too, the primitive feeling was displayed—"The warrior despised the toil of husbandry, and held all labor beneath him." Even the unwarlike Esquimaux is said to exhibit a like aversion. "He hunts and fishes, but having brought his booty to land troubles himself no further about it; for it would be a stigma on his character, if he so much as drew a seal out of the water." There being, perhaps, for this usage a plea like that possessed by the usage of the Chippewayans, among whom, "when the men kill any large beast, the women are always sent to bring it to the tent"—the plea, namely, that the chase, whether on sea or on land, is extremely exhausting.

Passing to South America we meet with facts of kindred

meaning. Men of the Guiana tribes take no share in industry, save in making clearance for the growing of food: each lies "indolently in his hammock until necessitated to fish, or use the more violent exercise of the chase, to provide for the wants of his family." And then of the Araucanians, warlike but agricultural (apparently because there is but little scope for the chase), we are told that "the 'lord and master' does little but eat, sleep, and ride about."

In the wording of this last statement, as by implication in the other statements, we may see that in early stages the egoism of men, unqualified by the altruism which amicable social intercourse generates, leads them to devolve on women all exertions which, unaccompanied by the pleasures of achievement, are monotonous and wearisome. "The lord and master" does what he likes; and he likes to make the woman (or his woman as the case may be) do all the dull and hard work. Proofs of this are multitudinous. America furnishes instances in the accounts of the Chippewayans, Creeks, Tupis, Patagonians; as witness these extracts:

"This laborious task [dragging the sledges] falls most heavily on the women: nothing can more shock the feelings of a person, accustomed to civilized life, than to witness the state of their degradation."

"The women perform all the labor, both in the house and field, and are, in fact, but slaves to the men."

"When they removed, the women were the beasts of burthen, and carried the hammocks, pots, wooden pestles and mortars, and all their other household stock."

The lives of the Patagonian women are "one continued scene of labor. . . . They do everything, except hunting and fighting."

Here, again, are testimonies given by travelers in Africa concerning the Hottentots, Bechuanas, Kaffirs, Ashantis, people of Fernando Po and the Lower Niger:

The wife "is doomed to all the toil of getting and dressing provisions for" her husband, "herself and children . . . . and to all the care and drudgery within doors, with a share of the fatigue in tending the cattle."

"The women build the houses; plant and reap the corn; fetch water and fuel; and cook the food. It is very rarely that the men are seen helping the women, even in the most laborious work."

"Besides her domestic duties, the woman has to perform all the hard work; she is her husband's ox, as a Kafir once said to me—she has been bought, he argued, and must therefore labor."

"It may be remarked, that the weightiest duties generally devolve upon the wife, who is to be found 'grinding at the mill,' transacting business in the market, or cultivating the plantation."

"The females in Fernando Po have a fair portion of work assigned to them, such as planting and collecting the yam . . . but they are certainly treated with greater consideration and kindness than in any part of Africa we visited."

On the lower Niger, "women are commonly employed in the petty retail trade about the country; they also do a great deal of hard work, especially in the cultivation of the land."

Of which extracts it may be remarked that the latter ones, which concern races of more advanced kinds, carrying on more settled industries, show that with them the slavery of women is less pronounced.

Beyond that dishonorableness which, in early stages, attaches to labor because it can be performed by women, who in most cases are incapable, or considered to be incapable, of war and the chase; there is the further dishonorableness which attaches to it because, as above pointed out, it is carried on also by conquered men or slaves—by men, that is, proved in one or other way to be inferior. In very early stages we sometimes find slaves thus used for the nonpredatory occupations which their masters find irksome. Even of the Chinooks we read that "slaves do all the laborious work"; and they are often associated with the women in this function. Says Andersson: "The Damaras are idle creatures. What is not done by the women is left to the slaves, who are either the descendants of impoverished members of their own tribe or . . . captured Bushmen." Describing the people of Embomma on the Congo, Tuckey writes: "The cultivation of the ground is entirely the business of slaves and women, the King's daughters and princes' wives being constantly thus employed." Burton tells us that in Dahomey "agriculture is despised, because slaves are employed in it"; but a great deal of it seems to be done by women. And similarly of the Mishmis in Asia, we read that "the women and slaves do all the cultivation."

Naturally, then, and, indeed, we may say necessarily, there grows up in these early stages a profound prejudice against labor—a proethical sentiment condemnatory of it. How this proethical sentiment, having the sanction of ancestral usages, assumes this or that special character according to the habits which the environment determines, we are variously shown. Thus we read that the Bushmen "are sworn enemies to the pastoral life. Some of their maxims are, to live on hunting and plunder"; "The genuine Arabs disdain husbandry, as an employment by which they would be degraded." In which examples, as in many already given, we may see how a mode of life long pursued, determines a congruous set of feelings and ideas. And the strength of the prejudices which maintain inherited customs of this class, is shown by sundry anomalous cases. Livingstone tells us of the East Africans that "where there are cattle, the women till the land, plant the corn, and build the huts. The men stay at home to sew, spin, weave, and talk, and milk the cows."

Still more strange is the settled division of labor between the sexes in Abyssinia. According to Bruce, "It is infamy for a man to go to market to buy anything. He cannot carry water or bake bread; but he must wash the clothes belonging to both sexes, and, in this function, the women cannot help him." In Cieza's account of certain ancient Peruvians, the Cañaris, we find a kindred system:

> [The women] are great laborers, for it is they who dig the land, sow the crops, and reap the harvests, while their husbands remain in the

houses sewing and weaving, adorning their clothes, and performing
other feminine offices. . . . Some Indians say that this arises from the
dearth of men and the great abundance of women.

Possibly such anomalies as these have arisen in cases where
surrounding conditions, causing decrease of predatory activities while the labors of women continued to suffice for
purposes of production, left the men to lead idle lives or lives
filled with easy occupations. We may safely infer that among
barbarous peoples, the men did not take to hard and
monotonous labor until they were obliged.

169. But where chronic militancy did not effectually keep
down population, increase of it made peremptory the devotion
of men to food production; and with this change in social life
there was initiated a change in the proethical sentiments respecting labor. The Khonds furnish an example. They "consider it beneath their dignity to barter or traffic, and . . . regard
as base and plebeian all who are not either warriors or tillers of
the soil." So of the Javans we are told that "they have a
contempt for trade, and those of higher rank esteem it disgraceful to be engaged in it; but the common people are ever
ready to engage in the labors of agriculture, and the chiefs
to honor and encourage agricultural industry." From
various sources we learn that the Germanic tribes, both in
their original habitats and in those which they usurped, became reconciled to husbandry as an alternative to hunting and
marauding: doubtless because by no other occupation could
adequate sustenance be obtained.

Concerning these and kindred transitional states, two passing remarks may be ventured. One is that since industry,
chiefly agricultural, is at first carried on by slaves and women,
working under authority, it results that when freemen are
forced by want of food to labor, they have a strong prejudice
against laboring for others, that is, laboring for hire; since
working under authority by contract, too much resembles
working under authority by compulsion. While Schomburgk
characterizes the Caribs as the most industrious race in

Guiana, he says that only the extremest need can induce a Carib so far to lower his dignity as to work for wages for a European. This feeling is shown with equal or greater strength by some peaceful peoples to whom subordination is unfamiliar or unknown. Speaking of southeast India, Lewin says: "Among the hill tribes labor cannot be hired; the people work each one for himself. In 1865, in this district, a road had to be cut; but although fabulous wages were offered, the hill population steadily refused to work." And still more decided is the aversion to working under orders shown by the otherwise industrious Sonthal:

> The Sonthal will take service with no one, he will perform no work except for himself or his family, and should any attempt be made to coerce him, he flies the country or penetrates into the thickest jungle, where unknown and unsought, he commences clearing a patch of ground and erecting his log hut.

The other remark is that the scorn for trade which, as above shown, at first coexists with the honoring of agriculture, is possibly due to the fact that it was originally carried on chiefly by unsettled classes, who were detached, untrustworthy members of a community in which most men had fixed positions. But the growth of trade slowly brought a changed estimate. As, in hunting tribes, agriculture, relatively unessential, was despised, but became respectable when it became an indispensable means to maintenance of life; so trade, at first relatively unessential (since essential things were mostly made at home), similarly lacked the sanction of necessity and of ancestral custom, but in course of time, while growing into importance, gradually ceased to excite that proethical sentiment which vents itself in contempt.

170. With the growth of populous societies and the more and more imperative need for agriculture, the honorableness for labor does not for long periods obtain recognition, for the reasons indicated at the outset: it is carried on by slaves, or by serfs, or in later days by men more or less inferior in body or

mind. A strong association in thought is thus established; and the natural repugnance to work is enforced by the belief that engagement in it is a confession of a low nature.

Though, in the literatures of ancient civilized societies, we find the duty of laboring insisted on, it seems mostly to be the duty of subject men. The injunction contained in the Code of Manu—"Daily perform thine own appointed work unweariedly," refers by implication to men under authority: "appointed" work implies a master. So, too, according to the *Book of the Dead* (cxxv), the Egyptian, when questioned after death, had to declare, "I have not been idle," and, "I have not made delays, or dawdled." From the phrasing of the last sentence we may fairly infer that the work diligently performed was work commanded. Of the Hebrews the same may be concluded. Remembering that, being originally pastoral, they long continued to regard the care of cattle as relatively honorable (like the existing Arabs among whom, when the men are not raiding, their only fit occupation is herding); we may similarly gather that the obligation to work was mostly the obligation imposed on servants or slaves: slaves being usually the proper word. Though the third commandment applies to masters as well as to servants, yet, even supposing the Commandments were indigenous, the fact that the life was still mainly pastoral, implies that the work spoken of was pastoral work, not manual labor. It is true that in the legend of Adam's condemnation, the curse of labor is imposed on all his descendants; but we have, in the first place, good reason for regarding this legend as of Babylonian origin, and we have, in the second place, the inference suggested by recent researches, that the Adami, a dark race, were slaves, and that the eating of the forbidden fruit reserved for the superior race, was a punishable transgression; just as was, in ancient Peru, the eating of coca, similarly reserved for the Inca class. So that possibly among the Hebrews also, the duty of working was imposed on inferior men rather than on men as such. In Persian literature we do, indeed, meet with more distinct recognition of the virtuousness of labor irrespective of conditions. Thus it is said—"A sower of seeds is as great in the eyes of Ormusd, as if he had given existence to a thousand creatures." And in *The Parsees*, by Dosabhoy Framjee, we read that "the Zoroastrian is taught by his religion to earn his bread by the sweat of his brow."

171. The peoples of Europe from early days down to our own, illustrate this relation between the kind of social activity and the prevailing sentiment about labor.

We have first the evidence which the Greeks furnish. Plato, showing his feeling towards traders by saying that the legislator passes them over, while for agriculturists he shows such respect as is implied by giving them laws, shows more fully in the *Republic* how degraded he holds to be all producers and distributors: comparing them to the basest parts of the individual nature. Similar is the belief expressed, and feeling manifested, by Aristotle, who says, "It is impossible for one who lives the life of a mechanic or hired servant to practice a life of virtue."

Nor has it been otherwise further West. In the Roman world, along with persistent and active militancy, there went an increasing degradation of the nonmilitant class—slaves and freedmen. And throughout "the dark ages," which collapse of the brutal civilization of Rome left behind, as well as throughout those ages during which perpetually recurring wars at length established large and stable kingdoms, this contempt for industry, both bodily and mental, continued; so that not only unskilled labor and the skilled labor of the craftsman, but also the intellectual labor of the educated man, were treated with contempt. Only in proportion as fighting ceased to be the exclusive business of life with all but the subject classes, and only as the subject classes, simultaneously growing larger, gained a larger share in the formation of opinion did the honorableness of industry become in some measure recognized: any praise of it previously given by the governing classes, being due to the consciousness that it conduced to their welfare.

In modern days, especially among ourselves and the Americans, the industrial part of society has so greatly outgrown the militant part, and has come to be so much more operative in forming the sentiments and ideas concerning industry, that these are almost reversed. Though unskilled labor is still regarded with something like contempt, as implying inferiority of capacity and of social position; and though the labor of the artisan, more respected because of the higher mental power it implies, is little respected because of its class associations; yet intellectual labor has in recent times acquired an honorable *status*. But the fact chiefly to be noted is that along with the advance of industrialism towards social supremacy, there has arisen the almost universal feeling that some kind of useful occupation is imperative. Condemnations of the "idle rich" are nowadays uttered by the rich themselves.

It may be noted, however, that even still, among those who represent the ancient regime—the military and naval officers—the old feeling survives; with the result that those among them who possess the highest culture—the medical officers, both military and naval, and the engineer officers— are regarded as standing on a lower level than the rest, and are treated with less consideration by the authorities.

172. Thus as in all the preceding chapters, so in this chapter, we see that the ethical conceptions, or rather the proethical conceptions, are determined by the forms of the social activities. Toward such activities as are most conspicuously conducive to the welfare of the society, sentiments of approbation are called forth, and conversely; the result being that the idea of right comes to be associated with the presence of them and wrong with the absence of them.

Hence the general contrast shown from the earliest stages down to the latest, between the disgracefulness of labor in societies exclusively warlike, and the honorableness of labor in peaceful societies, or in societies relatively peaceful. This contrast is significantly indicated by the contrast between the ceremonies at the inauguration of a ruler. Among uncivilized militant peoples, in the formal act of making or crowning a chief or king, weapons always figure: here he is raised on a shield above the shoulders of his followers, and there the sword is girded on or the spear handed to him. And since, in most cases, relatively peaceful societies have preserved in their traditions the ceremonies used in their exclusively militant days, it rarely happens that the inauguration of a ruler is free from symbols of this kind. But one significant case of freedom from them is supplied by that tribe in Africa, the Manansas, already named, who, driven by warlike tribes around into a hill country, have devoted themselves to agriculture, and who say: "We want not the blood of the beasts, much less do we thirst for the blood of men!" for among them, according to Holub, a new sovereign receives as tokens, some sand, stones, and a hammer, "symbolizing industry and labor."

There is one remaining fact to be named and emphasized. Out of the proethical sentiments which yield sanction to industry and make it honorable, there eventually emerges the ethical sentiment proper. This does not enjoin labor for its own sake, but enjoins it as implied by the duty of self-sustentation instead of sustentation by others. The virtue of work consists essentially in the performance of such actions as suffice to meet the cost of maintaining self and dependents and discharging social duties; while the disgracefulness of idleness essentially consists in the taking from the common stock the means of living, while doing nothing either to add to it or otherwise to further men's happiness.

CHAPTER 12

Temperance

173. Such ethical, or rather proethical, sentiments as attach to temperance, have primarily, like sundry of the associated proethical sentiments, religious origins. As shown in *The Principles of Sociology*, section 140, the bearing of hunger becomes in many cases a virtue, because it is a sequence of leaving food for the ancestor, and, at a later stage, sacrificing food to the god. Where food is not abundant, relinquishments of it involve either absolute fastings or stinted meals; and hence there arises an association in thought between moderation in eating and a subordination which is either religious or quasi-religious.

Possibly in some cases a kindred restraint is put on the drinking of liquors which are used as libations, since the quantities required for these also, restrict the quantities remaining for the sacrificers. If, as often happens, there is at every meal a throwing aside of drink, as well as food, for the invisible beings around, it tends to become an implication that one who exceeds so far as to become intoxicated, has disregarded these invisible beings, and is therefore to be blamed. It is true that, as we shall presently see, other ideas sometimes lead to contrary beliefs and sentiments; but it is possible that there may from this cause have originated the divine reprobation which is in some cases alleged.

467

Since the above paragraphs were written, I have found clear proof that the suspicion they express is well founded. From a people among whom ancestor-worship, and the habitual sacrificing to ancestors, have been through all known ages zealously carried on, we get evidence that moderation in both food and drink, pushed even to asceticism, is a consequence of regard for the dead, to whom oblations are constantly made. Said Confucius: "He who aims to be a man of complete virtue, in his food does not seek to gratify his appetite." Here we have the virtue enunciated apart from its cause. But Confucius also said: "I can find no flaw in the character of Yu. He used himself coarse food and drink, but displayed the utmost filial piety towards the spirits. His ordinary garments were poor, but he displayed the utmost elegance in his sacrificial cap and apron." Here we have the virtue presented in connection with religious duty: the last being the cause, the first the consequence.

Considered apart from supposed religious sanction, the virtue of temperance can of course have no other sanction than utility, as determined by experience. The observed beneficial effects of moderation and the observed detrimental effects of excess, form the bases for judgments, and the accompanying feelings.

Rational ideas concerning temperance—especially temperance in food—cannot be formed until we have glanced at those variations in the physiological requirements, entailed by variations in surrounding circumstances.

174. What would among ourselves be condemned as disgusting gluttony, is, under the conditions to which certain races of men are exposed, quite normal and indeed necessary. Where the habitat is such as at one time to supply very little food and at another time food in great abundance, survival depends on the ability to consume immense quantities when the opportunities occur. A good instance is furnished by Sir George Grey's account of the orgies which follow the stranding of a whale in Australia.

By and by other natives came gaily trooping in from all quarters: by night they dance and sing, and by day they eat and sleep, and for days this revelry continues unchecked, until they at last fairly eat their way into the whale, and you see them climbing in and about the stinking carcase choosing titbits . . . they remain by the carcase for many days, rubbed from head to foot with stinking blubber, gorged to repletion with putrid meat. . . . When they at last quit their feast, they carry off as much as they can stagger under.

Living as the Australians do in a barren country, and often half starved, those of their number who could not fully utilize an occasion like this would be the first to die during times of famine. Proof that this is the true interpretation, is furnished by Christison's account of a tribe of central Queensland. They are great eaters "only at first; but when they have become used to rations and regular meals, including bread or damper, they are very moderate eaters, perhaps more moderate than Europeans."

In other cases what seems to us extreme and almost incredible excess, is due to the physiological necessity for producing heat in climates where the loss of heat is very great. Hence the explanation of the following story.

From Kooilittiuk I learnt a new Eskimaux luxury: he had eaten until he was drunk, and every moment fell asleep, with a flushed and burning face, and his mouth open: by his side sat Arnalooa [his wife], who was attending her cooking pot, and at short intervals awakened her spouse, in order to cram as much as was possible of a large piece of half-boiled flesh into his mouth, with the assistance of her forefinger, and having filled it quite full, cut off the morsel close to his lips. This he slowly chewed, and as soon as a small vacancy became perceptible, this was filled again by a lump of raw blubber. During this operation the happy man moved no part of him but his jaws, not even opening his eyes; but his extreme satisfaction was occasionally shown by a most expressive grunt, whenever he enjoyed sufficient room for the passage of sound.

Another case, equally astonishing, comes from northern Asia. Mr. Cochrane says:

The Yakuti and Tongousi are great gluttons. I gave the child [a boy about five years old] a candle made of the most impure tallow, a second, and a third—and all were devoured with avidity. The steersman then gave him several pounds of sour frozen butter; this also he immediately consumed; lastly, a large piece of yellow soap; all went the same road . . . In fact, there is nothing in the way of fish or meat, from whatever animal, however putrid or unwholesome, but they will devour with impunity, and the quantity only varies from what they have, to what they can get. I have repeatedly seen a Yakut or a Tongouse devour forty pounds of meat in a day.

The following testimony of Capt. Wrangell shows the physiological results of this enormous consumption.

Even in Siberia, the Jakuti are called *iron-men,* and I suppose that there are not any other people in the world who endure cold and hunger as they do. I have seen them frequently in the severe cold of this country, and when the fire had long been extinguished, and the light jacket had slipped off their shoulders, sleeping quietly, completely exposed to the heavens, with scarcely any clothing on, and their bodies covered with a thick coat of rime.

And now observe the remarkable and significant fact that where survival primarily depends on this ability to eat and digest enormous quantities of food, this ability acquires an ethical or proethical sanction. According to Erman, a Yakut adage says: "To eat much meat and to grow fat upon it, is the highest destiny of men."

175. Passing from this extreme instance of the way in which the necessities of life generate corresponding ideas of right and wrong, and coming to the ordinary cases meeting us in temperate and tropical climates, where something like an ethical sanction, as we ordinarily understand it, comes into play; we find no connections between temperance in food and other traits, unless it be a general association of gluttony with degradation.

Even this qualified generalization may be held doubtful. Cook described the Tahitians as each consuming a "prodigious" quantity of food. Yet they were physically a fine race, intellectually superior to many, and, though licentious, were described by him as having sundry characteristics to be admired. Conversely, the Arabs are relatively abstemious in both food and drink. But while in their sexual relations they are about as low as the Tahitians, since they are continually changing wives, and say of themselves, "Dogs are better than we are," they are little to be admired in any respect: being fanatically revengeful and regarding skillful robbery as a qualification for marriage.

At the same time that the uncivilized at large present no definite relations between temperance or intemperance in food and their other traits, they display little or no sentiment in respect of one or the other which can be called ethical. Save in the above remarkable proverb quoted from the Yakuts, opinion on this matter has not taken shape among them.

In some ancient semicivilized societies, however, there had arisen the consciousness that excess in food is wrong. In the Code of Manu it is written:

> For gluttony is hateful, injures health,
> May lead to death, and surely bars the road
> To holy merit and celestial bliss.

The fact that in parts of the *Mahabharata* "heavenly blessedness" is described as without any kind of "sensual gratification," implies reprobation of excess in eating. This is of course implied also in the ascetic life on which the Indian sages insisted. The Hebrews, too, displayed this consciousness: there was occasional advocacy of abstemiousness, as shown in the proverb: "Be not among winebibbers: among riotous eaters of flesh: for the drunkard and the glutton shall come to poverty: and drowsiness shall clothe a man with rags" (*Prov.* xxiii 20–21). By the Egyptians gluttony was recognized as a vice, but was nevertheless deliberately practiced. On the one hand, excess in food was set down among the forty-two chief sins of the Egyptians, while on the other hand, at their

banquets the Egyptians do not seem to have been very moderate. Herodotus tells us (ii. 78) that a small wooden image of a mummy was carried round at their entertainments with the exhortion, "Look on this, drink and be merry. When dead, thou wilt be as this is!" This admonition was not without its results. In the pictures on monuments we find not only men, but women, throwing up the surfeit of food and wine.

But the general aspect of the evidence seems to imply that with the rise of settled societies, and with the generalizing of experiences, there arose a utilitarian condemnation of excess in food.

176. Excess in drinking is a phrase which, though applicable to drinking of unfermented liquors in injurious quantities, yet practically applies to liquors which are either fermented, and therefore intoxicating, or are otherwise intoxicating. Opinion concerning the taking of them is determined mainly by recognition of the effects they produce—regarded here with approbation and there with reprobation.

It is a mistake to suppose that the state of intoxication is everywhere condemned. Whether produced by alcohol or by other agent, it has been in early times lauded, and still is so in some places. An interpretation is suggested by the remark of an Arafura, who, when belief in the Christian God was commended to him and he was told that God is everywhere present, said: "Then this God is certainly in your arrack, for I never feel happier than when I have drunk plenty of it." The idea thus implied was distinctly and perpetually expressed by the ancient Indians in their praises of Soma-drinking. The god Soma was supposed to be present in the juice of the plant called soma; intoxication resulted from being possessed by him: and the exalted state desired, produced, and gloried in, was a state of religious blessedness: the gods themselves being supposed to be thus inspired by the god Soma. Says Max Müller:

> Madakyut=such a state of intoxication as was not incompatible with the character of the ancient gods. . . . We have no poetical word to express a high state of mental excitement produced by drinking the intoxicating juice of the Soma or other plants, which has not something opprobrious mixed up with it, while in ancient times that state of excitement was celebrated as a blessing of the gods, as not un-

worthy of the gods themselves, nay as a state in which both the warrior and the poet would perform their highest achievements.

So, too, by the Greeks it was believed that the god Dionysus was present in wine, and that "the Bacchic excitement," with its accompanying prophetic power, was due to possession by him. Hence there arose a religious sanction for drunkenness, as shown in the orgies. Nor are we without cases in our own times. The Dahomans, according to Burton, deem it a "duty to the gods to be drunk"; and the Ainos sanctify their intoxication under "the fiction of 'drinking to the gods' ": "the more *saké* the Ainos drink the more devout they are, and the better pleased are the gods." Kindred ideas and sentiments exist in Polynesia, in connection with the taking of the intoxicating *ava, kava,* or *yaqona.* In Fiji the preparation and drinking are accompanied by prayers to the gods and chants, and participation in the ceremonies is regarded as honorable.

Evidently then, drunkenness, instead of having in all cases religious condemnation, has in some cases religious sanction; and thus comes to have a proethical sentiment justifying it. This is very well shown by the Ainos, who refuse to associate with those who will not drink.

177. Either with or without this kind of sanction, intemperance, under one or other form, is widely spread among the inferior races.

Of the Kalmucks, Pallas tells us that they are intemperate in eating and drinking when they have the chance. "The festivities of the Khonds," says Campbell, "usually terminate in universal drunkenness." Brett writes that the drunkenness of the natives of Guiana takes the shape of "fearful excess at intervals." And we read of the existing Guatemalans that "the greatest happiness of these people consists in drunkenness, produced by the excessive use of . . . chicha." These last testimonies respecting American peoples at the present day, recall kindred testimonies respecting ancient American peoples. Garcilasso says of the Peruvians: "They brought liquor in great quantity, for this was one of the most prevalent vices among the Indians." Of the Yucatanese, Landa says: "The Indians were very debauched, and often got drunk"; "the women got intoxicated at the banquets, but by themselves." And Sahagun writes of the Mexicans that "they said that the bad effects of drunkenness were produced by one of the gods of wine. Hence it appears that they did not consider as a sin what they had done while being drunk."

But intemperance is by no means universal among the uncivilized and semicivilized: sobriety being shown by some of the utterly primitive as well as by some of the considerably advanced. Of the Veddahs we read—"They do not smoke, and are very temperate, drinking water only." Says Campbell: "Fond of fermented and spirituous liquors, the Lepchas are nevertheless not given to drunkenness." Of the Sumatran of the interior, only partially vitiated by contact with the Malays, Marsden tells us: "He is temperate and sober, being equally abstemious in meat and drink." Africa, too, supplies instances: "The Foolas and Mandingos very strictly abstain from fermented liquors, and from spirits, which they hold in such abhorrence, that if a single drop were to fall upon a clean garment, it would be rendered unfit to wear until washed." And Waitz makes the general remark that "except where they have had much intercourse with whites the Negroes cannot be accused of being specially addicted to intoxicating liquors."

This last statement, reminding us of the demoralization which Europeans everywhere produce in the native races whom they pretend to civilize, and reminding us more especially of the disastrous effects which follow the supplying of them with whiskey or rum, shows how cautious we must be in our inferences respecting the relations between drinking habits and social states. It is clear that in some cases, as in that of the Veddahs, sobriety may result from lack of intoxicants, and that in other cases insobriety does not naturally belong to the type or the tribe, but has been imported.

178. Perhaps among European peoples, with their long histories, we may with most chance of success seek for such

relation as exists between sobriety and social conditions. This relation seems but indefinite at best.

Brutal as was their social system, the Spartans were ascetic in their regimen; and remembering the lessons which drunken helots were made to inculcate, it is clear that originally the Spartans reprobated drunkenness and were ordinarily sober. Meanwhile the Athenians, much more civilized as they were in their social state, and far superior in culture, were by no means so sober. Some scanty testimonies imply that among the European peoples who at that time were socially organized in but low degrees, excesses in drinking were frequent. Of the early Gauls Diodorus says: "They are so exceedingly given to wine, that they guzzle it down as soon as it is imported by the merchant." And describing the primitive Germans, Tacitus tells us that "to pass an entire day and night in drinking disgraces no one." Of course not much has come down to us respecting men's drinking habits during "the dark ages"; but the prevalence of intemperance may be inferred from such indications as we have. One of the excesses occurring in the Merovingian period was that Bishop Eonius fell down drunk at mass; and we are told of Charlemagne that he was temperate: the implication being that temperance was something exceptional. Of France it may be remarked that even when intoxication was not produced, wine was taken in great excess during many later centuries. Montaigne, while saying that drunkenness was less than when he was a boy, tells us that: "I have seen a great lord of my time . . . who without setting himself to't, and after his ordinary rate of drinking at meals, swallowed down not much less than five quarts of wine." Evidently, from the days of Montaigne down to those of the modern French, the majority of whom water their ordinary weak wine, the decrease of intemperance has been marked. And among ourselves there has taken place, though with much irregularity, a kindred change. From old English and Danish times, when there was drunkenness among monks as well as others, down through the times of the Normans, who soon became as intemperate as those they had subjugated, and down through subsequent centuries, the excesses in drinks of the less potent kinds were great and general. At the beginning of the last century, when the consumption of spirits increased greatly, rising to nearly a gallon per head of the population annually, and producing scenes such as Hogarth depicted in his *Gin Lane,* there came the remedial Gin Act, which, however, was soon repealed after having done mischief. Then during the rest of the century, while "drunkenness was the common vice of the middle and lower orders," wealthier people indulged so largely in wine for their entertainments, as not unfrequently to improverish themselves.

179. Evidently the relations between drinking habits and kinds of social life are obscure. We cannot, as the teetotalers would like, assert a regular proportion between temperance and civilization, or between intemperance and moral degradation at large. Says Surgeon-General Balfour, "Half of the Asiatic races—Arab, Persian, Hindu, Burman, Malay, Siamese . . . are abstinents"; and yet no one will contend that, either in social type or social conduct, these races are superior to the races of Europe, who are anything but abstinents. Within Europe itself differences teach us the same lesson. Sober Turkey is not so high in its social life as whiskey-drinking Scotland. Yet, on comparing Italy and Germany, do we see that along with the contrast between the small potations of the one, and the great potations of the other, there goes contrast between their moral states of the kind that might be looked for. Putting on the one hand the Bedouin, who, habitual robber as he is and displaying numerous vices, nevertheless drinks no fermented liquors, and cries "Fie upon thee, drunkard!" and on the other hand the clever English artisan, who occasionally drinks to excess (and the clever ones are most apt to do this) but who is often a good fellow in other respects, we do not find any clear association between temperance and rectitude.

Some relation may reasonably be supposed to exist between drunkenness and general wretchedness. Where the life is miserable there is a great tendency to drink, partly to get what little momentary pleasure may be had, and partly to shut out unhappy thoughts about the future. But if we recall the drunkenness which prevailed among our upper classes in the last century, we cannot say that wretchedness, or at any rate physical wretchedness, was its excuse. *Ennui,* too, seems often an assignable cause, and may have produced the prevailing inebriety throughout Europe in early days, when there was difficulty in passing the time not occupied in fighting or hunting. Yet we find various peoples whose lives are monotonous enough, but who do not drink. Manifestly various influences cooperate; and it appears that the results of them are too irregular to be generalized.

180. But we are chiefly concerned with temperance and intemperance as ethically regarded. That intemperance, whether in food or drink, is condemned by the ethical sentiment proper, which refers, not to the extrinsic but to the intrinsic effects, as injurious alike to body and mind, goes without saying. But it is otherwise with the proethical sentiment. We have many cases showing that there comes either approbation or reprobation or intemperance, according to the religious ideas and social habits.

Already we have seen that intoxication may be sanctified by certain theological beliefs; and here we have to note that prevailing excess in drinking, and the current opinion which grows up along with it, may result in a social sanction. One of the uncivilized races shows us that a habit of taking a toxic agent may, where it is general, generate for itself not only a justification but something more. Says Yule of the Kasias:

> In the people perhaps the first thing that strikes a stranger, is their extreme addiction to chewing pawn, and their utter disregard of the traces which its use leaves on their teeth and lips. Indeed they pride themselves on this, saying that "Dogs and Bengalees have white teeth."

In records of ancient civilized races we find evidence of a kindred pride in excesses. Apart from its religious sanction, the drunken elevation which followed Soma-drinking was

gloried in by the Indian *rishi;* and among a neighboring
people, alcoholic excess was by some thought the reverse of
·disgraceful, as witness the epitaph of Darius Hystaspes, saying that he was a great conqueror and a great drinker, and as
witness the self-commendation of Cyrus, who "in his epistle
to the Spartans says, that in many other things he was more fit
than his brother to be a king, and chiefly because he could bear
abundance of wine." But modern Europe has yielded the
clearest proofs that prevailing inebriety may generate a sentiment which justifies inebriety. The drinking usages in Germany in past times, and down to the present time among
students, show that along with an inordinate desire for fermented liquor, and the scarcely credible ability to absorb it,
there had grown up a contempt for those who fell much below
the average drinking capacity, and a glory in being able to
drink the largest quantity in the shortest time. Among ourselves, too, in the last century, kindred ideas and feelings
prevailed. The saying "It is a poor heart that never rejoices"
was used as a justification for excess. The taking of salt to
produce thirst, the use of wine glasses which would not
stand, and the exhortation "No heel-taps," clearly showed
the disapproval of moderation which went along with
applause for the "three-bottle" man. There are some still living who have taken part in orgies at which after locking the
door and placing a number of bottles of wine on the
sideboard, the host announced that they had to be emptied
before rising: the refusal to take the required share causing
reprobation.*

But while, in past generations, there was thus a certain
proethical sentiment upholding intemperance, in our own

---

* The late Mr. John Ball, F.R.S., brought up in the neighborhood of Belfast, was,
when young, though nominally a Catholic, intimate with a wealthy family of Protes-
·tants, at the head of which was an old gentleman looked up to with reverence by his
descendants. Mr. Ball told me that this patriarch took a fancy to him; and one day,
when leaving the room after dinner, led him aside and patting him on the shoulder
said, "My good young friend, I want to talk to you about your wine. You don't drink
enough. Now take my advice—make your head while you are young, and then you
will be able to drink like a gentleman all your life."

generation temperance is upheld both by the ethical sentiment, and by a proethical sentiment. Not only is drinking
to excess universally reprobated, and to have been intoxicated even once leaves a stain on a man's reputation, but we
have now a large class by whom even moderate drinking is
condemned. While in America water is the universal bever-
age at meals and the taking of wine is regarded as scarcely
respectable.

CHAPTER 13

Chastity

181. Before we can understand fully the ethical aspects of chastity, we must study its biological and sociological sanctions. Conduciveness to welfare, individual or social or both, being the ultimate criterion of evolutionary ethics, the demand for chastity has to be sought in its effects under given conditions.

Among men, as among inferior creatures, the needs of the species determine the rightness or wrongness of these or those sexual relations; for sexual relations unfavorable to the rearing of offspring, in respect either of number or quality, must tend towards degradation and extinction. The fact that some animals are polygamous while others are monogamous is thus to be explained. In Part III of *The Principles of Sociology*, treating of "Domestic Institutions," it was shown that the relation between the sexes is liable to be determined into this or that form by environing conditions; and that certain inferior forms of the relation appear, under some conditions, to become necessary: nonadoption of them being fatal to the society. A natural connection was found to exist between polygamy and a life of perpetual hostilities, entailing great destruction of men: since of tribes which mutually slaughter their men, the one which, being monogamous, leaves many women unmarried and childless, must fail to maintain its population in face of the one which, being polygamous, utilizes all its women as mothers (sec. 307). We saw, too, that in some cases, especially in Tibet, polyandry appears more conducive to social welfare than any other relation of the sexes. It receives approval from travelers, and even a Moravian missionary defends it: the missionary holding that "superabundant population, in an unfertile country, must be a great calamity, and produce 'eternal warfare or eternal want' " (sec. 301).

These inferior forms of marriage are not consistent with that conception of chastity which accompanies the settled monogamy of advanced societies. As we understand it, the word connotes either the absence of any sexual relation, or the permanent sexual relation of one man with one woman. But we must not extend this higher conception of chastity to these lower societies. We must not assume that there exists in them any such ethical reprobation of these less-restricted relations as they excite in us. To see this clearly we must glance at the facts.

182. Already in section 120 I have given sundry illustrations of the truth, startling to those whose education has left them ignorant of multiform humanity, that the institution of polygamy is in various places morally approved, while the opposite institution is condemned. This truth, however, should not cause surprise, considering that from childhood all have been familiar with the tacit approval of the usage in the book they regard as divine. The polygamy of the patriarchs is spoken of as a matter of course, and there is implied approval of it by a wife who prompts her husband to take a concubine. But beyond this we see, in the case of David, both the religious and the social sanction for a harem: the one being implied by the statement that David, to whom God had given his "master's wives," was a man "after his own heart," and the other by the fact that when Nathan reproached him, the reproach was that he had taken the solitary wife of Uriah, not that he

had already many wives (1 *Samuel* xiii. 14; 2 *Samuel* xii). His many wives we may reasonably suppose constituted a mark of dignity, as do those of kings among savage and semicivilized peoples now. Clearly, then, under certain social conditions there is a proethical sentiment supporting polygamy, and that species of unchastity implied by it.

So, too, is it with polyandry. Various passages in the *Mahabharata* imply that it was a recognized institution among the early Indians, regarded by them as perfectly proper: practiced, indeed, by those who are upheld as models of virtue. The heroine of the poem, Draupadi, is the wife of five husbands. Each of them had a house and garden of his own, and Draupadi dwelt with them "in turn for two days at a time." Meanwhile, as we have already seen (sec. 117), one of the husbands, Yudhishthira, unfortunate notwithstanding his goodness, enunciates the doctrine that right is to be done regardless of consequences; while elsewhere Draupadi describes the virtues which she holds proper for a wife, and represents herself as acting up to them. Kindred evidence is yielded at the present time by some of the tribes in the valleys of the Himalayas—the Ladākhis, and the Chāmpās. Telling us that they practice polyandry, Drew says of the Ladākhis that they are "cheerful, willing, and good-tempered"; "they are not quarrelsome"; are "much given to truth-telling"; and he adds that the "social liberty of the women . . . I think it may be said, is as great as that of workmen's wives in England."

Rightly to interpret these facts, however, it should be added that the social state in which polyandry originally existed among the Indian peoples, had emerged from a social state still lower in respect of the sexual relations. Bad as were the gods of the Greeks, the gods of the ancient Indians were worse. In the *Puranas* as well as in the *Mahabharata* there are stories about the "adulterous amours" of Indra, Varuna, and other gods; at the same time that the "celestial nymphs are expressly declared to be courtesans," and are "sent by the gods from time to time to seduce austere sages." A society having a theology of such a kind, cannot well have been other than licentious. With the ascription even of incest to some of their gods, there naturally went an utter disregard of restraints among themselves. In the _Mahabharata_ we read: "Women were formerly unconfined, and roved about at their pleasure, independent. Though in their youthful innocence, they abandoned their husbands, they were guilty of no offense; for such was the rule in early times." And according to a tradition embodied in that poem,

> This condition of things was abolished by Svētakēhi, son of the rishi Uddalaka, who was incensed at seeing his mother led away by a strange Brahman. His father told him there was no reason to be angry, as: "The women of all castes of earth are unconfined: just as cattle are situated, so are human beings, too, within their respective castes."

Hence it may possibly be that polyandry arose as a limitation of promiscuity; and that therefore the ethical sentiment existing in support of it, was really in support of a relative chastity.

183. Returning now from this half-parenthetical discussion of those types of undeveloped chastity which are implied by low types of marriage, and resuming the discussion of chastity and unchastity considered in their simple forms, let us first look at the evidence presented by various uncivilized peoples. And here, in pursuance of the course followed in preceding chapters dealing with other divisions of conduct, I am obliged to name facts which in the absence of a strong reason should be passed over. They are not, however, more objectionable than many which are reported in our daily papers with no better motive than ministering to a prurient curiosity.

The absolute or relative deficiency of chastity may be conveniently exemplified by a string of extracts from books of travel. We may begin with North America. The testimony of Lewis and Clarke respecting the Chinooks, agreeing with that of Ross, is as follows: "Among these people, as indeed among all Indians, the prostitution of unmarried women is so far from being considered criminal or improper, that the females themselves solicit the favors of the other sex, with the entire approbation of their friends and connections." Concerning the Sioux, these same travelers give us a fact equally significant: "The Sioux had offered us squaws, but while we remained there having declined, they followed us with offers of females for two days."

Coming further south the Creeks may be named as, according to Schoolcraft, no better than the Chinooks. Like evidence is furnished by South American races, as the Tupis and Caribs: "Bands |of chastity] were broken without fear, and incontinence was not regarded as an offense"; Caribs "put no value on the chastity of unmarried women." These instances yielded by America, are associated with some in which the unchastity is of a qualified kind. To the fact that "among the Esquimaux it is considered a great mark of friendship for two men to exchange wives for a day or two," may be added a like fact presented by the Chippewayans: "It is a very common custom among the men of this country to exchange a night's lodging with each other's wives. But this is so far from being considered as an act which is criminal, that it is esteemed by them as one of the strongest ties of friendship between two families." The Dakotas supply an example, like many found elsewhere, of the coexistence of laxity before marriage with strictness after it: "There are few nations in the world amongst whom this practice, originating in a natural desire not to 'make a leap in the dark,' cannot be traced. Yet after marriage they will live like the Spartan matrons a life of austerity in relation to the other sex." In ancient Nicaragua, as in various countries, there was another kind of compromise between chastity and unchastity: "On the occasion of a certain annual festival, it was permitted that all the women, of whatever condition, might abandon themselves to the arms of whomever they pleased. Rigid fidelity, however, was exacted at all other times." But there seems to have been no restraint at other times on the unmarried, as witness Herrera's statement: "Many of the women were beautiful, and their parents used, when the maidens were marriageable, to send them to earn their portions, and accordingly they ranged about the country in a shameful manner, till they had got enough to marry them off."

Asia furnishes illustrations of another usage common among the uncivilized. The Kamtschadales and Aleuts lend their wives to guests; and sundry others of the Northern Asiatic races do the like. Pallas tells us that the Kalmucks are little jealous of their wives, and freely give them up to acquaintances. And then of an adjacent people we read—"The relation between the sexes, among the Kirghizes, is altogether on a very primitive footing; mothers, fathers, and brothers regard any breach of morality with great leniency, and husbands even encourage their friends to close intimacy with their wives. . . . Like the Kirghizes, the Buruts are strangers to jealousy." So, too, of the Mongols Prjevalsky tells us that "adultery is not even concealed, and is not regarded as a vice." From peoples further south, two instances may be cited: "Among the Red Karens, chastity, both with married and unmarried, is reported as remarkably loose. The commerce of the sexes among young people is defended as nothing wrong, because 'it is our custom' "; "Prostitution is exceedingly common, while chastity is a rare virtue among Toda women; and the ties of marriage and consanguinity are merely nominal."

To all these instances from other regions may be added some from Africa. In his *Highlands of Ethiopia,* Harris writes: "The jewel chastity is here ⌊in Shoa⌋ in no repute: and the utmost extent of reparation to be recovered in a court of justice for the most aggravated case of seduction is but five-pence sterling!" The nature of the sentiment prevailing near the Upper Congo is shown by this extract from Tuckey: "Before marriage, the father or brothers of a girl prostitute her to every man that will pay two fathoms of cloth; nor does this derogate in any way from her character, or prevent her being afterwards married." And so is it with some unlike people further south. Among the Bushmen, "infidelity to the marriage compact is . . . not considered as a crime; it is scarcely regarded by the offended person. . . . They seem to have no idea of the distinction of girl, maiden, and wife; they are all expressed by one word alone."

In Polynesia we have the well-known evidence yielded by the Arreoi society of Tahiti; and from the same region, or rather from Micronesia, comes yet other evidence. In his account of the inhabitants of the Ladrone Islands, Freycinct writes: "Souvent on avoit vu les pères vendre sans rougir les prémices de leurs filles . . . les mères elles-mêmes engager leurs enfants à suivre l'impulsion de leurs sens. . . . On possède encore une des chansons qu'elles chantoient à leurs filles en pareille circonstance." The Pelew Islanders furnish a like case: the universal practice being for the mother to instruct her newly initiated daughter always to exact payment, and the explanation of the usage being "the avarice of parents as recognized by custom."

Of the opposite trait a good many examples are furnished by primitive or uncultured peoples. Two of them come from amid these generally lax tribes of North America. Catlin says of the Mandans: "Their women are beautiful and modest— and amongst the respectable families, virtue is as highly cherished and as inapproachable, as in any society whatever." And of the Chippewas Keating writes: "Chastity is a virtue in high repute among the Chippewas, and without which no woman could expect to be taken as a wife by a warrior." But he goes on to admit that there is a good deal of concealed irregularity. Africa, too, yields some instances. "A Kaffer woman is both chaste and modest": "instances of infidelity are said to be very rare"; and the like is said of the Bachassins. The most numerous examples of chastity come from the island races. Mariner tells us that in Tonga adultery is very rare. "Chastity prevails more perhaps among these [the Sumatrans] than any other people," says Marsden. Similar is the statement of Low about the inland people of Borneo: "adultery is a crime unknown, and no Dyak (Land) ever recollected an instance of its occurrence." So in Dory, New Guinea, according to Kops, "chastity is held in high regard. . . . Adultery is unknown."

And Erskine testifies that the women of Uea, Loyalty Islands, "are strictly chaste before marriage, and faithful wives afterwards." Some peoples who are in other respects among the lowest are in this respect among the highest. Snow says that the Fuegian women at Picton Island are remarkably modest; and a fact worthy of special note is that among the rudest of the Musheras of India, who have no formal marriage, "unchastity, or a change of lovers on either side, when once mutual appropriation has been made, is a thing of rare occurrence"; and when it does occur causes excommunication. The remaining two most marked instances are found among other peaceful tribes of the Indian hills. Says Hodgson of the Bodo and Dhimal—"Chastity is prized in man and woman, married and unmarried." And according to Dalton, "The Santál women are represented by all who have written about them as exceedingly chaste, yet the young people of the different sexes are greatly devoted to each other's society and pass much time together."

With these cases of indigenous chastity may be named cases of peoples who are being degraded by foreign influences. In a paper on the Veddahs, whose neighbors the Singhalese are extremely lax, Virchow quotes Gillings to the effect that adultery and polygamy are only heard of among them where attempts have been made to civilize them. And then, little as we should expect to meet with such a testimony from a clergyman concerning a race so low as the Australians, yet of one tribe we are told by the Rev. R. W. Holden, as quoted by Taplin, that

> The advent of the whites has made the aborigines much more degraded, more helpless, more—yea, much more—susceptible to all diseases. Before our coming amongst them their laws were strict, especially those regarding young men and young women. It was almost death to a young lad or man who had sexual intercourse till married.

But the like cannot be said of other Australian tribes.

As thus presented by the uncivilized races, the facts do not fall into clear generalizations: they do not show distinct relations between chastity or unchastity and social forms or types of race. The evidence does, indeed, preponderate in favor of the relatively peaceful or wholly peaceful tribes, but this relation is not without exception; and conversely, though the standard of chastity is low in most of the fighting societies it is not low in all. Nor, when we contemplate special antitheses, do we get clear proof. Of the atrocious Fijians, exceeding in their cannibalism all other peoples, and who glory in lying, theft, and murder, we read in Erskine that the women are modest and that "female virtue may be rated at a high standard," while according to Seemann, "adultery is one of the crimes generally punished with death." On the other hand, Cook describes the Tahitians as utterly devoid of the sentiment of chastity. He says they are "people who have not even the idea of indecency, and who gratify every appetite and passion before witnesses, with no more sense of impropriety than we feel when we satisfy our hunger at a social board with our family or friends." At the same time he speaks very favorably of their dispositions: "They seemed to be brave, open, and candid, without either suspicion or treachery, cruelty or revenge; so that we placed the same confidence in them as in our best friends."

Here are incongruities which appear quite irreconcilable with the ideas current among civilized peoples.

184. Throughout the foregoing sections the aim has been to ascertain by examination of the facts, what relations, if any, exist between chastity and social type, as well as between this virtue and other virtues; but we must now consider specifically the prevailing ethical sentiments which go along with observance and nonobservance of it. Already, in many of the quotations above given, these sentiments have been expressed or implied; but to complete the general argument it seems needful to observe definitely, the extreme deviations from what we may consider normal, which they sometimes undergo. I will give three instances—one from the un-

civilized, another from a semicivilized people now extinct, and a third from an existing civilized people.

Of the Wotyaks, a Finnish race, the German traveler Buch says:

> Indeed it is even disgraceful for a girl if she is little sought after by the young men. . . . It is therefore only a logical result that it is honorable for a girl to have children. She then gets a wealthier husband, and her father is paid a higher kalym for her.

Concerning the ancient Chibchas, of Central America, we read:

> Some Indians . . . did not much care that their wives should be virgins. . . . On the contrary, some, if they discovered that they had had no intercourse with men, thought them unfortunate and without luck, as they had not inspired affection in men: accordingly they disliked them as miserable women.

The civilized nation referred to as showing, in some cases, a feeling almost the reverse of that so strongly pronounced among Western nations, we find in the Far East. Says Dixon of the Japanese:

> It used to be no uncommon thing (and we have no clear evidence that the custom is obsolete) for a dutiful daughter to sell herself for a term of years to the proprietor of a house of ill-fame, in order that she might thus retrieve her father's fallen fortunes. When she returned to her home, no stigma attached to her; rather was she honored for her filial devotion.

Though, in a work just published, *The Real Japan*, Mr. Henry Norman denies this alleged return home with credit (in modern times at least) he verifies that earlier part of the statement, that daughters are sold for specific periods by their parents: the fact that such parents are tolerated being sufficiently indicative of the prevailing sentiment.

Here then we get proof that in respect of this division of conduct, as in respect of the divisions of conduct dealt with in preceding chapters, habits generate sentiments harmonizing with them. It is a trite remark that the individual who persists in wrongdoing eventually loses all sense that it is wrong-doing, and at length believes that it is rightdoing: and the like holds socially—must, indeed, hold socially, since public opinion is but an aggregate of individual opinions.

185. If, instead of comparing one society with another, we compare early stages of those societies which have developed civilizations with later stages, we find very variable relations between chastity and social development. Only in modern societies can we say that this relation becomes tolerably clear.

Already we have seen how low in their sexual relations were the people of India in early days, and how, promiscuity and polyandry having died out, poets and sages in later times endeavored to explain away the traditional transgressions of their gods, while existing Hindus show shame when reproached with the illicit amours of their ancient heroes and heroines. Here there seems to have been a progress of the kind to be looked for.

That, among adjacent societies, there took place some kindred changes, seems implied in the fact that prostitution in temples, which prevailed among Babylonians, Egyptians, &c., and which, like other usages connected with religion, more persistent than general usages, probably indicated certain customs of earlier times, disappeared partially if not wholly. It is to be observed, too, that along with woman-stealing, common during primitive stages of the civilized, as still among the uncivilized, there naturally went a degraded position of captured women (concubinage being a usual concomitant), and that therefore, with the cessation of it, one cause of low sexual relations came to an end. That in the case of the Hebrews further advances took place seems to be shown by the facts that though Herod the Great had nine wives, and though in the *Mishnah* polygamy is referred to as existing, yet the references in *Ecclesiasticus* imply the general establishment of monogamy.

The relevant changes in the course of Greek civilization

clearly do not warrant the assertion that better relations of the sexes accompanied higher social arrangements. The amount of concubinage implied by the *Iliad,* was less than that implied by the use of female slaves and servants in Athenian households; and the established institution of *hetairai,* with the many distinguished of whom coexisted a multitude of undistinguished, the adding to the public revenue by a tax on houses of ill-fame, and the continuance of authorized prostitution in the temples of Aphrodite Pandemos, further prove that the relations of the sexes had degenerated. On passing to Rome we meet with an undeniable case of retrogression in sexual arrangements and usages, going along with the kind of social progress which is implied by extension of empire and increase of political organization. The contrast between the regular relations of men to women in early Roman times, and the extremely irregular relations which prevailed in the times of the emperors, when the being modest was taken to imply being ugly, and when patrician ladies had to be stopped by law from becoming prostitutes, shows that moral degradation of this kind may accompany one type of advancing civilization.

The reaction which commenced after these most corrupt Roman times, was greatly furthered by Christianity. The furtherance, however, cannot be ascribed to a true conception of the relations of the sexes, and a sentiment appropriate to it, but rather to an asceticism which reprobated the acceptance of pleasures and applauded the submission to pains. The prompting motive was an other-worldly one more than an intrinsically moral one; though the other-worldly motive probably fostered the moral motive. But in this case, as in countless other cases, the general law of rhythm was illustrated. Following this violent reaction came in time a violent re-reaction; so that after a period of sexual restraints came a period of sexual excesses—a period in which the relation between action and reaction was further illustrated by the fact that the nominally celibate clergy and nuns became worse than the laity who were not bound to celibacy.

It should be added that the peoples of Northern Europe, among whom the relations of the sexes seem to have been originally good, also exhibited in course of time, though in a less marked degree, the sexual retrogression that may go along with some kinds of social progression. In modern days, however, the advance to higher political types and more settled social states, has been accompanied by an average improvement in this respect as in other respects.

186. Satisfactory interpretation of these many strange contrasts and variations is impracticable: the causation is too complex. We may, however, note certain causes which seem to have been occasionally influential, though we cannot say to what extent.

The extreme laxity of the Tahitians may possibly have been encouraged by the immense fertility of their habitat. Commenting on the abundance of food almost spontaneously produced by their soil, Cook says of the Tahitians: "They seem to be exempted from the first general curse, that 'man should eat his bread in the sweat of his brow.'" Where self-maintenance and, by implication, the maintenance of children, is thus extremely easy, it seems that comparatively little mischief results if a mother is left to rear a child or children without the aid of a father; and in the absence of those evil effects on both parent and offspring which result where the necessaries of life are difficult to get, there may not tend to arise that social reprobation of incontinence which arises where its mischievous consequences are conspicuous.

Africa furnishes us with the hint of another cause of laxity which may sometimes operate. The fact that "the Dahoman, like almost all semibarbarians, considers a numerous family the highest blessing"—a fact which recalls kindred ones implied in the Bible—becomes comprehensible when we remember that in early stages, characterized by constant antagonisms, internal and external, it is important to maintain not only the numbers of the tribe in face of other tribes, but also the numbers of the families and clans; since the weaker of these go to the wall when struggles take place. Hence it results that not only is barrenness a reproach but fertility a ground of esteem; and hence possibly the reason why in East Africa "it is no disgrace for an unmarried woman to become the mother of a family": the remark of one traveler, which I cannot now find, concerning another tribe, being that a woman's irregularities are easily forgiven, if she bears many children.

This fact seems to point to the conclusion, pointed to by many preceding facts, that there is a connection between unchastity and a militant regime; seeing that production of many children is a desideratum only where the mortality from violence is great. For suspecting this connection we find a further reason in the degraded position of women which uniformly accompanies pronounced militancy (see *Principles of Sociology,* Part III, chap. X, "The Status of Women"). Where, as among peoples constantly fighting, the hard work is done by slaves and women—where women are spoils of war to be dealt with as the victors please—where, when not stolen or gained by conquest, they are bought; it is manifest that the wills of women being in abeyance, the unchecked egoism of men must conflict with the growth of chastity. And in the settled polygamy of societies which lose great numbers of men in battle, the large harems of kings and chiefs, the buying of female slaves—all of them characteristic of the militant type—we similarly see relations of the sexes adverse to any moral restrictions. If we remember that the extreme profligacy of Rome was reached after long centuries of conquests; if we remember that there survived during the feudal organization resulting from war, the *jus primæ noetis;* if of Russia, exclusively organized for war, we read that any girl on his estate was until recently, at the lord's disposal; we see further reason for suspecting that the militant type of society is unfavorable to elevated relations of the sexes.

We must not conclude, however, that chastity always characterizes societies of the nonmilitant type. Though sundry of the above-named peaceful tribes are distinguished from uncivilized tribes at large by the purity of their sexual relations, it is not so with another peaceful tribe, the Todas: these are characterized rather by the opposite trait. The Esquimaux, too, among whom there is exchange of wives, do not even know what war is.

187. It remains only to emphasize the truth, discernible amid all complexities and varieties, that without a prevailing chastity we do not find a good social state. Though comparison of intermediate types of society does not make this clear, it is made clear by comparison of extreme types. Among the lowest we have such a group as the Ku-Ka-tha clan, inhabiting Western South Australia, whose chief characteristics are "treachery, ingratitude, lying and every species of deceit and cunning," who have "no property," "no punishment of offenders," "no idea of right and wrong," and who show absolute lack of the sentiment in question: "chastity or fidelity being quite unknown to them." At the other extreme come the most advanced societies of Europe and America, in which, along with a relatively high standard of chastity (for women at least), there exist high degrees of the various traits required for social life which are wanting in these Australians. Nor does comparison of different stages of civilized nations fail to furnish evidence; as witness the contrast between our own time and the time after the Restoration, in respect alike of chastity and of general welfare.

There are three ways in which chastity furthers a superior social state. The first is that indicated at the outset—conduciveness to the nurture of offspring. Nearly everywhere, but especially where the stress of competition makes the rearing of children difficult, lack of help from the father must leave the mother overtaxed, and entail inadequate nutrition of progeny. Unchastity, therefore, tends towards production of inferior individuals, and if it prevails widely must cause decay of the society.

The second cause is that, conflicting as it does with the establishment of normal monogamic relations, unchastity is adverse to those higher sentiments which prompt such relations. In societies characterized by inferior forms of marriage, or by irregular connections, there cannot develop to any great extent that powerful combination of feelings—affection, admiration, sympathy—which in so marvelous a manner has grown out of the sexual instinct. And in the absence of this complex passion, which manifestly presupposes a relation between one man and one woman, the supreme interest in life disappears, and leaves behind relatively subordinate interests. Evidently a prevalent unchastity severs the higher from the lower components of the sexual relation: the root may produce a few leaves, but no true flower.

Sundry of the keenest aesthetic pleasures must at the same time be undermined. It needs but to call to mind what a predominant part in fiction, the drama, poetry, and music, is played by the romantic element in love, to see that anything which militates against it tends to diminish, if not to destroy, the chief gratifications which should fill the leisure part of life.

CHAPTER 14

Summary of Inductions

188. Where the data are few and exact, definite conclusions can be drawn; but where they are numerous and inexact, the conclusions drawn must be proportionately indefinite. Pure mathematics exemplifies the one extreme, and sociology the other. The phenomena presented by individual life are highly complex, and still more complex are the phenomena presented by the life of aggregated individuals; and their great complexity is rendered still greater by the multiformity and variability of surrounding conditions.

To the difficulties in the way of generalization hence arising, must be added the difficulties arising from uncertainty of the evidence—the doubtfulness, incompleteness, and conflicting natures, of the statements with which we have to deal. Not all travelers are to be trusted. Some are bad observers, some are biased by creed or custom, some by personal likings or dislikings; and all have but imperfect opportunities of getting at the truth. Similarly with historians. Very little of what they narrate is from immediate observation. The greater part of it comes through channels which color, and obscure, and distort; while everywhere party feeling, religious bigotry, and the sentiment of patriotism, cause exaggerations and suppressions. Testimonies concerning moral traits are hence liable to perversion.

497

Many of the peoples grouped under the same name present considerable diversities of character: instance the Australians, of whom it is remarked that some tribes are quiet and tractable while others are boisterous and difficult to deal with. Further, the conduct, sentiments, and ideas of native peoples often undergo such changes that travelers between whose visits many years have elapsed, give quite different accounts. The original feelings and beliefs are frequently obscured by missionary influences, and, in a still greater degree, by contact with white traders and settlers. From all parts of the world we get proofs that aborigines are degraded by intercourse with Europeans. Here, then, are further causes which distort the evidence.

Yet again there are the complications consequent on changes of habitats and occupations. In this place tribes are forced into antagonism with their neighbors, and in that place they are led into quiet lives: one of the results being that conceptions and feelings appropriate to an antecedent state, surviving for a long time in a subsequent state, appear incongruous with it.

Thus we must expect to meet with anomalies, and must be content with conclusions which hold true on the average.

189. Before we can fully understand the significance of the inductions drawn, we must reconsider the essential nature of social cooperation. As we pointed out in section 48, from the sociological point of view, "ethics becomes nothing else than a definite account of the forms of conduct that are fitted to the associated state"; and in subsequent sections it was made clear that, rising above those earliest groups in which the individuals simply live in contiguity, without mutual interference and without mutual aid, the associated state can be maintained only by effectual cooperation: now for external defense, now for internal sustentation. That is to say, the prosperity of societies depends, other things equal, on the extents to which there are fulfilled in them the conditions to such cooperation. Whence, through survival of the fittest, it

follows that principles of conduct implying observance of these conditions, and sentiments enlisted in support of such principles, become dominant; while principles of conduct which concern only such parts of the lives of individuals as do not obviously affect social cooperation, do not acquire sanctions of such pronounced and consistent kinds.

This appears to be the explanation of the fact which must have struck many readers of the last two chapters, that the ideas and sentiments respecting temperance and chastity, display less intelligible relations to social type and social development, than do the ideas and sentiments concerning cooperative conduct, internal and external. For if, scattered throughout the community, there are men who eat or drink to excess, such evils as are entailed on the community are indirect. There is, in the first place, no direct interference with military efficiency, so long as within the armed force there is no such drunkenness or gluttony as sensibly affects discipline. And in the second place, there is no direct interference with the process of social sustentation, so long as one who eats or drinks to excess does not aggress upon his neighbor or in any way inconvenience him. While erring in either of these ways, a man may respect the persons and property of his fellows and may invariably fulfill his contracts—may, therefore, obey the fundamental principles of social cooperation. Whatever detriment society receives from his conduct arises from the deterioration in one of its units. Much the same thing holds with disregard of chastity; there is no necessary or immediate interference with the carrying on of cooperations, either external or internal; but the evil caused is an ultimate lowering of the population in number or quality. In both these cases the social consciousness, not distinctly awakened to the social results, does not always generate consistent social sentiments.

It is otherwise with those kinds of conduct which directly and obviously transgress the conditions to social cooperation, external or internal. Cowardice, or insubordination, diminishes in a very obvious way the efficiency of a fighting body; and hence, in respect of these, there are readily established consistent ideas and sentiments. So, too, the murdering or assaulting of fellow citizens, the taking away their goods, the breaking of contracts with them, are actions which so conspicuously conflict with the actions constituting social life, that reprobation of them is with tolerable regularity produced. Hence, though there are wide divergences of opinion and of feeling relative to such classes of offenses in different societies, yet we find these related to divergences in the types of social activities—one or other set of reprobations being pronounced according as one or other set of activities is most dominant.

Taken together, the preceding chapters show us a group of moral traits proper to a life of external enmity. Where the predominant social cooperations take the form of constant fighting with adjacent peoples, there grows up a pride in aggression and robbery, revenge becomes an imperative duty, skilful lying is creditable, and (save in small tribes which do not develop) obedience to despotic leaders and rulers is the greatest virtue; at the same time there is a contempt for industry, and only such small regard for justice within the society as is required to maintain its existence. On the other hand, where the predominant social cooperations have internal sustentation for their end, while cooperations against external enemies have either greatly diminished or disappeared, unprovoked aggression brings but partial applause or none at all; robbery, even of enemies, ceases to be creditable; revenge is no longer thought a necessity; lying is universally reprobated; justice in the transactions of citizens with one another is insisted upon; political obedience is so far qualified that submission to a despot is held contemptible; and industry, instead of being considered disgraceful, is considered as, in some form or other, imperative on every one.

Of course the varieties of nature inherited by different kinds of men from the past, the effects of customs sanctified by age, the influences of religious creeds, together with the circumstances peculiar to each society, complicate and qualify these relations; but in their broad outlines they are sufficiently clear—as clear as we can expect them to be.

190. Hence the fact that the ethical sentiments prevailing in different societies, and in the same society under different conditions, are sometimes diametrically opposed. Multitudinous proofs of this truth have been given in preceding chapters, but it will be well here to enforce it by a series of antitheses.

Among ourselves, to have committed a murder disgraces for all time a man's memory, and disgraces for generations all who are related to him; but by the Pathâns a quite unlike sentiment is displayed. One who had killed a Mollah (priest), and failed to find refuge from the avengers, said at length: "I can but be a martyr. I will go and kill a Sahib." He was hanged after shooting a sergeant, perfectly satisfied "at having expiated his offense."

The prevailing ethical sentiment in England is such that a man who should allow himself to be taken possession of and made an unresisting slave, would be regarded with scorn; but the people of Drekete, a slave-district of Fiji, "said it was their duty to become food and sacrifices for the chiefs," and "that they were honored by being considered adequate to such a noble task."

Less extreme, though akin in nature, is the contrast between the feelings which our own history has recorded within these few centuries. In Elizabeth's time, Sir John Hawkins initiated the slave trade, and in commemoration of the achievement was allowed to put in his coat of arms "a demi-moor proper bound with a cord": the honorableness of his action being thus assumed by himself and recognized by Queen and public. But in our days, the making slaves of men, called by Wesley "the sum of all villainies," is regarded with detestation; and for many years we maintained a fleet to suppress the slave trade.

Peoples who have emerged from the primitive family-and-clan organization, hold that one who is guilty of a crime must himself bear the punishment, and it is thought extreme injustice that the punishment should fall upon anyone else; but our remote ancestors thought and felt differently, as do still the Australians, whose "first great principle with regard to punishment is, that all the relatives of a culprit, in the event of his not being found, are implicated in his guilt": "the brothers of the criminal conceive themselves to be quite as guilty as he is."

By the civilized, the individualities of women are so far recognized that the life and liberty of a wife are not supposed to be bound up with those of her husband; and she now, having obtained a right to exclusive possession of property, contends for complete independence, domestic and political. But it is, or was, otherwise in Fiji. The wives of the Fijian chiefs consider it a sacred duty to suffer strangulation on the deaths of their husbands. A woman who had been rescued by Williams "escaped during the night, and, swimming across the river, and presenting herself to her own people, insisted on the completion of the sacrifice which she had in a moment of weakness reluctantly consented to forgo"; and Wilkes tells of another who loaded her rescuer "with abuse, and ever afterward manifested the most deadly hatred towards him."

Here, and on the Continent, the religious prohibition of theft and the legal punishment of it, are joined with a strong social reprobation; so that the offense of a thief is never condoned. In Beloochistan, however, quite contrary ideas and feelings are current. There "a favorite couplet is to the effect that the Biloch who steals and murders, secures heaven to seven generations of ancestors."

In this part of the world reprobation of untruthfulness is strongly expressed, alike by the gentleman and the laborer. But in many parts of the world it is not so. In Blantyre, for example, according to Macdonald, "to be called a liar is rather a compliment."

English sentiment is such that the mere suspicion of incontinence on the part of a woman is enough to blight her life; but there are peoples whose sentiments entail no such effect, and in some cases a reverse effect is produced: "unchastity is with the Wotyaks a virtue."

So that in respect of all the leading divisions of human conduct, different races of men, and the same races at different stages, entertain opposite beliefs and display opposite feelings.

191. I was about to say that the evidence set forth in foregoing chapters, brought to a focus in the above section, must dissipate once for all the belief in a moral sense as commonly entertained. But a long experience prevents me from expecting this. Among men at large, lifelong convictions are not to be destroyed either by conclusive arguments or by multitudinous facts.

Only to those who are not by creed or cherished theory committed to the hypothesis of a supernaturally created humanity, will the evidence prove that the human mind has no originally implanted conscience. Though, as shown in my first work, *Social Statics*, I once espoused the doctrine of the intuitive moralists (at the outset in full, and in later chapters with some implied qualifications), yet it has gradually become clear to me that the qualifications required practically obliterate the doctrine as enunciated by them. It has become clear to me that if, among ourselves, the current belief is that a man who robs and does not repent will be eternally damned, while an accepted proverb among the Bilochs is that "God will not favor a man who does not steal and rob," it is impossible to hold that men have in common an innate perception of right and wrong.

But now, while we are shown that the moral-sense doctrine in its original form is not true, we are also shown that it adumbrates a truth, and a much higher truth. For the facts cited, chapter after chapter, unite in proving that the sentiments and ideas current in each society become adjusted to the kinds of activity predominating in it. A life of constant external enmity generates a code in which aggression, conquest, revenge, are inculcated, while peaceful occupations are

reprobated. Conversely, a life of settled internal amity generates a code inculcating the virtues conducing to harmonious
cooperation—justice, honesty, veracity, regard for other's
claims. And the implication is that if the life of internal amity
continues unbroken from generation to generation, there
must result not only the appropriate code, but the appropriate
emotional nature—a moral sense adapted to the moral requirements. Men so conditioned will acquire to the degree
needful for complete guidance, that innate conscience which
the intuitive moralists erroneously suppose to be possessed
by mankind at large. There needs but a continuance of absolute peace externally, and a rigorous insistence on nonaggres-
sion internally, to ensure the molding of men into a form
naturally characterized by all the virtues.

This general induction is reinforced by a special induction.
Now as displaying this high trait of nature, now as displaying
that, I have instanced those various uncivilized peoples who,
inferior to us in other respects, are morally superior to us; and
have pointed out that they are one and all free from intertribal
antagonisms. The peoples showing this connection are of
various races. In the Indian hills, we find some who are by
origin Mongolian, Kolarian, Dravidian; in the forests of
Malacca, Burma, and in secluded parts of China, exist such
tribes of yet other bloods; in the East Indian Archipelago, are
some belonging to the Papuan stock; in Japan there are the
amiable Ainos, who "have no traditions of internecine strife";
and in North Mexico exists yet another such people unrelated
to the rest, the Pueblos. No more conclusive proof could be
wished than that supplied by these isolated groups of men
who, widely remote in locality and differing in race, are alike
in the two respects, that circumstances have long exempted
them from war and that they are now organically good.

The goodness which may be attained to under these conditions excites the wonder of those who know only such goodness as is attained by peoples who plume themselves on their
superiority. Witness General Fytche's comment on the report
of Mr. O'Riley concerning the Let-htas: "The account given by

him of their appreciation of moral goodness, and the purity of their lives, as compared with the semicivilized tribes amongst whom they dwell, almost savors of romance."

May we not reasonably infer that the state reached by these small uncultured tribes may be reached by the great cultured nations, when the life of internal amity shall be unqualified by the life of external enmity?

192. That the contemplation of such an eventuality will be agreeable to all, I do not suppose. To the many who, in the East, tacitly assume that Indians exist for the benefit of Anglo-Indians, it will give no pleasure. Such a condition will probably seem undesirable to men who hire themselves out to shoot other men to order, asking nothing about the justice of their cause, and think themselves absolved by a command from Downing Street. As, among anthropophagi, the suppression of man-eating is not favorably regarded; so in sociophagous nations like ours, not much pleasure is caused by contemplating the cessation of conquests. No strong desire for such a state can be felt by our leading General, who says that the duties of a soldier "are the noblest that fall to man's lot," and whose motto is—"Man is as a wolf towards his fellow man."

Nor, strange though it appears, will this prospect be rejoiced over even by those who preach "peace and goodwill to men"; for the prospect is not presented in association with their creed. The belief that humanity can be made righteous only by acceptance of the Christian scheme, is irreconcilable with the conclusion that humanity may be molded into an ideal form by the continued discipline of peaceful cooperation. Better far to our theologians seems the doctrine that man, intrinsically bad, can be made good only by promises of heaven and threats of hell, than does the doctrine that man, not intrinsically bad, will become good under conditions which exercise the higher feelings and give no scope for the lower. Facts which apparently show that unchristianized human nature is incurably vicious, give to them satisfaction as justifying their religion; and evidence tending to prove the contrary is repugnant as showing that their religion is untrue.

And it is by no means certain that their attitude is to be regretted; for there has to be maintained a congruity between the prevailing cult and the social state and the average nature. If any one says that the men who form the land-grabbing nations of Europe, cannot be ruled in their daily lives by an ethical sentiment, but must have it enforced by the fear of damnation, I am not prepared to contradict him. If a writer who, according to those who know, represents truly the natures of the gentlemen we send abroad, sympathetically describes one of them as saying to soldiers shooting down tribes fighting for their independence—"Give 'em hell, men"; I think those are possibly right who contend that such natures are to be kept in check only by fear of a God who will "give 'em hell" if they misbehave. It is, I admit, a tenable supposition that belief in a deity who calmly looks on while myriads of his creatures suffer eternal torments, may fitly survive during a state of the world in which naked barbarians and barbarians in skins are being overrun by barbarians in broadcloth.

But to the few who, looking back on the changes which past thousands of years have witnessed, look forward to the kindred changes which future thousands of years may be expected to bring, it will be a satisfaction to contemplate a humanity so adapted to harmonious social life that all needs are spontaneously and pleasurably fulfilled by each without injury to others.

PART III
THE ETHICS OF INDIVIDUAL LIFE

CHAPTER 1

Introductory

193.   The foregoing fourteen chapters have shown that ethical sentiments and ideas are, in each place and time, determined by the local form of human nature, the social antecedents, and the surrounding circumstances. Hence the question arises—How from all which is special and temporary shall we separate that which is general and permanent?

We have been shown, if not overtly yet tacitly, that the very language used in speaking of moral questions, so involves the current beliefs that men are scarcely able to think away from them: the words used are question-begging words. "Duty" and "obligation," for example, carry with them the thought of obedience, subordination, subjection to authority; and thus, imply that right and wrong conduct are not such by their intrinsic natures, but are such by their extrinsic enactments. How, then, shall we free ourselves from the influence of the particular code we have been brought up under, and the misleading connotations of our terms?

Evidently we must for a time ignore established doctrines and expressions. We must go direct to the facts and study them afresh, apart from all preconceptions. I do not mean that the old ideas and the old words are to be rejected. Far from it. We shall find that the greater part of them are well warranted and have to be reinstated: in some cases with added authority, and in other cases with more or less of qualification.

Ethical ideas and sentiments have to be considered as parts of the phenomena of life at large. We have to deal with man as a product of evolution, with society as a product of evolution, and with moral phenomena as products of evolution. Let no one anticipate any loss of authority. Instead of finding that evolutionary ethics gives countenance to lower forms of conduct than those at present enjoined, we shall find that, contrariwise, evolutionary ethics is intolerant of much which those who profess to have the highest guidance think harmless or justifiable.

194. Integration being the primary process of evolution, we may expect that the aggregate of conceptions constituting ethics enlarges, at the same time that its components acquire heterogeneity, definiteness, and that kind of cohesion which system gives to them. As fulfilling this expectation, we may first note that while drawing within its range of judgment numerous actions of men towards one another which at first were not recognized as right or wrong, it finally takes into its sphere the various divisions of private conduct—those actions of each individual which directly concern himself only, and in but remote ways concern his fellows.

Nearly all these actions are usually supposed to lie beyond ethical rule: not only those multitudinous ones which are indifferent, and, like our movements from minute to minute, may be as well one way as another, but those numerous ones which bring some good or evil to self. But a theory of right and wrong which takes no cognizance of nine-tenths of the conduct by which life is carried on, is a folly. Life in general is a desideratum or it is not. If it is a desideratum, then all those modes of conduct which are conductive to a complete form of it are to be morally approved. If, contrariwise, life is not a desideratum, the subject lapses: life should, not be maintained, and all questions concerning maintenance of it, including the ethical, disappear. As commonly conceived, ethics consists solely of interdicts on certain kinds of acts which men would like to do and of injunctions to perform certain acts which they would like not to do. It says nothing about the great mass of acts constituting normal life; just as though these are neither warranted nor unwarranted. So influential are traditional sentiments and expressions, that the mass of readers will even now be unable to conceive that there can be an ethical justification for the pursuit of positive gratifications.

Such private conduct as errs in the direction of sensual excess, like drunkenness, they do indeed include as subject to ethical judgment and resulting condemnation: a perceived injury, primarily to self and secondarily to others, being the ground for the condemnation. But they ignore the truth that if injury to self is, in this case, a reason for moral reprobation, then benefit to self (so long as there is no contingent injury to others or remote injury to self) is a reason for moral approbation.

195. Far above other creatures though he is, man remains, in common with them, subject to the laws of life; and the requirement for him, as for them, is conformity to these laws. By him, as by every living thing, self-preservation is the first requisite; since without self-preservation, the discharge of all other obligations, altruistic as well as egoistic, becomes impossible.

But self-preservation is effected only by the performance of actions which are prompted by desires. Therefore the satisfaction of these desires is to be enjoined if life should be maintained. That this is so with the sensations which prompt breathing, eating, drinking, and avoidance of extremes of temperature, needs no proof: pain and death result from disobedience and pleasure from obedience. And as taking each of our primary pleasures directly furthers the vital activities, so, taking each of our secondary pleasures furthers them indirectly.

Unquestionably, then, there is a division of ethics which

yields sanctions to all the normal actions of individual life, while it forbids the abnormal ones. This most general view, at once evolutionary and hedonistic, harmonizes with several more special views.

196. As was pointed out in the preface, a disastrous effect is produced on the majority of minds by presenting ethics as a stern monitor, denouncing certain kinds of pleasures while giving no countenance to pleasures of other kinds. If it does not openly assert that all gratifications are improper, yet, by forbidding a number of them and saying nothing about the rest, it leaves the impression that the rest, if not to be condemned, are not to be approved. By this one-sided treatment of conduct it alienates multitudes who would otherwise accept its teachings.

Assuming that general happiness is to be the aim (for if indifference or misery were to be the aim, nonexistence would be preferable), then the implication is that the happiness of each unit is a fit aim; and a sequent implication is that for each individual, as a unit, his own happiness is a fit aim. Happiness as experienced by him, as much adds to the total amount as does happiness experienced by another; and if happiness may not be pursued for self, why may it be pursued for anyone else? If the totality of happiness could be made greater by each pursuing another's happiness, while his own was pursued for him by others, something might be said for the theory of absolute altruism. But, in the first place, the greater part of the grateful consciousness possible for each is achievable only by himself—is a consciousness accompanying certain activities, and cannot exist without them. In the second place, even were it otherwise, loss would arise if each pursued only the happiness of others; since as each of the others would have to do the like, there would be required the same amount of effort joined with a further amount of effort consequent on misunderstandings from cross-purposes. Imagine A feeding B while B fed A, and so on with C, D, &c., and instead of increase of satisfactions there would be decrease. The like would happen with the majority of other wants to be satisfied. As shown at the outset (secs. 82, 91), a system of ethics which insists on altruism and ignores egoism, is suicidal.

Such a system is, if the expression may be admitted, doubly suicidal; since, while its immediate operation must be detrimental, its remote operation must be still more detrimental. A loss of capacity for happiness must be the effect produced on all. For many of our pleasures are organically bound up with performance of functions needful for bodily welfare; and nonacceptance of them involves a lower degree of life, a decreased strength, and a diminished ability to fulfill all duties.

197. A further implication, almost universally ignored, must be here again emphasized. Already, in section 71, I have drawn attention to the obvious truth that the individual is not alone concerned in the matter, but that all his descendants are concerned.

In the utter disregard of this truth we see more clearly than usual how low is the average human intelligence. Sometimes, when observing on the Continent how the women, with faces unshaded, are, to keep out the bright sunlight, obliged to half-close their eyes and wrinkle up the corners of them, so producing, by daily repetition, crows' feet some ten or twenty years earlier than need be; I have thought it astonishing that, anxious though these women are to preserve beauty, they should have failed to perceive so simple a relation between cause and effect. But it may be held that an instance of stupidity even more extreme (if the expression may pass), is furnished by the inability of people to see that disregard of self involves disregard of offspring. There are two ways in which it does this.

Inability to provide for them adequately is one evil consequence. Without bodily welfare in parents there cannot be effectual sustentation of children; and if the race should be maintained, then care of self with a view to care of progeny becomes an obligation. This normal egoism must be such as results not merely in continued life, but in that vigorous life which gives efficiency. Nor is due care of self demanded only because the duties of the breadwinner cannot otherwise be fulfilled; but it is demanded also by regard for educational duties. Ill-health brings irritability and depression; incapacities for right behavior to children; and, by souring their tempers and deadening their sympathies, injures them for life.

Still more closely, however, is the welfare of descendants bound up with self-welfare. Good or ill treatment of his or her body or mind by each person, influences for good or ill the constitutions of his or her progeny. Unless it be held that stalwart and robust men may be expected to come from stunted and unhealthy parents, or that high intelligences and noble characters are likely to be inherited from stupid and criminal fathers and mothers, it must be admitted that any treatment of self which furthers bodily or mental development tends towards the benefit of the next generation (I say "tends" because there are complicating influences due to atavism), and that any treatment of self which undermines bodily health or injures the mind intellectually or emotionally, tends towards a lowering of the nature in the next generation. Yet while people daily make remarks about the likenesses of children to parents, and note the inheritance of this or that defect of mind or body, their criticisms on conduct entirely disregard the implication. They fail to draw the inference that if constitutions are transmitted, the actions which damage constitutions or improve them influence for good or ill the physical and mental characters of children and of children's children.

In certain extreme cases there is, indeed, a distinct recognition of the mischiefs entailed by the transgressions of parents. Though reprobation of those who have transmitted acquired diseases to their children is not often heard, yet there can be no doubt that it is strongly felt. Probably most will agree that, if the amount of suffering inflicted be used as a measure, murder is a smaller crime than is the giving of offspring infected constitutions and consequent lifelong miseries. But even in its grossest form this transgression is thought little of by the transgressors. There are, indeed, kindred cases in which the sense of responsibility sometimes serves as a deterrent—cases, for example, where knowledge of the existence of insanity in the family causes abstention from marriage. Very generally, however, where the weaknesses, or disorders, or taints they are likely to communicate, are of less conspicuous kinds, people, in a lighthearted way, are ready to inflict uncounted evils on descendants.

Still less is an allied consciousness of responsibility. There is no recognition of the truth that such persistent misuse of body or mind as injures it, involves the injury of descendants; and there is consequently no recognition of the truth that it is a duty so to carry on life as to preserve all parts of the system in their normal states.

These further reasons for due care of self have to be insisted upon. Each man's constitution should be regarded by him as an entailed estate, which he is bound to pass on in as good a condition as he received it, if not better.

198. Beyond this special altruism which makes imperative a normal egoism, there is a general altruism which also makes it in a measure obligatory. The obligation has both a negative and a positive aspect.

Such care of self as is needful to exclude the risk of burdening others, is implied in a proper regard for others. As, from those rude groups in which men lead lives so independent that they severally take the entire results of their own conduct, we advance to developed nations, fellow men become more and more implicated in our actions. Under a social system carried on by exchange of services, those on whom undue self-sacrifice has brought incapacity are commonly obliged to break contracts partially or wholly, and so to inflict evil; and then any such incapacity as negatives breadwinning, ordinarily imposes, first on relatives and then on friends, or else on the public, a tax implying extra labor. Everyone, therefore, is bound to avoid that thoughtless unselfishness which is apt to bring evils on others—evils that are often greater than those which entire selfishness produces.

The altruistic justification of egoism referred to as of a positive kind, results, firstly, from the obligation to expend some effort for the benefit of particular persons or for the benefit of society—an obligation which cannot be properly discharged if health has been undermined. And it results, secondly, from the obligation to become, so far as inherited nature permits, a source of social pleasure to those around; to fulfill this requirement there must ordinarily be a flow of mental energy such as the invalid cannot maintain.

CHAPTER 2

Activity

199.   In a systematic treatise the express statement of certain commonplaces is inevitable. A coherent body of geometrical theorems, for instance, has to be preceded by self-evident axioms. This must be the excuse for here setting down certain familiar truths.

The infant at first feebly moves about its little limbs; by and by it crawls on the floor; presently it walks, and after a time runs. As it develops, its activities display themselves in games, in races, in long walks: the range of its excursions being gradually extended, as it approaches adult existence. Manhood brings the ability to make tours and exploring expeditions; including passages from continent to continent, and occasionally round the world. When middle life is passed and vigor begins to decline, these extreme manifestations of activities become fewer. Journeys are shortened; and presently they do not go beyond visits to the country or to the seaside. As old age advances, the movements become limited to the village and the surrounding fields; afterwards to the garden; later still to the house; presently to the room; finally to the bed; and at last, when the power to move, gradually decreasing, has ceased, the motions of the lungs and heart come to an end. Taken in its *ensemble,* life presents itself in the shape of movements which begin feebly, gradually increase up to maturity, and then culminating, decrease until they end as feebly as they began.

Thus life is activity; and the complete cessation of activity is death. Hence arises the general implication that since the most highly evolved conduct is that which achieves the most complete life, activity obtains an ethical sanction, and inactivity an ethical condemnation.

This is a conclusion universally accepted and needing no enforcement. Even from those who habitually evade useful activities, there comes reprobation for such of their class as are too inert even to amuse themselves; absolute sloth is frowned on by all.

200. The kind of activity with which we are here chiefly concerned, is the activity directed primarily to self-sustentation, and secondarily to sustentation of family.

In the order of nature the imperativeness of such activity effectually asserts itself. Among all subhuman creatures (excepting most parasites) individuals which lack it die, and after them their offspring, if they have any. Those only survive which are adequately active; and, among such, a certain advantage in self-sustentation and sustentation of offspring is gained by those in which activity is greater than usual: the general effect being to raise the activity to that limit beyond which disadvantage to the species is greater than advantage. Up to the time when men passed into the associated state, this law held of them as of the lower animals; and it held of them also throughout early social stages. Before the making of slaves began, no family could escape from the relation between labor and the necessaries of life. And the ethical sanction for this relation in primitive societies is implied in the fact that extreme inequality in the distribution of efforts and benefits between the sexes, must always have resulted in deterioration and eventual extinction.

Though, in the course of social evolution, there have arisen multiplied possibilities of evading the normal relation between efforts and benefits, so as to get the benefits without the efforts; yet, bearing in mind the foregoing general law of life, we must infer that the evasions call for reprobation more or less decided, according to circumstances.

Being here directly concerned only with the ethics of individual life, we need not take account of the implied relation between the idle individual and the society in which he exists. Ignoring all other cases, we may limit ourselves to those cases in which property equitably acquired by a parent, without undue tax on his energies, serves, when bequeathed, to support a son in idleness: cases in which there is no implied trespass on fellow citizens. On each of such cases the verdict is that though it is possible for the individual to fulfill the law of life, insofar as physical activities are concerned, by devoting himself to sports and games, and insofar as certain kinds of mental activities are concerned, by useless occupations; yet there lack those mental activities, emotional and intellectual, which should form part of his life as a social being; and insofar his life becomes an abnormal one.

201. The chief question for us, however, is—What are the ethical aspects of labor considered in its immediate relations to pleasure and pain? From this point of view of absolute ethics, actions are right only when, besides being conducive to the future happiness of self, or others, or both, they are also immediately pleasurable. What then are we to say of necessary labor; most of which is accompanied by disagreeable feelings?

Such labor is warranted, or rather demanded, by the requirements of that relative ethics which is concerned not with the absolute right but with the least wrong. During the present transitional state of humanity, submission to such displeasurable feeling as labor involves, is warranted as a means of escaping from feelings which are still more displeasurable—a smaller pain to avoid a greater pain, or to achieve a pleasure, or both.

The state necessitating this compromise is the state of imperfect adaptation to social life. The change from the irregular activities of the savage man to the regular activities of the civilized man, implies a remolding—a repression of some powers which crave for action, and a taxing of other powers beyond the pleasurable limit: the capacity for persistent effort and persistent attention, being one especially called for, and one at present deficient. This adaptation has to be undergone, and the accompanying sufferings have to be borne.

And here seems a fit place for commenting on the varying amounts of displeasurable feeling, often rising to positive pain, necessitated by fulfillment of the obligation to work. The majority of people speak of effort, bodily or mental, as if the cost of it were the same to all. Though personal experience proves to them that when well and fresh, they put forth with ease a muscular force which, when prostrate with illness or exhausted by toil, it is painful to put forth—though they find, too, that when the mental energies are high they think nothing of a continuous attention which, when enfeebled, they are quite unequal to; yet they do not see that these temporary contrasts between their own states, are paralleled by permanent contrasts between states of different persons.

Ethical judgments must take account of the fact that the effort, bodily or mental, which is easy to one is laborious to another.

202. We come now to a question of special interest to us—Can the human constitution be so adapted to its present conditions, that the needful amount of labor to be gone through will be agreeable?

An affirmative answer will, to most people, seem absurd. Limiting their observations to facts around, or at most extending them to such further facts as the records of civilized people furnish, they cannot believe in the required change of nature. Such evidence as that which, in the first part of this work (secs. 63–67), was assigned to prove that pleasures and pains are relative to the constitution of the organism, and that in virtue of the unlimited modifiability of constitution, actions originally painful may become pleasurable, does not weigh with them. Though they probably know some who so love work that it is difficult to restrain them—though here and there they meet one who complains that a holiday is a weariness; yet it does not seem to them reasonable to suppose that the due tendency to continuous labor, which is now an exceptional trait, may become a universal trait.

It is undeniable that there are various expenditures of energy, bodily and mental—often extreme expenditures—which are willingly entered upon and continued eagerly: witness field sports, games, and the intellectual efforts made during social intercourse. In these cases the energy expended is often far greater than that expended in daily avocations. What constitutes the difference? In the one class of actions emulation makes possible the pleasurable consciousness which accompanies proved efficiency, and the pleasurable consciousness of the admiration given to efficiency; while, in the other class, the absence of emulation, or at any rate of direct visible emulation, implies the absence of a large proportion of this pleasurable consciousness. Nevertheless, what remains may become a powerful stimulus, making continuous application agreeable. Hobbies exemplify this truth. I can name two cases in which occupations of this kind are, without need, pursued so eagerly as scarcely to leave time for meals. Though in these cases the pleasurable exercise of skill is a large factor, and though in many occupations there seems but small scope for this, yet, nearly everywhere, the satisfaction attendant on the doing of work in the most perfect manner, may be sufficient to render the work agreeable, when joined with that overflowing energy which is to be anticipated as the concomitant of a normally developed nature.

203. It remains to consider whether, concluding that labor up to a certain limit is obligatory, there is any reason for concluding that beyond that limit it is the reverse of obligatory. The present phase of human progress fosters the belief that the more work the more virtue; but this is an unwarranted belief.

Absolute ethics does not dictate more work than is requisite for efficient self-sustentation, efficient nurture of dependents, and discharge of a due share of social duties. As in the lowest creatures, so in the highest, survival is the primary end to be achieved by actions; and though, in an increasing degree as we ascend, actions themselves with their associated feelings become secondary ends, yet pursued to the detriment of the primary end in all its fulness—the leading of a life complete, not in length only, but in breadth and depth. The hedonistic view, which is involved in the evolutionary view, implies an ethical sanction for that form of conduct which conduces in the highest degree to self-happiness and the happiness of others; and it follows that labor which taxes the energies beyond the normal limit, or diminishes more than is needful the time available for other ends, or both, receives no ethical sanction.

If adaptation to the social state must in time produce a nature such that the needful labor will be pleasurable, a con-comitant conclusion is that it will not produce a capacity for labor beyond this limit. Hence labor in excess of this limit will be abnormal and improper. For as labor inevitably entails physical cost—as the waste involved by it has to be made good out of the total supply which the organic actions furnish; then superfluous labor, deducting from this supply more than is necessary, diminishes the amount available for life at large—diminishes the extent or the intensity of that life.

Obviously, however, this reasoning refers to that fully evolved form of life which absolute ethics contemplates, rather than to the present form, which has to be guided by relative ethics. In our transitional state, with its undeveloped capacity for work, frequent overstepping of the limit is requi-site, and must be regarded as incident to the further develop-ment of the capacity. All we may fairly say is that, at present, the limit should not be so transgressed as to cause physical deterioration, and that it should be respected where there exists no weighty reason for going beyond it.

204. Connected as each man's actions are with the actions of others in multitudinous ways, it follows that the ethics of

individual life cannot be completely separated from the ethics of social life. Conduct of which the primary results are purely personal, has often secondary results which are social. Hence we must in each case consider the ways in which acts that directly concern self indirectly concern others.

In the present case it scarcely needs saying that beyond that obligation to labor which is deducible from the laws of individual life, there is a social obligation reinforcing it. Though, in a primitive community, it is possible for an individual to take upon himself all the results of his inactivity; yet, in an advanced community, consisting of citizens not devoid of sympathy, it becomes difficult to let the idle individual suffer in full the results of his idleness, and still more difficult to let his offspring do this. Even should it be decided by fellow citizens that the extreme consequences of idleness shall be borne, yet this decision must be at the cost of sympathetic pain. In any case, therefore, evil is inflicted on others as well as on self, and the conduct inflicting it is, for this further reason, to be ethically reprobated.

Reprobation, though quite of another quality, is also deserved by conduct of the opposite kind—by the carrying of labor to such extreme as to cause illness, prostration, and incapacity. For by this conduct, too, burdens and pains are entailed on others.

Hence altruistic motives join egoistic motives in prompting labor up to a certain limit, but not beyond that limit.

CHAPTER 3

Rest

205. Though the ethically enjoined limitation of life-sustaining activities, specified towards the close of the last chapter, apparently implies that rest is ethically enjoined, and in a large measure does so, yet this corollary must be definitely stated and enlarged on for several reasons.

The first is that there are various activities, not of a life-sustaining kind, which may be entered on when the activities devoted to sustentation of life are ended; and hence the conclusion drawn in the last chapter does not involve insistence upon absolute rest.

Further, we have to observe the several kinds of rest, which, if not complete, are approximately so; and the need for each of these kinds must be pointed out.

Something has to be said under each of the several heads—rest at intervals during work; nightly rest; rest of a day after a series of days; and occasional long rest at long intervals.

206. Rhythm, shown throughout the organic functions as elsewhere, has for its concomitant the alternation of waste and repair. Every contraction of the heart, every inflation of the lungs, is followed by a momentary relaxation of the muscles employed. In the process of alimentation, we have

the short rhythms constituting the peristaltic motion, compounded with the longer rhythms implied by the periodicity
of meals. Far deeper, indeed, than at first appears, is the
conformity to this law; for some organic actions which appear
continuous are in truth discontinuous. A muscle which maintains for a time a persistent contraction, and seems in a uniform state, is made up of multitudinous units which are
severally alternating between action and rest—these relaxing
while those are contracting; and so keeping up a constant
strain of the whole muscle by the inconstant strains of its
competent fibres.

The law thus displayed in each organ and part of an organ,
from moment to moment, is displayed throughout the longer
and larger cooperations of parts. Combined muscular strains
which tax the powers of the system in any considerable degree, cannot with impunity be continually repeated without
cessation, even during the period devoted to activity. Waste in
such cases overruns repair to a considerable extent, and
makes needful a cessation during which arrears may be in
some measure made up—an interval for "taking breath," as
the expression is. Long unbroken persistence, even in
moderate efforts, is injurious; and though such unresting
action when occasional does no permanent harm, if it recurs
daily, loss of power is the final result. Scriveners' palsy illustrates a local form of this evil; as do also various atrophies of
overused muscles.

Nor is this true of bodily actions only. It is true of mental
actions also. A concentrated attention which is too continuous
produces, after a time, nervous disturbance and inability.
Daily occupation for many hours in even so simple a thing as
removing the small defects in machine made lace, not unfrequently brings on chronic brain disorder. Some single-line
railways in the United States, the movements of trains on
which are regulated by telegraph from a central office, furnish
a striking instance in the fact that the men who have thus to
conduct the traffic, and cannot for a moment relax under
penalty of causing accidents, never last for more than a few
years; they become permanently incapable.

These unduly persistent strains, bodily and mental, are always indicated more or less clearly by the painful feelings accompanying them. The sensations protest, and their protests cannot with impunity be ignored.

207. Insistence on the need for that complete rest which we call sleep, is not called for; but something may fitly be said concerning its duration—now too small, now too great.

Current criticisms on the habits of those around, imply the erroneous belief that for persons of the same sex and age, the same amount of sleep is required—a professed belief which is, nevertheless, continually traversed by remarks on the unlike numbers of hours of repose which different persons can do with. The truth is that the required amount of sleep depends on the constitution. According as the vigor is small or great, there may be taken many hours to little purpose or few hours to great purpose. To understand what are the vital requirements, and, by implication, the habits which, from our present standpoint, we regard as having ethical sanction, we must pause a moment to look at the physiology of the matter.

The difference between waking and sleeping is that in the one waste gets ahead of repair, while in the other repair gets ahead of waste. Proof that repair is always going on, but that it varies in rate, is furnished by what are known as photogenes. During early life, while the blood is rich and the circulation good, the destruction of nerve tissue produced by each impression the eye receives, is made up for instantaneously, so that the eye is at once ready to appreciate perfectly a new impression; but in later life diminished vigor is shown by the greater time required for restoring the sensitiveness of the retinal elements; and connected nerves, after each visual impression—a time which is quite appreciable when the impression has been strong. The result is that a new image received is to some extent confused by the persistence of the preceding image, presented in its complementary colors.

Now these differences in the rates of repair at different stages in the life of the same individual, are paralleled by differences in the rates of repair in different individuals; and hence the unlike amounts of sleep required. There is a double cause for the unlikeness. In the vigorous person repair during the waking state is relatively so rapid as not to fall very far in arrear of the waste caused by action; the consequence being that at the end of the day less repair is required. And then, from the same cause, it results that during sleep such repair as has to be made is more rapidly made. Conversely, in the individual with low nutrition and slow circulation, action is sooner followed by exhaustion, and the parts wasted by action take a longer rest to make them fit for action.

But while the implication is that not unfrequently one who is condemned as a sluggard is taking no more absolute rest than is required by him, and is rightly prompted to take it by his sensations, we must not infer that there is no such thing as sleep in excess. There is a very general tendency to take not only more than is needful but more than is beneficial. Passing a certain limit, the state of entire quiescence does not invigorate but prostrates. Lacking their stimuli the vital organs flag, and when the quiescence is continued after repairs have been effected, a further fall in their activities disables them from carrying on the repairs needed during working life at the ordinary rate: a sense of weariness being the consequence. Probably for those whose systems are so far in a normal state that they sleep soundly, the first complete waking marks the proper limit to the night's rest. Some times a day after sleep thus limited is a day of unusual vivacity.

Here we have to recognize a seeming exception to the general law that for maintenance of bodily welfare the sensations are adequate guides. This lack of adjustment is most likely associated with our transitional state, during which the average life is so uninteresting, and often so wearisome, that the prospective renewal of it on waking does not serve as a stimulus to get up, but rather the contrary; for everyone has found that when the forthcoming day promises an enjoyment, say an excursion, there is no difficulty in rising early. It may be, therefore, that greater adaptation to the social state and its needful occupations, will render easy that normal

abridgment of sleep which is now difficult. But for a long time
to come, it will be an implication of relative ethics that guidance by the sensations must here be supplemented by judgments based on experience.

208. Civilized mankind have fallen into the habit of taking a
further periodical rest—a weekly rest; and without accepting
their reasons given for taking it, we may admit the propriety
of taking it for other reasons.

Monotony, no matter of what kind, is unfavorable to life.
Not only does there need some discontinuity in the activities
carried on during the waking state, and not only must the
activities be made discontinuous by intervals of sleep, but that
continuity of activities which consists in repetition of days
similarly occupied, also seems to require breaking by days of
rest. There is a cumulative weariness which is not met by the
periodical cessations which nights bring: there require larger
periodical cessations at longer intervals. The persistent strain
of daily occupations is in all cases a strain falling on some parts
of the system more than on others; and that daily repair which
suffices to bring the system at large into working order again,
appears not to suffice for bringing into working order again
parts that have been specially taxed. So that a recurring day of
rest has, if not a religious sanction, still an ethical sanction.

We may, too, agree with the Sabbatarians so far as to admit
that a periodical cessation of daily business is requisite as a
means to mental health. Even as it is, most people largely fail
to emancipate themselves from those prosaic conceptions of
the world and life which mechanical routine tends to produce;
and they would fail utterly were all their days passed in
work. There require intervals of passivity during which the
vast process of things amid which we live may be contemplated, and receptivity of the appropriate thoughts and feelings fostered.

209. I need not insist on the physical and mental benefits
gained from those longer intermissions of labor which now

commonly recur annually. Not to dwell on the positive pleasures obtained by them (which, however, must be counted as
effects to be deliberately sought), it suffices to recall the rein-
vigoration and increased fitness for work which they usually
produce, to show that they are ethically sanctioned, or rather,
where circumstances permit, ethically enjoined.

Without further elaboration I pass to the altruistic reasons
which justify rest, and show the taking of it in due amount to
be obligatory. The claims of dependents and the claims of
fellow citizens with whom engagements have been made,
alike forbid excess of work: energy must not be so wastefully
expended as to jeopardize fulfillment of them. A sane judgment has to balance between the demand for such efforts as
are required to make these claims, and the demand for such
rest as will prevent exhaustion and incapacity. Duty to others
forbids overtax of self.

But strong as is the interdict hence arising, there is a still
stronger interdict—peremptory, if not for all, yet for those
who are likely to have offspring. As pointed out emphatically
in the preliminary chapter, preservation of a sound body, as
well as of a sound mind, is a duty to posterity. Deterioration of
physique must result from persistence in undue activity. To
suppose that whether a life which is physically normal has
been led by a parent, or one which is physically abnormal,
matters not to children, is absurd. If there has been habitual
deficiency of rest and consequent deficiency of repair, the
abnormality produced must, like every other, leave its trace in
descendants—not always conspicuously, since each child, besides inheriting from two parents, inherits from many lines of
ancestors; but, nevertheless, in due degree somewhere.

CHAPTER 4

Nutrition

210.   Except perhaps in agreeing that gluttony is to be rep-
         robated and that the *gourmet*, as well as the *gour-
mand*, is a man to be regarded with scant respect, most people
will think it is absurd to imply, as the above title does, that
ethics has anything to say about the taking of food. Though,
by condemning excesses of the kinds just indicated, they
imply that men *ought* not to be guilty of them, and by the use
of this word class them as *wrong*; yet they ignore the obvious
fact that if there is a wrong in respect of the taking of food there
must also be a right.

The truth appears to be that daily actions performed in ways
which do not obviously deviate from the normal, cease to be
thought of as either right or wrong. As the most familiar
mathematical truths, such as twice two are four, are not ordinarily thought of as parts of mathematics—as the knowledge
which a child gains of surrounding objects is not commonly
included under education, though it forms a highly important
part of it; so this all-essential ministration to life by food,
carried on as a matter of course, is dropped out of the theory of
conduct. And yet, as being a part of conduct which fundamentally affects welfare, it cannot properly be thus dropped.

How improper is the ignoring of it as a subject matter for

ethical judgments, we shall see on observing the ways in which current opinion respecting it goes wrong.

211. Already, in section 174, the extreme instances furnished by the Esquimaux, the Yakuts, and the Australians, have shown us that enormous quantities of food are proper under certain conditions, and that satisfaction of the seemingly inordinate desires for them is not only warranted but imperative: death being the consequence of inability to take a sufficient quantity to meet the expenditure entailed by severe climate or by long fasts. To which here let me add the experiences of Arctic voyagers, who, like the natives of the Arctic regions, acquire great appetites for blubber.

Mention of these facts is a fit preliminary to the question whether, in respect of food, desires ought or ought not to be obeyed. As already said, treatment of this inquiry as ethical will be demurred to by most and by many ridiculed. Though, when not food but drink is in question, their judgments, very strongly expressed, are of the kind they class as moral; yet they do not see that since the question concerns the effect of things swallowed, it is absurd to regard the conduct which causes these effects as moral or immoral when the things are liquid but not when they are solid.

Adaptation goes on everywhere and always, in the human race as in inferior races, and, among other results, is the adjustment of the desire for food to the need for food. Even were this not shown us by the extreme instances above given, it would be an inevitable corollary from the law of the survival of the fittest. Every maladjustment of the two must have been injurious, and, other things equal, the tendency must ever have been for maladjustment to cause the dying-out of individuals in which it existed. On the average, then, there must be a fair balance: what there is of deviation from the normal, bearing but a small ratio to what there is of normal.

Some deviation doubtless occurs. We still see inheritance of traits appropriate to the primitive wild life and inappropriate to settled civilized life; and among such traits is that tendency to take food in excess of immediate need, which was good in the irregularly living savage but which is not good in the regularly living European. Further, it may be admitted that men who lead monotonous lives, as most do, presenting much to bear and little to enjoy, are apt to prolong unduly the few actions which are pleasurable; and of these eating is one. When the occupation to be entered upon at the end of a meal is pleasurable, there is comparatively little wish to eke out the meal.

But the more or less of excess apt to result from these causes, is consequent not upon obedience to the sensations naturally arising, but rather from solicitation of the sensations: a perverting factor made possible by that imagination which has evil effects as well as good effects. It is not that an immediate desire prompts the action, but that the action is prompted by the hope of experiencing the agreeable feeling which accompanies fulfillment of a desire. There are kindred evils arising from sitting down to table when appetite does not suggest—partaking of periodically recurring meals whether hungry or otherwise. Very often people eat as a matter of course, not in conformity with their sensations but notwithstanding the protests of their sensations. And then, oddly enough, there comes from these transgressors the assertion that sensations are not fit guides! Having suffered from constantly disobeying them, they infer that they are not to be obeyed!

It is doubtless true that those who are out of health occasionally entail on themselves mischiefs by eating as much as they desire; and some who are not in obvious ways unwell, now and then do the like. But a demurrer drawn from these experiences is not sustainable. In such cases the adjustments between all the various needs of the organism, and the various sensations which prompt fulfillment of them, have been chronically deranged by disobedience. When by persistent indoor life, or by overwork, or by ceaseless mental worry, or by inadequate clothing, or by breathing bad air, the bodily functions have been perverted, guidance by the sensations ceases to be reliable. It then becomes needful either, as in some cases, to restrain appetite, or, as in other cases, to take food without appetite: an abnormal state having been brought about by physiological sins, artificial regulation is called for to supplement natural regulation. But this proves nothing. After prolonged starvation, satisfaction of ravenous hunger by a good meal is said to be fatal. The prostration is so great that any considerable quantity of food cannot be digested, and administration in small quantities is needful. But it is not thence inferred that satisfaction of appetite by a good meal will ordinarily be fatal. Similarly is it throughout. The evils which occasionally arise from taking as much as appetite prompts, must be ascribed to the multitudinous preceding disobediences to sensations, and not to this particular obedience to them.

While there is recognition of the evils resulting from excesses in eating, there is little recognition of the evils consequent on eating too little. The ascetic bias given by their religion and by their education, leads most people to think themselves meritorious if they do with as little food as possible and tempts them to restrict the food of others. Disastrous effects follow. Inadequate nutrition, especially while growth is going on, is an unquestionable cause of imperfect development, either in size, or in quality of tissue, or in both; and parents who are responsible for it are responsible for invalid lives. No cattle breeder or horse breeder dreams of obtaining a fine animal on a stinted diet. No possessor of a fine animal expects him to do good service on the road or in the field unless he is well fed. Science and common sense unite in recognizing the truth that growth and vigor are alike dependent on a good supply of the materials from which body and brain are built up when young and repaired when adult. The taking of an adequate quantity of food is insured if appetite is obeyed, while if the supply is restricted spite of the demands of appetite, there will inevitably be more or less of defect in size or in strength.

Speaking generally, then, we may say that there is an ethical sanction for yielding in full to the desire for food: both because satisfaction of the desire is itself one element to be counted among the normal gratifications life offers, and because satisfaction of it indirectly conduces to subsequent fullness of life and the power of discharging all the obligations of life.

212. One who complains of the monotony of his meals and is thereupon reproached for seeking the enjoyments which change of diet gives (I name a fact), is, by the reproach, tacitly condemned from a moral point of view. Whence the implication is that a doctrine of right and wrong has something to say respecting the propriety or impropriety of yielding to the wish for variety. Everyone, therefore, who does not agree in the opinion of the pious Scotchwoman just referred to, must hold the opposite opinion: the desire for variety of food should be gratified—has a sanction like that of the desire for due quantity of food.

This is of course not a fit place for entering on the topics of variety, quality, and preparation of food—topic the mere mention of which will seem out of place to those who have not accepted the doctrines implied in the first chapter of this work, that every part of conduct which directly or indirectly affects welfare has an ethical aspect. Here, what has to be said or hinted under the three head-named, may come under the one general head of satisfaction of the palate, as distinguished from the satisfaction of the appetite—distinguished in a measure but not wholly since the one serves as a normal stimulus to the other. Partly as a further sequence of asceticism, and partly as a reaction against the gross sensualism which history occasionally records from Roman days down to recent days, it has come to be thought that the pleasures of the table are to be reprobated; or, if not positively reprobated, yet passed over as not proper to be regarded. Those who take this view are, indeed, like others, discontent with insipid food; and are no less ready than others to dismiss cooks who cannot prepare enjoyable dinners. But while practically they pursue gastronomic satisfactions, they refuse to recognize their theoretical legitimacy.

Here, I cannot imitate this uncandid mode of dealing with the matter; and find myself obliged to assert that due regard for the needs of the palate is not only proper but disregard of them is wrong. The contrary view involves the belief that it matters not to the body whether it is the seat of pleasurable feelings, or indifferent feelings, or painful feelings. But it matters very much. As asserted in an early chapter (sec. 36), pleasures raise the tide of life while pains lower it; and among the pleasures which do this are gustatory pleasures. There are two reasons why, when food is liked, digestion of it is furthered, and when disliked is hindered. In common with every agreeable sensation an agreeable taste raises the action of the heart, and, by implication, the vital functions at large; while simultaneously, it excites in a more direct way the structures which secrete the digestive fluids. It needs but to remember the common observation that an appetizing odor makes the mouth water, to understand that the alimentary canal as a whole is made active by a pleasurable stimulation of the palate, and that digestion is thus aided. And since on good digestion depends good nutrition, and on good nutrition depends the energy needed for daily work, it follows that due regard to gratification of the palate is demanded.

Those who have had any experience of invalid life, know well how small a quantity can be eaten of food which is indifferent or distasteful, and how trying is the digestion of such food, while the converse holds of food which is grateful: the resulting adequate meals of such food better digested, being a condition to recovery and the resumption of responsibilities. And if the benefit of such ministrations to the palate is made thus manifest where the vitality is low, it unquestionably exists, though less manifestly, where the vitality is high.

Of course, as in respect of quantity so in respect of quality and variety, there may be, and often is, excess: the last kind of excess being conducive to the first. But no more in this case than in any other case is abuse an argument against use.

213. Before ending this chapter, which I must now do lest it should become a chapter on dietetics, I must say something

on the altruistic bearings of the conclusions drawn; only making, in further repudiation of the ordinary ascetic view, the remark that the Hebrew myth which represents the eating of the apple by Eve as prompted by the serpent, seems in many minds to have been expanded into a general theory of our relations to food: their asceticism tacitly implying that gustatory promptings are suggestions of the devil.

Of the altruistic bearings to be noted, the first concerns the indirect effects of excess, suffered by those around, from the occasional illness and more frequent ill-temper which it produces: injuries to others the prospect of which should serve as a deterrent, no less than prospective injury to self. And then a more remote altruistic bearing is seen in the effect wrought on the community if excess is general. Remembering that the stock of food which a community obtains is a limited quantity, it results that if its members consume more than is needful for complete self-sustentation, they diminish the amount of human life proper to the inhabited area. Clearly, if people at large eat, let us say, one-sixth more than is required for full life and vigor—if ten millions of people eat as much as would satisfactorily support twelve millions; then, assuming human life to be a desideratum, a wrong is done by thus preventing its increase. The share of each individual in the wrong may be inappreciable; but the aggregate wrong—preventing the existence of two millions of people—is appreciable enough.

The remaining altruistic bearing is that which concerns offspring. Chronic innutrition of parents injures children. In the case of mothers the inevitableness of this result is clear. Building up of the fetus has to go on simultaneously with the carrying on of material life, and nutritive materials are used up for both processes. Though, in the competition between the two, the first has a certain priority, and is effected at great cost to the second; yet, where the supply of nutritive materials is inadequate, fetal growth is checked, as well as maternal enfeeblement caused. A stinted development of the infant and a subsequent falling short of full life are the consequences. Regard for posterity thus peremptorily demands good feeding.

CHAPTER 5

Stimulation

214. To write sundry chapters on the ethics of individual life and to say nothing about the taking of stimulants is out of the question. While, on large parts of private conduct, most men pass no moral judgments, and assume that they are subject to none; over that part of private conduct which concerns the drinking of fermented liquors, most men, passing strong moral judgments, unhesitatingly assume that ethics exercises peremptory rule; and the inclusion within the domain of ethics of questions concerning alcoholic stimulants, is followed by inclusion of questions concerning opium-eating.

We may observe here, as we have observed before, that the reprobation of practices which, in excess, are certainly injurious, and are held by many to be injurious altogether, is practically limited to practices which are primarily pleasurable. A man may bring on himself chronic rheumatism by daily careless exposure, or an incurable nervous disorder by overapplication; and though he may thus vitiate his life and diminish his usefulness in a far greater degree than by occasionally taking too much wine, yet his physical transgression meets with only mild disapproval, if even that. But in these cases the transgression is displeasurable, whereas excess in wine is pleasurable; and the damnable thing in the misconduct is the production of pleasure by it.

If it be said that this contrast of moral estimates is due to the perception that there is danger of falling into injurious habits which are primarily pleasurable, while there is no danger of falling into injurious habits which are primarily painful; the reply is that though we naturally suppose this to be true, yet it is not true. The obligations men are under, or suppose themselves to be under, lead them in multitudinous cases to persist in sedentary lives, to work too many hours, to breathe impure air, and so forth, spite of the feelings which protest—spite of continual proofs that they are injuring themselves. Clearly it is the vague notion that gratification is vicious, which causes the condemnation of gratifying transgressions while ungratifying transgressions are condemned but slightly or not at all.

Here we have to consider the matter, as far as we can, apart from popular judgments, and guided only by physiological considerations.

215. It cannot, I think, be doubted that from the point of view of absolute ethics, stimulants of every kind must be reprobated; or, at any rate, that daily use of them must be reprobated. Few, if any, will contend that they play a needful part in complete life.

All normal ingesta subserve the vital processes either by furnishing materials which aid in the formation and repair of tissues, or materials which, during their transformations, yield heat and force, or the material—water—which serves as a vehicle. A stimulant, alcoholic or other, is neither tissue food, nor heat food, nor force food. It simply affects the rate of molecular change—exalting it and then, under ordinary circumstances, if taken in considerable quantity, depressing it. Now matters which can be used neither for building up the body nor as stores of force, do not increase the sum of vital manifestations, but only alter the distribution of them. And since, in a being fully fitted for the life it has to lead, the functions are already adjusted to the requirements, it does not seem that any advantage can be obtained by changing the established balance.

This inference is far reaching—carries us beyond the point to which the total abstainers from fermented liquors wish to go. Tea and coffee also must be excluded from dietaries. The vegeto-alkalies, to which they owe their effects, are just as little akin to food properly so called, as is alcohol; and, like alcohol, simply modify for a time the rate of molecular change, causing greater genesis of energy during one interval with the effect of diminishing it during another. From the physiological point of view, therefore, the use of these must be condemned if the use of alcohol is condemned.

Should it be said that the condemnation of the last is evoked by the liability to abuse, it may be replied that the liability to abuse holds of the others also; though the mischiefs wrought are neither so frequent nor so conspicuous. In France there are occasional deaths from coffee drinking, and in England undue drinking of tea not infrequently causes nervousness.

216. But while, from the point of view of absolute ethics, the use of stimulants seems indefensible, we may still ask whether relative ethics affords any justification for it— whether, under existing conditions, imperfectly adapted as we are to the social state, and obliged to diverge from natural requirements, we may not use stimulants to countervail the consequent mischiefs.

It is a fact of some significance that throughout the world, among unallied races and in all stages of progress, we find in use one or other agent which agreeably affects the nervous system—opium in China, tobacco among the American Indians, bang in India, hashish in sundry Eastern places, a narcotic fungus in Northern Asia, kava among the Polynesians, chica and coca in Ancient Peru, and various fermented liquors besides the wine of Europeans, and the beer of various African tribes—the soma of the primitive Aryans and the pulque of the Mexicans. Not that this universality of habits of stimulation justifies them in face of the evidence that diseases often result; but it suggests the question whether there is not a connection between the use of some exciting or sedative agent, and the kind of life circumstances entail—a life here monotonous, there laborious, and in other places full of privations. Possibly these drugs and liquors may sometimes make tolerable an existence which would be otherwise intolerable; or, at any rate, so far mitigate the bodily or mental pains caused, as to diminish the mischiefs done by them.

Various testimonies are to the effect that where the daily life is one entailing much wear and tear of brain, the sedative influence of tobacco is useful—serves to check that nervous waste which otherwise the continuance of thought and anxiety would produce. In a normal state, those parts of the system which have been taxed cease to act when the strain is over: the supply of blood is shut off, and they become quiescent. But in the abnormal states established in many by overwork, it is otherwise. The parts which have been active become congested, and remain active when action is no longer demanded. Thinking and feeling cannot be stopped, and there occurs an expenditure which is not only useless but injurious. Hence a justification for using an agent which prevents waste of tissue and economizes the energies.

Again, where the constitutional powers are flagging, and a day's work proves so exhausting that the ability to digest partially fails, it may be held that vascular action and nervous discharge may advantageously be raised by alcohol to the extent needful for effectually dealing with food; since a good meal well digested serves to render the system fit for another day's work, which otherwise it would not be.

There are those, too, in whom undue application establishes a state of nervous irritation which is mitigated or ended by a dose of opium; and the life may sometimes be such that the state thus dealt with frequently recurs. If this happens the use of the remedy appears justified.

217. Even total abstainers admit that alcoholic beverages may rightly be used for medicinal purposes; and their admission, consistently interpreted, implies that, as above con-

tended, stimulants in general may properly be employed, not only where positive illness exists, but where there is inability to cope with the requirements of life. For if a very conspicuous departure from the normal state may often be best treated by brandy or wine, it cannot well be denied that a less conspicuous departure, occurring perhaps daily, may similarly be treated. Constitutional debility, or the debility which comes with advancing years, may, like the debility of an invalid, be advantageously met by temporarily raising the power of the system at times when it has to do work conducive to restoration—that is, when food has to be digested, and sometimes when sleep has to be obtained. But there hence results a defense only for such uses of stimulants as aid the system in repairing itself. When, as by taking alcoholic liquors between meals, or by the hypodermic injection of morphia, there is achieved a temporary exaltation of power or feeling, which conduces to no restorative end, reprobation rightly takes the place of approbation. In the order of nature, normal pleasures are the concomitants of normal activities, and pleasures which are achieved by gratuitous deviations from the normal have no ethical sanctions.

One exception only should be made. Stimulants may be taken with advantage when the monotony of ordinary life is now and then broken by festive entertainments. As implied in a preceding chapter, daily repetition of the same activities, which in our state are inevitably specialized, necessitates undue taxing of certain parts of the system. Breaches in the uniformity therefore yield benefits by furthering restoration of equilibrium. The functions, chronically kept out of balance, are aided in returning to a balance. Hence it happens that social meetings at which, along with mental exhilaration, there goes the taking of abundant and varied food, and wine even in large quantity, often prove highly salutary—are not followed by injurious reactions but leave behind invigoration. Such means used for such ends, however, must be used but occasionally: if often repeated they defeat themselves.

218. To sum up what has been said in a tentative way on this difficult question: we may, in the first place, conclude that absolute ethics, insofar as it concerns individual life, can give no countenance to the daily use of stimulants. They can have no place in a perfectly normal order.

In such approximately normal life as that enjoyed during their early days by vigorous persons, there is also no place for them. So long as there is nothing to prevent the full discharge of all the organic functions, there can be no need for agents which temporarily exalt them. What ethics has to say in the matter must take the form of an interdict.

Only when the excessive obligations which life often entails produce more or less of daily prostration, or when from constitutional feebleness or the diminished strength of old age, the ordinary tax on the energies is somewhat greater than can be effectually met, does there seem a valid reason for using exciting agents, alcoholic or other; and then only when they are taken in such wise as to aid reparative processes.

Beyond this there is a defense for such occasional uses of these agents as serves, when joined with raised nutrition and enlivening circumstances, to take the system out of its routine, which in all cases diverges somewhat, if not much, from a perfect balance.

CHAPTER 6

Culture

219. Taken in its widest sense, culture means preparation for complete living. It includes, in the first place, all such discipline and all such knowledge as are needful for, or conducive to, efficient self-sustentation and sustentation of family. And it includes, in the second place, all such development of the faculties at large, as fits them for utilizing those various sources of pleasure which nature and humanity supply to responsive minds.

The first of these two divisions of culture has more than an ethical sanction: it is ethically enjoined. Acquisition of fitness for carrying on the business of life is primarily a duty to self and secondarily a duty to others. If under the head of this fitness we comprise, as we must, such skill as is needful for those who are to be manually occupied, as well as skill of every higher kind, it becomes manifest that (save with those who have sustentation *gratis*) lack of it makes a healthy physical life impracticable, and makes impracticable the nurture of dependents. Further, the neglect to acquire a power of adequately maintaining self and offspring necessitates either the burdening of others in furnishing aid, or else, if they refuse to do this, necessitates that infliction of pain upon them which the contemplation of misery causes.

Concerning the second division of culture, peremptory obligation is not to be alleged. Those who take an ascetic view of life have no reason for that discipline of faculties which aims to increase one or other refined pleasure; and, as among the Quakers, we see that there does in fact result a disregard of, and often a reprobation of, such discipline, or of parts of it. Only those who accept hedonism can consistently advocate this exercise of intellect and feeling which prepares the way for various gratifications filling leisure hours. They only can regard it as needful for attaining complete life, and as therefore having an ethical sanction.

From these general ideas of culture, essential and nonessential, let us go on to consider the several divisions of it.

220. There is a part of culture, usually neglected, which should be recognized alike by those to whom it brings means of living and by those who do not seek material profit from it, which may fitly stand first. I mean the acquirement of manual dexterity.

That this is a proper preparation for life among those occupied in productive industry, will not be disputed; though at present, even the boys who may need it are but little encouraged to acquire manipulative skill: only those kinds of skill which games give are cultivated. But manipulative skill and keenness of perception ought to be acquired by those also who are to have careers of higher kinds. Awkwardness of limb and inability to use the fingers deftly, continually entail small disasters and occasionally great ones; while expertness frequently comes in aid of welfare, either of self or others. One who has been well practiced in the uses of his senses and his muscles, is less likely than the unpracticed to meet with accidents; and, when accidents occur, is sure to be more efficient in rectifying mischiefs. Were it not that this obvious truth is ignored, it would be absurd to point out that, since limbs and senses exist to the end of adjusting the actions to surrounding objects and movements, it is the business of every one to gain skill in the performance of such actions.

Let it not be supposed that I am here advocating the extension of *formal* culture in this direction: very much to the contrary. The shaping of all education into lessons is one of the vices of the time. Cultivation of manipulative skill, in common with expertness in general, should be acquired in the process of achieving ends otherwise desired. In any rationally conducted education there must be countless occasions for the exercise of those faculties which the artisan and the experimenter bring perpetually into play.

221. Intellectual culture under its primary aspect links on to the culture just described; for as discipline of the limbs and senses is a fitting of them for direct dealings with things around, so intelligence, in its successive grades, is an agent for guiding dealings of indirect kinds, greater and greater in their complexity. The higher acquisitions and achievements of intellect have now become so remote from practical life, that their relations to it are usually lost sight of. But if we remember that in the stick employed to heave up a stone, or the paddle to propel a boat, we have illustrations of the uses of levers; while in the pointing of an arrow so as to allow for its fall during flight, certain dynamical principles are tacitly recognized; and that from these vague early cognitions the progress may be traced step by step to the generalizations of mathematicians and astronomers; we see that science has gradually emerged from the crude knowledge of the savage. And if we remember that as this crude knowledge of the savage served for simple guidance of his life-sustaining actions, so the developed sciences of mathematics and astronomy serve for guidance in the workshop and the countinghouse and for steering of vessels, while developed physics and chemistry preside over all manufacturing processes; we see that at the one extreme as at the other, furtherance of men's ability to deal effectually with the surrounding world, and so to satisfy their wants, is that purpose of intellectual culture which precedes all others.

Even for these purposes we distinguish as practical, that intellectual culture which makes us acquainted with the natures of things, should be wider than is commonly thought needful. Preparation for this or that kind of business is far too special. There cannot be adequate knowledge of a particular class of natural facts without some knowledge of other classes. Every object and every action simultaneously presents various orders of phenomena—mathematical, physical, chemical—with, in many cases, others which are vital; and these phenomena are so interwoven that full comprehension of any group involves partial comprehension of the rest. Though at first sight the extent of intellectual culture thus suggested as requisite may seem impracticable, it is not so. When education is rightly carried on, the cardinal truths of each science may be clearly communicated and firmly grasped, apart from the many corollaries commonly taught along with them. And after there has been gained such familiarity with these cardinal truths of the several sciences as renders their chief implications comprehensible, it becomes possible to reach rational conceptions of any one group of phenomena, and to be fully prepared for a special occupation.

That division of intellectual culture which comprises knowledge of the sciences, while having an indirect ethical sanction as conducing to self-sustentation and sustentation of others, has also a direct sanction irrespective of practical ends. To the servant girl, the ploughboy, the grocer, nay even to the average classical scholar or man of letters, the world, living and dead, with the universe around it, present no such grand panorama as they do to those who have gained some conception of the actions, infinite and infinitesimal, everywhere going on, and can contemplate them under other aspects than the technical. If we imagine that into a gorgeously decorated hall a rush light is brought, and, being held near to some part of the wall, makes visible the pattern over a small area of it, while everything else remains in darkness; and if, instead of this, we imagine that electric lights turned on reveal simultaneously the whole room with its varied contents; we may form some idea of the different appearance under which nature is contemplated by the utterly uncultured mind and by the highly cultured mind. Whoever duly appreciates this immense contrast will see that, rightly assimilated, science brings exaltation of mental life.

One further result must be recognized. That study of all orders of phenomena which, while it gives adequate general conceptions of them, leads, now in this direction and now in that, to limits which no exploration can transcend, is needful to make us aware of our relation to the ultimate mystery of things; and so to awaken a consciousness which we may properly consider germane to the ethical consciousness.

222. In its full acceptation, knowledge of science includes knowledge of social science; and this includes a certain kind of historical knowledge. Such of it as is needful for political guidance, each citizen should endeavor to obtain. Though the greater parts of the facts from which true sociological generalizations may be drawn, are presented only by those savage and semicivilized societies ignored in our educational courses, there are also required some of the facts furnished by the histories of developed nations.

But beyond the impersonal elements of history which chiefly demand attention, a certain attention may rightly be given to its personal elements. Commonly these occupy the entire attention. The great-man theory of history, tacitly held by the ignorant in all ages and in recent times definitely enunciated by Mr. Carlyle, implies that knowledge of history is constituted by knowledge of rulers and their doings; and by this theory there is fostered in the mass of minds a love of gossip about dead individuals, not much more respectable than the love of gossip about individuals now living. But while no information concerning kings and popes, and ministers and generals, even when joined to exhaustive acquaintance with intrigues and treaties, battles and sieges, gives any insight into the laws of social evolution—while the single fact that division of labor has been progressing in all advancing nations regardless of the wills of lawmakers, and unobserved by them, suffices to show that the forces which mold societies work out their results apart from, and often in spite of, the aims of leading men; yet a certain moderate number of leading men and their actions may properly be contemplated. The past stages in human progress, which every one should know something about, would be conceived in too shadowy a form if wholly divested of ideas of the persons and events associated with them. Moreover, some amount of such knowledge is requisite to enlarge adequately the conception of human nature in general—to show the extremes, occasionally good but mostly bad, which it is capable of reaching.

With culture of this kind there naturally goes purely literary culture. That a fair amount of this should be included in the preparation for complete living, needs no saying. Rather does it need saying that in a duly proportioned education, as well as in adult life, literature should be assigned less space than it now has. Nearly all are prone to mental occupations of easy kinds, or kinds which yield pleasurable excitements with small efforts; and history, biography, fiction, poetry, are, in this respect, more attractive to the majority than science—more attractive than that knowledge of the order of things at large which serves for guidance.

Still, we must not here forget that from the hedonistic point of view, taking account of this pleasure directly obtained, literary culture has a high claim; and we may also admit that, as conducing to wealth and force of expression by furnishing materials for metaphor and allusion, it increases mental power and social effectiveness. In the absence of it conversation is bald.

223. In culture, as in other things, men tend towards one or other extreme. Either, as with the great majority, culture is scarcely pursued at all, or, as with the few, it is pursued almost exclusively, and often with disastrous results.

Emerson says of the gentleman that the first requisite is to be a good animal, and this is the first requisite for every one. A course of life which sacrifices the animal, though it may be defensible under special conditions is not defensible as a general policy. Within the sphere of our positive knowledge we nowhere see mind without life; we nowhere see life without a body; we nowhere see a full life—a life which is high alike in respect of intensity, breadth, and length—without a healthy body. Every breach of the laws of bodily health produces a physical damage, which eventually damages in some way, though often in an invisible way, the mental health.

Culture has therefore to be carried on subject to other needs. Its amount must be such as consists with, and is conducive to, physical welfare; and it must be also such as consists with, and is conducive to, normal activity not only of the mental powers exercised, but of all others. When carried to an extent which diminishes vivacity, and produces indifference to the various natural enjoyments, it is an abuse; and still more is it an abuse when, as often happens, it is pushed so far as to produce disgust with the subjects over which attention has been unduly strained.

Especially in the case of women is condemnation of overculture called for, since immense mischief is done by it. We are told that the higher education, as now carried on at Girton and Newnham, is not inconsistent with maintenance of good health; and if we omit those who are obliged to desist, this appears to be true. I say advisedly "appears to be true." There are various degrees of what is called good health. Commonly it is alleged and admitted where no physical disturbance is manifest; but there is a wide space between this and that full health which shows itself in high spirits and overflowing energy. In women, especially, there may be maintained a health which seems good, and yet falls short of the requirements of the race. For in women, much more than in men, there is constitutionally provided a surplus vitality devoted to continuance of the species. When the system is overtaxed the portion thus set aside is considerably diminished before the portion which goes to carry on individual life is manifestly trenched upon. The cost of activity, and especially of cerebral activity, which is very costly, has to be met; and if expenditure is excessive it cannot be met without deduction from that reserve power which should go to race maintenance. The reproductive capacity is diminished in various degrees— sometimes to the extent of inability to bear children, more frequently to the extent of inability to yield milk, and in numerous cases to a smaller extent which I must leave unspecified. I have good authority for saying that one of the remoter results of overculture, very frequently becomes a cause of domestic alienation.

Let me add that an adequately high culture, alike of men and women, might be compassed without mischief were our *curriculum* more rational. If the worthless knowledge included in what is now supposed to be a good education were omitted, all that which is needful for guidance, most of that which is desirable for general enlightenment, and a good deal of that which is distinguished as decorative, might be acquired without injurious reactions.

224. To the egoistic motives for culture have to be added the altruistic motives. A human being devoid of knowledge, and with none of that intellectual life which discipline of the faculties gives, is utterly uninteresting. To become a pleasure-yielding person is a social duty. Hence culture, and especially the culture which conduces to enlivenment, has an ethical sanction and something more.

Especially is this true of aesthetic culture, of which no note has thus far been taken. While it is to be enjoined as aiding that highest development of self required for the fullest life and happiness, it is also to be enjoined as increasing the ability to gratify those around. Though practices in the plastic arts, in music, and in poetry, are usually to be encouraged chiefly as producing susceptibility to pleasures, which the aesthetically uncultured cannot have; yet those who are endowed with something more than average ability, should be led to develop it by motives of benevolence also. In the highest degree this is so with music; and concerted music, subordinating as it does the personal element, is above all other kinds to be cultivated on altruistic grounds. It should be added, however, that excess of aesthetic culture, in common with excess of intellectual culture, is to be reprobated: Not in this case because of the overtax entailed, but because of the undue expenditure of time—the occupation of too large a space in life. With multitudes of people, especially women, the pursuit of beauty in one or other form is the predominant pursuit. To the achievement of prettiness much more important ends are sacrificed. Though aesthetic culture has to be recognized as ethically sanctioned, yet instead of emphasizing the demand for it, there is far greater occasion for condemning the excess of it. There needs a trenchant essay on aesthetic vices, which are everywhere shown in the subordination of use to appearance.

CHAPTER 7

Amusements

225. I have closed the last chapter with a division, the subject matter of which links it on to the subject matter of this chapter. We pass insensibly from the activities and passivities implied by aesthetic culture, to sundry of those which come under the head of relaxations and amusements. These we have now to consider from the ethical point of view.

To the great majority, who have imbibed more or less of that asceticism which, though appropriate to times of chronic militancy and also useful as a curb to ungoverned sensualism, has swayed too much men's theory of life, it will seem an absurd supposition that amusements are ethically warranted. Yet unless, in common with the Quakers and some extreme evangelicals, they hold them to be positively wrong, they must either say that amusements are neither right nor wrong, or, they must say that they are positively right—are to be morally approved.

That they are sanctioned by hedonistic ethics goes without saying. They are pleasure-giving activities; and that is their sufficient justification, so long as they do not unduly interfere with activities which are obligatory. Though most of our pleasures are to be accepted as concomitants of those various expenditures of energy conducive to self-sustentation and

sustentation of family; yet the pursuit of pleasure for pleasure's sake is to be sanctioned, and even enjoined, when
primary duties have been fulfilled.

So, too, are they to be approved from the physiological
point of view. Not only do the emotional satisfactions which
accompany normal life-sustaining labors exalt the vital
functions, but the vital functions are exalted by those satisfactions which accompany the superfluous expenditures of
energy implied by amusements: much more exalted in fact.
Such satisfactions serve to raise the tide of life, and taken in
due proportion conduce to every kind of efficiency.

Yet once more there is the evolutionary justification. In
section 534 of *The Principles of Psychology*, it was shown that
whereas, in the lowest creatures, the small energies which
exist are wholly used up in those actions which serve to
maintain the individual and propagate the species; in creatures of successively higher grades, there arises an increasing
amount of unused energy: every improvement of organization achieving some economy, and so augmenting the surplus
power. This surplus expends itself in the activities we call play.
Among the superior vertebrata the tendency to these superfluous activities becomes conspicuous; and it is especially
conspicuous in man, when so conditioned that stress of competition does not make the sustentation of self and family too
laborious. The implication is that in a fully developed form of
human life, a considerable space will be filled by the pleasurable exercise of faculties which have not been exhausted by
daily activities.

226. In that division of *The Principles of Psychology* above
referred to (secs. 533–40), in which I have drawn this distinction between life-sustaining activities and activities not of a
life-sustaining kind, which are pursued for pleasure's sake, I
have not drawn the further distinction between those of the
sensory structures and those of the motor structures. There is
a distinction between gratifications which aesthetic perceptions yield and those yielded by games and sports. This dis-

tinction it was left for Mr. Grant Allen to point out in his
Physiological Aesthetics. It cannot be made an absolute distinction, however; since gratifications derived from certain
excitements of the senses are often associated with, and dependent upon, muscular actions; and since the gratifications
of muscular actions, whatever their kind, are achieved under
guidance of the senses. Moreover, with each of them there
usually exists a large emotional accompaniment more important than either. Still the division is a natural one, and Mr.
Grant Allen has established it beyond question.

Even ascetically minded people do not repudiate those enjoyments, intellectual and emotional, which traveling yields.
Pursuit of the aesthetic delights derived from beautiful scenery, the mountains, the sea—primarily those due to the visual
impressions which forms and colors give, but secondarily and
mainly those due to the poetical sentiments aroused by
association—is approved by all. So, too, in a measure, is
pursuit of the gratifications yielded by exploration of the
unknown forms of human life and its products—foreign
peoples, their towns, their ways. One is sometimes saddened
to think what a vast majority of men come into the world and
go out of it again knowing scarcely at all what kind of world it
is. And this thought suggests that while it is to be sanctioned
for gratification's sake, traveling is to be further sanctioned for
the sake of culture; since the accompanying enlargement of
the experiences profoundly affects the general conceptions
and rationalizes them. Modern social changes and changes of
belief, are in considerable measure due to facilitation of intercourse with unlike forms of life, and character, and habit,
which railways have brought about.

After the pleasures given by actual presentations of new
scenes, may fitly be named the pleasures yielded by pictorial
representations of them. While in many cases these fall short
of those which the realities give, in many other cases they
exceed them. By its reproduction on canvas there is given to a
rural view or a domestic interior an artificial interest; so that
something intrinsically commonplace is transfigured into

something beautiful: possibly because the mind in presence of the object itself was so much occupied with its other aspects as to give no attention to its aesthetic aspects. Be the cause what it may, however, works of art open new fields of delight, and by hedonism acceptance of this delight is sanctioned, or rather enjoined. Few pleasures are more entirely to be approved, and less open to abuse, than those yielded by paintings, and of course also by sculptures.

It seems undesirable to insist that there is an ethical sanction for the pleasures given by light literature, seeing that there is so general a tendency to excess in the pursuit of them. Perhaps such exaltation of feeling as the reading of good poetry produces, is not sought in an undue degree; but, unquestionably, there is far too much reading of fiction; often excluding, as it does, all instructive reading, and causing neglect of useful occupations. While ethical approval must be given to occasional indulgence in that extreme gratification produced by following out the good and ill fortunes of imaginary persons made real by vivid character drawing; yet there much more needs ethical reprobation of the too frequent indulgence in it which is so common: this emotional debauchery undermines mental health. Nor let us omit to note that while sanction may rightly be claimed for fiction of a humanizing tendency, there should be nothing but condemnation for brutalizing fiction—for that culture of bloodthirst to which so many stories are devoted.

Of course much that has just been said concerning fiction may be said concerning the drama. Higher even than the gratification yielded by a good novel, is that yielded by a good play; and the demoralization caused by excess of it would be still greater were there the same opportunity for continuous absorption. Pleasures which are intense must be sparingly partaken of. The general law of waste and repair implies that in proportion to the excitement of a faculty must be its subsequent prostration and unfitness for action—an unfitness which continues until repair has been made. Hence, overwhelming sympathy felt for personages in a fiction or drama, is felt at the cost of some subsequent callousness. As the eye by exposure to a vivid light is momentarily incapacitated for appreciating those feeble lights through which objects around are distinguished; so, after a tearful fellow feeling with the sufferers of imaginary woes, there is for a time a lack of fellow feeling with persons around. Much theatergoing, like much novel reading, is therefore to be ethically reprobated.

Perhaps among gratifications of the aesthetic class, that which music yields is that which may be indulged in most largely without evil consequences. Though after a concert, as after a fiction or a play, life in general seems tame; yet there is a less marked reaction, because the feelings excited are more remotely akin to those associated with daily intercourse. Still, the pleasures of music are frequently enjoyed to an excess which, if not otherwise injurious, is injurious by the implied occupation of time—by the filling of too large a space in life.

227. Throughout the foregoing class of pleasures, resulting from the superfluous excitements of faculties, the individual is mainly passive. We turn now to the class in which he is mainly active; which again is subdivisible into two classes—sports and games. With sports, ethics has little concern beyond graduating its degrees of reprobation. Such of them as involve the direct infliction of pain, especially on fellow beings, are nothing but means to the gratification of feelings inherited from savages of the baser sort. That after these thousands of years of social discipline, there should still be so many who like to see the encounters of the prize ring or witness the goring of horses and riders in the arena, shows how slowly the instincts of the barbarian are being subdued. No condemnation can be too strong for these sanguinary amusements which keep alive in men the worst parts of their natures and thus profoundly vitiate social life. Of course in a measure, though in a smaller measure, condemnation must be passed on field sports—in smaller measure because the obtainment of food affords a partial motive, because the infliction of pain is less conspicuous, and because the chief plea-

sure is that derived from successful exercise of skill. But it cannot be denied that all activities with which there is joined the consciousness that other sentient beings, far inferior though they may be, are made to suffer, are to some extent demoralizing. The sympathies do, indeed, admit of being so far specialized that the same person who is unsympathetic toward wild animals may be in large measure sympathetic toward fellow men; but a full amount of sympathy cannot well be present in the one relation and absent in the other. It may be added that the specializing of the sympathies has the effect that they become smaller as the remoteness from human nature becomes greater; and that hence the killing of a deer sins against them more than does the killing of a fish.

Those expenditures of energy which take the form of games, yield pleasures from which there are but small, if any, drawbacks in the entailed pains. Certain of them, indeed, as football, are as much to be reprobated as sports, than some of which they are more brutalizing; and there cannot be much ethical approbation of those games, so-called, such as boat races, in which a painful and often injurious overtax of the system is gone through to achieve a victory, pleasurable to one side and entailing pain on the other. But there is ethical sanction for those games in which, with a moderate amount of muscular effort, there is joined the excitement of a competition not too intense, kept alive from moment to moment by the changing incidents of the contest. Under these conditions the muscular actions are beneficial, the culture of the perceptions is useful, while the emotional pleasure has but small drawbacks. And here I am prompted to denounce the practice, now so general, of substituting gymnastics for games— violent muscular actions, joined with small concomitant pleasures, for moderate muscular actions joined with great pleasures. This usurpation is a sequence of that pestilent asceticism which thinks that pleasure is of no consequence, and that if the same amount of exercise be taken, the same benefit is gained: the truth being that to the exaltation of the vital functions which the pleasure produces, half the benefit is due.

Of indoor games which chiefly demand quickness of perception, quickness of reasoning, and quickness of judgment, general approval may be expressed with qualifications of no great importance. For young people they are especially desirable as giving to various of the intellectual faculties a valuable training, not to be given by other means. Under the stress of competition, the abilities to observe rapidly, perceive accurately, and infer rightly, are increased; and in addition to the immediate pleasures gained, there are gained powers of dealing more effectually with many of the incidents of life. It should be added that such drawbacks as there are, from the emotions accompanying victory and defeat, are but small in games which involve chance as a considerable factor, but are very noticeable where there is no chance. Chess, for example, which pits together two intelligences in such a way as to show unmistakably the superiority of one to the other in respect of certain powers, produces, much more than whist, a feeling of humiliation in the defeated, and if the sympathies are keen this gives some annoyance to the victor as well as to the vanquished.

Of course, such ethical sanction as is given to games, cannot be given where gambling or betting is an accompaniment. Involving, as both do, in a very definite way, and often to an extreme degree, the obtainment of pleasure at the cost of another's pain, they are to be condemned both for this immediate effect and for their remote effect—the repression of fellow feeling.

228. Before passing to the altruistic aspect of amusements, there should be noted a less familiar egoistic aspect. Unless they have kept up during life an interest in pastimes, those who have broken down from overwork (perhaps an overwork entailed on them by imperative duties) usually find themselves incapable of relaxing in any satisfactory way: they are

no longer amusable. Capacities for all other pleasures are atrophied, and the only pleasure is that which business gives. In such cases recovery is, if not prevented, greatly retarded by the lack of exhilarating occupations. Frequently dependents suffer.

This last consideration shows that these, like other classes of actions which primarily concern the individual, concern, to some extent, other individuals. But they concern other individuals in more direct and constant ways also. On each person there is imposed not only the peremptory obligation so to carry on his life as to avoid inequitably interfering with the carrying on of others' lives, and not only the less peremptory obligation to aid under various circumstances the carrying on of their lives, but there is imposed some obligation to increase the pleasures of their lives by sociality, and by the cultivation of those powers which conduce to sociality. A man may be a good economical unit of society, while remaining otherwise an almost worthless unit. If he has no knowledge of the arts, no aesthetic feelings, no interest in fiction, the drama, poetry, or music—if he cannot join in any of those amusements which daily and at longer intervals fill leisure spaces in life—if he is thus one to whom others cannot readily give pleasure, at the same time that he can give no pleasure to others; he becomes in great measure a dead unit, and unless he has some special value might better be out of the way.

Thus, that he may add his share to the general happiness, each should cultivate in due measure those superfluous activities which primarily yield self-happiness.

CHAPTER 8

Marriage

229. U p to the present point there has been maintained, if not absolutely yet with tolerable clearness, the division between the ethics of individual life and the ethics of social life; but we come, in this chapter and the chapter which follows it, to a part of ethics which is in a sense intermediate. For in the relations of marriage and parenthood, others are concerned, not contingently and indirectly, but in ways that are necessary and direct. The implied divisions of conduct, while their primary ethical sanctions refer to the proper fulfillment of individual life, are yet inseparable from those divisions which treat of conduct that is to be ethically approved or disapproved because of its effects on those around.

Let us glance first at the general obligation under which the individual lies to aid in maintaining the species, while fulfilling the needs of his own nature.

230. In *The Principles of Biology* (secs. 334–51) was explained the necessary antagonism between individuation and reproduction—between the appropriation of nutriment and energy for the purposes of individual life, and the appropriation of them for the initiation, development, and nurture of other lives. Extreme cases in which, after an existence of a few

hours or a day, the body of a parent divides, or else breaks up into numerous germs of new individuals, and less extreme cases in which a brief parental existence ends by the transformation of the skin into a protective case, while the interior is wholly transformed into young ones, illustrate in an unmistakable way the sacrifice of individual life for the maintenance of species life. It was shown that as we ascend to creatures of more complex structure and greater activity, and especially as we ascend to creatures of which the young have to be fostered, the expenditure of parental life in producing and rearing other lives becomes gradually less. And then, in *The Principles of Sociology* (secs. 275–77), when considering the "diverse interests of the species, of the parents, and of the offspring," we saw that in mankind there is reached such conciliation of these interests that along with preservation of the race there go moderated individual sacrifices; and further, that with the ascent from lower to higher types of men, we tend toward an ideal family in which "the mortality between birth and the reproductive age falls to a minimum, while the lives of adults have their subordination to the rearing of children reduced to the smallest possible."

To the last, however, the antagonism between individuation and reproduction holds—holds in a direct way, because of the physical tax which reproduction necessitates, and holds in an indirect way because of the tax, physical and mental, necessitated by rearing children: a tax which, though it is pleasurably paid in fulfillment of the appropriate instincts and emotions, and is in so far a fulfillment of individual life, is nevertheless a tax which restricts individual development in various directions.

But here the truth which it chiefly concerns us to note is that, assuming the preservation of the race to be a desideratum, there results a certain kind of obligation to pay this tax and to submit to this sacrifice. Moreover, something like natural equity requires that as each individual is indebted to past individuals for the cost of producing and rearing him, he shall be at some equivalent cost for the benefit of future individuals.

In tribes and small societies, where maintenance of numbers is important, this obligation becomes appreciable; and, as we see in the reproach of barrenness, failure to fulfill it brings disapproval. But of course in large nations where multiplication is rather an evil than a benefit, this obligation lapses; and the individual may, in many cases, fitly discharge his or her indebtedness in some other way than by adding to the population.

231. Leaving here these considerations which pertain, perhaps, more to the ethics of social life than to the ethics of individual life, and returning to the consideration of marriage as a part of individual life, we have first to note its ethical sanctions as so considered. All activities fall into two great groups—those which constitute and sustain the life of the individual, and those which further the life of the race; and it seems inferable that if for full health the structures conducive to the one must severally perform their functions, so must the structures conducive to the other. Such part of the organization as is devoted to the production of offspring, can scarcely be left inert and leave the rest of the organization unaffected. The not infrequent occurrence of hysteria and chlorosis shows that women, in whom the reproductive function bears a larger ratio to the totality of the functions than it does in men, are apt to suffer grave constitutional evils from that incompleteness of life which celibacy implies: grave evils to which there probably correspond smaller and unperceived evils in numerous cases. As before remarked, there are wide limits of deviation in what we call good health; and there are everywhere, in men and women, many shortcomings of full health which are not perceived to be such—shortcomings, however, which may be recognized on remembering the contrast between the ordinary state of body and mind, and that which is shown after an invigorating holiday. That the physiological effects of a

completely celibate life on either sex are to some extent injurious, seems an almost necessary implication of the natural conditions.

But whether or not there be disagreement on this point, there can be none respecting the effects of a celibate life as mentally injurious. A large part of the nature—partly intellectual but chiefly emotional—finds its sphere of action in the marital relation, and afterwards in the parental relation; and if this sphere be closed, some of the higher feelings must remain inactive and others but feebly active. Directly, to special elements of the mind, the relation established by marriage is the normal and needful stimulus, and indirectly to all its elements.

There is in the first place to be recognized an exaltation of the energies. Continuous and strenuous efforts to succeed in life are often excited by an engagement to marry—efforts which had previously not been thought of. Then, subsequently, the consciousness of family responsibilities when these have arisen, serves as a sharper spur to exertion: often, indeed, a spur so sharp that in the absence of prudential restraints it leads to overwork. But the most noteworthy fact is that under these conditions, an amount of activity becomes relatively easy, and even pleasurable, which before was difficult and repugnant.

The immediate cause of this greater energy is the increased quantity of emotion which the marital relation, and after it the parental relation, excite; and there is to be recognized both a greater body of emotion, and a higher form of emotion. To the lower egoistic feelings which previously formed the chief, if not only, stimuli, are now added those higher egoistic feelings which find their satisfaction in the affections, together with those altruistic feelings which find their satisfaction in the happiness of others. What potent influences on character thus come into play, is shown in the moral transformation which marriage frequently effects. Often the vain and thoughtless girl, caring only for amusements, becomes changed into the devoted wife and mother; and often the man who is ill-tempered and unsympathetic, becomes changed into the self-sacrificing husband and careful father. To which add that there is usually exercised, more than before, the discipline of self-restraint.

Some effect, too, is wrought on the thinking faculties; not, perhaps, in their power, but in their balance. In women the intellectual activity is frequently diminished; for the antagonism between individuation and reproduction, which is in them most pronounced, tells more especially on the brain. But to both husband and wife there daily come many occasions for exercises of judgment, alike in their relations to domestic affairs, to one another, and to children—exercises of judgment which in the celibate state were not called for; and hence an increase of intellectual stability and sense of proportion.

It must, however, be remarked that the beneficial effects to be expected from marriage, as giving a sphere to a large part of the nature otherwise relatively inert, presuppose a normal marriage—a marriage of affection. If, instead, it is one of the kind to be ethically reprobated—a mercantile marriage—there may follow debasement rather than elevation.

232. But now comes a difficult question. If, on the one hand, as being a condition to fulfillment of individual life, marriage is ethically sanctioned and, indeed, ethically enjoined; and if, on the other hand, there is ethical reprobation for all acts which will certainly or probably entail evil—reprobation if the evil is likely to come on self, and still more if it is likely to come on others; then what are we to say of improvident marriage?

There needs no insistence on the truth that if domestic responsibilities are entered upon without a fair prospect of efficiently discharging them, a wrong is done: especially to children and, by implication, to the race. To take a step from which will result a poverty-stricken household, containing a half-starved and half-clothed family, is, if estimated by entailed miseries, something like a crime. When, after long years of pain, anxiety, cold and hunger, to adults and young, some out of the many born have been reared to maturity, ill-grown, unhealthy, and incapable of the efforts needed for self-support; it becomes manifest that there have been produced beings who are at once curses to themselves and to the community. Severe condemnation must be passed on the conduct which has such consequences.

And yet, on the other hand, what would happen if no marriages took place without a satisfactory prospect of maintaining a family? Suppose that an average delay of ten years were submitted to, so that there might be no such risks of evil as are now commonly run. The usual supposition is that such persistent self-restraint would be purely beneficial. This is far from being true, however.

I do not refer to the fact that ten years of partially abnormal life is a serious evil; although this should be taken account of in estimating the total results. Nor am I thinking of the increased liability to domestic dissension which arises when added years have given to each of the married pair greater fixity of beliefs and diminished modifiability of feelings. But I am thinking chiefly of the effects on progeny. The tacit assumption made by those who advocate the Malthusian remedy for overpopulation, is, that it matters not to children whether they are born to young parents or to old parents. This is a mistake.

Because many factors cooperate, the evidence is so obscured that attention is not commonly drawn to the effects indicated; but they certainly arise. The antagonism between individuation and reproduction implies, among other things, that the surplus vitality available for the maintenance of species life is that which remains after the maintenance of individual life. Hence the effects on offspring of early, medium, and late marriages, are not constant; because the surplus, though it has a general relation to age, is not constant at any age. But from this general relation it results, in the first place, that children born of very early marriages are injuriously affected; since where the development of parents, or more especially the mother, is not complete, the available surplus is less than that which exists after it is complete. It results also that where maternal vigor is great and the surplus vitality consequently large, a long series of children may be borne before any deterioration in their quality becomes marked; while, on the other hand, a mother with but a small surplus may soon cease altogether to reproduce. Further, it results that variations in the states of health of parents, involving variations in the surplus vitality, have their effects on the constitutions of offspring, to the extent that offspring borne during greatly deranged maternal health are decidedly feebler. And then, lastly and chiefly, it results that after the constitutional vigor has culminated, and there has commenced that gradual decline which in some twenty years or so brings absolute infertility, there goes on a gradual decrease in that surplus vitality on which the production of offspring depends, and a consequent deterioration in the quality of such offspring. This, which is an *a priori* conclusion, is verified *a posteriori*. Mr. J. Matthews Duncan, in his work on *Fecundity, Fertility, Sterility, and Allied Topics,* has given results of statistics which show that mothers of five-and-twenty bear the finest infants, and that from mothers whose age at marriage ranges from twenty to five-and-twenty, there come infants which have a lower rate of mortality than those resulting from marriages commenced when the mother's age is either smaller or greater: the apparent slight incongruity between these two statements, being due to the fact that whereas marriages commenced between twenty and five-and-twenty cover the whole of the period of highest vigor, marriages commenced at five-and-twenty cover a period which lacks the years during which vigor is rising to its climax, and includes only the years of decline from the climax.

Now this fact that infants born of mothers married between twenty and five-and-twenty have a lower rate of mortality than infants born of mothers married earlier or later, shows that the age of marriage is not a matter of indifference to the race, and that the question of early or late marriages is less simple than appears. While the children of a relatively early marriage improvidently entered upon, may suffer from inadequate sustentation; the children of a later marriage are likely to suffer from initial imperfection—imperfection which may be consistent with good health and fair efficiency, but yet may negative that high efficiency requisite for the best and most successful life. For especially nowadays, under our regime of keen competition, a small falling-short of constitutional vigor may entail failure.

Thus, except in the positive reprobation of marriages at an earlier age than twenty (among the higher races of mankind) ethical considerations furnish but indefinite guidance. Usually there has to be a compromise of probabilities. While recklessly improvident marriages must be strongly condemned, yet it seems that in many cases some risk may rightly be run, lest there should be entailed the evils flowing from too long a delay.

233. But what has ethics to say concerning choice in marriage—the selection of wife by husband and husband by wife? It has very decisive things to say.

Current conversation proves how low is current thought and sentiment about these questions. "It will be a very good match for her," is the remark you hear respecting some young lady engaged to a wealthy man. Or concerning the choice of some young gentleman it is said, "She is an accomplished girl and well connected; and her friends will help to advance him in his profession." Another engaged pair are described as well suited: he is a domestic man, and she does not care much for society. Or, perhaps, the impending marriage is applauded on the ground that the lady will be a good housekeeper, and make the best of a small income; or that the proposed husband is good-tempered and not too fastidious. But about the fitness of the connection as considered not extrinsically but intrinsically, little or nothing is said.

The first ground of ethical judgment is the reciprocal state of feeling prompting the union. Where there exists none of that mutual attraction which should be the incentive, evolutionary ethics and hedonistic ethics alike protest; whatever ethics otherwise derived may do. Marriages of this class are reversions to marriage of earlier types, such as those found among the rudest savages. The *marriage de convénance* has been called, with some show of reason, legalized prostitution.

But passing over the interdict which ethics utters on marriages which are mercantile, or which arise from other motives than affection, we have to notice its further interdicts physiologically originating. Here we see, as was pointed out in the preliminary chapter, how prevalent is the blindness to all effects save proximate ones; unquestionable as may be the genesis of remoter effects. Only in extreme cases do either those directly concerned or their friends, think of the probable quality of the offspring when discussing the propriety of a marriage. Disapproval, perhaps rising to reprobation, may be expressed when the proposed union is between cousins, or is a union with one who probably inherits insanity; but consideration of the effects to be borne by descendants goes scarcely beyond this. A feeble mind or a bad physique is but rarely thought a sufficient reason for rejecting a suitor. Thin, flat-chested girls, debilitated men perpetually ailing, some who are constitutionally wanting in bodily energy, others who have no activity either of intellect or feeling, and many who are from this or that defect so inferior as to be unfit to carry on the battle of life, are ordinarily considered good enough for marriage and parenthood. In a manner that seems almost deliberate there are thus entailed households in which illness and dullness and bad-temper prevail, and out of which there come unhealthy and incapable children and grand-children.

Ethical considerations should here serve as rigid restraints. Though guidance by the feelings is to be so far respected that marriages not prompted by them must be condemned, yet guidance by the feelings must not therefore be regarded as so authoritative that all marriages prompted by them should be approved. A certain perversion of sentiment has to be guarded against. Relative weakness, appealing for protection, is one of the traits in women which excites in men the sentiment of affection—"the tender emotion," as Bain styles it; and sometimes a degree of relative weakness which exceeds the natural, strongly excites this feeling: the pity which is akin to love ends in love. There are converse cases in which a woman of unusual power of nature becomes attached to a man who is feeble in body or mind. But these deviations from normal inclinations have to be resisted. Ethics demands that judgment shall here come in aid of instinct and control it.

234. There remains a question uniformly passed over because difficult to discuss, but the ignoring of which is fraught with untold disasters—a question concerning which ethics, in its comprehensive form, has a verdict to give, and cannot without falling short of its functions decline to give it.

The saying "the letter killeth but the spirit giveth life" not only is exemplified by the way in which observance of religious ceremonies replaces observance of the essential injunctions of religion, but is exemplified everywhere. As in the primitive legal system of the Romans, before it was qualified by infusion of the *Jus Gentium*, the essential thing was fulfillment of formalities rather than maintenance of right—as, among ourselves, the sacrifice of justice to the technicalities of law, led to the supplementary system of equity, intended to rectify the entailed injustices—as, again, in the system of equity the observance of rules and conforming to orders, ever complicating, became in course of time so burdensome that equity, lost sight of, was replaced by inequity, or iniquity; so is it throughout. Wherever requirements which have their roots in the order of nature, come to be enforced by an extrinsic authority, obedience to that extrinsic authority takes the place of obedience to the natural requirements.

It is thus in a considerable degree with marriage. I do not mean merely that unions of an essentially illegitimate kind are supposed to be legitimized by a church service or a registration; but I mean more. I mean that when the civil requirements have been fulfilled, and the ecclesiastical sanction has been obtained, it is supposed that no further control has to be recognized—that when the religious restraints and the social restraints on the relations of the sexes have been duly respected, there remain no other restraints. The physiological restraints, not having received official recognition, are not supposed to exist, or are disregarded. Hence a vast amount of evil.

The antagonism between individuation and reproduction comes into play throughout the entire process of race maintenance. It is true that the fulfillment of individual life largely consists in furthering species life; but it is nonetheless true that from beginning to end, the last puts a limit to the first. We have but to consider that, delighted as the mother is in yielding food to her infant, she yet suffers a serious physical tax in addition to the physical tax entailed by production of it, to see that great though the maternal gratification may be, it entails loss of gratifications which a more developed individual life might have brought; and that when many children are produced and reared, the sacrifices of individual life and of the pleasures which a higher development would bring, become very great. This law inevitably holds throughout the entire reproductive function from beginning to end—with the initial part as with the terminal part; and ignorance of, or indifference to, it entails profound injuries, physical and mental. If the physiological restraints are not respected the life is undermined in all ways.

When, out of the total resources which the sustaining organs furnish in materials and forces, the part required for the carrying on of individual life is trenched upon beyond the normal ratio, by the part constitutionally appropriated to species life, there comes a diminution of energy, which affects the vital processes and all dependent processes. Chronic derangements of health supervene, diminished bodily activity, decline of mental power, and sometimes even insanity. Succeeding the mischiefs thus caused, even when they are not so extreme, there come the mischiefs entailed on family and others; for inability to discharge obligations, depression of spirits, and perturbed mental state, inevitably injure those around. Several specialists, who have good means of judging, agree in the opinion that the aggregate evils arising from excesses of this kind are greater than those arising from excesses of all other kinds put together.

If, then, ethics as rightly conceived has to pass judgment on all conduct which affects the well-being, immediate or remote, of self or others, or both; then the lack of self-restraint which it condemns in other cases, it must condemn in this case also.

CHAPTER 9

Parenthood

235. The subject matter of this chapter is of course only in part separable from the subject matter of the last chapter. But though in discussing the ethics of marriage, as primarily concerning the relations of parents to each other, it has been needful to take account of the relations of parents to offspring, it has seemed best to reserve the full consideration of these last relations for a distinct chapter.

Already it has been pointed out that in the order of nature—"so careful of the type . . . so careless of the single life"—the welfare of progeny takes precedence of the welfare of those who produce them. Though the happiness or misery of the married pair is ordinarily the result chiefly contemplated, this result must be held of secondary importance in comparison with the results reached in offspring—the superiority or inferiority of the children born and reared to maturity. For in proportion as race maintenance is well- or ill-achieved in each case, must be the tendency of the species or variety to prosper or decline.

Hence all requirements touching the proximate end, marriage, are to be considered in subordination to requirements touching the ultimate end—the raising up members of a new generation. Evolutionary ethics demands that this last end shall be regarded as the supreme end.

236. Obviously the parental instincts in large measure se-cure fulfillment of this supreme end; since any species or variety in which they are not strong enough to do this, must presently become extinct. Here, then, we are introduced to the truth that achievement of those pleasures which par-enthood brings, has a double sanction—that which the ethics of individual life directly yields, and that which is yielded indirectly by the ethics of social life.

But satisfaction of the parental affections, while not to be ignored as an end in itself, is, as above implied, chiefly to be regarded as a spur to the discharge of parental responsibilities. The arrangements of things are dislocated if the two are not kept in relation—if the responsibilities, instead of being dis-charged by parents, are shouldered upon others. It might have been thought that this truth is too obvious to need enunciation; but, unhappily, it is far otherwise. We have fallen upon evil times, in which it has come to be an accepted doctrine that part of the responsibilities are to be discharged not by parents but by the public—a part which is gradually becoming a larger part and threatens to become the whole. Agitators and legislators have united in spreading a theory which, logically followed out, ends in the monstrous conclu-sion that it is for parents to beget children and for society to take care of them. The political ethics now in fashion, makes the unhesitating assumption that while each man, as parent, is not responsible for the mental culture of his own offspring, he is, as citizen, along with other citizens, responsible for the mental culture of all other men's offspring! And this absurd doctrine has now become so well established that people raise their eyebrows in astonishment if you deny it. A self-evident falsehood has been transformed into a self-evident truth! Along with the almost universal superstition that society is a manufacture and not a growth, there goes the unwavering belief that legislators, prompted by electors, can with advan-tage set aside one of the fundamental arrangements under which organic nature at large, and human nature in particular, has evolved thus far! Men who have proved cunning in business speculation, men who ride well to hounds and are popular in their counties, men who in courts of justice are skilled in making the worse cause appear the better, men who once wrote good Latin verses or proved themselves learned about the misbehavior of the Greek gods, unite in trying to undo organized dependencies resulting from millions of years of discipline. Men whose culture is so little relevant to the functions they have assumed, that they do not even see that everything in social life originates from certain traits of individual life, that individual human life is but a specialized part of life at large, and that therefore until the leading truths presented by life at large are comprehended, there can be no right comprehension of society—men who are thus ignorant of the great facts which it chiefly concerns them to know, have promised to do the behests of men who are ignorant not only of such facts but of most other things. The half-blind elected by the wholly blind take upon themselves the office of creation menders! Daily accustomed to discover that established laws are bad and must be repealed by act of Parliament, they have unawares extended their thought to laws not of human origin, and calmly undertake to repeal by act of Parliament a law of nature!

But this ignoring of the truth that only by due discharge of parental responsibilities has all life on the earth arisen, and that only through the better discharge of them have there gradually been made possible better types of life, is in the long run fatal. Breach of natural law will in this case, as in all cases, be followed in due time by nature's revenge—a revenge which will be terrible in proportion as the breach has been great. A system under which parental duties are performed wholesale by those who are not the parents, under the plea that many parents cannot or will not perform their duties—a system which thus fosters the inferior children of inferior parents at the necessary cost of superior parents and consequent injury of superior children—a system which thus helps incapables to multiply and hinders the multiplications of capables, or diminishes their capability, must bring decay and eventual extinction. A society which persists in such a system must, other things equal, go to the wall in the competition with a society which does not commit the folly of nurturing its worst at the expense of its best.

The ethical code of nature, then, allows of no escape of parents from their obligations. While under its hedonistic aspect it sanctions in an emphatic way the gratification of parental affections, under its evolutionary aspect it peremptorily requires fulfillment of all those actions by which the young are prepared for the battle of life. And if the circumstances are such that part of these actions must be performed by deputy, it still requires that the implied cost and care shall be borne, and not transferred to others' shoulders.

237. The time will come when, along with full recognition of parental duties, there will go an unyielding resistance to the usurpation of those duties. While the parent, as he ought to be, will conscientiously satisfy all the demands which his parenthood entails, he will sternly deny the right of any assemblage of men to take his children from him and mold them as they please. We have outgrown the stage during which the despot, with an army at his back, could impose his will on all citizens; but we have not yet outgrown the stage during which a majority of citizens, with police at their back, can impose their will, concerning all matters whatever, upon citizens not of their number. But when there has passed away this contemptible superstition that, having the power, the majority have the right, to do as they please with the persons and property and actions of those who happen to be in the minority—when it is understood that governmental orders are limited by ethical injunctions; every parent will hold his sphere as one into which the state may not intrude. And if under such conditions there occasionally, though rarely, happens a nonperformance of parental duties, the entailed evil brings, in nature's stern way, its own cure. For with mankind as with lower kinds, the ill-nurtured offspring of the inferior fail in the struggle for existence with the well-nurtured off-

spring of the superior; and in a generation or two die out, to the benefit of the species. A harsh discipline this, most will say. True; but nature has much discipline which is harsh, and which must, in the long run, be submitted to. The necessities which she imposes on us are not to be evaded, even by the joint efforts of university graduates and workingmen delegates; and the endeavor to escape her harsh discipline results in a discipline still harsher. Measures which prevent the dwindling away of inferior individuals and families, must, in the course of generations, cause the nation at large to dwindle away.

At the same time that intrusion into the parental sphere must, in a normal social state, be resented as a trespass, it will be further resented as a deprivation of those daily pleasures yielded by furthering the development of the young in body and mind. For when there have died out the stupidities of an education which may be briefly described as denying the mind that which it wants and forcing upon it that which it does not want, there will have come a time when the superintendence of education, at any rate in all its simpler parts, will be at once easy and enjoyable. The general law that through successive stages of organic evolution, there is an elongation of the period during which parental care is given, shown finally in the contrast between the human race and inferior races, as well as in the contrast between uncivilized and civilized, is a law which, involving as now a long and careful physical nurturing of the young by their parents, will hereafter involve a long and careful psychical nurturing by them; and though the higher and more special educational functions will have to be discharged by proxy, yet the proxy discharge will be under parental superintendence.

People feel no adequate pride in bringing to maturity fine human beings. It is true that the mother, exhibiting each infant with triumph, and during the childhood of each pleasing herself by presenting it to visitors prettily clothed and with hair on which much time has been spent morning and evening, is not wholly neglectful of diet, and takes care that the day's lessons are attended to. It is true, also, that the father, commonly leaving fashion to determine the places of education for his boys, sometimes makes inquiries and exercises independent judgment; and, moreover, looks with satisfaction on a well-grown youth and one who has brought home prizes. But it is nevertheless true that scarcely anywhere do we see proper solicitude. Grave mischiefs are daily done in almost every family by ignorance of physiological requirements; and in the absence of guiding knowledge in parents, innumerable children grow up with constitutions damaged for life. At the same time there is no such thoughtful ministration to the mind of each child as is called for—no search for a course of intellectual culture which is rational in matter and method, and nothing beyond a rough and ready moral discipline. On observing what energies are expended by father and mother to achieve worldly success and fulfill social ambitions, we are reminded how relatively small is the space occupied by the ambition to make their descendants physically, morally, and intellectually superior. Yet this is the ambition which will replace those they now so eagerly pursue; and which, instead of perpetual disappointments, will bring permanent satisfactions.

And then, following on the discharge of these high parental functions, will come that reward in old age consisting of an affectionate care by children, much greater than is now known.

238. Anything like due fulfillment of parental functions as thus conceived, is possible only under conditions commonly disregarded—conditions the disregard of which is supposed not to fall within the range of ethical judgments.

"Providence has sent me a large family," is a remark which may occasionally be heard from one who has more children than he can provide for. Though, in other directions, he does not profess an oriental fatalism, in this direction he does. "God has willed it so," appears to be his thought; and thinking this, he holds himself absolved from blame in bringing about the distresses of a poverty-stricken household.

If, however, improvident marriages are to be reprobated—if to bring children into the world when there will probably be no means of maintaining any, is a course calling for condemnation; then there must be condemnation for those who bring many children into the world when they have means of properly rearing only a few. Improvidence after marriage cannot be considered right, if improvidence before marriage is considered wrong.

The stunted and ill-formed bodies of dwellers in the East end of London, tell of the meager diet and deficient clothing from which the many children of parents with narrow means, have suffered during their early days; and even in country villages, where the sanitary conditions are relatively good, one may see in feeble and sickly people, the results of attempting to rear large families on small wages. This reckless multiplication, while it inflicts the daily-recurring pains of unsatisfied appetites and the miseries of insufficient warmth—while it is to be debited with that lack of bodily strength which makes efficient work impracticable, commonly involves also a stupidity which negatives all but the most mechanical functions; for mental power cannot be got from ill-fed brains. Unhappy and wearisome lives are thus entailed by parents who beget more children than they can properly bring up.

Matters are made worse, too, by the undue tax brought on the parents themselves—on the father, if he is conscientious by an injurious amount of labor; and still more on the mother, whose system, exhausted by the bearing of many children, is still further exhausted by the cares which all day long the many children need. Manifestly hedonistic ethics if we regard it as contemplating, more especially, immediate effects on happiness, severely denounces conduct which thus creates miseries all round; while evolutionary ethics, if we consider it as more especially contemplating future results, severely denounces conduct which thus bequeaths lower natures instead of higher to subsequent generations.

Even where parents have means sufficient to provide abundantly for the bodily welfare of many children, there must still be an insufficient provision for their mental welfare. Though, in a family of several, the children amuse and teach one another, and thus mutually aid mental growth; yet, when the number is large, the parental attention they severally need becomes too much subdivided; and the daily display of parental affection, which is a large factor in the moral development of children, cannot be given in adequate amount to each.

239. With the ethical censure of this improvident multiplication, must be joined a like censure of an improvidence habitually associated with it, and in large measure the cause of it. The nature of this will best be shown by citing some facts furnished by races which, being uncivilized, are regarded as therefore in all respects our inferiors.

The first of them comes from a society utterly brutal in most of its usages—Uganda: "The women rarely have more than two or three children, and the law is that when a woman has borne a child she must live apart from her husband for two years, at which age the children are weaned."

In a still more brutal society—that of the Fijians—we meet with a kindred fact. Says Seemann:

> After childbirth, husband and wife keep apart for three, even four years, so that no other baby may interfere with the time considered necessary for suckling children. . . . I heard of a white man, who being asked how many brothers and sisters he had, frankly replied, "Ten!" "But that could not be," was the rejoinder of the natives, "one mother could scarcely have so many children." When told that these children were born at annual intervals, and that such occurrences were common in Europe, they were very much shocked, and thought it explained sufficiently why so many white people were "mere shrimps."

In these cases, however, polygamy prevails: in Uganda, for instance, the enormous preponderance of women, due partly to the destruction of men in war and partly to the capture of women by war, rendering it almost universal. Here, therefore, the usage, insofar as it affects men, is not so remarkable. But in two leading districts of New Guinea, there are monogamous peoples among whom a like rule holds. The Rev. J. Chalmers tells us that in Motu-Motu, the parents, after the birth of a child, "do not live together again until the child is strong, walking, and weaned, and all that time he [the husband] sleeps in dubu. His friends cook food for him." Similarly of the Motu tribe, he tells us that the parents keep apart "until the child walks and is weaned." To ascertain the current opinion on the matter he asked the question, "If another child is born before the first is big and able to walk, are they ashamed?" To which he got the answer, "Yes, terribly; and all the village will be talking about it."

Even these warlike and sanguinary peoples then, and still more these trading, peaceful, and monogamous tribes of New Guinea, show us a deep consciousness of the truth that too frequent childbearing is injurious to the race—tells against the fullest development of both the already born child and the child to be presently born. Beyond that constant surplus vitality which, in the female economy, remains after meeting the expenditure of individual life, there is also what we may call a reserve of vital capital, accumulated during intervals in which the surplus is not being demanded. This reserve, used up during the interval in which an infant is being developed, takes some time to replace—a time shorter or longer according as the constitutional vigor is great or small. And if, much before the end of that time, the reproductive system is again called into action, the double result is an overtax of the maternal system, and an infant which falls short of the fullest development; at the same time that its predecessor is too early deprived of its natural supply of food. These are necessary consequences. They are collateral results of that general cause which makes reproduction impossible before and after certain ages.

Here then, as in sundry preceding cases, evolutionary ethics utters an interdict which current ethics, from whatever source derived, shows no signs of uttering.

240. How then are there to be reconciled the interests of the individual and the interests of the race? This question, which

here unavoidably presents itself, is one difficult, if not impossible to answer—perhaps they cannot be reconciled.

As already many times said, men have been long in course of acquiring fitness for that social state into which increase of numbers has forced them, and have still but partially acquired fitness for it. In multitudinous ways the survival of instincts appropriate to the presocial stage, has been a chronic cause of miseries; and in multitudinous ways the lack of sentiments appropriate to the social stage, has been a chronic cause of other miseries.

While it has continually increased that pressure of population which has been a cause of progress, excess of fertility has been among the chief factors in the production of these miseries, and must long continue to be such; but, as is shown in *The Principles of Biology,* sections 373–74, the implication of the general law traceable throughout the whole animal kingdom, is that still a higher development of mind, brought about by still increasing pressure of population, and still greater cerebral activity entailed by it, will gradually diminish the fertility, until the excess practically disappears: the highest degree of individuation entailing the lowest degree of reproduction. And the further implication, there pointed out, is that this degree of individuation, especially shown in a more exalted mental life—wider intelligence and more intense feelings—will not involve conscious stress, but will be the natural outcome of an organization adjusted to the requirements of a more costly self-sustentation. Hence, if there are deprivations which ethics dictates, they must step by step be accompanied by compensations, probably greater in amount.

Only in the slow course of ages, however, can any such change of balance be wrought. Whether, in the meantime, there may arise any qualifications of the process, it is impossible to say. One thing, however, is certain. No conclusion can be sustained which does not conform to the ultimate truth that the interests of the race must predominate over the interests of the individual.

CHAPTER 10

General Conclusions

241. The title of this division—"The Ethics of Individual Life"—has excited a publicly expressed curiosity respecting the possible nature of its contents. Nothing beyond prudential admonitions could, it was thought, be meant; and there was evident surprise that ethical sanction should be claimed for these.

The state of mind thus implied is not, I believe, exceptional. Ordinary individual life, when it is such as not directly to affect others for good or evil, is supposed to lie outside the sphere of ethics; or rather, there is commonly entertained no thought about the matter. Ethics, as usually conceived, having made no formal claim to regulate this part of conduct is assumed to be unconcerned with it. It is true that now and then come expressions implying a half-conscious belief to the contrary. "You *ought* not to have overtaxed your strength by so great an exertion"; "you *ought* not to have gone so long without food"; are not unfrequent utterances. "You were quite *right* to throw up the situation if your health was giving way," is said to one; while on another is passed the criticism, "He is *wrong* in idling away his time, wealthy though he may be." And we occasionally hear insistence on the *duty* of taking a holiday to avoid an illness: especially in view of responsibilities to be discharged. That is to say, the words *ought, right, wrong, duty* are used in connection with various parts of private conduct; and such uses of these words, which in other cases have ethical significance, imply that they have ethical significance in these cases also.

Moreover, as pointed out in the opening chapter, there are some modes of individual life concerning which ethical convictions of the most pronounced kinds prevail—excess in drinking, for example. Recognition of the immense evils entailed by this prompts strong reprobation. But there is no consciousness of the obvious truth that if, because of its mischievous consequences, this deviation from normal life is to be condemned; so, too, are all deviations which have mischievous consequences, however relatively small. It must be admitted that, conceived in its fully developed form, ethics has judgments to give upon all actions which affect individual welfare.

Throughout the foregoing series of chapters, it has, I think, been made sufficiently manifest that there is great need for ethical rule over this wider territory.

242. Doubtless this rule must be of an indefinite kind—may be compared rather with that of a suzerain than with that of an acting governor. For throughout the greater part of this territory, there have to be effected compromises among various requirements; and in the majority of cases ethical considerations can do little more than guide us toward rational compromises.

This will probably be regarded as a reversion to the ancient doctrine of the mean—a doctrine expressed in a manner generally vague, but occasionally distinct, by Confucius, and definitely elaborated by Aristotle. And it must be admitted that throughout most classes of actions which do not directly affect other persons, paths lying between extremes have to be sought and followed. The doctrine of the mean is not, as Aristotle admitted, universally applicable; and its inapplicability is conspicuous in respect of that part of conduct which stands above all others in importance—justice; not, indeed, justice as legally formulated, nor justice as it is conceived by communists and others such, but justice as deducible from the conditions which must be maintained for the carrying on of harmonious social cooperation. Ethics does not suggest partial fulfillment of a contract, as being the mean between non-fulfillment and complete fulfillment. It does not countenance moderate robbery of your neighbor, rather than the taking from him everything or the taking nothing. Nor does it dictate the assault of a fellow man as intermediate between murdering him and not touching him. Contrariwise, in respect of justice ethics insists on the extreme—enjoins complete fulfillment of a contract, absolute respect for property, entire desistance from personal injury. So likewise is it with veracity. The right does not lie between the two extremes of falsehood and truth: complete adherence to fact is required. And there are sundry kinds of conduct classed as vices, which are also not contemplated by the doctrine; since they are to be interdicted not partially but wholly. In respect of ordinary private life, however, the doctrine of the mean may be considered to hold in the majority of cases.

But admitting this, there still presents itself the question—How to find the mean? Until the positions of the extremes have been ascertained, the position of the mean cannot be known. As has rightly been remarked, "It is impracticable to define the position of that, which is excessive on the one hand, and defective on the other, till excess and defect have been themselves defined." And here it is that the ethics of individual life finds its subject matter. The guidance of uncultured sense, ordinarily followed throughout private conduct, it replaces by a guidance which, though still mainly empirical, is relatively trustworthy; since it results from a deliberate and methodic study of the requirements—a study which dissipates misapprehensions and reduces vague ideas to definite ones. In respect of nutrition, for instance, it is doubtless true that abstinence on the one hand, and gluttony on the other, are to be avoided—that food is to be taken in moderation. But it may rightly be contended that eating is not to be guided by observation of the mean between these two extremes; but is to be guided by reaching that which may, in a sense, be called an extreme—the complete satisfaction of appetite. And here we are shown the need for critical inquiry. For the conception of a mean between abstinence and gluttony, is confounded with the conception of a mean between no satisfaction of appetite and complete satisfaction of appetite; and in consequence of the confusion this last mean is by some prescribed. But the notion, not infrequently expressed, that it is best to leave off eating while still hungry, would never have been enunciated were there not so many people who lead abnormal lives, and so many people who eat before appetite prompts. In that state of health which exists where there has not been, on the part of either self or ancestors, a chronic disregard of physiological needs, proper nutrition is achieved not by partial fulfillment of the desire for food but by entire fulfillment of it—by going up to the limit set by inclination.

Remembrance of the various conclusions drawn in preceding chapters, such as those which concern activity and rest, culture and amusement, will make it clear that it is everywhere the business of the ethics of individual life thus to dissipate erroneous beliefs, by systematic observation and analysis of private conduct and its results.

243. Remembrance of these conclusions suggests that beyond giving a definite conception of the mean, when the mean is to be adopted, the ethics of individual life gives definiteness to a kindred idea—the idea of proportion. I do not refer to that proportion which is implied by the doctrine of the mean, and connotes a just estimation of excess and defect; but I mean that proportion which obtains among different parts of conduct.

While, within each division of the activities, the middle place may be duly regarded, there may be no due regard for proportion among the several divisions of the activities. There are various kinds of bodily action, some needed for self-sustentation and some not; there are various kinds of mental action, aiding in different ways and degrees the maintenance of individual life, and various others which do not aid this maintenance, or do so in but remote ways. And then, beyond the preservation of a right proportion between the life-subserving occupations and the occupations which do not directly subserve life, there is the preservation of right proportions among the subdivisions of these last—right proportions between culture and amusement and between different kinds of culture and different kinds of amusements. The conception of a mean does not touch the numerous problems thus presented; since it implies a compromise between two things, and not a number of compromises among many things.

Any one on glancing round may see that the great majority of lives are more or less distorted by failure to maintain balanced amounts of the activities, bodily and mental, required for complete health and happiness; and that there are here, therefore, many problems with which the ethics of individual life has to concern itself.

244. But while this division of ethics which has the control of private conduct for its function, may, by its ordered judgments, serve to prevent each kind of activity from diverging very far on either side of moderation; and while it may serve to prevent extreme disproportions among the different kinds of activities; it cannot be expected to produce by its injunctions a perfectly regulated conduct.

Only by the gradual remolding of human nature into fitness for the social state, can either the private life or the public life of each man, be made what it should be. In respect of private life, especially, the problems presented are so complex and so variable, that nothing like definite solutions of them can be reached by any intellectual processes, however methodic and however careful. They can be completely solved only by the organic adjustment of constitution to conditions. All inferior creatures, incapable of elaborating reasoned codes of conduct, are guided entirely by the promptings of instincts and desires, severally adapted to the needs of their lives. In each species the feelings are kept duly adjusted in their strengths to the requirements, and duly proportioned to one another, by direct or indirect equilibration, or by both; since, inevitably, the individuals in which the balance of them is not good, disappear, or fail to rear progeny. There are many who, while they recognize this necessity as operative throughout subhuman life, tacitly deny that it is operative throughout human life, or, at any rate, ignore its operation; and they do this notwithstanding their knowledge of the immense divergences of habits and sentiments, which multiform human nature itself has acquired under the different circumstances it has been subject to. Any one, however, who contemplates the contrast between those who witness with pleasure the tortures of men and animals, and those who cannot be induced to witness such tortures because of the sympathetic pain they experience, may infer from this single contrast, a capacity for modification which makes possible an approximately complete adjustment of the nature to the life which has to be led—an adjustment towards which there will be appreciable progress, when there have died out the fatuous legislators who are continually impeding it.

Eventually, then, the degree of each of the activities constituting private conduct, and the proportions among the different activities, must be spontaneously regulated by the natural promptings. In the meantime, all which the ethics of individual life can do, is to keep clearly in view, and continually to emphasize, the needs to which the nature has to be adjusted.

245. Finally, there must be uttered a caution against striving too strenuously to reach the ideal—against straining the nature too much out of its inherited form. For the normal re-molding can go on but slowly.

As there must be moderation in other things, so there must be moderation in self-criticism. Perpetual contemplation of our own actions produces a morbid consciousness, quite unlike that normal consciousness accompanying right actions spontaneously done; and from a state of unstable equilibrium long maintained by effort, there is apt to be a fall towards stable equilibrium, in which the primitive nature reasserts itself. Retrogression rather than progression may hence result.

REFERENCES

To find the authority for any statement in the text, the reader is to proceed as follows: Observing the number of the section in which the statement occurs, he will first look out, in the following pages, the corresponding number, which is printed in conspicuous type. Among the references succeeding this number, he will then look for the name of the person, tribe, people, or nation concerning which the statement is made (the names in the references standing in the same order as that which they have in the text); and that it may more readily catch the eye, each such name is printed in italics. In the parentheses following the name, will be found the volume and page of the work referred to, preceded by the first three or four letters of the author's name; and when more than one of his works has been used, the first three or four letters of the title of the one containing the particular statement. The meanings of these abbreviations, employed to save the space that would be occupied by frequent repetitions of full titles, is shown at the end of the references; where will be found arranged in alphabetical order, these initial syllables of authors' names, &c., and opposite to them the full titles of the works referred to.

REFERENCES TO VOLUME I

13. Aristotle (Arist. Nicom. Ethics, I, 7; *Ib.* I, 8, Gillies' translation). **14.** Hutcheson (Hutch, ch. IV). **14.*** Blessed (Matthew v. 7, 9; Psalms xli. 1). **18.** Dymond (Dym. pref. ix; ch. II). **52.** Bodo and Dhimals (J.A.S.B. xviii, 741). **60.** Plato (Pla. Rep., Davies and Vaughan's trans. xxix)—Aristotle (Arist. Nic. Eth. I, 8; *Ib.* X, 7)—*Jews* (Psalms xvii. 2)—*Early Christians* (Collossians iv. 1)—*Aristotle* (Arist. Nic. Eth. V, 1). **74.** "Love thy neighbor" (Leviticus xix. 18). **89.** Kant (Kant, 54–5). **106.** Socrates (Xen. Mem. III, 9)—*Plato* (Grote, Plato, i, 420, 479)—Aristotle (Arist. Nic. Eth. III, 4, Williams' trans.)—*Stoics* (Zeller, *The Stoics, Epicureans, and Sceptics,* translated by Reichel, pp. 253–4)—*Epicurus* (Zeller, 456)—*Kant* (Kant, 54–5). **112.** Veddahs (Bailey in T.E.S.L. n.s. ii, 302)—*Zulus* (Call. pt. ii, 146–7)—*Australians* (Smyth, i, 107)— *Tongans* (Mar. ii, 100)—*Gold Coast* (Ellis, T-S.P. 11)—Anc. Mexicans (Zur. 138–141)— *Hebrews* (Schenk, v, 431; Bruch, 368; Fritz. v, *xxxiv*)—*Rig-Veda* (R.V. i, 33, 4, 5; vi, 14, 3; x, 81, 7; iv, 17, 16)—*Rameses* (R.P. ii, 70)—*Chryses* (Hom. "Iliad," Lang, bk. i, 2)—Med. Europe (Brace, 230). **113.** Assyrians (R.P. N.S. iv, 56; R.P. v, 8; xi, 49; ix, 42)—*Egyptians* (R.P. ii, 70–72). **114.** Karens (Mason in J.A.S.B., xxxvii, Pt. ii, 143)—*Dakotas* (Scho. iv, 70)—*Iroquois* (Morg. 119)—Anc. Indians (Maha. xiii, 3880; Bhàravi, in Wil. 459; Cural, in Con. 220)—*Chinese* (Alex. 117, 254–5)—*Egyptians* (Renouf, 72). **115.** Bp. of Durham (Herald of Peace, Dec. 1890)—*L.* Cranbrook (*Standard,* July 12, 1889)—*Dr. Moorhouse* (*Manchester Examiner,* May 14, 1887)—*German Emperor* (Daily Papers, June 18, 1888). **116.** Malagasy (Drury, 192)—*Hebrews* (Bruch, 311)—*Egyptians* (Poole in Cont. Rev. Aug. 1881, p. 286)—*Mill* (Mill, 124). **117.** Otaheitans (Hawke. ii, 101–2)—Anc. Indians (Maha. iii, 1124, etc.)—*Ramayana* (Rich. 149)—*Chinese* (Edkins, 85, 179). **120.** Arabs (Palg. 10–11)—*Russians* (Niemo. ii, 167)—*Matelhapces* (Licht. ii, 306)—*Arabs* (Baker, 263)—*Makololo* (Liv. Zamb. 285)—*Eq.* Africans (Reade, 260)— *Araucanians* (Smith, 214)—*Chinooks* (Lewis & C. 439)—*Chukchi* (Erm. ii, 530, *note*)— *Mahabharata* (Wheel. i, 121)—*French* (Leber, xiii, 10–11)—*Patagonians* (Falk. 125)— *Dakotas* (Irving, 134)—*Esquimaux* (Crantz, i, 154)—*Caffers* (Thomp. ii, 354)—*Mayorunas* (Reade, 158)—*Bambarans* (Caillié, i, 398)—*Wa-kavirondo* (Thom. 487)—*Arabs* (Peth. 151)—*Khonds* (Macpherson in Perc. 345)—*Tahitians* (Cooke in Hawke. ii, 203)—*Vateans* (Turn. "P.R." 450)—*Fijians* (Wilkes, iii, 100). **121.** Innuits (Hall, ii, 315)—*Ancient Peruvians* (Garci. bk. ii, ch. 12). **126.** Bushmen (Liv. "Miss. Trav." 159)—*Uganda* (Wils. & Fel. i, 224)—*Bedouins* (Burt. "Pilg." iii, 246–7)—*Kukis* (Rown. 187)—*Pathans* (Temp. "Rep." 63). **127.** Ancient Indians (R.V. i, 74; vii, 6, 2; vii, 32, 7; Maha. xii, 5290; v. 5617)—*Assyrians* (R.P. i, 49, 78; v, 9; *Ib.* N.S. ii, 137, 143, 153; iv, 61)—*Sucvi* (Caesar, iv, 2; vi, 21)—*Mottoes* (Various Peerages)—*Wolseley* (Wolse. 5). **128.** Ancient Indians (Maha. xiii, 5571, in Wil. 448; Jones, Works, iii, 242)—*Persians* (Sadi, i, st. 33; ii, st. 4)—*Chinese* (Lao-Tsze, xxxi; Conf. Anal. xii, 19; Mencius, bk. i, pt. i, ch. 6; *Ib.* iv, i, 14)—*Sumatrans* (Mars. 173)—*Thârus* (Nesfield in *Calc. Rev.* 1885, lxxx, 41)—*Iroquois* (Morg. 92, 330). **129.** Fijians (Ersk. 247; Will. i, 218, 246–7)—*Waganda* (Wils. & Fel. i, 201)— *Charlemagne* (Hallam, 16). **131.** Comanches (Möll. i, 185)—*Patagonians* (Snow, ii, 233)—*E.* Africans (Liv. "Miss. Trav." 526)—*Kalmucks* (Pallas i, 105) *Kirghis* (Atkin. "Amoor," 206: *Ih. Sib. 500*) *Merv Turcomans* (O'Don. ii, 407, 278)—*Pathans* (Temp. "Rep." 62)—*Afridi* (Rown. 123–4)—*Kukis* (Dalt. 45)—*Mongols* (Gil. 273)—*Angamis* (Stewart, in J.A.S.B. xxiv, 652)—*Chinooks* (Waitz, iii, 337)—*Waganda* (Wils. & Fel. i, 224)—*Fijians* (Will. i, 127). **132.** Vishnu (R.V. i, 61, 7)—*Tvashtri & Indra* (Muir, O.S.T. v, 229; Wheel. i, 244)—*Norse* (Dasent, xxxiv)—*Prim.* Germans (Caesar, vi, 21)—*French* (Ste. Pal. ii, 47)—*Thirty Years' War* (Gind. ii, 393–7). **133.** Wood-Veddahs (Hartshorne in *Fort. Rev.* Mar. 1876, p. 416)—*Esquimaux* (King in J.E.S. 1848, i, 131)—*Fuegians* (Darwin in Fitz. iii, 242; Snow, i, 328)—*New Guinea* (Macgil. i, 270; Earl, 80)—*Lette* (Kolff, 61)—*Vera Cruz Indians* (Baker in P.R.G.S. Sept. 1887, p. 571)—*Thârus* (Nesfield in *Calc. Rev.* lxxx, 1, 41)—*Iroquois* (Morg. 333). **135.** Australians (Grey, ii, 240)—*Sioux*

(Burt. C.S. 125)—*Guiana* (Schom. i, 158)—*Fijians* (Will. i, 186)—*New Zealanders* (Thoms. ii, 86)—*Kukis* (Macrae in As. Res. vii, 189)—*Arabs* (Peth. 27)—*E. Africans* (Burt. C.A. ii, 329)—*Japanese* (Dening, pt. ii, 81)—*Anc. Indians* (R.V. x, 87; vii, 104; Wheel. i, 287–8, 290). **136.** *Anc. Indians* (Manu, ii, 161; vi, 47–8, in Wil. 283; Cural, in Con. 427)—*Persians* (Con. 226; Sadi, ii, st. 41; Hafiz, in Jones, iii, 244)—*Chinese* (Lao-Tsze, lxiii; Mencius, bk. v, pt. i, ch. iii; Conf. Anal. xiv, 36). **137.** *Lepchas* (Campbell in J.E.S.L. July, 1869, pp. 150–1). **139.** *Philip. Islands* (Fore. 213)— *Quianganes* (P.S.M. July, 1891, p. 390)—*Arabs* (Burck. 84–5). **140.** *Guiana* (Im Thurn, 213–4). **141.** *Anc. Indians* (Wheel. i, 102, 103 *note*)—*Todas* (Shortt in T.E.S.L. N.S. vii, 241)—*Bodo & Dhimáls* (J.A.S.B. xviii, pt. ii, 744)—*Hos* (Hayes in Dalt. 194)—*Pueblos* (Ban. i, 555, 547)—*Manansas* (Holub, ii, 206–11)—*Thârus* (Nesfield in *Calc. Rev.* lxxx, 41)—*Let-htas* (Fytche, i, 343). **144.** *Arabs* (Palg. i, 37)—*Kirghiz* (Atkin. Sib. 506)—*E. Africans* (Burt. C.A. ii, 274)—*Fijians* (Wilkes, iii, 77; Jackson, in Ersk. 460)—*Ainos* (Bird, ii, 101)—*Australians* (T.E.S.L. N.S. iii, 246)—*Samoans* (Jackson, in Ersk. 415)—*Kaffirs* (Licht. i, 272)—*Africans* (Wint. i, 213)—*N. American Indians* (Morg. 327)—*New Zealanders* (Angas, ii, 22; Thoms. i, 191, 98)—*St. Augustine Island* (Turn. Samoa, 292–3). **145.** *Bushmen* (Burch. ii, 54)—*Hottentots* (Burch. ii, 349; Kolben, i, 165)—*East Africans* (Liv. "Miss. Trav." 601)—*Loango* (Proyart in Pink. xvi, 565)—*Australians* (T.E.S.L. N.S. iii, 271)—*Sand. Islanders* (Van. iii, 21)—*Guiana* (Brett, 276)—*Thibet* (Bogle, 110). **146.** *Australians* (Eyre, i, 278; Sturt, i, 114; ii, 105)—*Tasmanians* (Mered. i, 201)—*Tongans* (Mar. i, 228). **147.** *Anc. Indians* (R.V. x, 107, 2, 5, &c.; Manu, iii, 105, 106; iv, 29; iii, 98)—*Apastamba* (Bühler, 114, 119)—*Persians* (Shâyast, xii, 4, in West, 341; Sadi, viii, 60; *Ib.* viii, 2)—*Chinese* (Conf. Anal. vi, 28; viii, 11; x, 15). **148.** *Early Germans* (Tac. *Germ.* xxi)—*Christians* (Lecky, ii, 93; Browne, pt. ii, sec. 2). **149.** *New Zealanders* (Angas, i, 312; Cook in Hawke. iii, 447; Thoms. i, 149)—*East Africans* (Burt. C.A. ii, 333)—*Fijians* (Will. i, 55, 133)—*Dacotas* (Burt. C.S. 124–5)—*Nagas* (Butler, 58)—*Steins* (Colq. Shans, 160)—*Chrysê* (Colq. *Chrysê*, ii, 120, 268)—*Malayan Tribes* (Favre, 97–100, 8, 73, 72, 100–2)—*Arafuras* (Kolff, 161–3). **150.** *Bushmen* (Moffat, 58; Licht. ii, 195; Moffat, 156)—*Hottentots* (Kolben, i, 332, 165, 142, 318)—*Dyaks* (Boyle, 223.) **151.** *Karens* (Mason in J.A.S.B. xxxvii, pt. ii, 144)—*Honduras* (Herr. iv, 141)— *Loando* (Monte, i, 244)—*Dahomans* (Burt. "Miss." i, 195, *note*; *Ib.* ii, 190, *note*)— *Ashantees* (Burt. W. & W. 121, 128)—*Damaras* (Baines, 243; Galt. 190)—*Dahomans* (Burt. "Miss." i, 345)—*Marutse* (Holub, ii, 297)—*West Africans* (Wolseley in *Fort. Rev.* Dec. 1888)—*Prairie Indians* (Burt. C.S. 124–5)—*Comanches* (Bollaert in J.E.S. 1850, ii, 269). **152.** *Greeks* (Grote, ii, 32). **153.** *Veddahs* (Tenn. ii, 445)—*Tannese* (Turn. "P.R." 92)—*Papuans* (Jukes, ii, 248)—*Dyaks* (Boyle, 215)—*Malagasy* (Drury, 230)—*Esquimaux* (Hall, ii, 312)—*Iroquois* (Morg. 171)—*Chippewas* (Scho. ii, 139)—*Araucanians* (Thomps. i, 416, 403)—*Mandingos* (Park in Pink. xvi, 871)—*Luan* (Kolff, 127). **154.** *Anc. Indians* (Maha. iii, 16782, 16796, 16619, &c.)—*Zend-Avesta* (Haug, 242)—*Persians* (Sadi, i, st. 10)—*Egyptians* (Dunck. i, 203; Poole in *Cont. Rev.* Aug. 1881, p. 287)—*Chinese* (Legge, R. of Ch. 224; Conf. D. of Mean, ch. xx; Mencius, bk. ii, pt. i, ch. 6; bk. i, pt. i, ch. 7). **155.** *Karens* (Mason in J.A.S.B. xxxvii, pt. ii, 152)—*Afridis* (MacGreg. i, 27)— *Fijians* (Will. i, 128–9)—*Veddahs* (Tenn. ii, 444; Prid. 460). **157.** *Dakotas* (Burt. C.S. 130)—*Mishmis* (Grif. 40)—*Kirghiz* (Vali. 279)—*Fijians* (Will. i, 124)—*Uganda* (Wils. & Fel. i, 224)—*Cent. Americans* (Laet, bk. ix, ch. 2; Dun. 336)—*Philip. Islands* (Fore. 186–7). **158.** *Greeks* (Mahaf. 27, 150)—*Merovingian Period* (Mart. ii, 709; Salv. iv, c. 14)—*Early Feudal Period* (Mart. ii, 709)—*French Monarchy* (Crowe, ii, 201)—*Lecky* (Lecky, i, 138). **159.** *Kois* (Morris, 89)—*Sowrahs* (Shortt, pt. iii, 38)—*Cent. Indians* (Fors. 164)—*Ramosis* (Sinclair in I.A. July, 1874, 186)—*Sontháls* (Sherwill in J.A.S.B. xx, 554; Man, 21)—*Puluyan* (Oppert in M.J.L.S. 1887–8, p. 104)—*Wood-Veddahs* (Bailey in T.E.S.L. N.S. ii, 291)—*Ostiaks, &c.* (Rev. Sib. ii, 130)—*Hottentots* (Barrow, i, 101; Kolben, i, 59)—*Iroquois* (Morg. 335)—*Patagonians* (Snow, ii, 233)—*Khonds* (Macpherson in J.R.A.S. vii, 196)—*Kolîs* (Sinclair, in I.A. July, 1874, p. 188)—*Khonds* (Macph. Report,

27). **160.** *Mexicans* (Tern. v, 102)—*E. Africans* (Liv. Zamb. 309)—*Egyptians* (St. John, 77)—*France* (Mich. i, 341)—*English* (Kirkus in *Fort. Rev.* Nov. 1866, p. 644). **162.** *Araucanians* (Smith, 201)—*Arawaks* (Hillhouse in J.R.G.S. ii, 229)—*Dakotas* (Burt. C.S. 131)—*E. Africans* (Burt, C.A. ii, 333)—*Bedouins* (Burck. 201, 56)—*Chippewayans* (Hear. 345)—*Kamtschadales* (Kotze. ii, 16)—*Dakotas* (Burt. C.S. 131)—*Fijians*, Will. i, 177)—*Hottentots* (Kolben, i, 123)—*Zulus* (Thomp. ii, 418)—*Karens* (Mason in J.A.S.B. xxxvii, pt. ii, 144)—*Esquimaux* (Hall, ii, 314). **163.** *Assyrians* (Smith, 14)—*Hindus* (Müller, H.L. 333–4)—*Chinese* (Conf. Anal. i, 2; Edkins, 155; Legge, R. of Ch. 104)—*Egypt* (Poole in *Cont. Rev.* Aug. 1881, p. 286). **164.** *Khonds* (Rown. 101)—*Bhils* (Hunter in J.R.A.S. viii, 189; Mal. C.I. ii, 180)—*Kalmucks* (Pallas, i, 106)—*Sgaus* (Mason in J.A.S.B. xxxv, pt. ii, 12)—*Chinese* (Conf. Anal. I, 7; X, 4)—*Persians* (Sadi, i, st. 28, 31; *Ib.* I, 25)—*Anc. Indians* (Manu, vii, 8)—*Egyptians* (R.P. N.S. iii, 21; Dunck. i, 184)—*Mottoes* (Burke's & Debrett's Peerages). **165.** *Mexicans* (Herr. iii, 203; Tern. ii, 195; Herr. iv, 126)—*Fijians* (Ersk. 208, 456; Will. i, 30)—*Dahomans* (Ellis, E.-S.P. 162–3; Dalzel, 69; Ellis, *l.c.*)—*Frederick II* (Gould, ii, 302)—*France.* **168.** *Chippewas* (Scho. v, 150)—*Snakes* (Lewis, 308)—*Dakotas* (Burt. C.S. 126)—*Iroquois* (Morg. 329)—*Esquimaux* (Crantz, i, 154)—*Chippewayans* (Hear. 90)—*Guiana Tribes* (Brett. 27)—*Araucanians* (Smith, 214)—*Chippewayans* (Frank. Journey, 161)—*Creeks* (Scho. v, 272)—*Tupis* (Sou. i, 250)—*Palagonians* (Falk. 125)—*Hottentots* (Kolben, i, 159)—*Bechuanas* (Burch. ii, 564)—*Kaffirs* (Shoo. 79)—*Ashanti* (Beech. 129)—*Fernando Po* (J.E.S. 1850, ii, 114)—*Lower Niger* (Allen & T. i, 396)—*Chinooks* (Ross, Oregon, 92)—*Damaras* (And. Ngami, 231)—*Congo* (Tuck. 120)—*Dahome* (Burt. "Miss." ii, 248)—*Mishmees* (Coop. 207)—*Bushmen* (Spar. i, 198)—*Arabs* (Niebuhr, in Pink. x, 131)—*E. Africans* (Liv. Zamb. 67)—*Abyssinia* (Bruce, iv, 474)—*Canaris* (Cieza, ch. 44). **169.** *Khonds* (Camp. 50)—*Javans* (Raf. i, 246)—*Caribs* (Schom. ii, 427–8)—*S.E. India* (Lew. 90–1)—*Santals* (Sherwill in J.A.S.B. xx, 554). **170.** *Manu* (Manu iv, 238, in Wil. 285)—*Book of the Dead* (Bunsen, v, 254–5)—*Persians* (Alb. 21; Fram. 48). **171.** *Greeks* (Arist. Pol. bk. iii, ch. 5). **172.** *Manansas* (Holub, ii, 211). **173.** *Confucius* (Anal. I. 14; VIII. 21). **174.** *Australians* (Grey, ii, 277–8; Christison in J.A.I. vii, 148)—*Esquimaux* (Lyon, 181–2)—*Yakuts, etc.* (Coch. i, 254; Wrang. 384; Erm. ii, 361). **175.** *Tahitians* (Cook in Hawke. ii, 202)—*Arabs* (Palg. i, 10)—*Ancients* (Manu, ii, 57; Muir, O.S.T. v. 324)—*Egyptians* (Dunck. i, 225). **176.** *Arafuras* (Kolff, 161)—*Ancient Indians and Greeks* (Müller, R.V. i, 118; Muir, O.S.T. v, 260)—*Dahomans* (Burt. "Miss." ii, 250)—*Ainos* (Bird, ii, 96, 102)—*Polynesians* (Will. i, 141–5)—*Ainos* (Bird, ii, 68). **177.** *Kalmucks* (Pallas, i, 131)—*Khonds* (Camp. 164)—*Guiana* (Brett, 349)—*Guatemalans* (Haef. 406)—*Peruvians* (Garci. bk. vi, ch. 22)—*Yucatanese* (Landa, secs. xxii, xxxii)—*Mexicans* (Saha. bk. i, ch. 22)—*Veddahs* (Bailey in T.E.S.L. N.S. ii, 291)—*Lepchas* (Campbell in J.E.S.L. July, 1869, p. 147)—*Sumatrans* (Mars. 173)—*Foolas, etc.* (Wint. i, 72)—*Negroes* (Waitz, ii, 86). **178.** *Gauls* (Diod. v, 2)—*Prim. Germans* (Tac. xxii)—*Eonius* (Greg. v, 41)—*Charlemagne* (Egin. ch. 24)—*French* (Mont. 14)—*English* (Massey, ii, 60). **179.** *Asiatics* (Balf. i, 164)—*Bedouins* (Burt. Pilg. iii, 12). **180.** *Kasias* (Yule in J.A.S.B. xiii, 620)—*Cyrus* (Plut. *Symp.* lib. I. qu. iv). **181.** *Thibet* (Wilson, 235). **182.** *Early Indians* (Wheel. i, 131–6, 142; Maha. v, 14667, &c.)—*Ladākhis* (Drew, 287, 239, 240, 250)—*Ancient Indians* (Muir, O.S.T. iv, 41; v, 324; Maha. i, 4719–22, in Muir, O.S.T. ii, 336). **183.** *Chinooks* (Lewis, 439; Ross, 92)—*Sioux* (Lewis, 77)—*Creeks* (Scho. v, 272)—*Tupis* (Sou. i, 241)—*Caribs* (Waitz, iii, 382)—*Esquimaux* (Lubb. 556)—*Chippewayans* (Hear. 129)—*Dakotas* (Burt. C.S. 142)—*Nicaragua* (Pala. 120; Herr. iii, 340–1)—*Kamtschadales, &c.* (Ploss, i, 293)—*Kalmucks* (Pallas, i, 105)—*Kirghizes* (Vali. 85)—*Mongols* (Prjev. i, 70)—*Karens* (Masons in J.A.S.B. xxxv, pt. ii, 19)—*Todas* (Shortt in T.E.S.L. vii, 240)—*Shoa* (Harris, iii, 167)—*Upper Congo* (Tuck. 181)—*Bushmen* (Licht. ii, 48–9)—*Ladrone Isl.* (Frey. ii, 369)—*Pelew Isl.* (Kubary, 50–1)—*Mandans* (Cat. i, 121)—*Chippewas* (Keat. ii, 165)—*Kaffirs* (Barrow, i, 160)—*Tongans* (Mar. ii, 161)—*Sumatrans* (Mars. 222)—*Borneo* (Low, 300)—*Dory* (Kops in Earl, 81)—*Loyalty Isl.* (Ersk. 341)—

Fuegians (Snow in T.E.S.L. i, 262)—*Musheras* (Càlc. Rev. April, 1888, p. 222)—*Bodo & Dhimáls* (Hodgson in J.A.S.B. xviii, 719)—*Santals* (Dalt. 217)—*Veddahs* (Virchow in A.k.A.W. 1881, 21)—*Australians* (Tap. 19)—*Fijians* (Ersk. 255; Sec. 191–2)—*Tahitians* (Cook in Hawke. ii, 196, 188). **184.** *Wotyaks* (Buch, 45)—*Chibchas* (Simon, 254)—*Japanese* (Dixon, 472–3). **186.** *Tahitians* (Cook in Hawke. ii, 186)—*Dahomans* (Burt. "Miss." i, 83)—*E. Africans* (Burt. C.A. ii, 332). **187.** *Ku-ka-tha* (Tap. 101, 94, 95, 93). **190.** *Patháns* (Oliv. 139–40)—*Fijians* (Ersk. 461–4)—*Australians* (Grey, ii, 239)—*Fijians* (Ersk. 228)—*Bilochs* (Oliv. 29)—*Bantyre* (MacDon. i, 185)—*Wotyaks* (Buch, 46). **191.** *Bilochs* (Oliv. 24)—*Ainos* (Bird, ii, 103)—*Let-htas* (Fytche, i, 343). **192.** *Wolseley* (Wolse. 5; Debrett). **239.** *Uganda* (Wils. and Fel. i, 186–7)—*Fijians* (See. 190)—*Motu-Motu* (Chalm. 162–3). **242.** *Mean* (I.G. Smith, 57).

TITLES OF WORKS

A.k.A.W.—*Abhandlungen der Königlichen Akademie der Wissenschaften.* Berlin.
Alb.—Albitis (F.) *The Morality of All Nations.* 1850.
Alex.—Alexander (G.G.) *Confucius, the Great Teacher.* 1890.
Allen.—Allen (Wm.) and Thomson (T.R.H.) *A Narrative of the Expedition to the River Niger in 1841.* 2 vols. 1848.
And.—Andersson (C.J.) *Lake Ngami.* 1856.
Angas.—Angas (G.F.) *Savage Life and Scenes in Australia and New Zealand.* 1847.
Arist.—Aristotle's *Politics.*
Arist.—Aristotle's *Nicomachean Ethics.*
As. Res.—*Asiatic Researches.*
Atkin.—Atkinson (T.W.) *Oriental and Western Siberia.* 1858.
Atkin.—Atkinson (T.W.) *Travels in the Regions of the Upper and Lower Amoor, etc.* 1860.
Baines.—Baines (T.) *Explorations in South-West Africa.* 1864.
Baker.—Baker (Sir S.) *The Nile Tributaries of Abyssinia.* 1867.
Balf.—Balfour (E.) *Cyclopoedia of India.* 3rd Ed. 3 vols. 1875.
Ban.—Bancroft (H.H.) *Native Races of the Pacific States of North America.* 5 vols. 1875.
Barrow.—Barrow (Sir J.) *Travels into the Interior of Southern Africa.*
Beech.—Beecham (J.) *Ashantee and the Gold Coast.* 1841.
Bird.—Bird (Isabella) *Unbeaten Tracks in Japan.* 2 vols. 1880.
Bogle.—Bogle, *Narratives of the Mission of George Bogle to Thibet, &c.* Ed. C.R. Markham. 1876.
Boyle.—Boyle (F.) *Adventures among the Dyaks of Borneo.* 1865.
Brace.—Brace (C.L.) *Gesta Christi.* 2nd Ed. 1886.
Brett.—Brett (Rev. W.H.) *The Indian Tribes of Guiana.* 1868.
Browne.—Browne (Sir T.) *Religio Medici.* 1656.
Bruce.—Bruce (J.) *Travels to Discover the Source of the Nile.* 1804.
Bruch.—Bruch (J.Fr.) *Weisheitslehre der Hebräer.* Strassburg, 1851.
Buch.—Buch (M.) *Die Wotjäken.* Helsingfors, 1882.
Bühler.—Bühler (G.) *The Sacred Laws of the Aryas.* Oxf.
Bunsen.—Bunsen (Baron C.C.J.) *Egypt's Place in Universal History.* Trans. by C.H. Cottrell. 5 vols. 1848–67.
Burch.—Burchell (W.J.) *Travels in the Interior of Southern Africa.* 2 vols. 1822–4. 4 to.
Burck.—Burckhardt (J.L.) *Notes on the Bedouins and Wahábys.* 1829. 4 to.
Burt.—Burton (R.F.) *The City of the Saints, &c.* 1861.
Burt.—Burton (R.F.) *The Lake Regions of Central Africa.* 2 vols. 1860.
Burt.—Burton (R.F.) *A Mission to Gelele, King of Dahome.* 1864.

Burt.—Burton (R.F.) *Personal Narrative of a Pilgrimage to El-Medinah and Meccah*. 3 vols. 1855, etc.
Burt.—Burton (R.F.) *Wit and Wisdom from West Africa*. 1865.
Butler.—Butler (Maj. J.) *Travels and Adventures in the Province of Assam*. 1855.
Caesar.—Caesar (C. Jul.) *Commentarii de Bello Gallico*.
Caillié.—Caillié (Réné) *Travels through Central Africa to Timbuctoo*. 2 vols.
Calc. Rev.—*The Calcutta Review*.
Call.—Callaway (Rev. H.) *The Religious System of the Amazulu*. 3 Parts. Natal, 1869.
Camp.—Campbell (Maj.-Gen. J.) *A Personal Narrative of Thirteen Years' Service amongst the Wild Tribes of Khondistan*. 1864.
Cat.—Catlin (G.) *Letters and Notes on the Manners, Customs, and Condition of the North American Indians*. 2 vols. 1841.
Chalm.—Chalmers (J.) *Pioneering in New Guinea*. 1887.
Cieza.—Cieza de Leon (P. de) *Travels, A.D.* 1532–50. Trans. by C.R. Markham. 1864.
Coch.—Cochrane (J.D.) *A Narrative of a Pedestrian Journey through Russia and Siberian Tartary*. 4th Ed. 2 vols. 1825.
Colq.—Colquhoun (A.R.) *Across Chrysê.* 2 vols. 1883.
Colq.—Colquhoun (A.R.) *Among the Shans*.
Con.—Conway (M.D.) *The Sacred Anthology*. 1874.
Conf.—Confucius, *The Analects* and *The Doctrine of the Mean*. (In Legge's *Chinese Classics*. Vol. I.)
Cont. Rev.—*The Contemporary Review*.
Coop.—Cooper (T.T.) *The Mishmee Hills*. 1873.
Crantz.—Crantz (D.) *History of Greenland*. Translated. 2 vols. 1820.
Crowe.—Crowe (E.E.) *The History of France*. 5 vols. 1858–68.
Dalt.—Dalton (E.T.) *Descriptive Ethnology of Bengal*. Calc. 1872.
Dalzel.—Dalzel (A.) *The History of Dahomey*. 1793. 4 to.
Dasent.—Dasent (Sir G.W.) *The Story of Burnt Njal*. 2 vols. 1861.
Dening.—Dening (W.) *The Life of Miyamoto Musashi*. 2 Pts. 1887.
Diod.—*Diodorus Siculus, The Historical Library of*, made English by G. Booth. 2 vols. 1814.
Dixon.—Dixon (W.G.) *The Land of the Morning*. Edin. 1882.
Drew.—Drew (F.) *The Jummoo and Kashmir Territories*. 1875.
Drury.—Drury (R.) *Madagascar*. 1729.
Dunck.—Duncker (Max) *The History of Antiquity*. Trans. by E. Abbott. 6 vols. 1879, etc.
Dun.—Dunlop (R.G.) *Travels in Central America*. 1847. 4 to.
Dym.—Dymond (J.) *Essays on the Principles of Morality*. 7th Edit.
Earl.—Earl (G.W.) *Native Races of the Indian Archipelago: Papuans*. 1853.
Edkins.—Edkins (J.) *The Religious Condition of the Chinese*. 1859.
Egin.—Eginhardus, *Life of the Emperor Karl the Great*. Trans. by W. Glaister. 1877.
Ellis.—Ellis (A.B.) *The Ewe-Speaking Peoples of the Slave Coast of West Africa*. 1890.
Ellis.—Ellis (A.B.) *The Tshi-Speaking Peoples of the Gold Coast of West Africa*. 1887.
Erm.—Erman (G.A.) *Travels in Siberia*. Trans. by Cooley. 2 vols. 1845.
Ersk.—Erskine (J.E.) *Journal of a Cruise among the Islands of the Western Pacific*. 1853.
Eyre.—Eyre (E.J.) *Journal of Expeditions of Discovery into Central Australia*. 2 vols. 1845.
Falk.—Falkner (T.) *A Description of Patagonia*. Hereford, 1774.
Favre.—Favre (Abbé) *An Account of the Wild Tribes Inhabiting the Malayan Peninsula*. Paris, 1865.
Fitz.—Fitzroy (Adm. R.) *Narrative of the Surveying Voyages of His Majesty's Ships Adventurer and Beagle*. 3 vols. 1839–40.
Fore.—Foreman (J.) *The Philippine Islands*. 1890.
Fors.—Forsyth (Capt. J.) *Highlands of Central India*. 2nd Ed.
Fort Rev.—*The Fortnightly Review*.

Fram.—Framjee (Dosabhoy) *The Parsees.* 1858.

Frank.—Franklin (Capt. J.) *Narrative of a Journey to the Shores of the Polar Sea.* 1823. 4 to.

Frey.—Freycinet (L.C.D. de) *Voyage autour du Monde.* Paris, 1827.

Fritz.—Fritzsche (O.F.) & Grimm (C.L.W.) *Kurzgefasstes exegetisches Handbuch zu den Apocryphen des Alten Testaments.* 6 Parts. 1851–60.

Fytche.—Fytche (Gen. A.) *Burma, Past and Present.* 2 vols. 1878.

Galt.—Galton (F.) *Narrative of an Exploration in Tropical South Africa.*

Garci.—Garcilasso de la Vega, *First Part of the Royal Commentaries of the Yncas* [1604]. Tran. by C.R. Markham. 2 vols. 1869–71.

Gil.—Gilmour (J.) *Among the Mongols.*

Gind.—Gindely (A.) *History of the Thirty Years' War.* Trans. by Ten Brook. 2 vols. N.Y. 1884.

Gould.—Gould (S. Baring-) *Germany Present and Past.* 2 vols.

Greg.—Gregory (of Tours) *Histoire ecclésiastique des Francs.* Translated. 3 vols. Paris, 1836–8.

Grey.—Grey (Sir G.) *Journals of Two Expeditions of Discovery in North-West and Western Australia.* 2 vols. 1841.

Grif.—Griffith (W.) *Journals of Travels in Assam.* Calc. 1847.

Grote.—Grote (G.) *History of Greece.* 4th Ed. 10 vols. 1872.

Haef.—Haefkens (T.) *Centraal Amerika.* Dordrecht, 1832.

Hall.—Hall (Capt. C.F.) *Life with the Esquimaux.* 2 vols. 1864.

Hallam.—Hallam (H.) *Europe during the Middle Ages.* 4th Ed. 1869.

Harris.—Harris (Sir W.C.) *The Highlands of Ethiopia.* 3 vols. 1844.

Haug.—Haug (M.) *Essays on the Sacred Language, Writings, and Religion of the Parsees.* 1878.

Hawke.—Hawkesworth (J.) *An account of the Voyages undertaken . . . by Comm. Byron, Capt. Wallis, Capt. Carteret, and Capt. Cook, etc.* 3 vols. 1773. 4 to.

Hear.—Hearne (S.) *Journey from Prince of Wales's Fort, etc.* Dub. 1796.

Herr.—Herrera (A. de) *The General History of the Vast Continent and Islands of America* [1601]. Trans. by J. Stevens. 6 vols. 1725–6.

Holub.—Holub (Emil) *Seven Years in South Africa.* 2 vols. 1881.

Hom.—Homer, *The Iliad,* done into English prose by A. Lang and others. 1883.

Hutch.—Hutcheson (F.) *A System of Moral Philosophy.*

I.A.—*The Indian Antiquary.* Bombay.

Irving.—Irving (Washington) *Astoria.* 1850.

J.A.I.—*Journal of the Anthropological Institute.*

J.A.S.B.—*Journal of the Asiatic Society, Bengal.*

J.E.S.L.—*Journal of the Ethnological Society, London.*

Jones.—Jones (Sir Will.) *Works.* 13 vols. 1807.

J.R.A.S.—*Journal of the Royal Asiatic Society, London.*

J.R.G.S.—*Journal of the Royal Geographical Society, London.*

Jukes.—Jukes (J.B.) *Narrative of the Surveying Voyage of H.M.S. "Fly,"* 1842–6. 2 vols. 1847.

Kant.—Kant (E.) *Critique of Practical Reason and Other Works on the Theory of Ethics.* Trans. by T.K. Abbott.

Keat.—Keating (W.H.) *Narrative of an Expedition to the Source of St. Peter's River, Lake Winnepeck, etc. in 1823.* 2 vols. 1825.

Kolben.—Kolben (P.) *The Present State of the Cape of Good Hope.* Trans. by Medley. 2 vols. 1731.

Kolff.—Kolff (D. H.) *Voyages of the Dutch Brig the "Dourga."* Trans. by Earl. 1840.

Kotze.—Kotzebue (Otto von) *New Voyage Round the World.* 1830.

Kubary.—Kubary (J.S.) *Ethnographische Beiträge zur Kenntniss der Karolinischen Inselgruppe.* Berlin, 1885.

Laet.—Laet (J. de) *Novus Orbis*. 1633.

Landa.—Landa (D. de) *Relation des choses de Yucatan* [1566]. Texte et Traduction par Brasseur de Bourbourg. Paris, 1864.

Lao-Tsze.—Lao-Tsze, *The Tao-têh-king*. Various translations.

Leber.—Leber (J.M.C.) *Collection des meilleures dissertations . . . relatifs à l'histoire de France*. 20 vols. Paris, 1826–38.

Lecky.—Lecky (W.E.H.) *History of European Morals*. 3rd Ed. 2 vols. 1877.

Legge.—Legge (James) *The Chinese Classics*. 5 vols. 1869, etc.

Legge.—Legge (James) *The Religions of China*. 1880.

Lew.—Lewin (Capt. T.H.) *Wild Races of South Eastern India*. 1870.

Lewis.—Lewis (Capt. M.) & Clarke, *Travels to the Source of the Missouri River*. 1814. 4 to.

Licht.—Lichtenstein (H.) *Travels in Southern Africa in the Years 1803–1806*. 2 vols. 1812–15. 4 to.

Liv.—Livingstone (D.) *Missionary Travels and Researches*. 1857.

Liv.—Livingstone (D. & C.) *Narrative of an Expedition to the Zambesi*. 1865.

Low.—Low (Hugh) *Sarawak, Its Inhabitants and Productions*. 1848.

Lubb.—Lubbock (Sir J.) *Pre-Historic Times*. 2nd Ed.

Lyon.—Lyon (Capt. G.F.) *Private Journal*. 1824.

MacDon.—MacDonald (Duff) *Africana*. 2 vols. 1882.

Macgil.—Macgillivray (J.) *Narrative of the Voyage of H.M.S. Rattlesnake . . .* 1846–50. 2 vols. 1852.

MacGreg.—MacGregor (Gen.) *Central Asia. Part I*. 2 vols. Calc. 1873.

Macph.—Macpherson (Lieut.) *Report on the Khonds of Ganjam and Cuttack*. Calc. 1842.

Maha.—*The Mahabharata*. Various translations.

Mahaf.—Mahaffy (J.P.) *Social Life in Greece*. 1874.

Mal.—Malcolm (Sir. J.) *Memoir of Central India*. 1823.

Man.—Man (E.G.) *Sonthalia and the Sonthals*. 1867.

Manu.—*The Laws of Manu*. Various translations.

Mar.—Mariner's (W.) *An Account of the Natives of the Tonga Islands*. By J. Martin. 2 vols. 1818.

Mars.—Marsden (W.) *The History of Sumatra*. 1783. 4 to.

Mart.—Martin (H.) *Histoire de la France*. 1884.

Massey.—Massey (W.N.) *A History of England during the Reign of George III*.

Mencius.—*The Works of Mencius*. (In Legge's *Chinese Classics*. Vol. II.)

Mered.—Meredith (Mrs. C.L.A.) *My Home in Tasmania*. 2 vols.

Mich.—Michelet (J.) *History of France*. 2 vols. Trans. by G.H. Smith.

Mill.—Mill (J.S.) *An Examination of Sir William Hamilton's Philosophy*. 3rd Ed. 1867.

M.J.L.S.—*The Madras Journal of Literature and Science*.

Moffat.—Moffat (R.) *Missionary Labours and Scenes in Southern Africa*. 4th Ed. 1842.

Möll.—Möllhausen (B.) *Diary of a Journey from the Mississippi to the Coasts of the Pacific*. 2 vols. 1858.

Mont.—Montaigne (M. de) *Essays*. Trans. by Cotton. 3 vols.

Monte.—Monteiro (J.J.) *Angola and the River Congo*, 2 vols. 1875.

Morg.—Morgan (L.H.) *League of the . . . Iroquois*. Roch. U.S.A. 1851.

INDEX TO VOLUME I

Tibor R. Machan teaches at Chapman University, California. He is a research fellow at the Hoover Institution on War, Revolution and Peace, Stanford University, California.

The Palatino typeface used in this volume is the work of Hermann Zapf, the noted European type designer and master calligrapher. Palatino is basically an "old style" letterform, yet it is strongly endowed with Zapf's distinctive exquisiteness. With concern not solely for the individual letter but also for the working visual relationship in a page of text, Zapf's edged pen has given this type a brisk, natural motion.

Printed on paper that is acid-free and meets
the requirements of the American National Standard
for Permanence of Paper for
Printed Library Materials, Z39.84, 1984 ⊚

Book Design by JMH Corporation, Indianapolis, Indiana
Typography by Weimer Typesetting Co., Inc., Indianapolis, Indiana
Printed and bound by Edwards Brothers, Inc., Ann Arbor, Michigan